Propaganda and Persuasion

Propaganda and Persuasion

THE COLD WAR AND THE CANADIAN-SOVIET FRIENDSHIP SOCIETY

JENNIFER ANDERSON

UNIVERSITY OF MANITOBA PRESS

21 20 19 18 17 1 2 3 4 5

University of Manitoba Press
Winnipeg, Manitoba, Canada
Treaty 1 Territory
uofmpress.ca

Cataloguing data available from Library and Archives Canada
ISBN 978-0-88755-742-2 (PAPER)
ISBN 978-0-88755-512-1 (PDF)
ISBN 978-0-88755-510-7 (EPUB)

Cover design by Frank Reimer
Interior design by Karen Armstrong Graphic Design
Cover images from the *Northern Neighbours* magazine of February, March, and May 1981.

Printed in Canada

The University of Manitoba Press acknowledges the financial support for its publication program provided by the Government of Canada through the Canada Book Fund, the Canada Council for the Arts, the Manitoba Department of Sport, Culture, and Heritage, the Manitoba Arts Council, and the Manitoba Book Publishing Tax Credit.

Funded by the Government of Canada | Canada

Contents

Illustrations

Abbreviations

ATIP	Access to Information and Privacy
AUUC	Association of United Ukrainian Canadians
BBC	British Broadcasting Corporation
CBC	Canadian Broadcasting Corporation
CCF	Cooperative Commonwealth Federation
CNR	Canadian National Railway
CPC	Communist Party of Canada
CPSU	Communist Party of the Soviet Union
CRCR	Centre for Research on Canadian-Russian Relations
CSFS	Canadian-Soviet Friendship Society
CSIS	Canadian Security Intelligence Service
DEA	Department of External Affairs
DEW	Distant Early Warning
FOC	Finnish Organization of Canada
FRC	Federation of Russian Canadians
FSU	Friends of the Soviet Union
GARF	*Gosudarstvennyi arkhiv Rossiiskoi Federatsii/* State Archives of the Russian Federation
HCA	Housewives' Consumers' Association
ID	International Department (of the CPSU Central Committee)
KGB	*Komitet gosudarstvennoy bezopasnosti/*Committee of State Security, USSR
LAC	Library and Archives Canada
LPP	Labor-Progressive Party
MP	Member of Parliament
MPP	Member of Provincial Parliament
NATO	North Atlantic Treaty Organization
NCCSF	National Council for Canadian-Soviet Friendship

NHL	National Hockey League
RCMP	Royal Canadian Mounted Police
RNWMP	Royal North-West Mounted Police
SSOD	*Soyuz sovetskyi obshchestvo druzhbi i kulturnoi sviazi s zagranitsei*/Union of Soviet Friendship Societies and Cultural Relations with Foreign Countries
TASS	*Telegrafnoe Agentstvo Sovetskovo Soyuz*/Telegraph Agency of the Soviet Union
TVO	TVOntario
UJPO	United Jewish People's Order
ULFTA	Ukrainian Labour Farmer Temple Association
USSR	Union of Soviet Socialist Republics
VOKS	*Vse soiuznoe obshchevstvo kul'turnoi sviazi s zagranitsei*/ All-Union Society for Cultural Relations with Foreign Countries
YMCA	Young Men's Christian Association

Acknowledgements

It is hard for me to remember a time when I was not interested in Russia. It all started in a library. One book on the Russian Revolution led to another, which led to investigations of Soviet and Russian culture, international relations, and Cold War antipathies. Most of my high school history projects dealt in some way with the USSR and North American perceptions of it, facilitated by the mass of information made public in those heady days of Mikhail Gorbachev. By the time that I got to university, the USSR was no more, and my goal was to get over there so that I could balance my bookish learning with real experiences. Immediately following the completion of a master's degree in Central/Eastern European and Russian-Area Studies, I found a job in Kyiv, Ukraine. What was meant to be a summer internship turned into a five-year hiatus in Ukraine, where I lived in Kyiv and Kharkiv, travelled throughout the region, met and married my husband, and spent the best part of a year with my oldest son. Although as foreigners we lived in privileged conditions, the economic and social aspects of life in the former USSR had an impact on our everyday lives. The people whom I met there were struggling to overcome seventy-five years of poor policy with limited success. I have nothing but admiration for what they have achieved in the face of enormous obstacles.

If on one level I can understand the motivation of some Canadians to join the Canadian-Soviet Friendship Society (CSFS), a group that allowed them to visit the USSR, on another level I cannot ignore the fact that they were co-opted into legitimizing a message that was part of a larger Soviet Potemkin village. Negotiating these two levels of understanding, and balancing an appreciation for idealism with a realistic and healthy dose of scepticism, have comprised ongoing conversations throughout this project.

For deepening these discussions, I would particularly like to thank my doctoral supervisors, J.L. Black and Duncan McDowall. I am also grateful to Larry Black for arranging to have copies of the rich VOKS documents brought to Canada, and to the Centre for Canadian-Russian Relations at Carleton University for hiring me to produce the finding aid for these papers. These papers have since been at Georgian College in Barrie, Ontario, and are now at Cameron Library, University of Alberta Archives.

Several of the chapters in this book have benefited greatly from comments and suggestions offered by members of the Canadian Historical Association and the Canadian Association of Slavists, to whom I presented early versions of the research. A version of Chapter 4 appeared in the *Journal of the Canadian Historical Association* 18, 1 (2007): 179–206, and part of Chapter 5 was published in *Re-Imagining Ukrainian Canadians: History, Politics, and Identity*, edited by Rhonda L. Hinther and Jim Mochoruk (Toronto: University of Toronto Press, 2011), 279–328. I am grateful to the editors of these publications for their input and validation.

I would like to thank the librarians, archivists, and resource staff at Library and Archives Canada, the Osler Library (McGill University), the Thomas Fisher Rare Book Library (University of Toronto), the Cameron Library (University of Alberta), the Canadian Museum of History, the Gravenhurst Public Library, and Special Collections and Archives (Carleton University). A particular thanks to Myron Momryk, a stellar scholar, archivist, and colleague.

I also wish to thank Leonard Stern, *Ottawa Citizen* editor, who inadvertently offered me the title when he responded to my e-mail about the fact that a Canadian version of the American-Soviet Friendship Society did, indeed, exist.

I owe a great deal to the individuals who agreed to speak to me about their experiences with the CSFS and their knowledge of its leaders, contacts, members, and activities. They helped me to understand the links between individuals' lives and their social and political engagements. Although they might not all agree with my conclusions, I hope that they can appreciate my point of view.

A special debt of gratitude is owed to David Carr, Glenn Bergen, and the team at the University of Manitoba Press. Since completing the dissertation upon which this book is based, I have been working full time as an archivist and museum curator and raising a family. David has been the most supportive and patient of editors. I am grateful, too, to the anonymous peer reviewers whose comments improved my work.

Finally, a thank you to my family and friends for their encouragement on this journey.

Propaganda and Persuasion

Introduction

The stone building is on a busy Toronto street corner. A streetcar passed by; there were upscale shops all around, and merchants were selling jewellery on the wide sidewalk. To gain entry, one had to buzz using an intercom and wait for the ornate metal door to be remotely unlocked. I pushed the door open and stood in a hallway—stairs up to the left, down to the right.

Going downstairs, I was attracted by the tourism posters showing places that I had visited or had yet to visit: Crimea, St. Petersburg, Uzbekistan. The large room at the bottom of the stairs had several smaller antechambers and a kitchen, resembling in many ways a church or town hall basement. Except, of course, for the red banners with gold writing displayed along the walls proclaiming "Back to the USSR." A Soviet flag stood in the corner.

I felt as if I had stumbled back in time or fallen into one of the history books on the library shelf. This could have been a meeting in the former Soviet Union or—minus the banners—a gathering of Communist Party members in downtown Winnipeg in the 1930s.

But, no, it was Toronto in the twenty-first century. And despite what one might think, the room was not full of old-timers with a quaint nostalgia for the USSR and communism, nor was it full of adolescents play-acting their rebellion by wearing Soviet relics and spouting Stalinist slogans. Instead, the room was filled with a multi-generational, multi-lingual, articulate crowd of people who appeared to believe deeply that the world needed to bring the USSR back into existence as a model for countries like Canada and that this feat was, in fact, possible. I was witness to a Soviet friendship meeting in modern-day downtown Toronto. This group traced its lineage back to the early twentieth century.

The contrasts in the room were striking. A grandfatherly man across the table from me spoke about his deep admiration for Josef Stalin, dismissing as "lies" any criticism of him. Meanwhile, a young man at the back of the room told me that I had an obligation to tell the "truth" about the group. There were photos on the walls of people whose names I had seen on lists in the archives kept by the Soviets but also, likely, by the RCMP. Putting faces to names, I became aware that these lists were related to real people with real experiences. Any action that they had taken based upon their beliefs would have had real consequences for them, but no doubt the lists had held consequences for them as well. I thought about the infamous "blacklisting" of the Cold War era and about Len Scher's oral history interviews with Canadians who found themselves so listed.[1] Accessing these archival lists, naming these people, and making connections based upon musty documents was not just about making history; telling their stories could "out" them in a way that I had not previously realized. Were these people still vulnerable, could they be targets, even though the Cold War was over?

For some, it seemed that the Cold War was not over at all. I was told that they had been alerted to my visit by a CSIS agent. Was this meant primarily to frighten me? The fact that I came from Ottawa aroused suspicion, and when I paid for my lunch I was given a receipt for a "contribution" to the organization. Some were reluctant to speak with me at all, and others agreed to do so as long as the conversations were not recorded. This was not a purely academic exercise, I realized. My own name had likely just been added to a list.

When I asked about the group's archival papers, I was told that a fire had destroyed them. The traditional historian/archivist in me asked how, without these archives, they could expect their version of the truth to be told. The historical record was central to their self-identities and to the history that I would tell. Clearly, oral history would play a role too as the listed spoke back to the lists, with all of the ethical complications that doing so entailed. So it was that I embarked on a project that focussed on perception, persuasion, and propaganda.

During the early Cold War, thousands of Canadians attended events organized by the Canadian-Soviet Friendship Society (CSFS) and subscribed to its publications. Although scholarship on Cold War Canada and the Communist Party of Canada (CPC) has grown, the CSFS, led by Dyson Carter from 1949 to 1960, has received relatively little attention from historians. Moreover, few historians have noted the important role played by the Soviet All-Union

Society for Cultural Relations with Foreign Countries (VOKS) in encouraging and supporting parts of the Canadian left. This book looks at the CSFS as a blend of social and political activism in which gender, class, ethnicity, linked communities, and ideology had significance. The CSFS was clearly associated with the CPC (or Labor-Progressive Party [LPP], as it was called for some time). The book also deals with an example of foreign influence in Canada, for the elaborate pro-Soviet performances staged by the CSFS were part of a larger campaign orchestrated from Moscow to manage perceptions.

At the meeting in Toronto, and from the archives, I learned that groups calling themselves "friends" of the USSR could be found in Canada as early as 1921, when a branch of the American Friends of Soviet Russia was founded in Toronto. Subsequently, they were known variously as the Aid to Russia campaign, Friends of the Soviet Union, CSFC, and Canada-USSR Association. From 1941 on, when the USSR was invaded by Nazi Germany, the National Council for Canadian-Soviet Friendship received widespread popular support, and some of the country's leading figures, including Prime Minister W.L. Mackenzie King, attended events and contributed to the cause of "friendship" with the Soviets. But after the defection of cipher clerk Igor Gouzenko from the Soviet Embassy in Ottawa became public in 1946, friendship with the USSR abruptly fell out of style. Around this time Sir Ellsworth Flavelle, head of the friendship society in Toronto, complained that "radical elements" were trying to take over the cause.[2] In 1946, the RCMP reported that few members of the "progressive" groups in Canada were accepting invitations to visit the USSR and concluded that this reluctance was directly related to the investigation of individuals identified as communist spies by Gouzenko.[3]

That is when Carter emerged as president of the friendship society. His involvement with the CSFS is framed by the Gouzenko defection and the disillusionment among the Canadian left after 1956. In 1945, the Labor-Progressive Party (Communist Party of Canada) claimed to be at the height of its membership, with 20,000 members, but immediately following the Gouzenko revelations hundreds left the party, and many who remained questioned their decision to do so.[4] Disillusionment over links between the LPP and the Soviet Union compounded earlier feelings of resentment among party members and fellow travellers in regard to the Nazi-Soviet Pact of 1939 and the flip-flop that the CPC had been forced to perform when it came to support for the Second World War. After 1946, Soviet authorities posted in Canada no longer recommended reaching out to the wider Canadian public via the LPP.[5]

The CSFS was meant to shore up confidence among progressives in the Soviet experiment and, as a front organization, to bolster support for policies advanced by the CPC-LPP in a neutral, apparently non-partisan, forum. Canadian-Soviet friends were part of an elaborate *mise-en-scène* presenting an unfailingly positive view of the USSR to fellow Canadians. But the dynamic changed once more in 1956. Disenchantment caused many Canadian leftists to cut ties with the progressive groups. The membership of the LPP was severely reduced;[6] the CSFS also lost members. As Merrily Weisbord has suggested, "until 1956 the nature of this relationship [between the Communist Party of the Soviet Union and the Labor-Progressive Party] would remain obscured by an almost mythological belief in Soviet communism."[7] For some LPP members and fellow travellers, it was not until Nikita Khrushchev's denunciation of Stalin's policies that they realized the full import of the revelations made public by Gouzenko a decade earlier. The Soviet response was to change its strategy. Almost immediately after 1956, the CSFS was reorganized, a new journal was introduced, and the same was done in Moscow for its parent organization, VOKS. In 1960, the LPP replaced Carter as head of the CSFS with Les Hunt, but Carter continued to publish the pro-Soviet magazine, *Northern Neighbors*. The popularity of *Northern Neighbors* was one reason that Carter was untouchable. In 1957, partly because of illness, he moved from Toronto to Gravenhurst, but he also had a new work plan in mind.

The CSFS created and distributed Soviet propaganda for Canadian (and some American) readers not from across the Arctic Circle but from within Ontario. Carter was paid in in-kind support and benefits to serve as a Soviet propagandist. He frequently travelled to the USSR and the Soviet Embassy in Ottawa as a guest of honour. Although Carter eventually recognized that the message he had been disseminating did not correspond with reality, he did so only after Mikhail Gorbachev's policy of glasnost made speaking openly about Soviet "falsifications" possible. In 1990, Carter wrote that he had spent forty years producing "bullshit."[8] Even this admission was completely in line with the official policy of Moscow.

The end of the Cold War made previously classified documents available to researchers, but it also made it possible for former activists to tell their side of the story. Documents copied from the State Archives of the Russian Federation (GARF), previously held by the Centre for Research on Canadian-Russian Relations (CRCR) at Carleton University, then at Georgian College, and today at the University of Alberta, show how the CSFS worked with VOKS. Some restricted documents from the collections of the RCMP and the Department of External Affairs are now available. Individuals who chose to speak about their involvement with the CSFS at once support and counter the documentary evidence. The narrative is complicated by individuals' responses to the use of official archives from Canada and the USSR, formerly secret, documenting different perspectives on the same group and reporting on the same individuals for different reasons.

In a letter to his friend John Boyd in February 1990, Carter spoke sarcastically about the establishment at Library and Archives Canada of the Dyson Carter fonds. He mentioned that it would be flattering to have such a collection in his name if it did not contain so many false claims about Soviet superiority. Yet, read in this light, the collection is invaluable. It has proven important particularly in assessing how *Northern Neighbors* was put together and readers' responses to it. Hundreds of readers' letters to Carter are in the collection, and these handwritten notes, often sent by elderly individuals who might not have used English as a first language, are a testimony to his appeal to the non-party left. The letters show that many Canadians sincerely believed that the USSR represented a shining example of socialism in practice.

But most fascinating for me was that a few key individuals had used archives to speak back to the historical record of the Canadian left and the CSFS. Dorise Nielsen's and Louis Kon's daughters chose to comment on material in their parents' archival collections and to include these notes in the fonds. Ted Baxter held on to archival material, referred to photographs when recalling events, and gave me both originals and copies. John Boyd has submitted documents to online collections and created and circulated texts that openly refer to events once shrouded in Cold War secrecy and innuendo. And Dyson Carter himself was constantly rewriting his story. Key actors in the CSFS wanted their story told, and they were actively engaged in preparing the archival record to be "discovered" later by historians.

But, like all archivists, I continue to feel haunted by gaps. If an RCMP file specifically on Carter exists, it has not yet been opened to researchers. We know too little about how the CSFS functioned in Quebec, partly because of the lack of archival resources, partly because activists there have not been interested in participating in oral history interviews. No doubt there are errors of omission and counter-narratives mixed into this story as well, for the same reasons. Photographs of CSFS events remain largely in private collections, and some individuals are still leery about telling their stories. Still, what we know today of the Canadian-Soviet Friendship Society allows for a better understanding of Cold War Canada.

The book unfolds roughly by time period. The following chapters outline the Friends of the Soviet Union during the 1930s, the Soviet perspective on friendship groups abroad, and CSFS publications from 1949 to 1989. Discussion also focuses on how ethnicity, class, and gender played roles in the

CSFS appeals and how leaders used cultural diplomacy, if always predictably from a pro-Soviet perspective. The final chapter outlines in broad strokes how the Canadian Communist Party and authorities in Moscow tweaked the image of Soviet friendship in Canada following the events of 1956 while maintaining the emphasis on building sympathy through cultural exchange.

CHAPTER 1

Who's Who of the Canadian-Soviet Friendship Society

Between 1949 and 1960, the Canadian-Soviet Friendship Society aimed its message at an audience of progressive leftists in North America, hoping to convince them that the USSR was indeed the epitome of an enlightened and egalitarian state. Attempting to soften, define, and redirect the antagonistic narratives of the day, the CSFS used propaganda and persuasion in Cold War Canada.[1]

Members of the CSFS were fellow travellers.[2] They were Soviet sympathizers, attracted to socialism, who saw in the USSR an example of social principles that they wished to see applied in Canada. They were associated with, but not always members of, the Canadian Communist Party. At the height of the Cold War during the 1950s, CSFS members continued to admire the USSR when such admiration was unpopular, and they actively campaigned for more "friendly" Canadian policies on the Soviet Union. A large number of non-CPC "progressives"[3] found in the cause of "friendship" an activist role. The Soviets encouraged them and even provided the necessary material and funding for many of their projects.

The CSFS was led by Dyson Carter, a Sovietophile and member of the Communist Party who spent most of his career promoting the USSR to North Americans. He served as president of the CSFS from 1949 to 1960, edited the CSFS newsletter *News-Facts about the USSR* from 1950 to 1956, and published the popular pro-Soviet magazine *Northern Neighbors* from 1956 to 1989. His work was supported by the Soviet All-Union Society for Cultural Relations with Foreign Countries (*Vse soiznoe obshchestvo kul'turnoi sviazi s zagranitsei,*

Figure 1. Dyson Carter, n.d.

or VOKS) and by the Communist Party of Canada, and his writing had wide appeal on the Canadian left. This story of propaganda[4] and persuasion offers a new perspective on the history of Cold War Canada.

Founded in 1949 by Carter and former Member of Parliament Dorise Nielsen, the CSFS was clearly meant to provide an alternative (positive) view of the USSR, just a few years after the defection of Igor Gouzenko signalled the beginning of Cold War tensions in Canada. Concerned by the negative press, the Soviets saw the CSFS as a way to improve Canadians' opinions of the USSR, but after the events of 1956 damaged the Soviet image enough for leading communists worldwide to leave the movement, the CSFS and its Moscow-based parent organization were reorganized. In the intervening years, CSFS members were presented as "average" Canadians seeking more "truthful" and balanced reports of life in the USSR, and they disseminated material sent from the Soviet Union in publications and at public events. In pre-Internet days, when information about life in the USSR was hard for Westerners to come by, Carter and the CSFS tapped into a sincere desire to learn more about

Soviet realities. The material they presented was vetted by Soviet organizations, and intended to propagate a particular point of view.

The CSFS was in constant liaison with VOKS, the Soviet organization responsible for public relations abroad, monitored by the Soviet Ministry of Foreign Affairs and the International Department of the Communist Party of the Soviet Union Central Committee. The CSFS also worked closely with the Communist Party of Canada (called the Labor-Progressive Party from 1943 to 1959) and the progressive "ethnic" groups associated with it. In the early 1940s, Carter, a well-known progressive writer and member of the Communist Party since 1931, wrote to Louis Kon, who had headed the Friends of the Soviet Union in Montreal before the war, asking for a contact at the Soviet Embassy. Kon advised Carter that the moment was ripe to reorganize the friendship society. After the Gouzenko defection, most of the high-profile supporters of wartime Canadian-Soviet friendship withdrew their support, and when Carter was suggested as head of the new organization, the Soviets were enthusiastic.

In 1953, a secret RCMP report identified the CSFS as a communist-front organization organized and financed by the Communist Party of Canada (or Labor-Progressive Party).[5] Undoubtedly, it was. The links between the CSFS and the CPC-LPP have been confirmed by documentary and oral history evidence. The CSFS mission was twofold, said the RCMP report: first, the society served as a "clearing-house" for invitations to the USSR and Soviet propaganda; second, it attempted to persuade many "innocent" Canadians to view Soviet-style communism favourably. The CSFS was indeed engaged in propaganda and persuasion, acting as a proxy for the Communist Party of Canada and as an attractive forum for leftists interested in Soviet culture, everyday life, scientific and sociopolitical innovation, and international relations. The RCMP worried that in a "stressful" situation (i.e., war) Canadians influenced by the CSFS message might support the wrong side. The CSFS contact at the Soviet Embassy in Ottawa was likely working in connection with the KGB, and individual CSFS members have been accused in the Mitrokhin Archive of having been involved in espionage. However, rank-and-file members were probably not aware of any nefarious dealings, hence "innocent" or "naive" from the point of view of Canadian officials. Today former CSFS members recall the meaningful activism that they found in countering the prevailing rhetoric about the USSR as the enemy. Rather than as potential enemies within Canada's borders, these individuals saw themselves as having attempted to "warm" Cold War international relations. They saw their activities as attempts to create a more peaceful world by presenting positive arguments about the USSR and encouraging other Canadians to see the Soviet Union in more friendly terms.

Herbert Dyson Carter was born in 1910 in New Brunswick, moved to Winnipeg with his parents as a child, and died in 1996 in Gravenhurst, Ontario. In his autobiography,[6] Carter explains how he came to an understanding that he was a "red." His parents were active in the Salvation Army and ran a reformatory school and residence in Winnipeg. Carter credits attempts by his parents to mediate between the youngsters accused of criminal activities, most of whom came from poor neighbourhoods of new immigrants, and the authorities who accused them of such activities; the sometimes harsh and random reactions of the latter radicalized Carter. He claims that he was deeply influenced by seeing his parents, especially his father, come to question whether religious faith was enough to effect real change in a society that clearly discriminated against women, non–Anglo Saxons, and the poor. He explains that his respect for the Soviet Union came from a combination of socialist conviction and admiration for the scientific and technological advances made in the USSR. Later this techno-utopian view of socialism set him apart at times from his party peers, but he was held in high regard by Soviet authorities.

Carter was well educated. Home-schooled and a voracious reader, he entered university ahead of his peers and studied science, eventually obtaining a master's degree in chemistry and physics.[7] He was motivated by the desire to discover cures similar to the vitamin D that had allowed him to leave his bed finally, where he had been imprisoned for years by *osteogenesis imperfecta*, and embark on a more independent life. His conviction that only in a socialist system could scientific discoveries have an immediate impact for citizens might have been reinforced by the premature deaths of two women important to him: his first wife, around 1944 from a rare virus, and his second wife, in 1972 from cancer. Carter also discovered another gift: he could write with flair yet in a way that made complex ideas accessible to the non-initiated. He used this talent to praise scientific and technological advances, particularly—and most flamboyantly—those made in the USSR.

Carter was active for years on the left before heading the CSFS, and he was known primarily as a writer with progressive views. The RCMP believed that he had joined the Communist Party of Canada in 1946,[8] but according to him he had joined it in 1931, in the same Winnipeg group as John Boyd.[9] Carter published in *Saturday Night* and *Maclean's*, and his book *Russia's Secret Weapon*[10] was noted by Canadian dailies. He was made a fellow of the Royal Canadian Geographical Society in 1941 for his book on Canadian sovereignty in the North, entitled *Sea of Destiny: The Story of Hudson Bay, Our Undefended Back Door* (1940).[11] In the 1930s, Carter published in *New Frontier*, a Toronto journal that attempted to "integrat[e] Communist writing with the mainstream of Canadian culture," using the pseudonym "Jack Parr."[12] As a gifted orator and writer, he also spoke and wrote for the Communist Party. In 1946, Carter moved to Toronto to work for the new communist daily the *Canadian Tribune*.[13] During the summer of 1948 and 1949, he taught at the LPP Training School in Long Branch, Ontario.[14] Well-known Canadian progressive activists such as Quebec communist Jeanne Corbin and Robert Mendel Laxer admired his work. A biography of Corbin notes that she was captivated by Carter's writings and that the CSFS president and publicist "offered hope to his many and faithful readers."[15] James Laxer has similarly described how his father considered Carter "Canada's greatest novelist."[16] In later years, many of Carter's books were translated into Russian and published in Moscow, and his articles were frequently featured in Soviet newspapers.[17]

Literary critic James Doyle has noted that, when Carter proclaimed publicly in 1945 that he was a member of the LPP, he effectively marked "the end of his association with the mass media."[18] He did, however, publish an article on heart disease and new transplant treatments in the Toronto weekly *New Liberty* in 1952.[19] Although Carter claims that he was ostracized by the mainstream press because of his political views,[20] he no longer needed that outlet. He worked for the LPP on publicity throughout the late 1940s, until founding the CSFS at the request of the LPP in 1949.[21] By the 1950s, Carter was on the national executive of the LPP.[22] In addition, his radical politics, writing talent, and interest in the Soviet Union brought him to the attention of Soviet authorities,[23] who assured him an audience until he stopped publishing in 1989.

Carter claimed that he had a certain charm with women. In his fictionalized memoirs, *Fatherless Sons*, he refers to himself as something of a Casanova, able to attract women with his talk of how love could save the world.[24] Later he refers to certain party insiders advising him to calm his love life down. In the book, Carter has one of his "motherly" party figures say that "many a time I thought he was a son-of-a-bitch" because of his sexual promiscuity.[25] Although it is hard to say if these details were truly autobiographical, today his former comrades still refer to him variously as a "womanizer," a man with an enormous sexual appetite, surrounded by beautiful women, or a "horrible man."

As is the case while reading most of Carter's writing, it is difficult to sort fact from fiction. For example, it is not clear how many times Carter was married. In his memoirs, he describes his first wife, "Shirley Anne Northway," as a nurse whom he claims to have met in Winnipeg in the mid-1930s while he was in the hospital after having been beaten up. Carter implies that it was the police who beat him up for being a "red."[26] They were married secretly because their acquaintances feared that her family would not approve of Dyson, but "Shirley" died soon after from encephalitis caught from a patient.[27] This first marriage has not been confirmed by interviewees. There might have been another short-lived marriage after this one. In 1944, Louis Kon sent his congratulations to Dyson and "Lina,"[28] but this marriage might have been annulled.[29] Could the "Shirley" in his memoirs have been Charlotte, in fact a nurse? It appears from the archival record that Dyson married Charlotte Breckham Carter in the late 1940s, and from then on she co-authored his books and ran his publications when he was unwell.[30] Many acquaintances spoke admiringly of her, of her patience and willingness to put up with Dyson, apparently a very difficult man. In 1953, they had a son, Breck. At first, it seemed that he did not suffer from the same condition as his father,[31] but as he aged it became apparent that he did. On one trip to Crimea, the waves crashing in on the beach broke his leg.[32] The Carters occasionally travelled on party business, but otherwise they were able to work from home. This might have been a necessity since Dyson at times was able to get around on crutches or in a wheelchair, and at other times he was on bed rest. When they were away, young Breck was often cared for by Dorise Nielsen's daughter, Sally. She remembers that later, when Breck was a young man, father and son would sometimes have passionate arguments and that Dyson was as arrogant with Breck as he was with others in his life.[33]

The other main character in the story of the early years of the CSFS is Dorise Nielsen. Born in 1902 in London, England, she emigrated to Canada in 1927 with a teacher exchange program called the Fellowship of the Maple Leaf, organized by the Church of England.[34] While teaching and then raising a young family in Saskatchewan, Nielsen became active with farmers' movements during the Depression. The RCMP reported that she was expelled from the Cooperative Commonwealth Federation (CCF) in 1939 because of her efforts to merge the party with other left-wing groups, including communists, and say that "soon after she secretly joined the Communist Party of Canada."[35] Her biographer writes that Nielsen and her good friend and political collaborator Bob Paul were probably "courted by communists who recognized their ability and their legitimacy in the English-speaking community. This period of courtship may have occurred early in the 1930s, but more likely it took place in 1934 or 1935 when the communist push to unite the left began."[36] In 1940, Nielsen was elected as an independent member of Parliament for the North Battleford, Saskatchewan, riding. In 1943, she became an executive member of the Labor-Progressive Party, and in the 1945 federal election she ran on the LPP ticket.[37] When she was not re-elected, she moved to Toronto to work for the Communist Party. That work often involved travelling with Carter to promote the LPP and its publications *National Affairs Monthly* and the *Canadian*

Figure 2. Dorise Nielsen, 1940.

Tribune. In 1946, when the news finally hit the headlines that Igor Gouzenko had defected, naming Fred Rose and other key personnel in Ottawa as Soviet spies, Nielsen was touring the country with Carter.

Nielsen was not present in November 1949 for the founding of the CSFS because she was in Moscow attending a conference hosted by the Women's International Democratic Federation, another organization supported by the LPP.[38] However, on her return in January 1950, she immediately began a tour of western Canada, again with Carter, to drum up support for the newly reformed CSFS. She was elected its national secretary in 1952.[39] While executive secretary, she did most of the organizational and publicity work, arranging visits and attempting to have new branches set up. Carter was responsible for editing *News-Facts about the USSR* and corresponding with VOKS, but by 1953 Nielsen was complaining resentfully that he was "managing the organization like his own private fiefdom."[40] In particular, she was bothered by the fact that Carter received a higher salary than she did. She was disappointed by how the party treated her, using her as a spokesperson but not giving her the plum jobs.[41] Her party colleagues did not value her leadership potential, arguing that she was "'not theoretically developed'" and labelling her a populist.[42] Faith Johnston has noted that, "in a Marxist party, populists are regarded as rather fuzzy-headed individuals."[43] Nielsen was resentful that the party had passed her over in favour of James Endicott for leadership of the peace movement and in favour of Dyson Carter for the CSFS. In 1953, Nielsen resigned from the CSFS, and Ted Baxter took over most of her work. The party did not offer her a better post. In 1955, she left Canada for Britain, where she hoped to find a more satisfying role, and in 1957 she went to China, where she lived the rest of her life doing publicity work for the Mao regime. When Carter criticized her in 1962 for her pro-Chinese, anti-Soviet views, Nielsen called him "the highest-paid Soviet agent in Canada."[44] Dorise's daughter, Sally, is uncomfortable calling her mother a "communist" despite her political affiliations; she prefers to use the term "progressive."[45]

In 1952, well-known LPP activists Dewar Ferguson and Romeo T. Lafond were elected at the CSFS convention as vice-presidents of the organization. Ferguson also organized for the Canadian Seamen's Union, supported by the LPP, and Lafond ran a camp on his property near L'Annonciation, north of Montreal, used by the LPP youth and members for educational retreats.[46] References to Ferguson and Lafond are made throughout the VOKS papers. Lafond wrote to VOKS in French, and his letters were often typed on Camp Lafond letterhead. Ferguson passed away in the 1970s, and Lafond died in Montreal in 1981.[47]

Ted Baxter has said that in the summer of 1953 Stanley Ryerson, historian and leading theorist for the Labor-Progressive Party, approached him and asked him to take over from Nielsen as national secretary of the CSFS in Toronto.[48] He joined the team in October that year, and in November he gave a talk to a Hamilton CSFS book club about his three-week trip to the USSR as a Canadian youth group member.[49] Baxter said that he was paid forty dollars a week for his CSFS work from 1953 to 1956, though at one time there were not enough funds to pay him, so he split his time between the CSFS and the Canadian Peace Congress. During his time with the CSFS, Baxter counted the reception organized for Ambassador Chuvakhin and his wife at the Royal York Hotel in Toronto the major success. Baxter said that at first the Royal York had refused to host the reception, but when Carter wrote directly to the head of Canadian National Railways and Canadian Airways the CSFS received permission to host a reception for the Soviet ambassador at the exclusive hotel. Baxter also recalled the visit of Soviet performing artists in 1954 as a highlight of his work with the CSFS: "Everybody agreed that this visit

Figure 3. In 1954 the CSFS hosted a banquet at the Royal York Hotel in Toronto in honour of the Soviet Ambassador to Canada, Dmitri Chuvakhin. Pictured in this photo (L-R) are Vladimir Burdin, Cultural Attaché at the Soviet Embassy; his spouse; the Ambassador's spouse; Ted Baxter, national secretary of the CSFS; Ambassador Chuvakhin; and Paul Pauk, executive member of the CSFS.

was really a great success," he said.[50] It was "a first step in cultural exchange between the two countries" and might have "set the stage for Glenn Gould's visit to the USSR" in 1957, he added.[51] John Boyd travelled with the Soviet artists across Canada. Boyd and Baxter had first met on their trip to China in 1952, and Baxter said that Boyd, as secretary of the Slav Committee, and an activist in the LPP and Association of United Ukrainian Canadians (AUUC), was a skilled spokesman and master of ceremonies. Baxter also visited the Soviet Embassy in Ottawa with Carter for the anniversary of the Bolshevik Revolution every 7 November.[52]

Understanding what motivated Baxter to become involved with the CSFS and the Canadian left in the first place might shed some light on the motivations of other activists. He preferred to say that he was a "fellow traveller" rather than a communist because he was never actually an LPP member. He was attracted to socialism because of its similarity to the Christian Social Gospel that he had absorbed as a child and young man. He understood the mandate of the CSFS to be "to show Canadians the Soviet Union in a positive

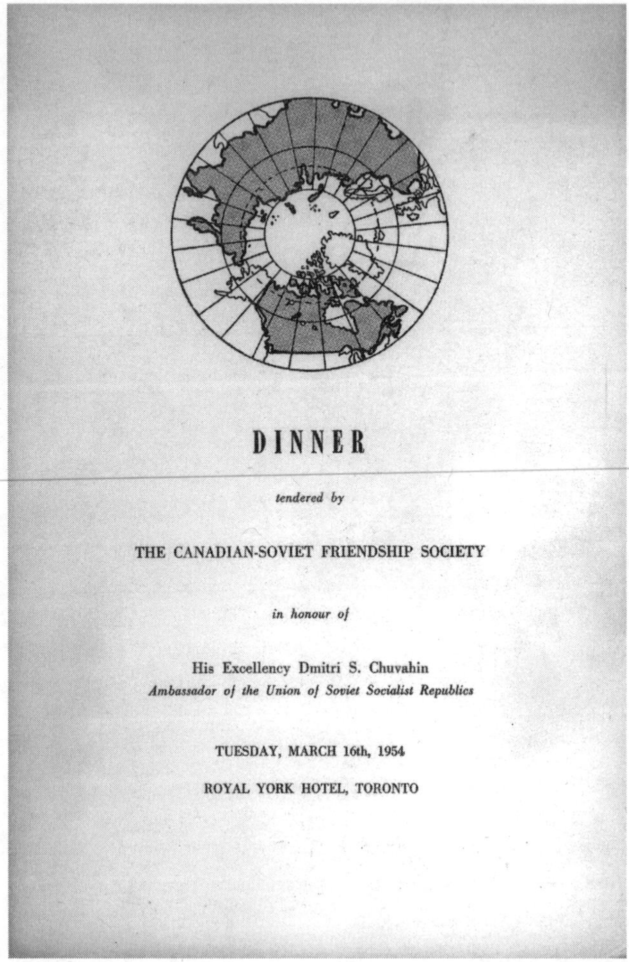

DINNER

tendered by

THE CANADIAN-SOVIET FRIENDSHIP SOCIETY

in honour of

His Excellency Dmitri S. Chuvahin
Ambassador of the Union of Soviet Socialist Republics

TUESDAY, MARCH 16th, 1954

ROYAL YORK HOTEL, TORONTO

Figure 4. Program for the banquet hosted by the Canadian-Soviet Friendship Society for Ambassador Chuvakhin, 16 March 1954, Toronto, Ontario.

light because there was no shortage of people showing it in a negative light" and particularly to show "the human side" of life in the USSR.[53] He said that they were "not suggesting Canada should have a Soviet style government" but that there should be trade, cultural exchange, and increased contact between the two countries in order to diminish Cold War tensions.[54]

But in 1956, things changed for Baxter. In reference to the events of that year, Nikita Khrushchev's criticism of Stalin, the Soviet invasion of Hungary, and the Suez Crisis, he said that "everything fell apart, blew apart."[55] Many LPP members in Montreal left the movement, including Gui Caron, and especially the Jewish members, some of whom were Baxter's friends: "It didn't bother me as much as others—some felt very guilty for having involved other people. I hadn't done anything that was injurious to anyone or to Canada."[56] But coincidentally at this time, Ted and Barbara Baxter decided to adopt twin boys, and he thought it best for his family to distance himself from the movement. He became a high school teacher of French, first in Port Perry on Lake Scagog, then in North York. His *VOKS Bulletin* subscription, and presumably his subscriptions to CSFS publications, were cancelled in August 1956.[57]

Baxter did experience further effects of his "radical youth" later in life. He (and his employers) were visited by police officers inquiring about his political activities, and he thought that this affected his career. In general, the constant surveillance bothered him, and he worried about his family.[58] In the late 1980s, he was not allowed on a flight to the United States and later was questioned when crossing the border by train. He had never had any trouble crossing the border by car. Later he wanted to fly to visit people in Seattle, so he drove to the US border, before he bought the ticket, and asked the border officer to tell him whether he would be allowed to do so. The officer went into a back room, and another officer came out to speak to Baxter. He said that, judging from what he had seen, he would allow Baxter to go, but another officer might not. He advised Baxter to phone a certain number in Toronto. He later did so and was assured that there was no longer a problem, and he travelled to Seattle without incident. He figured that he had been on an old list prohibiting him from entering the United States, and with a simple phone call his name had been deleted from this Cold War relic.

Meanwhile, Carter continued his work. For forty years, he published pro-Soviet magazines (first *News-Facts about the USSR* and, after 1956, *Northern Neighbors*), as well as other collections and monographs, by rewriting and building on articles sent to him by Soviet press agencies, taking every policy turn in step with the official Moscow line. For example, discussion of Nikita Khrushchev's 1956 "secret speech" distancing the Communist Party of the Soviet Union from Josef Stalin did not appear in Carter's publication until the 1980s when Mikhail Gorbachev's glasnost allowed discussion of that theme in the USSR. The invasions of Hungary in 1956 and Czechoslovakia in 1968 were presented from the Soviet (i.e., "liberation") point of view, and especially in the 1980s the magazine had a strong anti-American slant. Traditional "left" issues such as women's rights, claims that Jews and other ethnic/national groups in the USSR were free, environmental protection, and natural health remedies were given considerable space in the magazine but always with a strong positive spin on the USSR's advanced social policies.

The CSFS attempted to attract readers, participants, and delegates to the USSR from among progressive Canadians, many of whom had lived through the Depression and had come to admire the USSR as a symbol of socialism in practice. A good number of these individuals were also members of the left-wing Association of United Ukrainian Canadians, United Jewish People's Order, or Labor-Progressive Party itself. The CSFS was never a large group: in 1951, there were roughly fifty people listed as members of the National Council for Canadian-Soviet Friendship, most of whom were in Ontario.[59] There were five executive officers: the president was Dyson Carter, Major Romeo T. Lafond was listed as the vice-president for French Canada, Dewar Ferguson was his English Canadian counterpart, William Tweedale was the treasurer, and Dorise Nielsen was the executive secretary. Four years later Carter claimed that the CSFS had 400 members and, in 1957, 800 members. Although the membership was relatively small, the readership of the CSFS publications grew substantially over the years. In 1950, *News-Facts about the USSR* had four paid subscriptions, but in 1989 Carter claimed that *Northern Neighbors* was sent to 10,000 subscribers in eighty-one countries. The link between subscribers and members was close. In 1952, Nielsen said that every subscriber was automatically a member of the CSFS. In her "Report on Organization," she broke down the numbers of attendees at CSFS events by province, concluding that "some 10,000 Canadians have heard an account of Soviet life." She lamented the fact that, though in the Maritimes "we have many readers of *News-Facts*, as yet we have no functioning committees," and she pointed to the limited success in Quebec, explaining that in that province "real difficulties exist, caused by the Duplessis government and its Padlock Law."[60] Still, she noted, a Quebec CSFS committee had been established, and members were both anglophone and francophone.[61] The claim to represent "alternative" news about the USSR did have an appeal.

An examination of the CSFS offers historians a fascinating glimpse of how some fellow travellers responded to the ideological tensions that they perceived in early Cold War Canada. Under Carter's leadership, the CSFS made a serious attempt to change the prevailing negative view of the USSR, apparent in mainstream press and political statements in Canada during those years. Moscow provided support in quantity and quality, and CSFS efforts were monitored by high-level officials in the USSR. Producing propaganda that appealed largely to left-leaning Canadians who already admired the USSR, the group did not sway the vast majority of Canadians to view the Soviet Union as a politically neutral friend. However, its attempts at persuasion were consistently in the public eye, and its calls for cultural and information exchanges appealed to many Canadians for whom Russia had long been fascinating. Explicating the relationship among the CSFS, the CPC-LPP, and VOKS adds to our understanding of how individual Canadians contributed and responded to the rhetoric of Cold War international relations.

CHAPTER 2

Setting the Stage: The Soviet Friendship Phenomenon, 1917–49

Russians and Canadians have long been fascinated with one another as northern neighbours separated by Arctic waters. The Bolshevik Revolution of 1917 heightened considerably the political and ideological aspects of this relationship since the USSR appeared to be a symbol of socialism in action.[1] For Soviet sympathizers, 1917 appeared to herald a new era in political affairs and international relations; for others, the symbol was more menacing, and a red scare in Canada was heightened in 1919 when a general strike gripped Winnipeg.[2] Organizers of the strike were suspected, in some cases rightly so, of Soviet sympathies. There were also Canadians who advocated engagement with the Soviet Union for pragmatic reasons: political recognition of and increased trade with the USSR were seen by these Canadians as a practical approach to international affairs. The period was marked by the founding of numerous "aid to Russia" groups that promoted both friendship and, to a limited extent, political links with the Soviets.

From 1917 to the end of the 1920s, the plight of the "Russians" made headlines in Canada. The Bolshevik government was fighting a civil war against the imperial White Army, with Canadian troops supporting the Whites. Tsar Nicholas II and his immediate family had been executed by the Reds. Newspapers reported on clashing ideological entreaties to consolidate or resist the revolution and in 1921–22 on a famine so severe that Vladimir Lenin and Maksim Gorky appealed for international aid. Some refugees who had escaped the revolution and war arrived in Canada in 1924, and other Doukhobor and Russian immigrants came to this country throughout the

1920s. Their impressions and experiences affected the Canadian mainstream view of the USSR.[3] In 1919, Canadian troops were among those who went to the aid of the Whites, fighting from the eastern city of Vladivostok, in the northeast at Archangelsk and Murmansk, and in the Caucasus. From the perspectives of Canadians of all political stripes, the Soviet people did appear to be in need of international support, foreign aid, and friendship.[4] Groups were organized to send provisions.[5] Others, such as the Winnipeg Society for Technical Assistance for the Soviet Union and the Toronto-based Progressive Russian Club, sent workers to help repair the Russian economy.[6]

Among the most active in promoting trade with the Russians was Colonel Herbert J. Mackie; along with Dana Wilgress, he had been considered as a representative to the Canadian Trade Commission in Russia before the plan to send a commission was scrapped in the early 1920s. Mackie went on to found in 1926 a group called the Society for Cultural Relations with the USSR, which boasted more than 200 members. Although he was constantly in contact with the All-Union Society for Cultural Relations with Foreign Countries in Moscow, it distrusted him. The Soviets thought that his interest in the USSR was primarily commercial rather than political, and they suggested that it would be better to find another contact in Canada.[7]

In the 1920s, left-leaning Canadians considered it important to support not only the troubled Soviet people but also the Bolshevik government. Workers worldwide were attracted to the New Economic Policy with which the Bolshevik government was experimenting, though they had little information about what was happening "on the ground" in the USSR. Campaigns for "friendship" with the USSR allowed Soviet supporters in the West to channel leftist sympathies toward admiration of the USSR while providing some distance from the more "political" communist parties. Cultural exchanges gave the impression that Mackie's organization was apolitical, but archival documents show that Canadian authorities were nonetheless concerned that admiration for the USSR included a desire to imitate the Soviet system in Canada. Indeed, the authorities were suspicious of "friends" of the USSR from the beginning.

The RCMP reported retrospectively in the 1950s that the first Soviet friendship organizations arrived in Canada in 1921 when a branch of the American Friends of Soviet Russia was founded in Toronto. An undated RCMP report entitled "Brief: The Canadian Soviet Friendship Society" said that

> the fall of 1921 saw the formation of the "Canadian Friends of Soviet Russia" . . . as a branch of the Friends of Soviet Russia in the United States. By 1939, this Canadian section, never having

> gathered any significant support, had dwindled in strength to the point where only one small group remained, that at Montreal under the leadership of Louis Kon. The American organization was formed August 7th, 1921, in New York City, with one of its main purposes the soliciting of funds and supplies for the relief of famine in Russia. In carrying out this task, a considerable quantity of pro-Soviet propaganda was circulated.[8]

Another organization mentioned earlier, the Society for Technical Aid to Soviet Russia, took shape in June 1921. The Mounties said that this group "was formed for the purposes of carrying out policies laid down by Soviet Russia and the Communist International," and researchers have noted that Ukrainians living in Canada could return to the USSR with the help of this organization.[9] Although the Mounties reported that the society did not attract much support during the 1930s, several activists from the Cold War period speak of their radicalization during the Depression and of how the economic situation in Canada at that time convinced them of Soviet superiority. The RCMP kept files on the organization through the 1930s and reported on the wartime National Council for Canadian-Soviet Friendship when being a friend of the USSR gained a certain political acceptance.

From today's perspective, we might question whether RCMP attention to these individuals was warranted, but at the time there was real concern that the Soviets could convince some Canadians to import politics along with cultural products. And some did. To this day, groups in Canada and the United States who support the re-establishment of the Soviet Union trace their roots back to 1918 and the "Hands off Russia" campaign. They recall that the first "Friends" sent funds to Soviet Russia and lobbied Western governments not to interfere in the Russian Civil War (1917–19), in which White imperial troops bolstered by some foreign units fought Red Bolshevik troops under the leadership of Leon Trotsky. The groups, called the US Friends of the Soviet People and the International Council for Friendship and Solidarity with Soviet People (based in Toronto), celebrated the eightieth anniversary of the 1918 campaign in New York, where a banner proclaiming "Back to the Future . . . Restore the Soviet Union" was featured prominently.[10]

Typical of this trend was Louis Kon, who dated his involvement from 1919. Born in Moscow in 1881, he left Russia after having been involved in the 1905 revolution,[11] emigrated to Canada, and became a citizen in 1907. Working for the Grand Trunk Pacific Railway as an immigration and colonization officer, he met his wife, Elsa, in Brussels in 1910 while attending the Universal and International Exhibition for his employer. The couple had two children, both born in Winnipeg. Irene was born in 1911 and William in 1914. It is not clear what Kon was doing during the First World War, but in 1918 he returned to Russia as secretary of the Canadian Economic Commission under the supervision of Dana Wilgress, for whom he wrote several important reports.[12] Upon their return to Canada in 1919, Wilgress reported Kon to the RCMP for his "Bolshevik-like" views, noting that he had "contemplate[d] the trouble which can be caused ... by men of the type of Mr. Kon."[13] From then on, the RCMP kept a file on Kon, which essentially amounted to a blacklisting. The reports called Kon a "Bolsheviki propagandist" who spoke at radical immigrant meetings, presumably drawing funds from this activity.[14] In August 1919, the Civil Service Commission declared that it would "take every precaution in its power to guard against Mr. Kon's receiving any employment in the Public Service."[15]

Kon claimed that he was involved in organizing the Winnipeg General Strike of 1919, and his daughter, Irene, wrote that, "when the strike was broken and severe reprisals [were] in store for those who had supported it, he took his wife and two small children to Montreal."[16] He worked for the Canadian Electrical Association and the Montreal Light, Heat, and Power Corporation until he was offered a job by the Soviet government in 1926 to promote trade with the USSR. He was sent as a representative of the Canadian Pacific Railway to the Soviet Union in 1929 to try to sell the wider-gauged rails to the Soviet government, but once the Depression hit he found himself unemployed.

Kon served as head of the Montreal-based Friends of the Soviet Union (FSU) until the Second World War broke out, writing countless letters to the editors of local newspapers and organizing events. A main attribute that he brought to his work was his command of languages. At some meetings, Kon was said to have spoken French, at others "Jewish," and he was fluent in English and Russian.[17] In 1935, he organized a Soviet art exhibition sponsored by the FSU in Montreal, complained that it was "the object of the [Montreal] city authorities to prevent the French Canadian workers from learning the truth about Soviet Russia," and, even before the infamous "Padlock Law" was officially passed, served time in jail for having run a meeting in a hall without the necessary police permit.[18] He introduced Norman Bethune to the Communist Party of Canada[19] and encouraged Dyson Carter to re-establish the CSFS after the Second World War.[20] Kon was a supporter of Josef Stalin in the early 1950s,[21] attended events at the Soviet Embassy in Ottawa, and received letters from the leader of the Communist Party of Canada, Tim Buck.[22] Irene Kon wrote that "throughout the thirties and until the end of his life he worked tirelessly without money, trying to educate people to the momentous changes taking place in the world."[23] Kon's son, William, worked as an organizer for

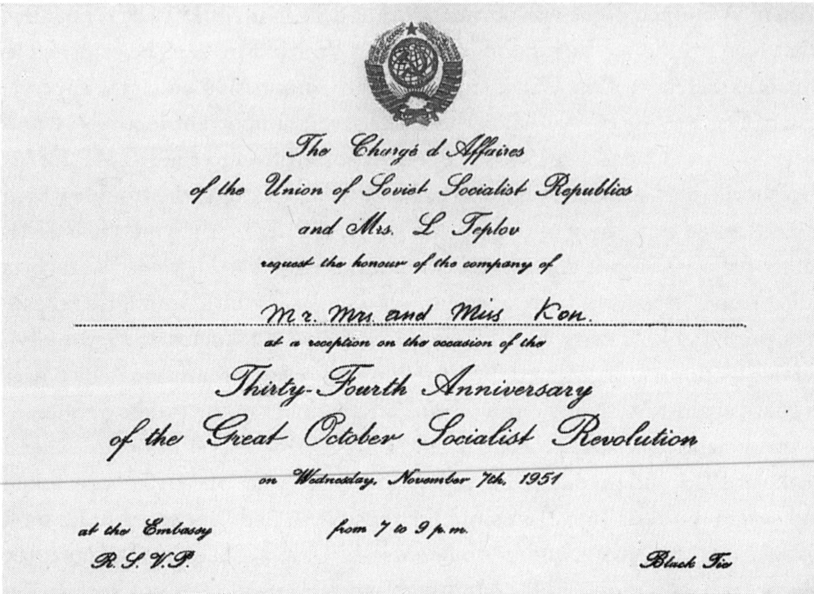

The Chargé d'Affaires
of the Union of Soviet Socialist Republics
and Mrs. L Teplov
request the honour of the company of
Mr. Mrs. and Miss Kon.
at a reception on the occasion of the
Thirty-Fourth Anniversary
of the Great October Socialist Revolution
on Wednesday, November 7th, 1951
at the Embassy from 7 to 9 p.m.
R.S.V.P. Black Tie

Figure 5. Invitation to Louis Kon and family to attend a party at the Soviet Embassy, Ottawa, Ontario, 7 November 1951.

the CPC, but as a member of the Canadian Forces he was killed overseas in 1945.[24] Irene is remembered fondly by progressives in Montreal as one of their most active members in the postwar years.

The Friends of the Soviet Union included a number of well-known Canadian communists and fellow travellers and was certainly what the RCMP would have called a "Communist Party front." The political nature of the prewar Soviet friendship movement was not disguised. Kon was probably a member of the Communist Party of Canada. Irene wrote to her father in a confessional manner in the late 1930s promising to approach the party herself soon about becoming a member, and he made the arrangements for CPC meetings throughout the 1930s.[25] In that decade, an RCMP report placed several other prominent communists at Soviet friendship events in Toronto. At the National Conference of Friendship with USSR held at the Odd Fellows Temple on College Street in Toronto in June 1935, speakers included party organizers Sam Carr and A.A. McLeod; Annie Buller and Bella Gauld were also present.[26] The secretary of the Conference Committee, Jack Cowan, began his remarks by addressing the audience as *comrades*,[27] a choice of words that Carter would consistently avoid in favour of *friends*. The context of the 1930s was important to the delegates. Reverend C.C. Wellerman, a Protestant minister from

Figure 6. In the 1930s, Canadians attending Soviet Friendship events were not necessarily communists, but neither was the political messaging hidden. Conference participants at the Canadian Soviet Congress Arts Panel included Paraskeva Clark and Sir Ernest MacMillan (right), Toronto, Ontario, around 1934.

Holland Centre, spoke at the event, explaining that "membership in the church was in itself no reason for not admiring the splendid achievements of the Soviet Union." He said that "his sympathies were with the working-class, and with the Soviet Union, which has been doing so much for the working class, and for the cause of peace."[28] The Depression of the 1930s and the social alternative that the USSR appeared to represent were important factors here. This context was later cited by several former CSFS activists as being an important influence in their decision to become involved with left-wing groups in Canada.

The rhetoric at the meetings in the 1930s showed overt admiration for both the cultural and the social advances made in the USSR and the political situation that made these advances possible. As Libbie Park, an active attendee of Friends of the Soviet Union events, noted, "the FSU was a lively organization attracting Communists and non-communists curious about life in the Soviet Union."[29] In 1935, the group organized talks given by Bethune, who had just come back from the USSR, by leading CPC theorist Stanley Ryerson, and by Kon's son, William, who spoke about Soviet writer Gorky and the "new democracy" in the USSR.[30] However, at their congress in June 1935, it was noted that a different strategy was needed in appealing to Canadians outside left-wing groups. For example, J.F. White said that the message needed to be pitched differently to "intellectuals, and liberals, with a small 'l,' of all descriptions," than to members of the CCF, Canadian Labor Defense League, Friends of the Soviet Union, and unions:

> In dealing with delegates and observers from these outside organizations, it is necessary to use a slightly different technique than in dealing with the regular inside ones. After all, we have to realize that as we make contact with larger numbers of people who have been outside the left-wing or revolutionary or even mildly socialist movement, that these people will know very much less about the U.S.S.R., and will be more or less in the kindergarten class. When we are talking to regular delegates who have been going to these meetings for years, we can use revolutionary technique[s], and have a regular sort of hell-fire meeting, but that sort of thing is not proper for delegates from the other organizations, who are gradually becoming interested and sympathetic towards the developments in the U.S.S.R.[31]

He suggested that the FSU had begun in Canada as a small group, but now that it had its own journal, members could aspire to greater things. He even dreamed of one day hosting events in Maple Leaf Gardens.[32]

The argument that support for the USSR meant support for peaceful coexistence was used in the interbellum period as it was during the Cold War. In 1934, the RCMP reported that Kon gave a speech to the French-language FSU branch in Montreal entitled "The Danger of War against the Soviet Union" attended by 250 people. Beatrice Ferneyhough, who would remain active in the postwar CSFS, was pulled from the platform by police in Montreal while speaking against the rise of Hitler and fascism in Europe.[33] At the FSU congress in 1935, White argued that the ranks of pro-Soviet Canadians could only grow since "the Soviet Union offers the one hope of an alternative system to capitalism,"[34] the one solution to fascism, and, "although it is quite a long time since the Great War has finished, there are still thousands, tens of thousands, hundreds of thousands of people who remember quite clearly what war means to the working-class."[35] A.A. McLeod, who would later serve as a member of the Legislative Assembly in Ontario, brought greetings to the congress from the Canadian League against War and Fascism, recognizing that "the Soviet Union is the greatest force for peace in the world."[36]

The rhetoric of the truth about the Soviet Union and its universal achievements, also used in the postwar period, was a feature of many FSU speeches. Sam Carr brought greetings from the Communist Movement of Canada to the FSU congress: "I am certain that the gathering in this hall will again prove that there are tens of thousands of people in Canada who, though they do not agree with what they believe is Communism, admire the great deeds of the people of the U.S.S.R. and the contribution the Soviet Union is making towards a better universe. . . . I feel confident that you will elaborate the necessary plans to further disseminate the truth about what is going on in that one-sixth of the earth, the U.S.S.R."[37] Perhaps foreshadowing Carter's emphasis on the scientific and technological achievements of the USSR, J.F. White said that "one of the disadvantages of living as we do under a capitalist system is that nothing can be done about the weather, and it is probably due partly to the unfavorable weather that we have such a small gathering of delegates and observers here this morning. Now, in the Soviet Union, they have already begun to investigate the possibility of channeling the weather to suit themselves. . . . As Comrade Stalin has said, 'There are no fortresses too difficult for a Bolshevik to conquer.'"[38]

In the mid-1930s, the policy of the Comintern, laid out at its congress in Moscow in 1935 and then adopted by all international Communist Parties, was to present a "united front": that is, to co-opt all progressive, left-leaning groups and individuals into a larger forum that would be friendly to the USSR. The Comintern press related that CPC delegates to the USSR in the 1930s were encouraged to promote, on their return to Canada, the Friends of the Soviet Union.[39] Several aspects of the 1935 friendship convention point to the development of this policy, adopted directly from the Comintern platform. Cables from Friends of the Soviet Union congresses in Sweden, Holland, France, and Norway were read at the convention, and participants were encouraged to feel that they were part of a larger, international movement.[40] W. Sydney, representing the National Committee of the FSU, began his speech as if at a wedding:

> To-day, when we are gathered here, representatives of 75 or 80 organizations, we must understand that our role is in relation to the Soviet Union. We must understand that we have a very definite role to play and that we by showing our friendship with the Soviet Union . . . contribute to the success of the Soviet Union both at home and abroad. That is why it is necessary that we, to-day, reaffirm our friendship with the Soviet Union. There are representatives here from various organizations; some are as yet not clear on the aims and objects of the Friends of the Soviet Union. We will

> try ... during this Conference and Convention to clarify what we stand for, and by doing this, we feel certain that we will draw them into our ranks, and greatly extend the ranks of those friends of the Soviet Union in Canada. We must be clear that our object here must be of the broadest possible nature, that we must not in any way do anything that will narrow our sphere of activities. We will not be doing the Soviet Union any good by trying to duplicate the work of other organizations. We have certain functions to perform.[41]

These functions involved spreading the good news of the USSR, telling Canadians about Soviet achievements and policies "in the interest of the working class." "We have to bring the truth to them, and have them realize what the Soviet Union is doing," Sydney indicated.[42]

The duty of the FSU was also to respond to attacks against the USSR from the bourgeoisie, according to Sydney, because these attacks "weaken not only the Soviet Union, but they weaken the working-class the world over." "As a result of this Conference, we want to see greatly added strength to the Friends of the Soviet Union, whether as members or as affiliates," said Sydney. "We want to see ever larger sections of the Canadian people rally to support the work that the workers and farmers are doing in the Soviet Union, and to answer every slander and attack against it."[43] This was the kind of language later used by Carter in *News-Facts about the USSR* and *Northern Neighbors*, as well as in the book that he published in 1951 with Charlotte Carter, *We Saw Socialism*.[44] The emphasis was always on promoting the USSR in the most positive light and countering critiques of it by presenting "facts" and personal testimonies to the contrary.

In celebrating their success, the friendship magazine *Soviet Russia To-Day*, published in Canada from August 1933, was held up as an example.[45] Its circulation was said to have increased from the original 3,000 to 8,000 in two years. This magazine might have been a Canadian version of the publication by the same title published by the New York–based FSU from February 1932 to January 1951. In its first issue, the editors noted that it was published by the "Canadian section of the F.S.U.," and it carried greetings from the American and British sections of the same organization.[46] The last issue appears to have been published in January 1936, carrying an article written by Aleksei Stakhanov, the young Soviet miner known as the inspiration for the Stakhanovite movement in the USSR.[47] Articles purporting to reveal "The Truth about the Soviet Union,"[48] and large photographs of Soviet people and technological might, suggest that the magazine was an example for Carter, who later spent his career publishing this type of pro-Soviet literature. The

1935 conference resolved that *Soviet Russia Today* "has been an important instrument in spreading knowledge about the Soviet Union to a wide reading public. This magazine also constantly reflects in its columns ... organizational activities of the Friends of the Soviet Union."[49] In 1933, the magazine was ten cents an issue, but in 1936 the price was reduced to only five cents. No direct information was given on where the financing for this magazine came from, though trouble overcoming financial difficulties was discussed.

At the congress, J. Cowan, national secretary of the Friends of the Soviet Union, denied that funding for the FSU came from Moscow yet suggested that Soviet investment would be justified:

> Our enemies have reiterated that our financing is done on "Moscow Gold." I make so bold as to express my opinion that if it were true, it would be no crime, as the Soviet Union has as much and more right to finance movements in her favor in other countries as have all other countries of the world who maintain propaganda agents of all kinds, including lobbyists, trade representatives, spies, and others to further their own interests in every country. I say, therefore, if it were true that the Soviet Union finances our work, I would see no crime in it. The fact of the matter is however, not only that it is a lie deliberately spread by our enemies for their own purpose, but that on the other hand, the sections of the F.S.U. throughout the world finance the maintenance of its International headquarters in Amsterdam, Holland, by means of annual Levy Stamps, and that not one penny either directly or indirectly has come into our funds from other than the working-class and friends in Canada.

Cowan complained that photos, pamphlets, notes, and books had been confiscated by the RCMP, and provincial police visits were intimidating members and hall owners into not allowing FSU events to be hosted.[50] The 1935 Conference Resolution on the Friends of the Soviet Union concluded that, "in spite of the unfriendly and often hostile attitude on the part of the Canadian Government and of certain powerful industrial and financial interests, this Conference records a growing feeling of friendship among the people of Canada for the people and government of the Soviet Union."[51]

Being friends of the USSR might have allowed individuals to combine political idealism with a sense of active participation on the world stage. Certainly, an interest in Soviet culture was sincere. Lobbying for international recognition of the Soviet Union was a rallying cry. Soviet leaders had powerful celebrity status for leftists in this period. For instance, in 1936 Louis Kon wrote a letter to Josef Stalin asking for photographs of him for the FSU office in Montreal. The letter is striking in its naive suggestion that Stalin was approachable: "We are addressing you, of course, as the symbol of the realism and ideal of human life as understood and lived by those who proudly call themselves Friends of the Soviet Union."[52] Despite all the rhetoric, the main attraction of Soviet friendship events during the Depression might well have been as a venue for idealistic Canadians to share dismay at the economic problems on their own doorsteps rather than a more politically driven desire to replace the Canadian political system with a Soviet alternative.[53]

The signing of the non-aggression pact between Stalin and Hitler in 1939 threw communist and progressive groups worldwide into disarray. For years, their message had been that the USSR represented the only alternative to fascism, yet now Moscow had negotiated a deal to remain neutral if war broke out between the Allies and Nazi Germany. It was a hard pill for many communists to swallow, but within a few weeks the Canadian Communist Party instructed its members to oppose the war—and to blame it on imperialism sponsored by the United Kingdom and France.[54] Communists and Soviet sympathizers in Canada found themselves considering the argument that a Nazi victory would "liberate" Canada from its colonial status and were therefore accused of being traitors. Suddenly, the FSU took a hiatus. Kon stopped organizing friendship events in 1939, and RCMP documents reveal little information on the groups in Montreal or Toronto until the Soviet Union entered the war following Hitler's invasion in 1941. In 1945, the RCMP reported that the FSU was already in decline in the late 1930s, noting that the numbers "had dwindled considerably to small groups in Montreal and Toronto" by 1937 and 1938. By 1939, just the group in Montreal under Kon was left, and by 1940 even that group had dissipated, the report stated.[55]

However, once the USSR entered the war, Soviet friendship became broadly palatable as it never had before. In Canada as in Britain, mass support for Soviet friendship was enthusiastically popular by 1942.[56] A BBC documentary produced in 1980 and aired on TVO in Canada illustrates the extent to which the swing toward friendship with the Soviet Union was a result of international events and changing interpretations of them in the West between the 1930s and the 1950s.[57] Starting in 1941, non-governmental, often voluntary, groups across Canada began to organize once more to send aid to "Russia" and lobby for the opening of a second front in Europe to help the Soviets. The RCMP were still convinced that some of these small organizations were put together by communists of long standing. One of these groups, called the Information Bureau, Soviet Union at Peace and War, formed in Montreal with a "membership comprised [of] many of those formerly connected with the Friends of the Soviet Union," apparently joined the Labor-Progressive Party in 1944.[58] The Russian Medical Aid Committee, also set up in Montreal in 1941, was sponsored by "persons close to the Communist movement," but it also attracted "prominent citizens in Montreal" to its events.[59] In December 1941, Joseph H. Davies, former American ambassador to the USSR and White House–supported spokesman for the war effort, spoke at one of its events, and the money raised was donated to the Canadian Red Cross with instructions to use it for medical supplies for the USSR. Davies had become well known for his positivist views on the USSR published in his 1941 bestseller, *Mission to Moscow*,[60] made into a Warner Brothers film in 1943. In March 1942, the Montreal group sponsored a talk by American communist Anna Louise Strong, founder in the 1920s of the English-language Soviet newspaper for foreign audiences, *Moscow News*. The RCMP reported that a separate Montreal-based organization called the Association of Canadian Citizens of Russian Origin, also set up in 1941, had 5,000 people at its first event in July that year, 75 percent of whom were "communist sympathizers," but that it "ceased to exist" sometime in 1942.[61] These groups might have been merging into others. A fourth group, originally called the Society for the Study of Modern Russia and largely made up of university professors, was organized in March 1943, later changed its name to the Canada Russia Society, and became the Montreal branch of the National Council for Canadian-Soviet Friendship later that year.[62]

Gregory S. Kealey and Reginald Whitaker have commented that the RCMP "were sometimes not very careful about painting people Red or Pink who were associated with such alleged fronts. For instance, their discussion of the National Council for Canadian-Soviet Friendship contains names of many persons who were probably never influenced by Communism at all."[63] This is likely what the RCMP meant when they spoke of "innocent" people attracted to the event suggesting an assumption of ideological "guilt" in the case of other attendees. It is worth noting the degree to which communists and fellow travellers remember the Canadian-Soviet friendship group as a forum for the expression of political and fraternal sympathies for the USSR. Fraternal, good neighbourly, relations were in style while the Soviets were with the Allies, and within this environment, communists and fellow travellers found an outlet for their activism and some shelter from social judgement.

In 1942, Carter, already well known in progressive circles, wrote to Kon in Montreal to thank him for material that Kon had sent and for his compliments on Carter's recent pro-Soviet book, *Russia's Secret Weapon* (1942).[64] Carter said that he was receiving material from the Soviet Embassy in Washington, DC, and asked Kon for a connection at the Soviet Embassy in Ottawa. He also requested a recommendation on Friends of the Soviet Union letterhead, which he said "would be very helpful."[65] This might have been his initiation into Soviet friendship events, and Carter would remain involved with the wartime group until he himself became head of the postwar National Council. But his interest in things Soviet did not set him apart from many Canadians at that time. Throughout the war, the Canadian Wartime Information Board used Soviet films and discussed the use of Canadian culture as a means of promoting Canadian contributions to the war effort to the Soviets.[66] Kon was among those who approached the Wartime Information Board about publishing Canadian material in the Soviet publication *International Literature*.[67] This focus on the wartime use of culture also meant that the Canadian ambassador, Dana Wilgress, on behalf of the Canadian people, donated a collection of Canadian art to the city of Leningrad via VOKS in Moscow.[68]

The RCMP reported that "on June 22nd, 1943, the National Council for Canadian-Soviet Friendship"[69] was formed in Toronto. Wartime public opinion in support of the Allies meant that the council was supported by elite politicians and businesspeople in Canada. The first public function was a large rally at Maple Leaf Gardens under the chairmanship of Prime Minister W.L. Mackenzie King. This was the second anniversary of the attack on the USSR by Nazi Germany. It was said that the main purpose of the new organization was to dispel misunderstanding and distrust of the Soviet Union in an effort to strengthen the military alliance. The affairs of the newly formed council were conducted from the offices of *Vestnik*, the organ of the Federation of Russian Canadians.[70] The RCMP did not believe that the National Council had a "connection with any of its predecessors," nor did they think that it was sponsored by the CPC, but they did note that "the Communist Party is very interested in its activities and has several members and sympathizers listed as patrons."[71] An undated leaflet from the CSFS and *News-Facts about the USSR* told a similar story but with some spin: "The National Council for Canadian-Soviet Friendship *was formed in June 1943*, at a rally of 17,000 people in Toronto, with the late Hon. W. Mackenzie King as Chairman, and hundreds of prominent citizens and organizations taking part. *For years* the Council was made up mainly of prominent business men, professional people and others of high prestige. Much valuable work was done in publicizing facts about the USSR's war effort as Canada's ally."[72]

The list of the wartime executive of the National Council for Canadian-Soviet Friendship contained the names, addresses, and phone numbers of

Figure 7. A worker installs decorations for a wartime rally at Maple Leaf Gardens, Toronto, 1940s.

eighty Canadians and was followed by a list of the members of the Arts, Science, Education, Agriculture, and Labour Committees.[73] The national executive included John David Eaton of the Thomas Eaton Company; L.W. Brockington of the Canadian Broadcasting Corporation, also serving at the Ottawa branch of the United Kingdom Information Office; Dr. Wilder Penfield, renowned Montreal-based neurosurgeon; and "renegade lawyer" J.L. Cohen.[74] Also listed were the heads of two universities, Dr. Carleton Stanley, president of Dalhousie, and Dr. G.P. Gilmour, chancellor of McMaster, as well as professors from the University of New Brunswick, University of Western Ontario, Laval University, Queen's University, and University of Alberta. Dr. Barker Fairley of the Department of English at the University of Toronto and his wife, Margaret Fairley, well known for her work as a leftist literary critic, were on the executive. The mayor of Windsor, an alderman from Regina, Dorothy Burr Thompson, archeologist at the Royal Ontario Museum, and poet E.J. Pratt were members. Leo Malania of the Department of External Affairs was listed, as was I. Malania, secretary of the Federation of Russian Canadians. Mrs. Rae Luckock, MPP and president of the Housewives' Consumers' League, and Margaret Gould, associated with the CPC and an editorial writer at the

Toronto Daily Star, were also listed. David Shugar, noted as a "research physicist" from Ottawa, was on the executive. He would later be detained by the RCMP after the Gouzenko defection, and though he was eventually acquitted in court he did end up losing his job at the Department of Health and Welfare. Sir Ellsworth Flavelle,[75] Max Chic, and R.H. Davis, each of whom served as head of the National Council at various times until 1947, were predictably on the executive in 1943. Several people involved with worker and adult education, as well as cultural and festival groups, were among the members. Sergei Koudriavtzev, first secretary of the Soviet Embassy in Ottawa, was also on the executive.[76]

Famous Canadian composer and musician Sir Ernest Macmillan, as well as Group of Seven artists A.Y. Jackson and Lawren Harris, were on the Arts Committee. Fellow committee members John Grierson,[77] Nat Taylor,[78] Andrew Allan of the CBC,[79] and Herbert Allen of Columbia Pictures[80] were—as one would imagine—particularly interested in film exchanges. Barker Fairley was also on the Arts Committee.[81] The Science Committee had seventeen members, thirteen of whom were professors at Canadian universities. Dr. H.B. Speakman, director of the Ontario Research Foundation, was chairman of the Science Committee, and David Shugar was listed as a member.[82] The Education Committee was chaired by Dr. J.A. Long of the College of Education in Toronto, and its eighteen members included the president of the University of British Columbia, Norman A. Mackenzie, and provincial ministers of education from Ontario, Quebec, Saskatchewan, and New Brunswick. Members of municipal boards of education, teacher councils, and home and school councils were represented on this committee.[83] The Agriculture Committee was chaired by V.S. Mulburn of the Ontario Federation of Agriculture, and members included representatives of the federal Department of Agriculture, as well as provincial agricultural federations. There was representation from the Ontario Milk Control Board, as well as the Ontario Whole Milk Producers League, the Ottawa Experimental Farm, the Saskatchewan Co-op, tobacco farmers in Simcoe, Ontario, and journalists who specialized in agricultural matters.[84]

With almost sixty members, the Labour Committee was by far the largest of all the National Council committees, and included in its membership were many openly associated with the Canadian left. Among these individuals were J.L. Cohen, A.A. MacLeod, communist MPP Bruce Magnusson of Port Arthur, and Pearl Wedro of Toronto, all of whom were LPP members. Most of those listed included their union affiliations. Some of these individuals would remain involved in the CSFS under Carter's leadership. For instance, Dewar Ferguson, of the Canadian Seamen's Union, would appear on the letterhead of the postwar society as an executive member. Bruce Magnusson was head of the trade union delegation sent by the CSFS to the USSR in the early 1950s, and Pearl Wedro later subscribed to the CSFS publications.[85] This particularly interested the RCMP in 1951, and in submitting these lists to his superior in Ottawa, the Toronto Special Section inspector wrote that, "although the documents refer to the activities of the Council in 1943, 1944 and 1945, they are being submitted to augment our file and attention is drawn to the fact that the names of several persons who are at present prominent in subversive activities are mentioned therein."[86]

In November 1943, the National Council hosted another rally in Maple Leaf Gardens.[87] Introducing the rally, L.K. Brockington of the United Kingdom Information Office in Ottawa said that

> this great building, like many little homes which are to-night joined with it in sympathy and experience, echoes with the noble harmony of thanksgiving which has just ended. And if the Maple Leaf Gardens and the room in which you hear these words echo with the sound of that thanksgiving, it is because for many months, sometimes dark, always grim, always glorious, many hundreds of thousands of British and Canadian hearts have also been filled with thankfulness—thankfulness for the men and women of the Soviet Republics. To mark that thankfulness and to try to translate it into something real and enduring, in the spirit of Canadian-Soviet friendship and in the name of the society dedicated to that high purpose, it is my duty to bring before you who listen a proposal to draw two pioneer northern peoples closer together in neighbourly and kindly company.[88]

Brockington spoke poetically, reciting the names of Soviet cities such as Stalingrad, Leningrad, Kharkov, Rostov, and Kiev that had fought back the Nazis and "will ring through the ages like Thermopylae and Marathon, Lapanto, Trafalgar, Waterloo, Vimy Ridge and El Alamein."[89] He called on Canadians to do as their British brothers and sisters had done—adopt Soviet cities, send much-needed provisions to the Soviets, and be ready to exchange information, experience, and services with them. Edgar Snow, an American journalist who had visited the war-torn USSR, urged his audience "to hammer out" a partnership with the USSR "on the broad anvil of honest democratic discussion" because the "Soviet peoples want our friendship and our co-operation," and they had earned it with their wartime sacrifices.[90]

The cause of Soviet friendship can be seen, therefore, to have enjoyed its widest popularity and legitimacy during the Second World War, while the USSR was one of the Allies. The red scare of 1919 forgotten and the ideological battles of the Cold War not yet envisioned, the Soviets were admired and their political system tolerated or perhaps simply ignored. Fellow travellers within the organized friendship groups did not stand out greatly from other members, though the RCMP continued to track them. After 1945, left-leaning members stayed within the group, attempting to bolster its support as mainstream social and political elites reconsidered their affiliation. The war years were therefore something of a golden age for Canadian-Soviet friends in the chilly political climate of the decade following the end of the war.

In 1943, Louis Kon wrote to Dyson Carter to congratulate him on his admiring biography of Stalin, *Stalin's Life: At Last the True Story*.[91] The *Canadian Tribune*, newspaper of the Labor-Progressive Party, had given it a poor review, and Carter had written to the editor to complain. The paper apologized, saying that "Mr. Carter is doing invaluable work to explain the USSR and the social advantages modern science can bring to Canada, and we urge the readers of our paper to give him all their support. The *Tribune* review erred on the side of sectarianism, as Mr. Carter says, and we apologize for any harm we have done him or his publishers."[92] In his letter of congratulation, Kon suggested that the Friendship Society be re-established. With arguments reminiscent of the 1935 FSU convention, he proposed that a less overt political strategy was needed "if we are to cease just to talk to ourselves" and that the new organization be modelled on his own work to bring together "a group of likeminded persons ... coast-to-coast ... arranged in the larger centres with a real benefit to Canada."[93] He asked Carter to meet him in Montreal to discuss the idea.

Meanwhile, the minutes from a national executive meeting in January 1944 show that the council was meeting with success in its campaign to increase contact between Soviet and Canadian citizens. The Science Committee had been corresponding with Soviet scientists, the Labour Committee was urging Canadian unions to contact their Soviet counterparts directly, and Soviet and Canadian cities were being twinned. To facilitate this communication, the Education Committee had contacted all Canadian university language departments to ask them to promote the study of Russian.[94] Under the subtitle "Armed Forces," it was noted in the minutes that "various army contacts are enthusiastic about the use of the Council's services. Two poster exhibits are now on display at Camp Borden, Military District #1 recruiting officer has made use of poster exhibits [*sic*]. The Army's Ontario Educational Services ... and the Canadian Legion Educational Director for the armed forces have requested material. The Army Recreation Director, Captain Eisenhardt[,] is arranging for a Red Army Sports exhibit to tour Canadian army centers."[95] However, the council seemed to be having financial difficulties. In January, Sir Ellsworth Flavelle complained that money was being spent before it was raised,[96] and at the next meeting, in February, it was announced that "Sir Ellsworth regrets that he can no longer be responsible for further financing of the Council. All outstanding accounts to date will be taken care of. This is not to be construed as any lack of interest or support of the Council by Sir Ellsworth."[97] The Canadian Congress of Labour had apparently pledged $1,000, and a few hundred dollars had been sent by individual unions to fund the council's activities. It was decided that big industrialists and agricultural groups such as the wheat pools could be approached for further funding.[98] Although listed as members, most of the "big names" did not appear to attend the council's meetings.

The August 1944 issue of the *Council Bulletin* announced the dates of the next congress and congratulated local branches on their efforts to promote Soviet friendship.[99] In particular, Vancouver was praised for the "Odessa Week," sponsored by the mayor and local Soviet Friendship Council, during which pledges were made to help rebuild and restore Odessa. Fifteen thousand people attended an aid-Odessa concert in Stanley Park, and media helped to publicize the campaign.[100] Regina was said to be carrying out a similar campaign to help the Soviet city Kursk, and the telegram sent from Stalino thanking the mayor and citizens of Glace Bay for "adopting" it was quoted in full. The *Council Bulletin* also quoted a telegram sent from VOKS, Moscow's All-Union Society for Cultural Relations with Foreign Countries, urging Canadian authors to correspond with Soviet writers such as Boris Pasternak, Alexei Tolstoy, Ilya Ehrenburg, and Mikhail Sholokhov. "Fruitful cooperation between writers [from] our two countries who are using their art as weapons against Nazism—common enemy of progressive humanity—will serve to promote friendship and closer contact between Canadian and Soviet culture and to increase [the] mutual understanding of our two peoples," the telegram said.[101] The Agriculture Committee decided that a delegation to the USSR was needed, and it cabled the Canadian ambassador to the USSR, Dana Wilgress, to ask for more information on the Soviet agricultural situation.[102]

In October 1944, it looked like the Second Annual Congress for Canadian-Soviet Friendship might not go ahead as planned. Flavelle had been absent from a series of meetings because of "ill health," and he resigned in late October.[103] In addition, Dr. Malcolm Ross, Canadian literary critic with the National Film Board at that time, was to make the arrangements for the congress but had "been recalled to Ottawa," and the executive had to replace

Figure 8. Announcement of the Second Annual Congress for Canadian-Soviet Friendship, November 1944.

PATRONS

LIEUTENANT-GOVERNORS:

Hon. Albert Matthews (Ontario)
Major-Gen. Hon. Sir Eugene Fiset (Quebec)
Lt.-Col. Hon. Henry E. Kendall (Nova Scotia)
Lt.-Col. Hon. W. G. Clark (New Brunswick)
Hon. R. F. McWilliams (Manitoba)
Lt.-Col. Hon. W. C. Woodward (British Columbia)
Hon. Bradford W. LePage (Prince Edward Island)
Hon. Archibald P. McNab (Saskatchewan)
Hon. John Campbell Bowen (Alberta)

PRIME MINISTERS:

The Right Hon. W. L. Mackenzie King, Prime Minister of Canada
Hon. George A. Drew (Ontario)
Hon. A. Stirling MacMillan (Nova Scotia)
Hon. J. B. McNair (New Brunswick)
Hon. Stuart S. Garson (Manitoba)
Hon. John Hart (British Columbia)
Hon. William J. Patterson (Saskatchewan)

CHIEF JUSTICES:

The Rt. Hon. Sir Lyman Poore Duff, Chief Justice of Canada
Hon. Severin Letourneau (Quebec)
Hon. Sir Joseph Andrew Chisholm (Nova Scotia)
Hon. J. B. M. Baxter (New Brunswick)
Hon. James E. P. Prendergast (Manitoba)
Hon. David A. MacDonald (British Columbia)
Hon. Thane A. Campbell (Prince Edward Island)
Hon. W. Melville Martin (Saskatchewan)
Hon. Horace Harvey (Alberta)

Walter Abell
Mrs. Harvey Agnew
G. H. Aikens
W. F. Angus
Mrs. C. H. A. Armstrong
J. E. Atkinson
E. A. Baker
John Bassett
M. Banker Bates
John B. M. Baxter
DeGaspe Beaubien
Senator C. P. Beaubien
L. P. Belnap
Percy R. Bengough
A. B. Bennett
Boris Berlin
Acting Surgeon-Captain Charles H. Best
Andre Bieler
Prof. H. E. Bigelow
Rev. Dr. H. H. Bingham
Wm. Massey Birks
W. D. Black
John Boyd
Hon. John Bracken
Air-Marshal L. S. Breadner
Dr. Horace L. Brittain
John A. Brockie
Allan Bronfman
Samuel Bronfman
Mrs. Elizabeth Brown
John W. Bruce
Very Rev. D. Peter Bryce
E. E. Buckerfield
J. W. Buckley
Stanley Burke
W. H. Burnell
H. D. Burns
John Burns
George Burt
C. L. Burton
E. L. Bushnell
Morley Callaghan
C. H. Carlisle
Dyson Carter
William Casey
Mme. Pierre F. Casgrain
P. A. Chester
Lewis Clark
Brooke Claxton, M.P.
J. L. Cohen
M. J. Coldwell, M.P.
D. C. Coleman
Professor J. B. Collip
F. J. Conboy
Patrick Conroy
Dr. E. A. Corbett
John Counsell, M.C.
J. B. Coyne
Harold Crabtree
Jack Creed
Senator W. Rupert Davies
Aubrey Davis
R. H. Davis
S. L. de Carteret
Prof. Alfred T. de Lury
Elizabeth de Miribel
L. A. de Wolfe
Dora Dibney
Jackson Dodds
Mrs. Cameron E. Dow
Huntly R. Drummond
W. R. Drynan
J. S. Duncan
Mrs. Andrew Dunn
Hon. C. A. Dunning
J. H. Duplan
Michael Dushnitsky
John David Eaton
Lady Eaton
R. Y. Eaton
W. A. Eden
Wm. Edmiston
W. Sanford Evans
Lady Falconer
Grace M. Fairley
Gordon Farrell
Robert Fennell
Dewar Ferguson
G. V. Ferguson
Philip Fisher, D.S.O.
Sir Ellsworth Flavelle, Bart.
Lady Flavelle
Norman G. Foster
R. M. Fowler
Dr. W. Sherwood Fox
Mrs. W. Kaspar Fraser
Kat Shau Fung
Dr. W. E. Gallie
Aime Geoffrion
Dr. George Peel Gilmour
W. C. Good
Earl Gordon
Walter Gordon
Margaret Gould
Hon. Feodor Gousev
W. G. Graham
Mrs. W. L. Grant
Sir Edmund Wylie Grier
Dr. Donald W. Gullett
Major-General J. A. Gunn
Robert Haddow
Boris Hambourg
H. H. Hannam
Mrs. Edgar Drury Hardy
Lawren Harris
Major William Harty
Jean Charles Harvey
G. Russell Harvey
Major-Gen. H. F. H. and Mrs. Hertzberg
Herbert Higgins
Dr. C. M. Hincks
Mrs. W. B. Horkins
Hon. Clarence D. Howe, M.P.
Senator A. K. Hugessen
E. Ingles
J. L. D. Ives
R. G. Ivey
A. Y. Jackson
C. S. Jackson
Dr. F. Cyril James
Wilfred C. James
E. B. Jolliffe, M.P.P.
Col. C. H. L. Jones
Paul C. Jones
Walter D. Jones
Canon W. W. Judd, D.D.
Lady Kemp
A. J. Kelly
Rev. Dr. H. B. Ketchen
Senator James H. King
Mrs. George D. Kirkpatrick
Rabbi E. Kirzner
Fred Knowles
J. E. Labelle
Major-Gen. the Hon. L. R. LaFleche, M.P.
Senator Norman P. Lambert
Cecil Lamont
F. P. L. Lane
Louis L. Lang
Samuel Lapedes
Hugh H. Lawson
Ray Lawson
N. L. Leach
R. V. LeSueur
Ivor Lewis
Arthur Lismer
Mrs. R. M. Luckock, M.P.P.
D. S. Lyons
Harold W. Male
Alfred Marois
Dr. Paul J. J. Martin, M.P.
Major Raymond Massey
F. W. Maxted
C. H. Millard
Horatio Ray Milner
Hon. Humphrey Mitchell, M.P.
F. Cleveland Morgan
Nigel Morgan
F. M. Morton
A. R. Mosher
James Y. Murdoch
Walter M. Murdoch
W. G. Murrin
Rev. Dr. J. R. Mutchmor
P. D. McArthur
Hon. Leighton McCarthy
J. W. McConnell
H. O. McCurry
Mrs. Clara F. McEachren
His Excellency the Most Rev. J. C. McGuigan, D.D.
John J. McHale
Hugh A. MacKenzie
Hon. Ian A. Mackenzie, M.P.
Dr. Norman A. M. MacKenzie
Hon. James A. MacKinnon, M.P.
J. S. McLean
Rev. Dr. David MacLennan
Ross H. McMaster
Sir Ernest MacMillan
Harvey R. MacMillan
G. A. S. Nairn
Dr. Robert Newton
Hon. Jacob Nicol
Mrs. Dorise Nielsen, M.P.
Harry C. Nixon, M.P.P.
Gregory Okulevich
J. J. O'Grady
Commissioner Benjamin Orames
His Grace the Most Rev. Derwyn T. Owen, D.D.
Rev. Dr. F. W. Patterson
Wilfred Pelletier
L. R. Philie
W. H. Phillips
Hon. Charles G. Power, M.P.
Prof. E. J. Pratt
Harold Pritchett
F. W. Ransom
Mrs. W. C. Rean
B. H. Reiger
C. S. Riley
Sir Charles G. D. Roberts
Rabbi Samuel Sachs
Benjamin Sadowski
B. K. Sandwell
George Sangster
J. Ernest Savard
The Rt. Rev. Dr. J. R. P. Sclater
Dr. Duncan Campbell Scott
Dr. Fletcher B. Sharp
Mrs. Fletcher B. Sharp
L. E. Shaw
C. W. Sherman
Rev. Dr. T. T. Shields
Dr. Liu Shih Shun
Victor Sifton
Joseph Simard
C. F. Sise
Dr. Sydney E. Smith
Mrs. H. B. Spaulding
Christopher Spencer
George W. Spinney
Dr. W. Carleton Stanley
Joseph Star.
Taylor Statten
Mrs. N. C. Stephens
Rabbi H. J. Stern
James Stewart
Wm. Stewart
A. M. Sullivan
J. A. Patrick Sullivan
Herbert J. Symington
Dr. W. P. Thompson
Mr. Justice L. P. D. Tilley
Beryl Truax
Dr. George J. Trueman
Dr. Dorothy Turville
R. C. Vaughan
Squadron Leader Gregory Vlastos
Alex. Walker
Professor M. W. Wallace
Dr. Robert C. Wallace
Mrs. H. D. Warren
S. M. Wedd
Morris Wilson
North Winship
Margaret Wherry
Fred Whitehouse
Norman Wilks
Dr. Healey Willan
Senator Cairine Wilson
A. B. Wood
Samuel Zacks
W. P. Zeller

Figure 9. During the Second World War, Canadian–Soviet Friendship initiatives attracted broad support, as this list of patrons dated 27 October 1944 demonstrates.

him.[104] These changes were said to have caused "a certain amount of confusion" in the council office. Margaret Spaulding, "representing the national office," was charged with "explain[ing] a few of the difficulties."[105] What she did not admit, but what seems to have been happening, was that the less politically committed Soviet friends were dropping out of public association with the council.

The invitations sent out to council branches and "friendly organizations"[106] in October 1944 nevertheless included a page-long list of patrons. Nine lieutenant governors, Prime Minister Mackenzie King, six premiers, and prominent Canadians such as Samuel Bronfman, Dr. Charles Best, artist Arthur Lismer, and actor Raymond Massey were among those listed as patrons. Dyson Carter and Dorise Nielsen were also on the list.[107] Other problems notwithstanding, the congress was held at the Royal York Hotel in Toronto in November 1944. Mr. R.H. Davis, president of the Atlas Steel Company, was listed as national president on the program. He would remain involved with the society during Carter's tenure in the postwar years and initiated the Artkino exchange of films. After the playing of "God Save the King" and the Soviet national anthem, Davis presented Soviet Ambassador G. Zarubin with a combined map of Canada and the USSR showing twinned cities.[108] A series of panel discussions on art, agriculture, education, labour, science and medicine, and trade and commerce included presentations by professors at Canadian universities, a representative of the Ontario Agricultural College, the Central Experimental Farm in Ottawa, the Canadian Congress of Labour, the Ontario Research Foundation, and the federal Department of Trade and Commerce.[109] A representative of VOKS gave a report entitled "The U.S.S.R. Academy of Sciences," and the first secretary of the Soviet Embassy in Ottawa, Sergei Koudriavtzev, presented a paper on "Leo Tolstoy and Traditions of Russian Literature." Carter was in the audience.[110]

The emphasis throughout was on Canadian-Soviet cooperation during and after the war and the benefits that such cooperation would bring to both countries. Recently, Raymond Arthur Davies had published a book entitled *Canada and Russia: Neighbors and Friends* detailing a history of Canadian-Soviet friendship. The book was published in Toronto by the Communist Party's publication house, Progress Books.[111] A paper given at the congress by the Washington representative of the United Electrical, Radio, and Machine Workers of America was titled "The Significance of Our Friendship with the Soviet Union to Full Employment after the War." Other talks focussed on the importance of cooperation in science, trade, and medicine. On Sunday evening, the film *Wallace in Siberia* was shown, detailing American Vice-President Henry A. Wallace's trip to the USSR,[112] and at 9 p.m. a victory rally was held at Maple Leaf Gardens. The program was sponsored by unions, the progressive Serbian organization, the Niagara Falls branch of the Canadian-Soviet Friendship Council, and other progressive groups and individuals. The T. Eaton Company published a full-page advertisement on the front of the program asking people to give blood "to keep a flicker of life alive in a Canadian boy."[113] The emphasis was still very much on showing unified support for the Allies.

The congress received good coverage in the Toronto papers,[114] and one article reprinted the text of the speech given by journalist Edgar Snow at the Thanksgiving Service for Russian Victories held at Maple Leaf Gardens. Above the text was a photograph of Snow, Colonel Nikolai Zabotin, whom the *Toronto Star* called a "Red Army hero,"[115] and the Soviet chargé d'affaires, Gregori Tonkin.[116] Photographs of the main speakers appeared in the paper, as did the statements coming out of the congress, calling for more Russian to be taught at Canadian schools, exchanges and courses to be taught on Soviet agriculture, and emulation of Soviet anti-discrimination policies.[117] Poet E.J. Pratt, a member of the Canadian-Soviet Friendship Council, read a poem that he had composed entitled "A Victory Message and Pledge of Friendship from the Canadian People to the U.S.S.R." Privately, early in 1946, Pratt wrote that "good neighbourliness and mutual trust and decency are all we have left."[118]

Ironically, perhaps, considering that the summer of 1945 brought celebrations of Allied victory and a "Friendship for Russia Week" sponsored by Toronto's mayor,[119] the wartime Friendship Society was in definite decline by 1945. In the eyes of many of its mainstream patrons, the society's wartime value was now exhausted. Insiders complained that "radical elements" were trying to take it over.[120] The RCMP reported that, in contrast to the earlier wartime rallies, the 1945 rally held at Maple Leaf Gardens was mostly attended by known communists, and members of the Labor-Progressive Party were at every door handing out its literature.[121] Soviet friendship had retreated to its peacetime definition and utility. During the summer of 1945, in the political scandal dubbed the "Gestapo Affair" by the press, a police officer was accused of filing secret reports on leftists with the Ontario government, the Labor-Progressive Party was accused of receiving financial support from Moscow in Bay Street stocks, and the goals of the National Council for Canadian-Soviet Friendship were questioned. Many did not want to believe these stories. The *Ottawa Citizen*'s editorial "Groundless Story" of 6 July 1945 argued that "self-respecting diplomatic authorities do not indulge in underground political activities.... Nor is it entertained that the Russian embassy here or anywhere else would stoop to such crude practices within a friendly country."[122] But how "groundless" were these claims? The Gouzenko Affair, which broke in the press less than a year later, would make the *Citizen* editorial seem naive.

Meanwhile, membership of the council was changing. An RCMP report from 1945 listed Reverend R.H. Thomas of Deer Park United Church in Toronto as chairman of the Toronto Council, with Margaret Spaulding, Pearl Wedro, and Mrs. Malania also involved. The RCMP pointed out that Wedro was prominent in the LPP and that Malania was married to I. Malania of the Federation of Russian Canadians.[123] Spaulding and Wedro would remain active under Carter's leadership after 1949. R.H. Davis was still president of the National Council in 1945, but he was soon replaced by Max Chic. In 1945, the Toronto branch of the Friendship Council did away with membership fees, perhaps because there were not enough paying members, and instead solicited all names on its mailing list for donations.[124]

Dana Wilgress, now Canadian ambassador to the Soviet Union, spoke at the victory rally at Maple Leaf Gardens on 3 July 1945, welcoming Ukrainian and Belarussian delegates to the San Francisco conference.[125] A few months later 5,000 people were present to hear Hewlett Johnson, the "red dean" of Canterbury, discuss his impressions of the USSR at the Maple Leaf Gardens rally in November, though the RCMP reported that only about half of those present seemed to be interested in the proceedings.[126] The theme of the 1945 Soviet friendship congress was "The Effect on Canada's Post-War Progress of Trade and Cultural Relations with the Soviet Union," and agricultural, veterans' affairs, and labour representation from Ottawa was present. However, there were far fewer businesspeople in attendance. The featured talk on Saturday evening was given by Dr. Raymond Boyer on the theme of "Science and Peace."[127]

In 1945, Kon wrote again to Carter: "Congratulations to you and the L.P.P. for getting together on the inside."[128] Most likely he was referring to the public declaration by Carter in a December issue of the *Canadian Tribune*[129] that he was a communist because Kon spoke of framing it in gold. In the same letter, he asked, "don't you agree with me that we are making a considerable progress in Canada on the whole? After all, there is [*sic*] a lot of scientists in the Scientific Workers Association who must be forward looking, if they elected as their chairman one of our fellows—Raymond Boyer, and if the government does not dare to dismiss General Chisholm, facts that were unthinkable only a short few years ago!"[130] By then, Igor Gouzenko had defected from the Soviet Embassy in Ottawa, carrying papers with him that would point to Boyer's role in passing confidential information to the Soviets. Mainstream Canadian attitudes to the Soviet Union were about to experience a sea change, and the Soviet authorities were to find this a major concern.

Although Gouzenko left the Soviet Embassy on Charlotte Street in Ottawa for the last time on the evening of 5 September 1945, he and his family did not receive asylum from the Canadian government until several days later. He had documents proving that a Soviet espionage system existed in Canada and that Soviet spying was taking place in the United States and Britain. According to all accounts,[131] Gouzenko was not understood or believed when he first attempted to explain the importance of the information to the editor of the *Ottawa Journal*, and the various government officials who learned of his behaviour were not initially sure, or in agreement, on the action to be taken. It was only when the Gouzenkos' apartment was broken into and ransacked by several representatives from the Soviet Embassy that the RCMP took the family, who had been hiding in a neighbour's flat, to safety. Five more months were to pass before the Canadian government took any public action on Gouzenko's allegations, and even then the royal commission set up to investigate carried out its interrogations in secret. Six weeks' worth of documents during this crucial time are missing from related departmental records and personal archival collections, so there is considerable speculation among historians on how and why the government eventually made the decisions it did. This is all the more intriguing since these six weeks represent the few conspicuous gaps in Mackenzie King's diary. Soviet archives related to Gouzenko are still closed, so Canadian scholars are not able to benefit from Russian sources on the subject. The Canadian public became aware of the scandal in February 1946, in which thirteen people, including MP Fred Rose, were accused of spying for the Soviet Union, when the headlines splashed the news. The Soviet Union, an ally in the Second World War, had now, seemingly overnight, become the enemy.

The report of the Taschereau-Kellock Royal Commission[132] was released as three separate interim reports throughout 1946, and its final version was presented in June 1946. Each new revelation made headline news in Canada and abroad. Many of the people accused in the report of being "agents" had not even been to court yet, and several of them were later acquitted of all charges. Nonetheless, the sensational accusations proved to be indelible, and in some cases the individuals suffered job loss and insecurity for the rest of their lives.[133] Boyer, one of the speakers on science at the last NCCSF congress, was accused along with Rose and would later serve time in prison for espionage. Many others were caught in the ideological about-face that signalled the beginning of the Cold War in Canada. As historian Denis Smith has suggested, in this political climate, "post-war Canada thus found not security but new anxiety" with "the propagandist advantage that it played upon old fears of Bolshevism to produce a new myth of good and evil to replace the wartime myth" of an international alliance.[134] The NCCSF was caught up in this change as friendship with the Soviets lost any claim to political neutrality.

The embarrassment to Moscow caused by the Gouzenko revelations, and the importance that Soviet authorities placed on repairing the damaged Soviet image abroad, have been well documented.[135] The increased attention paid after this moment to supplying communist front organizations in the West with the material necessary to promote friendship with the USSR, rather than overt political admiration, is significant. The increasing inability of the LPP to attract mainstream Canadian members meant that the VOKS representative in the Soviet Embassy in Ottawa would play a greater role in facilitating and coordinating Canadian-Soviet friendship via apparently non-partisan ethnic and progressive groups.[136]

As the news of Gouzenko broke, the RCMP reported that few progressive Canadians were taking the Soviets up on invitations to tour the USSR,[137] and they suggested that this might be because of the effects of the "spy trials."[138] A few days after the royal commission began its hearings, the executive of the National Council held a meeting in Toronto to decide on its position vis-à-vis the negative publicity directed at the USSR and Canadian communists. A press statement was released on 22 February 1946 "addressed to all branches of Council and copy to P.M.":

> Our executive met today with Mrs. W.K. Fraser, Vice-President, in the chair and gave careful consideration to the statement issued last Friday by Prime Minister Mackenzie King. We were unanimous in expressing regret that the newspapers and radio commentators had failed to follow the advice of the Prime Minister to treat the whole matter with reserve and caution. The executive felt that unwarranted speculation indulged in by the press can only do grave injury to future relations between Canada and her northern neighbor. The executive urges the Council to avoid being drawn into the current wave of hysteria. In the circumstances, the [e]xecutive feels that there is no occasion whatever to lessen the activity of the Council and that it should be continued in the normal way.[139]

But it was not business as usual. The National Council had a revolving door. In August 1946, Max Chic was replaced as national director by Frank Park.[140] Park, well known as an LPP organizer and a lawyer, would later serve as editor of the party's theoretical journal, *National Affairs Monthly*, and travel to the USSR and Cuba, sending back reports to Dyson Carter and the CSFS, as well as to the LPP leadership.[141] Less than two years later the NCCSF leadership changed again. Even LPP members were dropping out of the NCCSF, perhaps because the discredited party made Soviet friends look suspicious and vice versa. By 1948, Park wrote that he was "no longer the director of that [friendship] organization."[142] A CSFS leaflet subsequently described the personnel change in this way: "*1946–1948* most of these Council members withdrew their support (many with sincere regrets) due to anti-Soviet hysteria."[143] The RCMP reported that in December 1946 "the Party had issued instructions for its members to sever their connection with the Council. Rev. Fern Sayles, prominent Party member and former leading official of the Council in Welland, alleged that the Council was spoiling the reputation of the Party, as it was built upon a high society level and most of its leading members were capitalists. Therefore, it had been decided to break away from the Council quietly by ignoring it."[144] It is more likely, however, that post-Gouzenko the compromised LPP reflected badly on the Soviet Union, and its overt support made it impossible for the NCCSF to claim any political neutrality.

By this time, the Canadian government, and particularly Under-Secretary of State for External Affairs Lester B. Pearson, were also drawing back from involvement with the National Council for Canadian-Soviet Friendship. What had been seen in wartime as expediently attractive was now tinged with ideological danger. Although the NCCSF continued to correspond with Pearson, and he was sent its publications,[145] External Affairs officials saw the president of the National Council, Leslie Roberts, as a "misguided fellow traveller" and attempted to persuade him to be more critical of the USSR and the Soviet message that he was receiving.[146] Pearson had also been warned that the establishment figures who had supported wartime Soviet friendship groups in the United States and Canada were no longer doing so. In fact, an adviser told Pearson that the Canadian organization appeared to be "a more or less Communist front organization of a mild kind, which tends to attempt to put forward the Soviet case in such a way as to gain the support of Left Wingers."[147] In effect, this observation was correct.

But the National Council did not die out entirely. A convention was held in Ottawa in April 1947, led by Barker Fairley and Clarence S. Jackson, whom the RCMP reported were "regarded as fellow travellers, at least."[148] Keynote speakers included Arctic explorer Vilhjalmur Stefansson, Vancouver journalist Kimore Philpott, and lecturer Dr. Watson Thomson, "all regarded as sympathetic to the Communist cause," according to the RCMP.[149] In January 1948, Mary Jennison, secretary of the National Council, argued that it needed to put forward a program to counter the negative publicity of the USSR in the Western press. This program, she said, "would be an attempt to turn the tide of Soviet-baiting, not for the sake of the Soviet Union which is quite able to take care of itself, but for the sake of Canada and the safeguarding of Canadian families from the horrors of another war."[150] The link between pro-Soviet groups in Canada and the theme of peace would become more important in the next few years.

The National Council continued to maintain that the USSR was worthy of admiration. Echoing official Soviet responses, the media coverage of Gouzenko's allegations was depicted by the National Council as anti-Soviet slander. His autobiography, which came out in 1948, set the tone for many of the earliest analyses of his defection and reflected the conclusions of the royal commission report, but from the perspective of Sovietophiles it was bad news. *This Was My Choice: Gouzenko's Story*[151] was the first book to deal with the defection and its consequences. Detailing his disaffection with the Soviet Union and the reasons for his decision to defect, Gouzenko concluded that, if he "had obediently packed up and gone to Moscow instead of to the Royal Canadian Mounted Police, Soviet agent Fred Rose would probably still be seated among the law makers of Canada and be reporting state secrets to the Soviet Union!"[152] Published while Sam Carr was still underground and before he was convicted in 1949, the book detailed how several of the accused Canadians, including Carr, came to be spies, used false passports, recruited other agents, and led study groups. Gouzenko affirmed that he was motivated only by the highest ideals and "had no thought, in making my break, of any financial returns to be derived from it.... The greatest gain is the one I feel deep down inside: that I did my duty toward the millions enslaved and voiceless in Russia today."[153] Showing how others appreciated his courage, he quoted letters from abroad thanking him for exposing the Soviet Union for what it was, Mackenzie King's statement that he had "accomplished a historic act," and the royal commission's comment about his sincerity and the "great public service" that he had performed. Gouzenko modestly wrote that "I think it is promising that such a small cog as myself in the vast Soviet machine could have done so much."[154] But the NCCSF did not like Gouzenko and, echoing Moscow, claimed that his "truths" were lies.

One of the Hollywood films based on Gouzenko's memoirs, *The Iron Curtain* (1948), starred Dana Andrews as Gouzenko and Gene Tierney as Gouzenko's wife, "Anna."[155] A May 1948 meeting of the National Council for Canadian-Soviet Friendship[156] in Toronto unanimously adopted a resolution condemning "this picture as deliberate war-mongering, based on distortion of facts. We protest its showing in Canada as against the basic interests of the people as an incitement of war."[157] Calling on Canadians to boycott the film, the National Council said that it "join[ed] hands with the American-Soviet Friendship Council and many other progressive groups in the United States in calling for the banning of this picture."[158]

In June 1948, the National Council published the first issue of its new bulletin entitled *These Are the Facts*. The "facts" put forward by the group were that world peace inevitably meant friendship and cooperation with the Soviet Union, and inviting Reverend Hewlett Johnson to speak once more in Canada about his impressions of the USSR would contribute to this spirit.[159]

A summary of the work of VOKS in Canada after 1946 from the Soviet perspective noted that the NCCSF was "hindered by the absence of leadership," the lack of significant funds, and an anti-Soviet campaign.[160] R.H. Davis, the report said, had been just a figurehead only interested in increased trade with the USSR, and Max Chic, active for years, had been forced to leave in 1945. Under Frank Park, the momentum could not be maintained, and the NCCSF "activity had almost stopped by 1946," except for the Vancouver branch, where a "deep sympathy" for the Soviet Union remained. The VOKS report concluded by saying that letters continued to come into the embassy from interested Canadians, proving that there was still value in maintaining a VOKS presence in Ottawa.[161]

In February 1949, the RCMP headquarters in Ottawa delivered a letter by hand to Lester B. Pearson, by then the minister of external affairs, responding to his request for information on the National Council for Canadian-Soviet Friendship. The RCMP assured him that the organization "is at present inactive. It has not formally gone out of existence but certain of its functions have been taken over by the Provisional Peace Committee."[162] An RCMP report filed in February showed that the financial affairs of the National Council and the Peace Congress were linked,[163] and later in 1949 Dr. James Endicott, head of the Canadian peace movement, was listed as "conducting" the friendship society.[164] In April 1949, a report sent to the RCMP commissioner stated that "it is interesting to note that the National Council of Canadian Soviet Friendship is apparently still active."[165] However, the inspector pointed out that "there appears to be little doubt that unless financial assistance is received the National Council . . . will be forced to cease activities in the near future."[166]

Accompanying his letter were the minutes from a council executive meeting held on 26 February 1949 at Secretary Mary Jennison's Hamilton home. Margaret Spaulding chaired the meeting, and others attending were Elizabeth Brown, Barker Fairley, Mrs. Rae Luckock, Mr. MacInnes, Stanley Ryerson, Mr. Mertunen, Mr. Sundqvist, and Mary Jennison. Plans for upcoming activities were discussed, in particular the possible visit to Canada of Soviet composer Dmitri Shostakovich. The executive decided to ask members to donate more than usual since the council had only $156 in the bank and owed money for bills and the payment of a loan recently received.[167] It looked to be on the verge of bankruptcy. However, rather than being absorbed or dying out, the friendship society was about to be rejuvenated.

On 7 November 1949, the thirty-second anniversary of the Bolshevik Revolution, the *Canadian Tribune* nostalgically published a large photograph of the 1943 rally in Maple Leaf Gardens, when the wartime National Council for Canadian-Soviet Friendship was founded. Below the photo ran this description:

> Many will recall this thrilling scene as over 17,000 Canadians jammed Toronto's Maple Leaf Gardens to pay tribute to the people of the Soviet Union and its Red Army which at that time was alone in action against the Hitler armies. . . . W.L. Mackenzie King, then premier and Liberal party leader[,] also spoke. He is the man who the moment victory was won over the Nazis joined Washington in a vile betrayal by launching a "cold war" against our Soviet ally, a "war" the St. Laurent government has intensified. The Tribune joins the National Council of Canadian-Soviet Friendship and all democratic Canadians in calling for a return to days when Canada proudly acclaimed the Soviet Union and her peoples, allies and friends.[168]

Under the photograph was an article inviting "all Canadians of good will" to a conference on 26 November 1949 at the Prince George Hotel in Toronto. Press releases were sent out from the National Council office,[169] the announcement was advertised in the English-language and "ethnic" left papers,[170] and RCMP detachments in large cities across Canada were instructed to find out who was attending.[171] The RCMP in Toronto reported that "it would appear that the Party will make a determined effort to revitalize this front organization on the theme of trade with the U.S.S.R. and friendly cooperation, thereby ensuring peace."[172] That observation proved to be correct.

At 2:30 p.m. on 26 November 1949, the meeting got under way. Dyson Carter gave an impassioned speech, arguing that it was high time for a renewed friendship society: "Ladies and Gentl[e]men . . . GONE ARE THE DAYS, FOREVER, when we have to APOLOGIZE for friendship with the Land of Socialism! Never again do we have to go, hat-in-hand, to people in high places, and ask them: 'Please won't you allow your name to be used for the sake of friendship . . . Important names will make people think the Russians are important!' . . . What we have to do NOW . . . is go to the Canadian people with the truth."[173] In leaving behind the wartime, elite-driven friendship society, Carter pointed to how "people in high places" had betrayed the trust of Canadians, and he urged his audience to take the cause directly to the "Canadian people"—particularly workers, farmers, and youth. He blamed Canada for "whipping up" the Cold War: "In recent years Canada has taking [*sic*] the LEADING part in trying to DESTROY world-wide friendship with the great Socialist land, the USSR. . . . Canada, with the notorious Spy Trials, OPENED the post-war campaign of hatred and hysteria against the S.U."[174] According to Carter, Canada had much to learn from the USSR in science, medicine, culture, economics, and northern affairs. That is why, he said, Canadians should take the cause of friendship into their own hands, so that "Canada COULD be the KEY nation in leading the great and small powers of the world towards a new spirit of international agreement and friendship."[175]

Following his speech, Carter was elected president of the new National Council of Canadian-Soviet Friendship. Apparently, he was the only candidate. Mary Jennison resigned as secretary of the National Council to become secretary of the Peace Congress,[176] replaced by William Tweedale of Toronto. Of the sixty people in attendance, Rae Luckock, Stanley Ryerson, Margaret Spaulding, Nora Rodd, John Weir, and Gregory Okulevich were among those who paid the one-dollar membership fee.[177] Vladimir Burdin, first secretary at the Soviet Embassy in Ottawa and representative of the All-Union Society for Cultural Relations with Foreign Countries, spoke about culture in the USSR, and a Soviet film called *Sports Parade* was shown. The meeting was glowingly reviewed in the left press. The *Ukrainian Canadian*, for instance, argued that Canadians would welcome the society's initiatives because they were becoming fed up with the Cold War rhetoric against the USSR, and "public pressure must mount to secure a change."[178]

The CSFS leaflet claiming that prominent members had been forced to withdraw their support "due to anti-Soviet hysteria" pledged that the new council elected in November 1949 would continue their work. The National Council renamed itself the Canadian-Soviet Friendship Society and called a convention for 1952, at which it approved a new constitution.[179] Although links to the wartime society were played up, the CSFS was essentially a new organization, founded less on wartime friendship with the USSR than on the determination to maintain friendly relations with a country that most Canadians now saw as a threat. Carter explained that the membership fee was two dollars a year, and members would get *News-Facts about the USSR* and the *VOKS Bulletin*. He wrote that the CSFS was looking for branches to be founded and would supply groups with exhibitions, films, and ideas, which "will make your committee a highly popular center for all who want inspiring, entertaining, informative meetings and social gatherings." In response to its self-formulated question "is there a Friendship Society in the USSR?" the CSFS answered potential members that "there is 'VOKS', the All-Union Society for Cultural Relations with Foreign Countries. Our Society exchanges publications with VOKS, and also sends Canadian books, magazines, cultural articles, music, etc. We hope to greatly increase this exchange."[180] This hope was shared by VOKS and other authorities in Moscow.

In 1946, VOKS had concluded that the National Council for Canadian-Soviet Friendship was down but not out: it was in need of reformulating and strengthening. In 1949, when Carter came forward to head up the new society, VOKS got what it sought. It is clear from the documentary evidence that, in writing to the Soviet Embassy in Ottawa, and in asking for a recommendation from Kon, Carter had volunteered in the early 1940s to play a more substantial role in promoting the USSR in Canada. The decision to lead the CSFS would have been taken in conjunction with the LPP, for which Carter was working at the time. Dorise Nielsen's reassignment to the CSFS as executive secretary from the LPP main office was naturally also a party decision.[181] The realities of the day meant that the LPP would have discussed and received approval for this strategy from authorities in Moscow, where the reputation of Carter as a pro-Soviet propagandist had certainly earned him praise.[182] A similar pattern of CPC-Soviet planning would be followed in 1960 when he was replaced as head of the society by Les Hunt.[183]

In November 1949, the new friendship society had more impetus than its lacklustre predecessor could muster, and it had renewed energy to fight anti-Soviet "slander." The combination of Carter's talent and energy and the backing from the CPC-LPP and VOKS made the new CSFS a much more pernicious group in the eyes of the RCMP than the groups that had come before, but it never regained the popular support that the wartime society had garnered. Ultimately, it did not reach beyond the stalwart left-wing supporters who had looked for years to the USSR as a positive role model in the world, and after 1956 even this group was diminished. The legacy of the CSFS includes its consistent attempts to soften Canadian antipathies toward the USSR, its promotion of exchanges between the Cold War combatants, and its views on Soviet social experimentation. In Carter and the CSFS, the Soviets found willing and energetic partners in promoting a positive image of the Soviet Union in the post-Gouzenko, postwar, chilly international climate.

CHAPTER 3

Institutionalizing Friendship: The All-Union Society for Cultural Relations with Foreign Countries

Copies of Soviet-era archival documents from the Russian State Archives, now available to researchers at the University of Alberta, placed alongside Canadian archival resources provide a deeper context for the activities of Dyson Carter and the CSFS, as well as the Soviet institutionalization of foreign "friendship" and the role of the VOKS representative in Ottawa. The All-Union Society for Cultural Relations with Foreign Countries was founded in Moscow in April 1925 to engage in international cultural diplomacy. In practice, VOKS served the dual function of disseminating Soviet propaganda and collecting information abroad to be used domestically. Although purportedly a voluntary, non-governmental organization, VOKS provided a direct link between international pro-Soviet leftist groups and the Soviet state apparatus, likely tapping into a genuine desire by Soviet intellectuals to connect with their counterparts abroad. It was overseen by the Soviet Ministry of Foreign Affairs and the International Department of the Communist Party of the Soviet Union. By 1928, VOKS had links with Soviet friendship societies in twenty countries;[1] by 1946, there were sixty VOKS-supported groups abroad, and a few years later they included both a large group in the United Kingdom[2] and the CSFS. VOKS-linked friendship societies located in Britain, Canada, Australia, and New Zealand were overseen by the British Countries division, and correspondence was coordinated via VOKS representatives in the Soviet Embassies. Once the CSFS was founded in 1949, it began to follow a pattern similar to other VOKS-supported groups: it organized Soviet Friendship Months, hosted film screenings and pro-Soviet discussion groups, published a pro-Soviet journal, and sponsored delegations of Canadians on visits to the USSR.[3] Soviet friendship societies in other countries had identical programs. For instance, in 1956, the Belgian-Soviet Friendship Society, founded in 1929 and linked with VOKS, followed a pattern remarkably similar to that of the CSFS, as shown by a feature article written by its president for the *VOKS Bulletin*.[4]

By the 1950s, the CSFS served as the main VOKS contact with the Canadian public as requests, correspondence, and supporting materials crossed the desk of the VOKS representative at the Soviet Embassy in Ottawa, at first Vladimir Burdin and later Aleksei Tovstogan. The Canadian Department of External Affairs paid attention to VOKS, as can be seen by documents in the departmental fonds at Library and Archives Canada. At the same time, the RCMP were certain that VOKS was supporting the CSFS. If in the early 1950s External Affairs was not aware that Burdin, first secretary at the Soviet Embassy, was also the VOKS representative in Canada, and that this might be a security issue, the link was made clear at least by 1963.[5] In 1958, when VOKS was renamed the Union of Soviet Friendship Societies and Cultural Relations with Foreign Countries (SSOD), its function remained the same.[6]

Olga Davidovna Kameneva, the sister of Leon Trotsky and the first wife of Lev Kamenev, both Old Bolsheviks and Politburo members, was one of the first VOKS chairpersons. The high political profile that she brought to the organization was reflective of the significance that Soviet authorities attributed to VOKS and its role in international relations.[7] Kameneva had been active in high politics for years, associated closely with Vladimir Lenin. Her activities had involved promoting culture domestically as a tool of education and enlightenment and representing women within the Communist Party of the Soviet Union (CPSU). Her work at VOKS was an extension of her earlier work representing Soviet culture abroad and coordinating links with Westerners who admired the USSR. In 1928, she published an article in the journal *Pacific Affairs* explaining the function of VOKS. Noting that the USSR had been surrounded for years by hostile states, she argued that the new Soviet culture to which the revolution had given birth deserved to be better known in the West. Particularly, she wrote that VOKS was satisfying the demands for information coming from "progressive intellectual elements in foreign countries [who had been led to] interest themselves in the question: what is it that has taken place in that mysterious country which used to be known as the 'Russian Empire.'"[8] After describing the functions of the various sections of VOKS, underscoring the volume of information sent abroad, including the distribution of 14,000 copies of Soviet books per month to foreigners in 1928,

Kameneva concluded with a simple statement: "At present there are 20 societies for cultural relations with U.S.S.R. in various countries."[9]

Like other Soviet cultural organizations, VOKS masqueraded as a voluntary association. In fact, the Soviet interpretation of art as necessarily serving the state made "servants of the state" out of individual writers and performers. If they wanted to be published and accepted, they cooperated with the authorities when asked to do so. The Soviet Writers' Union served as a clearing agency for all Soviet literature. Although the VOKS leadership was elected by its larger membership, and was represented abroad as a non-governmental organization, the fact that it reported directly to the Ministry of Foreign Affairs and the International Department of the Communist Party of the Soviet Union meant that it was not truly independent.[10] At the same time, it was not officially part of any government department.[11] A document prepared by the British mission to the USSR in 1955, seen by Canadian diplomats there and by the Department of External Affairs, suggested that VOKS was "undoubtedly heavily sponsored and controlled by the Soviet Government and the CPSU," with "its main activity up to the present [being] Soviet ideological and cultural propaganda abroad through the medium of foreign delegations to the USSR and various societies."[12] The report quoted the most recent edition of the *Great Soviet Encyclopedia*, which defined the role of VOKS as "acquainting the Soviet Society with the achievements of the culture of foreign countries and the popularization of the culture of the peoples of the USSR abroad, contributing thereby to the development and strengthening of friendship and mutual understanding between the peoples of the USSR and the peoples of other countries."[13] The encyclopedia definition remained unchanged in its third edition, published in 1971.[14]

The British remarked on the rapid growth of VOKS in the immediate postwar years as the organization expanded its contacts abroad and opened more offices within the Soviet republics. In 1946, VOKS opened branches in the capitals of Soviet Georgia and Ukraine and in 1954–55 in the Armenian, Belorussian, Uzbek, Kazak, and Azerbaijani republics. Monitoring references to VOKS in the Soviet press allowed the British to conclude that there was also an increase in visits by foreign delegations to the USSR sponsored by the organization. In 1950, VOKS claimed to have sponsored thirty-two delegations to the Soviet Union; in 1951, this number had risen to forty-one and included twenty-three individuals; in 1952, forty-seven delegations and thirteen individuals; and in 1953, fifty-three groups and forty-two individuals. The British report noted that "the figures show a pronounced upward trend." In general, the British concluded, the "main activities [of VOKS] seem to be the reception of foreign delegations and propaganda to attract national émigrés abroad."[15] The highest number of foreign delegations visiting the USSR was reported in 1956, coming just before negative international reactions to the Soviet invasion of Hungary in the fall of that year.[16] Western countries, including Canada, were in the process of negotiating cultural exchanges with the USSR at that time, but plans were cancelled or suspended after the events in Hungary.[17] VOKS was soon after reorganized and renamed.[18]

The involvement of Soviet organizations in the policy, planning, and monitoring of foreign leftist groups, especially Communist Parties abroad, was not new. From the 1920s on, the Communist International (Comintern), and later the International Department of the Central Committee of the CPSU, had coordinated policy among foreign Communist Parties. From its formation in 1943 to the late 1980s, the International Department was the most important Soviet organization dealing with foreign affairs. It monitored all incoming information gathered by the Departments of Foreign Affairs and Defence and the KGB and drew up policy papers for Soviet leaders.[19] It operated mostly in secret and had the same director, Boris Ponomarov, from 1955 to 1986.[20] It helped to set up the Communist Information Bureau (Cominform) in 1947 to ensure that Communist Parties in Europe followed the "correct" Soviet ideological path,[21] but the International Department took over responsibility for liaison with all Communist Parties and front groups abroad, and it published the *World Marxist Review* and the *New Times*.[22] It was also responsible for the Soviet news service, *Telegrafnoye agentstvo svazi i soobshcheniya* (TASS),[23] the Soviet Information Bureau (Sovinformburo), which worked abroad to distribute Soviet news with the desired perspective to foreign audiences, and VOKS.

The importance of VOKS to authorities in the USSR is hard to gauge, precisely because the inner system in the Kremlin relied so heavily on secrecy. Nevertheless, that many VOKS reports from Canada, among them information directly from and about the CSFS, were stamped *sekretno* ("secret") or *ves'ma sekretno* ("top secret") and copied directly to high-level personnel such as Andrei Vyshinsky, Vyacheslav Molotov, and Boris Ponomarev speaks volumes. The authority wielded by agencies run by these individuals had no counterpart in Canada. The chiefs were hand-picked for their posts by Josef Stalin and ranked the highest in the land in terms of authority, second only to him. Vyshinsky and Molotov ran the Ministry of Foreign Affairs, the most important department of the Soviet government. Molotov was the minister until 1949, when Vyshinsky took over the post. Vyshinsky had been Stalin's main trouble-shooter abroad. They both sat on the Politburo of the Central Committee of the CPSU, the most powerful committee in the country, even though it was not mentioned in the Soviet constitution.

Ponomarev had a different sort of power as the classic back-roomer. A member of the Central Committee Secretariat, he ranked higher than either Vyshinsky or Molotov within the party itself. As head of the semi-secret International Department for an astonishingly long period, he was the unchallenged interpreter of Marxism-Leninism for almost the entire postwar period. That Vyshinsky's successor as foreign minister, Andrei Gromyko, held office for nearly as long as Ponomarev (1957–85) ensured that these foreign specialists held a monopoly of authority within the USSR. Their interest in the CSFS, therefore, was no small matter.

How did all of this affect Canada? In 1954, for instance, the Sovinformburo bragged that it had arranged for the publication of 378 excerpts from Soviet official documents in sympathetic Canadian "progressive" journals and distributed more than 7,000 photographs dealing with 1,251 Soviet themes. In all, the Sovinformburo report claimed that "in 1954 it had performed a great service providing the progressive Canadian press with honest information about our foreign policy and the Soviet way of life."[24] The mandate of VOKS was to promote a positive image of the USSR abroad, but it involved itself less with official Communist Parties than with non-party leftist cultural and social groups in other countries. Its officers gathered information from its contacts and possibly cultivated friendships with the goal of gaining more useful contacts in the future. In Canada, VOKS maintained close contacts with the pro-Soviet Federation of Russian Canadians (FRC), Association of United Ukrainian Canadians (AUUC), other Eastern European progressive groups, and especially the CSFS. While the Sovinformburo provided these groups with material to condense or rewrite in their journals,[25] VOKS handled the logistics for the delivery of the subscriptions, books and objects that they requested, and corresponded with individual members of progressive groups and the general public. From the VOKS archive, large parts of which are copied and held at the Cameron Library, University of Alberta, it is clear that the VOKS representative in Canada was sending information to the International Department of the CPSU and the Soviet Ministry of Foreign Affairs. Authorities in Canada were also paying close attention.[26]

But if VOKS had existed as early as the 1920s, how can its sudden growth immediately following the Second World War be explained? It appears that the increased importance placed on the work of VOKS was related to changes in Soviet ideological concerns following the war. An emphasis on encouraging renewed ideological commitment within Soviet society, and especially the Communist Party, was led by Andrei Zhdanov, head of the International Department before he died in 1948.[27] Zhdanov, also in charge of propaganda and agitation (agitprop) for the CPSU, launched a purge of Soviet writers in 1946 that made ideological commitment a prerequisite to publication.[28]

A series of international incidents at about the same time was interpreted as damaging the Soviet image abroad. Research has established that perception of the Cold War at times affected international relations.[29] It has been argued that the American invitation to extend the Marshall Plan to Eastern Europe, and even to the Soviet Union, caused the Soviets some alarm, for Moscow feared that this was a Trojan horse.[30] After the defection of Igor Gouzenko from the Soviet Embassy in Ottawa became public in 1946, the Soviets complained constantly of heightening anti-Soviet campaigns in the West. In the next decade, other high-profile Soviet defections periodically made news, including most famously the defection of Vladimir Petrov in Australia in 1954. Like the Gouzenko defection, the Petrov case became known as an "affair," and its political implications had ripple effects internationally.[31] Although Western commentators have labelled the incidents the "Gouzenko Affair" and "Petrov Affair," in the Soviet Union the defection in Canada became known as the "King Affair" because of the perceived involvement of Prime Minister Mackenzie King in causing an exaggerated increase in anti-Soviet public opinion, inconsistent with the consequences of Gouzenko's actual revelations.[32] As one historian of the USSR has written, "by 1947 it would no longer be possible to print anything in the USSR about a foreign country without conveying at the same time a clear political, social or economic message."[33] This message invariably fit with the renewed importance placed on themes espoused in Vladimir Lenin's *Imperialism: The Highest Stage of Capitalism* (1916).[34]

Canada was important to the Soviets not only because it was in Ottawa that the Gouzenko Affair exploded into the headlines but also because the Soviets believed that Canada had great geopolitical importance. Because Canada was a northern hemispheric neighbour, was also a neighbour to and partner of the United States, and had historical ties to the other "great imperial power," Britain, Soviet authorities paid close attention to Canadian public opinion. Convinced that the West was ganging up on the USSR, and could provoke a Third World War directed against Moscow,[35] and aware that their country was weakened by the Second World War, and not prepared for another world conflict, Soviet leaders undertook diplomatic damage control. This strategy as applied to Soviet influence in Canada appears to have manifested itself in efforts to gather information on Canadian attitudes to the USSR and thereby attempt to influence the larger North American public against starting another war.

After the Gouzenko revelations, which resulted in the arrest of, among others, Fred Rose, member of Parliament and Labor Progressive Party member, the LPP suffered a considerable loss of legitimacy, and its leaders went underground. A VOKS report in 1946 complained that "Canada is among the most active leaders of the post World War II new reaction against the Soviet Union. The year 1946 was marked by the activation of anti-Soviet groups that organized a special legal process against the only parliamentary deputy who is a member of the Labor-Progressive Party . . . for the purpose of spreading lies and slanders against the Soviet Union."[36] The cultural attaché at the Soviet Embassy in Ottawa, N.D. Belokhvostikov, was particularly upset by how he and other Soviet officials were portrayed in Gouzenko's 1948 book about the defection, *This Was My Choice*, and sent Molotov, the Soviet foreign minister, the book, his complaints, and a copy of a book by Canadian Leslie Roberts, entitled *Home from the Cold Wars*, which received good Soviet reviews.[37]

Roberts was president of the National Council of Canadian-Soviet Friendship, but if the Soviets hoped that this group could keep relations friendly they were wrong. The National Council had received widespread Canadian support during the war, including that of Prime Minister Mackenzie King, but after the Gouzenko defection high-profile members left it. Other individuals involved in the National Council out of idealist concern for an ally felt uncomfortable because the Cold War climate in Canada made such associations seem disloyal.[38] As mentioned earlier, by 1947 Secretary of State for External Affairs Lester B. Pearson attempted to distance the Canadian government from this group, and he had been advised that a large number of prominent members no longer supported it, that it had increasingly taken an uncritical stance toward Soviet policy, and that the same developments were taking place in the United States.[39] In 1948, when Roberts was invited by VOKS to visit the USSR, he accepted the invitation, but his treatment in Moscow suggests that, among Soviet authorities, he was out of favour. His book, *Home from the Cold Wars*, fits into the genre of Westerners presenting the truthful facts about the Soviet Union, but Roberts also described the VOKS representative's reaction to Roberts' view that a Soviet film was "dreadful."[40] Possibly Roberts did not play the role the Soviets had expected of him.

The Roberts visit created a flurry of correspondence between the Canadian Embassy in Moscow and Ottawa. The secretary of state telegrammed Moscow saying that, "since Leslie Roberts seems to be a misguided fellow traveler but not repeat not so far as we know a member of the Communist party, anything that you could do to educate him would be well worth the effort in view of the wide public his articles are likely to reach."[41] From Moscow, John Holmes responded that, though VOKS was "looking after him," he was "not being treated as a particularly distinguished visitor" and had become sceptical of the storyline that he was receiving from his Soviet hosts.[42] Holmes was congratulated on his approach by Escott Reid,[43] who wrote that "it is not likely that the visit will result in any radical change in Mr. Roberts' views, but it may, I hope, lead him to a more realistic and critical approach."[44] In London, Roberts had lunch with G. Zarubin, who had been the Soviet ambassador to Canada until 1946, but he did not show up for his appointment with the Canadian chargé d'affaires in Prague.[45] The doubts and questions that Roberts expressed about the Soviet project, as well as the declining membership in the wartime NCCSF, helped to convince VOKS that the group needed reorganization. It was in reference to his role that VOKS concluded that the National Council was "hindered by the absence of leadership."[46]

We know that VOKS maintained contacts with friendly groups in Canada during the 1920s and 1930s,[47] but previously it had been the Communist Party of Canada that had most publicly expressed pro-Soviet views. However, Soviet "image-polishing" via Communist Parties abroad could not work in post-Gouzenko Canada. The Labor-Progressive Party was largely discredited, and with so many of its leaders affected by the arrests and trials it could not be looked to by the Soviets for support. A secret report prepared in 1955 by V. Loginov, a counsellor at the Soviet Embassy in Ottawa, and forwarded via the International Department to the Central Committee of the CPSU, suggested that Soviet authorities continued to be disappointed with the work of Canadian communists a decade after the defection. Loginov pointed to the party's weaknesses and inability to make serious inroads into unions, farmers' movements, or the Canadian intelligentsia.[48] In addition, Loginov criticized the fact that more than half of LPP members were "immigrants," the majority of them Ukrainian Canadians. Despite this, the nationalist Ukrainians in Canada still produced stronger propaganda and influenced a larger percentage of Ukrainian Canadians than the communists, he said.[49] According to Loginov, the CPC was clearly not in a position to reach out to mainstream Canadian society and thereby improve the image of the Soviet Union as a socialist state.

From the Soviet perspective, needed was an alternative organization that could appeal to a broader Canadian audience and promote Soviet friendship as a non-political avenue to closer relations. In 1949, a reshuffling of the wartime National Council, which retained its name and most of its pro-Soviet members, but became a front organization for the Labor-Progressive Party, resulted in more enthusiastic VOKS reports. This reorganization put Dyson Carter, already a well-known Soviet sympathizer, in charge of the friendship society and might have corresponded with the arrival of Vladimir Burdin as the VOKS representative at the Soviet Embassy.[50] A VOKS biography of Carter written in 1950 praised the LPP's choice of president of the friendship society, particularly because he was a propagandist for the Soviet system, a member of the Communist Party, and a "friend of the Soviet Union."[51]

At first, Carter and other active members corresponded directly with the VOKS headquarters in Moscow from the CSFS office in Toronto or from their homes, but from 1951 on, perhaps because of the increasing volume of mail, the VOKS representative in Ottawa asked that all further contact be directed via his office.[52] The representative, in turn, relayed messages to the VOKS headquarters, which passed them on to the government departments or ministries in Moscow, as deemed necessary. Carter thought it important to differentiate between VOKS and the Soviet government more generally. In 1955, when a telegram signed "the Soviet government" was sent by the VOKS headquarters to congratulate the CSFS on hosting a Soviet Friendship Month, Carter wrote to VOKS to ask it, in the interest of preventing "confusion" in Canadians' minds, to avoid signing cables in this way.[53] Yet the connection between VOKS and Soviet governing bodies was clear. When Carter wrote in 1956 to complain about a Soviet review of one of his books, his letter was forwarded to the Central Committee of the CPSU, and when he published another book in 1957 two copies were forwarded by VOKS to the Ministry of Foreign Affairs.[54] The VOKS representatives might have been "clean" diplomats, but they were in highly trusted positions. They might also have been KGB personnel with dual functions. Aleksei P. Makarov, who worked for years in the Soviet Embassy in Ottawa, has described the degree to which the activities of all Soviet diplomats were closely monitored by KGB staff, who doubled as embassy personnel.[55] The sensitive nature of their jobs meant that they and their Canadian contacts were under constant surveillance by both Soviet and Canadian security forces. In seeking sympathetic individuals and distributing and gathering information, the VOKS representatives warranted watching.

Vladimir Pavlovich Burdin, also the first secretary at the Soviet Embassy, served as the VOKS representative in Ottawa from December 1950 to June 1955. John Holmes, assistant undersecretary of external affairs for Canada at that time, described Burdin as a "slick operator,"[56] and Jules Léger, also of the Department of External Affairs, once thought him "cocky,"[57] but both Canadians noted that in 1953 Burdin suddenly became much more charming. He was involved in lobbying to have ambassadors reappointed in Moscow and Ottawa, replacing the chargés d'affaires who had been in place since the scandal over the Gouzenko defection.[58] In discussing ambassadorial appointments, Burdin had behaved so cordially that Léger believed that he had either taken him "for a ride" or "made a deliberate attempt to create an atmosphere favourable to discussing common problems. Or both."[59] Holmes also wondered whether his initial impression of Burdin had been mistaken and whether Canadian Chargé d'Affaires Robert Ford's belief that Burdin was in fact sincere was more correct. Holmes noted that Burdin had always had a "privileged position" at the Soviet Embassy and wondered if it was because of his character or his job.[60] He wondered also whether these changes were related to the recent death of Stalin, a topic that Burdin broached, saying that the USSR had since been making concessions that were not recognized or reciprocated by the United States. "It may of course be that recent trends in Moscow have given Mr. Bourdine [*sic*] a little more confidence in his license to speak if not freely at least more flexibly," wrote Holmes.[61]

Burdin worked both sides of the ocean. In 1952, while on leave in Moscow, he met several times with Robert Ford, introducing the Canadian diplomat to Soviet friends. Ford realized at the time that Burdin had been asked by his superiors to set up such contacts but argued that it might be worthwhile for Canadians to maintain these friendships with Soviet cultural figures for their own purposes.[62] Apart from his official job as first secretary at the Soviet Embassy, and his less well-known position as the VOKS representative in Canada, Burdin might well have had other tasks. He was accused by the KGB archivist Vasili Mitrokhin, in the well-known Mitrokhin Archive, of being an operator for the KGB.[63]

Throughout his tenure at the embassy in Ottawa, Burdin was active in corresponding with the CSFS and other Canadian progressive groups and in accompanying Soviet Chargé d'Affaires L.F. Teplov, and later Ambassador Dmitri Chuvakhin,[64] to pro-Soviet events. Ted Baxter, national secretary for the CSFS, remembered meeting Burdin and his wife together with the Chuvakhins at a CSFS friendship evening held at the Royal York Hotel in Toronto in 1954.[65] As a cultural representative of the USSR in Canada, he requested and received from VOKS materials to support him in the role. All sorts of "typical" Soviet objects, including a gramophone and music records, busts and small statues of Soviet figures, ashtrays, and vodka were sent from Moscow to Ottawa for Burdin's needs in entertaining.[66] In 1954, the VOKS headquarters promised to arrange for his writing to be published in Soviet journals since Burdin was an "official representative and cultural actor" in his own right.[67]

On the personal side, Burdin's four-year-old son Sergei was killed in a car accident in Montreal in 1949. In the spring of 1952, Burdin had to negotiate with the VOKS headquarters to have the ashes accepted at a crematorium in Moscow.[68] When meeting Ford later that year, Burdin's wife showed the Canadian pictures of her two sons, who she said had been born in Canada.[69] When Burdin was replaced by Alexei Tovstogan in June 1955, he headed to India, where he appeared in a film about Nikita Khrushchev and Nikolai Bulganin's visit to India in 1956.[70]

Tovstogan, too, ordered vodka, wine, tins of crabmeat, caviar, cigarettes, and other "representative products" from the VOKS headquarters to be used as gifts and decorations in his apartment.[71] After the fire that ravaged the Soviet Embassy on New Year's Day 1956, Tovstogan wrote to the VOKS headquarters to ask for his radio receiver to be replaced.[72] When attending CSFS events, he was referred to as the "second secretary" at the Soviet Embassy in Ottawa, though in his letters to VOKS in Moscow he called himself the "VOKS Representative in Canada." In November 1958, the RCMP reported that Tovstogan was not an effective speaker. Apparently, he "read a 22-page speech in very poor English" "made up entirely of statistics." The RCMP observer found that it was "hard enough to follow as given, but the fact that it was read too fast and into a very poor public address system left most of the audience more annoyed than informed."[73] Like Burdin, Tovstogan maintained contacts with the progressive groups in Canada, frequently forwarding their letters and requests to the branches of VOKS in Belorussia, Ukraine, Leningrad, Uzbekistan, and elsewhere or to the particular departments concerned.[74]

What kind of correspondence was forwarded from Canada to VOKS departments in Moscow? Because of his interest in health and science, a considerable amount of material from Carter was forwarded to the VOKS Medical Section, and this department responded with answers to his questions and requests. Requests for books or magazines were sent to the VOKS Book Exchange department, and subscriptions were sent to the Printing and Information department. A musical score composed by a Canadian, Sam Dolan, an English-language poem praising the Soviet Union, and requests for accordion music were sent to the Soviet Culture Section.[75] Other letters were forwarded to the Ministry of Culture, Ministry of Health, Academy of Sciences, Writers' Union, and Sovexportfilm, which in turn arranged to have letters answered by individual athletes, musicians, academics, and specialists.

Unlike in the Soviet Ministry of Culture, where the US portfolio was grouped together with Commonwealth nations in the Department of Countries of America and England, VOKS had a separate department for the Americas. Issues concerning Canada were dealt with by the British Countries division, but when American readers of the CSFS journal were discussed the correspondence was directed to K.A. Chugonov, chief of the American department.[76] In Moscow, letters from the Canadian VOKS representative passed through the office of V.S. Bogatyrev, chief of the British Countries department, or his deputy, Konstantin Perevoschikov. After 1954, A. Vertogradov served as chief of the department, with Inna Kulakovskaya as his deputy. Kulakovskaya went to work for the new VOKS journal, *Culture and Life*, in 1957, and G. Ioanisyan, who had been head of the VOKS Balkan Countries department, took over from Vertogradov. Responses to Burdin and Tovstogan frequently came from one of the acting chiefs or deputy chiefs of the same department. Infrequently, letters to the Ottawa VOKS representative came from V. Yakovlev, deputy head of the entire VOKS organization, or his superior, A. Denisov.

The main outward interest of the VOKS representatives was in Canadian culture, particularly where Canadian cultural interests intersected with Soviet ideological approaches. Some of this correspondence might have appeared mundane, but VOKS left nothing to chance. In a system in which secrecy was pervasive, all information was treated as sensitive and represented a valuable political currency. This was manifested in an enormous correspondence with leftist cultural groups in Canada, especially the FRC, the AUUC, the United Jewish People's Order, the Lithuanian and Yugoslav progressive groups, and others.[77] Shipments of goods, music, films, and photographs, but especially books, were arranged through the VOKS office for these groups. Requests were made for films to be in Ukrainian or Latvian with English subtitles, so as to avoid irritating the Canadian ethnic groups' sensitivities to Russian.[78] Only books whose authors were approved by Soviet authorities were sent, whether classified as Russian classics or new Soviet writers. Literature sent to Canada included the work of Leo Tolstoy, Aleksei Tolstoy, Mikhail Sholokhov, Alexander Herzen, Fyodor Dostoevsky, Nikolai Berensky, and of course, before 1956, Josef Stalin. The proceeds gained from selling these items appear to have been left in the CSFS coffers, and the shipment was made at no charge to the society. In response to a request from a Finnish member of the LPP, VOKS sent fifteen sets of *Stalin's Collected Works* in Finnish to Canada.[79] VOKS also made sure that any Canadian writers whose works were published in the USSR had boxes of their books to distribute at home. For instance, when CPC leader Tim Buck had his book *30 Years of the Communist Movement in Canada* published in Russian, 100 copies were sent for distribution in Canada.[80]

In the early 1950s, the work done by the VOKS representative appeared to be rather passive. Generally, he passed along requests and interesting material to his superiors, but he did not go out of his way to solicit such information. Much of the correspondence between Ottawa and Moscow consisted of lists of materials being sent to Canada and requests for information on how these materials were being used. In addition, Burdin fielded questions on a wide variety of themes, passing them on to headquarters for more detailed replies. Most of the correspondence came from members of "progressive" groups. For instance, in 1954, Burdin passed along a letter from Beatrice Ferneyhough, an activist in British Columbia, asking for a Soviet opinion on her master's thesis about Machiavellianism in Shakespeare.[81] VOKS arranged to send a CSFS member, Alfred Dewhurst, for a therapeutic rest at a Soviet sanatorium.[82] Progressive Jews in Toronto asked to set up a book exchange and donated Canadian books to the Lenin Library in Moscow.[83] The Federation of Russian Canadians addressed Burdin with a request for periodic updates on the Alekhinsky chess tournament in 1956, and VOKS complied.[84] Florence (Fel) Dorland of the CSFS asked VOKS to arrange a letter exchange between schoolchildren in Vancouver and those in Minsk. The request was granted, and a list of pioneers willing to write to Vancouver children was forwarded.[85] Leslie Morris, Labor-Progressive Party executive member and editor of the LPP newspaper *Canadian Tribune*, asked for twenty copies of the collected works of Peretz Markish, a Soviet Jewish writer who praised the Soviet Union, "to be used amongst prominent Jews in Canada."[86] The Association of United Ukrainian Canadians requested $600 to fund a film about the July 1956 All-Canadian Festival of Ukrainian Music, Song, and Dance, which the AUUC hoped to show at the Youth Festival in Moscow in 1958, and the request was forwarded to VOKS for consideration.[87] Photographs of the Winnipeg festival, and news of the Canadian progressive youths' preparations for the Moscow festival, were included. Burdin must have been asked in early 1953 to survey Canadian progressives about the success of the *VOKS Bulletin*, because both Dyson Carter and Avrom Yanovsky suggested improvements to the magazine. Their advice was sent to the VOKS headquarters.[88] Canadians sympathetic to the Soviet cause generally found their needs for cultural and ideological reinforcement promptly and generously satisfied by Moscow and VOKS, through the medium of the CSFS.

VOKS treated just as seriously correspondence from the wider Canadian public. That these requests are still on file, copied and/or translated in the archives, demonstrates the importance once attached to them. All information had value, every letter was placed in a file, answers were recorded, lists of names were compiled, follow-ups were made when appropriate. Not knowing whom to address, many of these people wrote directly to Premier Nikolai Bulganin. His office forwarded the letters to VOKS. Otherwise, they wrote to the Soviet Embassy in Ottawa, and Burdin and Tovstogan handled the correspondence. In 1950, VOKS prepared a list of twelve Canadians and the questions that

Figure 10. The House of Friendship located near the Arbat in Moscow, in a building that was originally built in 1899 and was the home of a theatre and cultural club after the October Revolution.

they had asked in the past year. There were requests for pen pals, souvenirs from the USSR, stamps and coins, medical and scientific advice, and general information.[89] A Toronto artist, G. Kingsford, wrote via the Soviet Embassy for information on a Dutch painting hanging in the Leningrad Hermitage Museum. The Soviet ambassador, Chuvakhin, suggested that VOKS forward the letter together with a sketch that Kingsford had done of the work to the Leningrad VOKS branch. He got his answer in March 1955 and sent a thank-you note.[90] In 1955, a horticulturalist from Duncan, British Columbia, N.A. English, sent seeds for the "cascara tree" to Moscow and in return was sent some seeds from the Academy of Sciences Main Botanical Garden.[91] In April 1956, Raymond Arthur Davies, a left-wing book dealer in Toronto and the author of a book on Canada and Russia,[92] asked for information on material about Canada in the Soviet archives. VOKS responded that it did not deal with archival matters but forwarded the request to several archives. Eventually, the Ministry of Foreign Affairs answered Davies, listing several holdings related to Canada.[93] In October 1956, a representative of the World University Service of Canada wrote to Premier Bulganin asking for a display of Uzbek hats for one of its events. VOKS handled the request and sent the hats in January 1957.[94] Teachers frequently requested information to supplement their class curricula, and students sometimes wrote for class projects.[95] Someone asked about mushroom-picking in the USSR, and others wanted to know more about the Soviet chess champions.[96] Burdin translated the chess tournament between Canadian chess champion Frank Anderson and Igor Bondarevsky in 1954 by cable and sent clippings of the Canadian coverage to the VOKS headquarters.[97] A Canadian asked for information on Soviet nursery school designs, another asked about cinema design, and a man calling himself a "proletarian scientist" sent VOKS a book called the *Mysteries of the Cosmos*. VOKS might not have responded to all correspondence.[98]

VOKS also received letters of thanks and personal correspondence from Canadians who had visited the USSR or were interested in it. Carter cabled VOKS to make announcements about important CSFS events, such as the performance of a Shostakovich oratorio in 1951.[99] VOKS sent telegrams of congratulations to Carter and the CSFS to be read at CSFS events. For example, in 1952, VOKS cabled participants in the CSFS Friendship Month wishing them success and international peace.[100] After their visit to the USSR in 1951, Fagel and Emil Gartner, Jeanette Brunelle, artist Frederick Taylor, and Winnipeg alderman Jacob Penner each wrote glowing thank-you notes to VOKS.[101] The tone of these letters was very friendly, and clearly personal ties had been established during the visit. Several members of the Cooperative Commonwealth Federation who visited the Soviet Union in 1956 wrote thank-you letters to VOKS on their return.[102] Harold Bronson, a CCF member from Lethbridge, Alberta, claimed that his photographs of the USSR were causing a stir in Canada and boasted of his struggle with the "monopoly big business daily newspaper" in Edmonton. VOKS responded and asked for clippings of the Canadian press opinions of the CCF visit. A former CCF member of Parliament, William Irvine, wrote to VOKS on Alberta CCF executive letterhead and mentioned that his "speeches in the Soviet Union created quite a furor in the capitalist press." A month later VOKS wrote to suggest that Irvine write an article for the Soviet magazine *New Times*,[103] and in 1960 he was chosen as honorary chairman of the successor of the CSFS, the Canada-USSR Association.[104] Another CCF delegate, Otto Wobick, praised socialism over capitalism in his thank-you letter, and VOKS responded by asking him to send material on farming practices in Canada.[105] The interest that VOKS took in CCF members was maintained.

Chatty, personal letters were sent to VOKS personnel by CSFS member Romeo Lafond in 1957,[106] and Carter frequently addressed his correspondents by first name, asking about their spouses and children. The Cysz family in Edmonton wrote "Long Live Great Rus" in Russian on their New Year's card to VOKS in 1957.[107] When Louis Kon fell ill, his friend Louise Harvey wrote to VOKS to let it know. VOKS responded with a get-well letter and informed Kon about his financial holdings in the USSR.[108] On his death in October 1956, Tovstogan informed headquarters.[109] This correspondence was personal but also official. In 1951, when the USSR celebrated its thirty-fourth anniversary, Carter sent a letter of congratulations to A. Denisov at VOKS.[110] On the death of Andrei Vishinsky, famous as the chief prosecutor (or "hanging judge") during the show trials of the Stalin period, and the Soviet representative to the United Nations, Carter sent condolences to Denisov at VOKS.[111]

Occasionally, VOKS dealt with official government information. The VOKS representative in Ottawa routinely forwarded Canadian Department of External Affairs bulletins to Moscow and sent shipping guides for the Accounting department, presumably so that the costs of sending packages could be calculated. In 1957, the Fisheries Research Board of Canada requested an exchange of information on fisheries. W.E. Ricker explained that Canadians had been sending material for some years to the USSR and would like to receive some in return.[112]

The VOKS representatives in Ottawa and the Moscow headquarters also put the CSFS in contact with other Soviet friendship societies abroad and informed them of the Canadian-Soviet friendship evenings hosted in Moscow. For example, Carter's 1951 letter to the Sino-Soviet Friendship Society was directed via VOKS.[113] Many American progressives received the CSFS journal and other mailings and corresponded with Carter. In 1952, he forwarded VOKS a glowing letter to "Dear, dear Joseph Stalin" from a "rank and file U.S. citizen" praising socialism, as well as a poem written in English by an American CSFS member, which included an odd phrase given the USSR's official atheism: "God Bless the Soviets."[114]

VOKS representatives in Ottawa also sent material to headquarters related to Canadian culture, society, and politics. Often these packages included newspaper clippings and magazine articles, the Canadian *Who's Who*[115] or biographical descriptions of Canadian figures, and books showing the USSR in a favourable light.[116] Gregory Okulevich's book *Russkye v Kanade* (Russians in Canada) was sent to VOKS in 1957. In addition, any letters from CSFS readers or members who spoke in favour of Soviet policies in Hungary and elsewhere, and material such as Carter's information on housing in Canada, which described homes as status symbols, were forwarded to interested parties in the USSR.[117] A package of brochures, probably anti-communist, written in German and Ukrainian, was sent by VOKS to the Institute of Marx-Engels-Lenin-Stalin in Moscow.[118] Inna Kulakovskaya wrote to editors of mainstream

Canadian magazines asking if they would be interested in a magazine exchange. The editors of *Canadian Art*, *Liberty*, *Phoenix*, *Canadian Forum*, and *Maclean's* agreed to exchanges, and the VOKS Book Exchange department coordinated them.[119] All this correspondence shows just how important publicly available information and personal contacts were to the Soviet authorities in the pre-internet days.

But in 1956, the VOKS representative reported to his superiors on the difficulties of exhibiting Soviet photographs and declining attendance at Soviet friendship events caused by the 20th Party Congress announcements in February. After Khrushchev's famous "Secret Speech" denouncing Stalin in 1956 became public in the West,[120] and the Soviet invasion of Hungary in the autumn of that year, the pro-Soviet communist movement suffered an enormous attrition worldwide. In Canada, not only did great numbers of long-time Communist Party members disassociate themselves from their former comrades, but also the purportedly more mainstream CSFS suffered. One of the most important CSFS administrators, Jim Leech, was "freed from his duties" because of his "incorrect behaviour" following the 20th Party Congress,[121] and another, Ted Baxter, admitted that after 1956 police intimidation and fear became too much to bear, and he left the movement.[122] Baxter's subscription to the *VOKS Bulletin* was cancelled in August 1956.[123] Charlotte Carter's comments that the 20th Party Congress had made the idea of Soviet friendship unpopular in Canada were duly reported by Tovstogan to the VOKS headquarters.[124] Apparently, it was not only Canadian-Soviet friendship that suffered: in the summer of 1957, when more issues of the VOKS magazine were requested for Canada, the head of the VOKS Book Exchange department was instructed to take the copies from the supply earmarked for the New Zealand Society for Closer Relations with the USSR.[125]

The Soviet response was again to reshuffle and reorganize, as had been done after the Gouzenko defection. The *VOKS Bulletin*, the in-house magazine for foreign readers, became the more lively and colourful *Culture and Life*, sent from January 1957 on to all *VOKS Bulletin* readers. CSFS members had written for the *VOKS Bulletin*,[126] and Carter had periodically sent VOKS comments on and suggestions for the publication. In November 1956, he was asked to promote the new magazine and to give VOKS a list of Canadians who should receive a free subscription.[127] It was probably not a coincidence that the first issue of *Northern Neighbors* appeared in December 1956. Carter continued to organize tours and promote Soviet literature through the journal's pages.

Increasingly, perhaps as a result of the suspension of high-level Soviet and Canadian discussions of cultural exchanges in late 1956, the VOKS representative at the Soviet Embassy began to travel in Canada, interviewing individuals about the possibility of organizing tours of Soviet performing artists. Tovstogan's notes on these interviews were sent to the VOKS headquarters in Moscow. For instance, in March 1957, Tovstogan visited Walter Homburger, the director of International Artists, representing pianist Glenn Gould, soprano Lois Marshall, conductor Jack Bowdrie, and other Canadian performing artists. They discussed Gould's upcoming European tour, which would include a visit to the USSR.[128] Gould was the first Canadian performer to visit the Soviet Union, where he had a large fan base, and this was his first trip to Europe. Homburger said that naturally Gould was slightly nervous but that preparations were on schedule. Tovstogan then asked Homburger about the possibility of organizing a tour of Soviet artists to Canada, and Homburger responded positively, saying that a few concert performers or a ballet troupe would be feasible. Tovstogan concluded his report by saying that he thought Homburger had the experience and capability to organize such a tour.[129]

In April 1957, Jules Léger suggested to Lester B. Pearson, minister of external affairs, that "the time has come for us to reconsider our present policy" on cultural exchanges with the USSR.[130] He mentioned that the Soviets had been pressing "for a resumption of those exchanges which were planned before the events in Hungary" and, in response to Canadian hesitation, had "now taken the line that they will have to make alternative plans if they cannot count on us for an early decision." Rather than allow this to happen, Léger suggested, a strictly non-political performing tour that would interest Canadians—perhaps of a ballet troupe—might be in order, provided that the Soviets negotiated all details with External Affairs first.[131] In June 1957, the new undersecretary of state, John Holmes, renewed the suggestion that negotiations be revived.[132] In early 1958, the Canadian government promised the Soviets that it would discuss further exchange programs, but a federal election caused some delays. Ambassador Chuvakhin was told in February that "pressure from the Soviet side on these matters during the pre-election period would be embarrassing," but once the election was over, the cabinet agreed.[133] The Soviet Embassy in Canada was informed of the Canadian proposals for high-level exchanges in August.[134]

In the meantime, Tovstogan continued sounding out Canadian impresarios on the theme of exchanges. In July 1957, he interviewed impresario Nicholas Koudriavtsev, president of Canadian Concerts and Artists, about a Soviet performing art group coming to Canada.[135] Koudriavtsev also agreed in principle that having a Soviet group visit Canada after they had finished their tour of the United States was possible. He noted that there was a "weak cultural market in Canada" and that his company could guarantee only six or seven concerts of Soviet artists in eastern Canada. He suggested, then, that it would be best to arrange a tour of North America in cooperation with American companies. He further suggested that a group of fifty to sixty artists might consider participating in Montreal's annual festival of music and dance or perhaps the Stratford Music Festival. On the financial side, Koudriavtsev noted that he had good connections at the Department of External Affairs, especially with Deputy Minister Jules Léger, and it would be necessary to make sure that visas were issued before contracts were signed.[136]

Not surprisingly, given Koudriavtsev's recommendation, Tovstogan visited Louis A. Applebaum in October 1957 to discuss the possibility of Soviet participation in the Stratford Music Festival.[137] Applebaum was one of the initiators of the festival in 1954, and he spoke at length with Tovstogan about organizing a music seminar at which internationally renowned musicians would mix with newer talents. He suggested to Tovstogan that some Soviet musicians might attend that seminar and promised to let the Soviet Embassy know when the plans were better formed. In December, Ambassador Chuvakhin wrote to Yury Zhukhov, head of the State Committee for Cultural Relations with Foreign Countries, officially suggesting that Soviet music groups be sent to participate in the music festivals in Montreal, Stratford, and British Columbia in 1958. Chuvakhin added that Sydney Smith, Canadian secretary of state for external affairs, had said publicly that greater cultural exchanges between the USSR and Canada were needed.[138]

In October 1957, Tovstogan also sent a letter to V.A. Bony at the Soviet Ministry of Culture giving details about the upcoming visit of Canadian conductor Jack Bowdrie to Moscow.[139] Bowdrie would be arriving from Brussels and Paris, and Tovstogan reported that he had agreed to do six concerts as the director of Soviet symphony orchestras in November and December. Tovstogan also sent along information about Lois Marshall's visit to the USSR in 1958.[140]

It has been suggested that changes in how the International Department (ID) of the CPSU Central Committee functioned after this time were directly related to post-1956 management of perceptions.[141] In the spring of 1957, the ID was relieved of its supervision of ruling Communist Parties abroad, and this task was handed over to a new Central Committee department, Liaison with Communist and Workers' Parties of Socialist Countries.[142] The new State Committee for Friendship established in 1957 could have been intended to replace the ID in its responsibility for the foreign communist-front friendship groups. Also at this time, the Return to the Homeland project was initiated, appealing directly to individuals abroad who had roots in the Soviet territories to return "home."[143]

By the end of the 1950s, the State Committee for Cultural Relations with Foreign Countries dealt with high-level exchanges agreed to between the Soviet government and governments abroad, and it was "commonly recognized and tacitly admitted" to be in charge of VOKS.[144] A memorandum prepared by the Canadian Embassy in Moscow in 1957 explained that the recent establishment of this committee, linked to the USSR Council of Ministers, was the "most recent indication of Moscow's desire to break out of the isolation imposed by its actions in Hungary and the Suez Crisis. The USSR has been conducting a vigorous campaign to restore contacts at all levels with the West."[145] At the head of the committee was G.A. (Yuri) Zhukhov, the former deputy editor of *Pravda* and a man whom the Canadian mission described as "a skilled propagandist" who had "acted on many occasions as an unofficial spokesman for the Soviet government."[146] Therefore, establishment of the committee signalled the beginning of changes to VOKS and its sponsored groups.

In February 1958, VOKS was dissolved, and a new organization mandated to deal with friendship abroad was set up in Moscow. This new institution was called the Union of Soviet Societies for Friendship and Cultural Relations with Foreign Countries, known by its Russian acronym SSOD. Despite the new moniker, the head of VOKS, N.V. Popova, carried on in the post of president for the SSOD, two of her deputies kept the position of vice-chairmen in the new organization, the same building was used as a headquarters, and the SSOD continued to publish the journal *Culture and Life*.[147] A memorandum prepared by the European Division of the Canadian Department of External Affairs in April 1958 declared "that the new union is merely VOKS under another name."[148] The Canadian memorandum also clearly identified this change as part of the Soviet appeal for greater cultural exchange, by which it meant not "the abolition of their censorship, radio jamming and restrictions on the import of books and newspapers but the stepping up of such cultural activities as the exchange of ballet companies." Apparently, foreign governments had complained to authorities in Moscow about the VOKS sponsorship of unofficial communist-led groups in their countries, and Popova "admitted that some of VOKS' past activities have embarrassed the Soviet Government and prejudiced its relations with other countries."[149] Renaming the organization the Union of Soviet Societies gave the impression that these groups were themselves non-governmental organizations within Soviet society and could therefore negotiate freely with other unofficial non-governmental groups like them abroad. The definition of its mandate did not change in the Soviet encyclopedia or in the speech given by its "new" president in February 1957. In 1959, the Canadian Department of External Affairs discussed the fact that the

VOKS headquarters had had within it a KGB office and expressed concern that a corresponding individual working directly for the KGB often held a position within the friendship societies abroad.[150] Indeed, it appeared that certain types of information forwarded to VOKS were probably prepared with KGB interests in mind.[151] The Defence Liaison Division of External Affairs suggested that this overlap of intelligence with friendship would continue under the SSOD.[152]

The Department of External Affairs and its embassy in Moscow followed these developments closely and sceptically, particularly in the SSOD's organization of special friendship evenings linked to Western countries. In February 1959, a memorandum from the Canadian ambassador in Moscow, David M. Johnson, to Ottawa noted that the SSOD had established groups in Moscow that specialized in the promotion of culture and friendship with France and Italy and anticipated that the SSOD would soon approach the Canadian Embassy with a proposal for a Moscow-based Canadian friendship group.[153] He also indicated the reactions of American, British, and German diplomats in Moscow to the activities of the SSOD.[154] The North Atlantic Treaty Organization (NATO) in Paris was also pondering the line to be taken in relation to this group. Ottawa advised its representatives to NATO that, "if the Canadian ambassador is invited to attend or to be represented at an inaugural meeting of any Soviet-Canadian Friendship Society, he should make it clear to VOKS [SSOD] that the Canadian-Soviet Friendship Society, as it is at present constituted, is unrepresentative and unrespected and would not repeat not enjoy the cooperation of the Canadian government in any effort to play any role in cultural exchanges between Canada and the USSR."[155]

The SSOD established a Moscow-based USSR-Canada Society on 28 December 1959, and it was announced in *Pravda* the next day.[156] The first president of the society was Soviet actor Mikhail I. Tsarev, who had once visited Canada, and the general secretary was Igor A. Tikhomirov of the SSOD, who later went to work for the State Committee on Cultural Relations with Foreign Countries.[157] In 1962, D.M. Zabrodin, who had arranged teacher exchanges between Canada and the USSR for the Union of Education, Higher Education, and Scientific Workers, took over from Tikhomirov.[158] Ambassador Johnson was instructed by External Affairs to send junior representatives to the inaugural meeting but not to attend himself. External Affairs explained that this was because the new Moscow group was intent on propagandizing the Soviet Union in Canada, had used Canadian visitors to do so, and maintained contact with sympathetic groups in Canada, "possibly through the Soviet embassy." Still, External Affairs concluded that the society could be useful to Canadian diplomats in the USSR if treated carefully, so it would not "cold-shoulder" the group as long as the USSR-Canada Society did not make any specific mention of supported groups in Canada.[159] The SSOD was informed of these conditions and appears to have respected the Canadian Embassy's request.[160]

Given the expressed distrust of the Canadian-based CSFS, as well as the changes in VOKS/SSOD, it is not surprising that the CSFS was dissolved and reformed in 1959–60. The RCMP reported that, in the spring of 1959, Tim Buck, leader of the Labor-Progressive Party, travelled from Canada to Moscow for discussions about establishing a new Soviet-Canadian friendship link. Apparently, he was urged by "Soviet officials" to find a new leader from within the Canadian party and to re-establish the society soon after its Moscow link was formed. In late 1959, the recently renamed Communist Party of Canada decided to change the name of the CSFS to the Canada-USSR Association, and in March 1960 Leslie Hunt was chosen to head up the new group.[161] The association was officially launched in December 1960 at the King Edward Hotel in Toronto.[162] Although the Canada-USSR Association would publish its own newsletter, Dyson Carter was encouraged to continue publication of *Northern Neighbors*.[163] He continued to be a frequent guest at the Soviet Embassy in Ottawa, and his relationship with embassy and Moscow-based officials remained close.[164] The association cooperated and corresponded with Moscow via the Soviet Embassy in Ottawa. In 1962, the RCMP confirmed that a Soviet official at the embassy, responsible for liaising with the new Canadian group and dealing with cultural affairs, had been with the USSR-Canada Society in Moscow and "had been firmly identified as a K.G.B. careerist officer" with previous foreign experience in that field.[165] The work of Soviet image-spinning in Canada carried on as before.[166]

In a society that placed great importance on managing contacts with Westerners, VOKS had a special significance. The weight placed on its activities is clear not only from the high-profile individuals who headed the organization but also from the people selected as representatives in Ottawa. Burdin and Tovstogan, if not actually KGB officers, benefited from official Soviet trust and were given cover unusual even in Soviet Embassies, where many of the diplomats held such dual positions. The KGB would have kept close track of their activities. The RCMP and Department of External Affairs were correct in their concern about the security risks to Canadians. As an authoritative and sympathetic contact, Carter and perhaps some of the other CSFS activists provided information that the Soviets craved, and in turn their demands were also satisfied.

In 1956, Carter asked VOKS to send him a special camera that took miniature photographs: "I have long wanted to send certain 'micro-film' copies of letters, etc., to VOKS," he wrote.[167] Whether or not he received this camera is uncertain, but his request is suspicious. Why did Carter need to microfilm his letters? If he was not engaged in spying, then why would he reference a technique commonly known to be used by spies to send secret messages? He did not otherwise seem to be naive and politically unaware, so it is difficult to escape the implication that Carter was at least flirting with clandestine activities. Several of his former collaborators wonder if Carter was trustworthy. Would he have informed on other Canadian communists? Unfortunately, the documentary evidence available does not provide the answers.

What is clear is that Canadian historians have overlooked for too long the importance of VOKS in negotiating both high and grassroots cultural exchanges, and as an actor in international relations, just as "ordinary" Canadians might have overlooked the sensitive nature of their contacts with VOKS. The promotion of Soviet culture abroad and the establishment of contacts with sympathetic individuals were the main goals of VOKS representatives in Ottawa. The Soviet image was polished by pro-Soviet Canadians during the Cold War using information and opportunities provided by VOKS. The message was disseminated by progressive groups in Canada, who found it appealing.

CHAPTER 4

The Pro-Soviet Message: Dyson Carter and the CSFS Literature and Photographs

For forty years, Dyson Carter[1] produced literature that mixed a radical political message with articles on Soviet science and medical advances. This literature, which he claimed was sent to thousands of subscribers internationally,[2] maintained the Soviet political line from the first issue of *News-Facts about the USSR* in 1950 to the last issue of *Northern Neighbors* in 1989 and promised readers an upbeat alternative view to that of the mainstream press. Arguing that Western governments were censoring or twisting information provided to their citizens, he claimed to be a beacon in the night, allowing his readers an inside view of the enlightened and altruistic Soviet experiment. He combined text and photographs to produce this message. As president of the CSFS from 1949 to 1960, he organized events that disseminated the pro-Soviet message orally and in photograph and film exhibitions. Using Soviet sources, Carter produced what was essentially Soviet propaganda.[3] Carter attempted to persuade progressives that the USSR represented the realization of their ideals of gender, class, and ethnic equality and scientific and technological superiority.

The history of the CSFS and Carter's role as a promoter of the Soviet Union is linked to the history of the Canadian left.[4] Carter was a member of the Communist Party of Canada from the 1930s on,[5] as were several core CSFS organizers and members, but the rank-and-file CSFS membership and readership were drawn mostly from the non-party left. Little has been written on fellow travellers in Canada.[6] This story hints at the radical aspirations and goals of some Canadians during the Cold War, individuals who might have appeared to be "normal"[7] but who "lived otherwise"[8] and interpreted Cold War international relations differently. Ironically, the demise of the USSR makes it possible to tell this story today.

"Telling the *truth* about the Soviet Union" was the constant theme of the literature, speeches, and cultural exchanges sponsored by the CSFS. Through its publications, and in distributing Soviet magazines published specifically for foreign readers, the CSFS challenged the discourse of truth that characterized Cold War rhetoric in mainstream Canadian society. Upon returning from tours of the Soviet Union, members took part in cross-Canada speaking engagements organized by the CSFS, arguing that the prevalent Western view of the Soviet Union as sinister and backward was false. These arguments were built using the language of progress and enlightenment, and the USSR was held up by foreign admirers as the only state willing and able to construct a truly progressive society.[9] The cost of this project was not up for consideration. CSFS members were "high modernists," a term used by James C. Scott to denote faith in the possibility that scientific rationalism can cure all social ills and admiration of highly rational, scientific state planning done in the name of egalitarianism.[10] CSFS members visited Soviet hospitals, sanatoriums, prisons, factories, collective farms, and schools, and everywhere they admired the order and egalitarianism that they saw. They were interested in how "average" people lived and in the workings of "everyday socialism" in the Soviet Union.[11] They were interested in how Soviet women were treated. They were interested in peace. They never appeared to notice that much of what they saw was purposely prepared for them as Potemkin villages.[12] Instead, they reported back on their observations, emphasizing that, like scientific observers, they were witnesses and could attest to the truth of these social experiments. The CSFS newspaper *News-Facts about the USSR* and Carter's *Northern Neighbors* magazine published information on old age and health in the USSR, innovations in the treatment of cancer, sport and physical culture, greetings from Moscow schools, and Soviet innovations and inventions. The CSFS thus appeared as a projector of social idealism, acted out through friendship with the Soviet Union.

How do we understand this techno-utopian view of the future and the Soviet Union's prominent place in it? It might help to know that Carter himself was something of a science-miracle boy. Raised by Salvation Army parents in a home for the rehabilitation of juvenile delinquents, young Dyson had the condition *osteogenesis imperfecta*, which no amount of prayer was able to overcome. The rare bone disorder meant that the slightest impact or pressure could break his bones, and Carter did not walk until he was fourteen and only after he accidentally took a superdose of vitamin D. Doctors were just learning that vitamin D aided in the absorption of calcium and could be useful in curing rickets and other bone disorders. In 1932, Carter earned a master's degree in chemistry from the University of Manitoba, and his articles on popular science and engineering were published in mainstream journals through the 1930s and 1940s.[13] He was convinced that cures for many common ailments and diseases were just around the corner, but though he had full confidence in scientists he worried that, because of press bias, North Americans might not be informed of Soviet scientific advances in a timely fashion. His wife, Charlotte,[14] died of cancer in 1972, and this might have played a role in his publication of numerous articles on research on and treatments for cancer, at home and especially in the USSR. Publishing this material, knowledge apparently hidden by Western governments from their denizens,[15] became his raison d'être. Rejecting the religious evangelism of his parents, Carter took up secular evangelism. His was a belief in the ability of science, Soviet science in particular, to solve society's problems.

The USSR held symbolic significance for many Canadian leftists at this time. As Merrily Weisbord and James Laxer have suggested, in looking to the Soviet Union, Canadian communists and sympathizers were seeking a concrete example of how their beliefs could be implemented, and at times they were willing to close their eyes to unflattering evidence of Soviet reality in order to maintain this ideal.[16] Progressive Canadians with ethnic roots in Eastern Europe saw the Soviet Union as embracing and promoting the cultures of the various peoples and republics.[17] But likely these Canadians were constantly negotiating a compromise between their ideals and the practical realization of them in Canada and abroad. In oral interviews, former friendship society activists spoke about the need for researchers to understand that the Depression was a terrible time in Canada and that the Communist Party was the only group that stood up for the working person. References to philosophical similarities between Christianity and communism were frequently made in letters written to Carter and in oral interviews. The Soviet Union appeared to these people to be the only nation in the world that had successfully established a system that did not exploit the lower classes, and for this it was admired. But when, over the years, evidence from Moscow showed the USSR to be less than ideal, some members left the party, the friendship society, and the movement, while others hung on. These decisions were not made lightly, and many felt disillusionment, anger, and even betrayal in the process.[18]

What many CSFS members and readers might not have known is that, despite the seeming altruism of his activism, Carter made a living as a propagandist for the USSR. He received materials from the Soviet Union via the All-Union Society for Friendship and Cultural Relations with Foreign

Countries and its successor, the Canada-USSR Society, and he took every policy turn in step with Moscow. His income consisted of subscription payments, generous donations sent by readers, as well as payment for books purchased from him, all of which he had received at no cost from Moscow.[19] In addition, his wife and collaborator, Sally Nielsen, remembers that Soviet Embassy staff themselves periodically brought him cash bonuses and that he received some financial support from the Communist Party of Canada.[20] With these funds, Carter said he invested in Bay Street stocks and bought real estate. When he sold the warehouse that he used for his journal and books, he apparently turned a profit on the deal. He lived in a comfortable home in Gravenhurst, Ontario. But this is not to say that Carter did not sincerely believe in the USSR and its brand of socialism. Sally Nielsen, who was the daughter of one of the original CSFS leaders, Dorise Nielsen, had known Dyson for many years before she married him in 1980, and she said that he was greatly disappointed with Mikhail Gorbachev's reforms but "quickly changed his tune in order to keep his job."[21]

The Soviets were pleased when Carter was chosen as president of the CSFS in 1949, praising him as a propagandist of long standing.[22] In 1952, an article about him in the Soviet magazine *Ogonyok* called the picture of the USSR given by Dyson and Charlotte Carter in *We Saw Socialism* "correct."[23] *Ogonyok* gave a favourable review of Carter's latest book, *Tomorrow Is With Us* (translated as *The Future Is Ours*), and compared one of his characters to the mother figure in Maksim Gorky's *Mother* (high praise from the Soviets) for her exclamation that the radical pamphlets that she printed were "pure truth! Like the holy scriptures!"[24] The review pointed to the popularity of Carter's books in left-wing American circles and noted that the action in the novel could be taking place in Canada or the United States. The Soviets clearly saw Carter and the CSFS as a kind of information bridge to American, as well as Canadian, audiences, and American readers of his publications often wrote to him.[25]

Carter was already relatively well known in Canada during the Second World War for his writings on science and for his descriptions of the Soviet Union as an ally. For instance, his *Sea of Destiny*, published in 1940, warned that Canada's undefended North could leave it open to Nazi invasion, and *Russia's Secret Weapon* (1943) suggested that the power of the USSR was its ethos of positivism in the promotion of science and universal well-being.[26] For the Soviets, it did not hurt that Carter also wrote an admiring biography of Josef Stalin,[27] and in 1945 he published an account of why he became a member of the Labor-Progressive Party.[28] Other books that Carter published, sometimes co-authored with Charlotte, included comparisons of the medical care and health of Canadians and Soviets, stories about the difficult living conditions of Canadian miners and their families, and the discrimination affecting poor Americans and Ukrainian Canadians and Blacks in the Prairies.[29]

The style and themes of Carter's writing led many on the Canadian left to find in his work a reflection of their own ideals. For instance, Robert (Mendel) Laxer, an organizer with the LPP, called Carter "Canada's best writer."[30] It appears as well that his combination of scientific and technological articles had particular appeal to subscribers of *News-Facts about the USSR* and later *Northern Neighbors*. When near the end of the 1950s the Communist Party of Canada put a new person in charge of the CSFS and renamed the group the Canada-USSR Association, Carter continued to publish *Northern Neighbors*.[31]

The friendship society based its perceptions of the Soviet Union on a very Thucydidean notion of "being there" and "seeing the facts for oneself" combined with a special talent for seeing through "Western propaganda." Its perspective was presented as the basis for true knowledge of the Soviet reality, a knowledge that could and should be passed on to other Canadians. For example, in its draft constitution of January 1952, the aim of the CSFS was to "develop friendship between the peoples of Canada and the peoples of the Soviet Union," which would "be realized by bringing to the Canadian peoples, in every possible way,"

> a) Information about all aspects of life in the Soviet Union today;
>
> b) The truth that the Soviet peoples and their Government want peace and friendship with all countries;
>
> c) Facts concerning the great advantage Canada can gain by economic, cultural and scientific exchange and co-operation between our country and the Soviet Union.[32]

This aim was to be accomplished using the CSFS journal *News-Facts about the USSR* as "the chief means for building the Society and achieving its aims."[33] Leading members of the CSFS repeatedly argued that any suggestion that the society served Moscow's interests was the result of anti-Soviet sentiments that had taken root in Canada since the beginning of the Cold War. Rather than appealing exclusively to convinced communists in Canada, the CSFS emphasized that its membership included Canadians of all political stripes, those who simply wished to see a warmer international climate. For instance, in his "President's Speech," given at the first CSFS conference in 1952, Carter said that

> no doubt there will be efforts, by those whose aim is to promote hatred, not friendship, efforts to make people think the Friendship

> Society has aims which are not made public in our constitution. For example: some people will say the aim of the Friendship Society is to bring about Socialism in Canada, to do away with the capitalist system in our country. This is not true. . . . True, the Friendship Society *does include* people who would like to see Socialism in Canada. But the majority of Friendship supporters are people who believe in the economic and political system we have in Canada, the capitalist system.[34]

Carter was probably exaggerating these claims to some extent. As we have seen, the idea of friendship with the USSR had broader appeal between 1941 and 1945, while the Soviet Union was an ally, but after the defection of Igor Gouzenko, a cipher clerk at the Soviet Embassy in Ottawa in late 1945, prominent "friends of the USSR" became sceptical about such claims. In adopting the rhetoric of earlier times, Carter probably hoped to convince those on the non-party left that they were in good company. As it was, the CSFS gained most of its positive press from the established left-leaning papers.[35]

Still, Carter frequently used the truth argument. He argued that "the Canadian people want the truth, the facts. The job ahead is to get the truth, the facts, into their hands! . . . What is the greatest, most inspiring truth brought forward at this convention?—that friendship with the Soviet Union is a means to preserving world peace."[36] Frequently referring to negative reports on the USSR as "slander," the CSFS worked to produce information to disprove claims that it saw as untruthful. For example, Carter wrote that "a flood of fantastic anti-Soviet slanders [has been] poured on the Canadian people for so long. Truth has been virtually excommunicated from the press. But the love of truth and reason is deeply engrained in Canadian [sic] character, founded as it is upon intermingling of French and British democratic traditions and the freedom-loving spirit of millions of immigrant European workers and peasants. Today the Canadian people are becoming sharply curious about life in the Socialist world."[37] Education was seen to be the best way to combat this slander because it brought enlightenment: "The main features of anti-Soviet opinion in Canada today are utter stupidity and gross ignorance. People with such weaknesses of thought in time become hungry for truth. . . . Over and above all facts about the Soviet Union there stands the profoundly impressive truth that the land of Socialism is the most faithful, most determined, most powerful guardian of peace for all peoples. This truth, without a doubt, is wearing away the foundations of anti-Soviet propaganda."[38]

The CSFS emphasized this theme in all its publications, and the distribution figures were celebrated as proof that the truth was spreading. The tone of reports to VOKS in Moscow was enthusiastic, and sales figures for *We Saw Socialism* were put forward as evidence that the Canadian public was increasingly sympathetic to the USSR. In October 1951, Carter claimed that the first 4,000 copies of the book had sold out, and another 4,000 copies were being printed.[39] Similarly, he proclaimed that the CSFS bulletin *News-Facts about the USSR*, "Canada's Authoritative Information Service," was increasing its circulation in the United States and in Canada "continues to be popular"; moreover, the distribution of "Anti-Slander 'Photo-Facts'" cards ("little bullets of truth"[40]) was spreading positive information about the Soviet Union.[41]

Photography played an important role in the message produced by Carter and the CSFS. In the USSR, creating images of the progress and technological advance of socialism was a task that the photographer performed for the state. The CSFS used this technique, and photos received from the USSR, to educate Canadian audiences on the Soviet reality. *Photo-Facts*, published by the CSFS in 1951, was a set of twelve cards with photos of the Soviet Union on one side and Soviet factoids on the other. The CSFS printed 4,000 sets of these cards and had their branches across Canada distribute them. Carter had hit on the idea of publishing photo-cards in 1951 and argued that "tens of thousands more" needed to be sent out.[42] Playing on the resemblance to collectible sports cards, *Photo-Facts* offered alternative statistics on the USSR. For instance, one card showed a worker smiling at the camera, and under the photo was the phrase "Freedom for the Working Man." On the back were three categories. First, "The Papers Say: Soviet workers have to work where they're told to, their wages are low and working conditions are bad." Second, "The Photo Shows: This machinist of Soviet Latvia, U. Masulis, has been elected [a] member of his country's Supreme Parliament." Third, "The Facts Are," under which several comparisons between Soviet and American workers were made. Holders of the card were encouraged to write to *News-Facts about the USSR* for a subscription so that they could have "proof" of these facts. Each card finished with the phrase "let's get to know our neighbors—we can live in peace!"[43] Other cards dealt with "Freedom from Rising Prices," "Freedom from War Propaganda," and "Freedom from Farm Debts." Writing to VOKS, Carter suggested sending sets of these cards to other Soviet friendship societies, such as those in Australia and New Zealand, and, if needed, he was willing to have more printed, presumably for a fee. In April 1952, an article on the cards ran in the *Toronto Telegram*, calling them "straight, undiluted Communist propaganda" that was ultimately unconvincing.[44] John Yaremko, Ontario MPP, made fun of the cards, which he had received unsolicited in his mail, when he spoke at the annual meeting of the Women's Progressive Conservative Association in February 1952.[45] But Carter

Figure 11. The Photo-Facts *cards distributed by the CSFS in 1951.*

called the cards "a new development in fighting against anti-Soviet slanders."[46] Members were encouraged to buy *Photo-Facts* to distribute to friends and to leave them in public places where other Canadians would find them.

Similarly, in their book *We Saw Socialism*, the Carters put images to the text describing their highly orchestrated trip to the USSR.[47] The text is arranged around thematically oriented large photographs that usually include one of the Carters. The message clearly is here in the evidence that the Carters were there and that they investigated the truth about the USSR. Captions under the photos included "Mr. and Mrs. Carter saw hundreds of apartments like these," "Mr. and Mrs. Carter shopped in splendid stores like these," "the Carters saw mass-production of these big welding generators," "the Carters witnessed this

Victory Day Anniversary scene," and "Charlotte Carter was deeply impressed by the cleanliness and care provided for workers' children."[48] The shopping photo appeared in the chapter "Paradise or Poverty?" subtitled "Here's What We Saw."[49]

News-Facts about the USSR was first published in 1950. It was a small folded newsletter that contained snippets of interesting (and always positive) facts about the Soviet Union. Sixty-eight issues were published between 1950 and September 1956. Dorise Nielsen, as co-founder and executive secretary of the CSFS, said in a November 1950 promotional address that, by becoming subscribers, individuals would automatically become members of the CSFS. The RCMP reported her as having said "all that is necessary to become a member is to subscribe to the Society's publication which is edited by Dyson Carter."[50] Written in what has been described as the "U.S. News and World Report" style that Carter always used in his publications,[51] they were snappy, concise, and enthusiastic reports on Soviet medical and scientific advances. In addition to publishing articles that praised all things Soviet, Carter responded to critiques of the USSR. Armed with "facts" and "the truth about the USSR," he urged readers to engage friends and neighbours in discussion and to write to political leaders advocating trade with the USSR, and he argued that mainstream domestic newspapers must be read with scepticism. The first issue included greetings to Stalin on his seventieth birthday, declaring that "history is not changed by falsehood, and history records forever the truth that the Canadian people owe to you immeasurable gratitude for your leadership in the historic battles of Moscow, Leningrad and Stalingrad."[52] In 1956, reports on and photographs of people born in the USSR who had been relocated as "displaced persons" to Western Europe and North America, and who had subsequently "returned to the homeland," were published.[53] The overall impressions that readers got from *News-Facts about the USSR* have been described in this way:

> A subscription fee of one dollar would cover twelve issues, mailed in a plain brown envelope. When they opened their plain brown envelopes, subscribers could read about the latest wonders of Soviet science: "famed Soviet scientist finds way to double production of sheep . . . daring new airplane flies with no fuel." They could be assured that they were in good company: that in Britain, Vivien Leigh, Laurence Olivier, and Arthur Rank were members of the British-Soviet Friendship Society. And they could have some of those hard questions answered. Why, for example, had the Soviet Union refused to allow the UN to investigate charges of slave labour

camps? No, answered Carter, the Soviets had not refused, they had proposed a commission to investigate prisons in all countries.[54]

By 1953, a page or two of photographs appeared monthly, and the quantity and size of the photos grew steadily. Initially, Carter wrote to VOKS asking for photos "showing different sides of life of the Soviet people" to be used in *News-Facts about the USSR*,[55] but increasingly he began to request photos of specific subjects. In the April–May 1953 issue, captions to photographs of Soviet development and smiling faces read thus: "These new, exclusive *News-Facts* photographs show life inside the Soviet Union today. *News-Facts* welcomes readers' suggestions for topics to be shown in future photo pages."[56] On the same page under the headline "Canadian Trade Unionists on Visit to U.S.S.R." were photos of smiling delegates. Their names were printed in the captions, thus attesting to the truth of the images, and the locations were noted in terse phrases: "Arrival in Moscow, Aug. '52, Tom Applegarth of Toronto receives welcoming bouquet"; "Up from the Coal Mine, K. Hladiy, C. Leech"; "On Moscow's Metro. K. Hladiy, J. Goldman, J. Hines, B. Magnuson, C. Leech, J. Leech."[57] In February 1954, a line at the bottom of a page said that "the *News-Facts* camera takes you visiting; a Soviet hockey game with 80,000 in attendance; opening of Moscow's new university; and a New Year party in the Kremlin," alerting readers to the exciting photos inside. Pictures of the opening of Moscow State University present a spectacular skyscraper of knowledge and classrooms packed with studious proletarian youths. The enormity of the building and its modern architecture are impressive, and readers are informed that "in all there are 27 academic and 10 subsidiary buildings, 148 auditoriums, over 1,000 laboratories, and a 1,200,000-volume library."[58] In April 1955, under the headline "Just Arrived in Canada: They Saw for Themselves: Seven Canadians in the Soviet Union," another delegation, including R.L. Patriquin, Morris Biderman, and Louis Kon, is shown in conversation with citizens of the "worker's state."[59] In its photographs, *News-Facts about the USSR* presented Canadians as witnesses to "real" life there.

After returning from visits to the USSR, CSFS delegates toured regions of Canada speaking about their experiences. The location and number of people attending each of these meetings were duly recorded and reported to VOKS. The RCMP also paid close attention to the numbers of attendees at these functions. After returning from the USSR in May 1951, Jacob Penner apparently spoke to 500 people in Toronto and 600 in Winnipeg; Mr. and Mrs. Gartner spoke to 500 people in Toronto, 800 more in Toronto at a later date, and smaller groups of musicians and artists, university people, housewives, Jewish adults

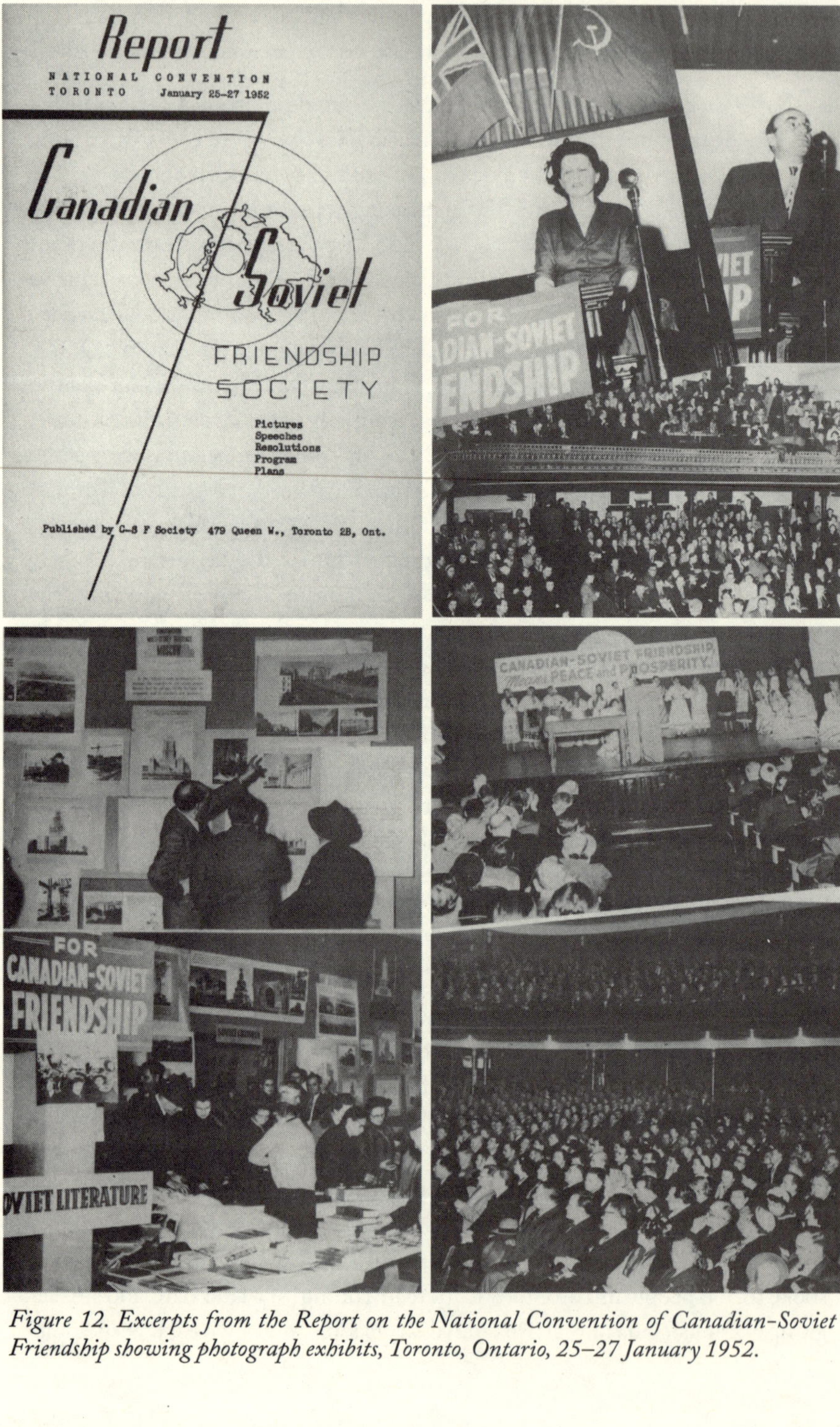

Figure 12. Excerpts from the Report on the National Convention of Canadian-Soviet Friendship showing photograph exhibits, Toronto, Ontario, 25–27 January 1952.

and children at a United Jewish People's Order meeting and summer camp; Frederick Taylor and Jeannette Pratte, restricted from speaking to public meetings by "conditions in . . . Quebec," reportedly spoke at five or six small private meetings each.[60] Dorise Nielsen, former MP and co-founder of the CSFS, argued that in terms of delegations sent to the USSR "the most important thing . . . is NOT how big they are, nor HOW MANY we send. . . . It is that every member is prepared to give of their time and energy in telling the truth about the Soviet Union to Canadians when they return. Even if this means personal sacrifice, it becomes the most important thing about any member of a delegation, that they are prepared to defeat the Big Lie, and give of their best effort to help maintain peace and friendship with the Soviet people."[61] Nielsen quoted from the journals of the Italian-Soviet Society—"today the centre of our struggle for peace . . . and the future of our nation is the struggle against anti-Soviet propaganda"—and the Iceland-Soviet Society, in which a member had pledged to "work persistently and honestly, everywhere, and all the time, to strengthen world peace, to defend the truth that comes to us from the great land of Russia."[62] Nielsen asked members of the CSFS to heed these words in their own work and to appreciate the "profound truth" contained therein.[63]

Photo exhibits sent by VOKS for exhibition by the CSFS were titled "Vacation below Moscow," "A Day at a Kolkhoz," and "Science and Religion," and a slide show called "Along the Halls of the Museum of the History of Religion and Atheism" was sent in 1957.[64] VOKS was eager to get feedback on how the photos and films were being used. It wanted to know not only who saw these materials where and when but also whether progressive groups had any comments or wishes to express to the organizers of these exhibits for future reference. Films also fit the bill of objectively showing Soviet realities to Canadians. In 1953, the RCMP reported that Nielsen toured Saskatchewan "to organize cultural groups throughout the province . . . and to make arrangements for the screening of Soviet movies." At her talk in Kamsack, *The Leading Soviet Athletes in Training* was shown, and in Winnipeg *Construction Sites of Moscow*, *Republic of Kazakhstan*, and *Girl at the Circus* were shown.[65]

Films and photo exhibits were often used to supplement other activities, such as handicraft sales or lectures. At one showing, a room meant to hold 250 people was so full that some people were refused entry. The VOKS representative in Ottawa reported to his Moscow office that the audience responded to the film and Carter's speech "very warmly." Carter had pointed out to VOKS that this report "shows once more that the Canadian public is interested in the life of the Soviet people . . . [and] willingly attends suitable events[,] and the Society (CSFS), because of this ready cooperative desire, is able to find the necessary audience amongst Canadians."[66] But at times the Russian language used in the Soviet films offended the Canadian audience, many of whom were of Ukrainian background. A letter sent to VOKS in December 1956 requested that films in Ukrainian and Latvian sent to Canada have English subtitles (not Russian ones) because members of Canadian progressive organizations found the Russian subtitles displeasing. It was further suggested that Ukrainian Canadian nationalists could use these Russian language materials to advance "anti-Soviet propaganda" about the Russification of the USSR.[67] In forwarding this letter to the Ukrainian cultural organization, a request was made that action be taken "in alleviating the uncomfortable situation for Ukrainian-Canadian progressive organizations."[68]

In October 1951, Carter reported to VOKS that 35 percent of new subscribers to *News-Facts about the USSR* were residents of the United States.[69] By 1956, with the subscription to the magazine, readers were entitled to receive *Moscow News*,[70] and many also subscribed to the *VOKS Bulletin*, a Soviet magazine prepared especially for a foreign audience and available in English, French, and other languages. International events in 1956, which included the Suez Crisis, the Soviet invasion of Hungary, and Nikita Khrushchev's famous speech denouncing Josef Stalin's personality cult, damaged the Soviet image abroad. Most likely as a response to the resulting crisis in leftist circles worldwide, both VOKS and the CSFS produced a new journal shortly afterward. In January 1957, VOKS changed the name of its magazine to *Culture and Life*, and the VOKS representative in Ottawa was told that his task was to "popularize the journal . . . and use links to Canadian intelligentsia and the progressive organizations of the Russian and Ukrainian diaspora" to do so, while the CSFS was also asked to "propagandize" the journal.[71] Carter advertised subscriptions to other Soviet magazines on sport, women, literature, and photography, and lists of addresses in the VOKS files show that many took out subscriptions. One ad included the promise that any canvasser who found two new subscribers for *News-Facts about the USSR* would receive a free map of the Soviet Union.[72]

In December 1956, the first issue of *Northern Neighbors* appeared, replacing *News-Facts about the USSR.* Readers were automatically switched over to the new publication.[73] Subscribers would have noticed that, from its first issue, *Northern Neighbors*[74] was much fuller, with bigger pictures, more like mainstream magazines. The new magazine did not call itself a CSFS publication and instead was published by the Northern Neighbors Publishing Company, Carter's own initiative. A few years later, when the Carters moved from Toronto to the more northerly town of Gravenhurst, Dyson gave up his presidency of the CSFS to devote his time to the magazine and book house

Figure 13. The covers of the Northern Neighbors *magazine published by Dyson Carter were colourful and featured photographs supplied to him by authorities in Moscow.*

work. Leslie Hunt was asked by the CPC to take over the society, soon after renamed the Canada-USSR Association, and Carter kept on with his work on *Northern Neighbors*.[75]

The initial price of the new magazine was one dollar for ten issues, and even in 1989 it was still affordable at ten dollars for ten issues. The first issue featured an interview with Soviet ballerina Galina Ulanova, photos of the International Seminar on the Equality of Rights of Women in the USSR, and photos of the CCF delegation and Canadian lumbermen visiting the USSR. The page on the lumbermen was headlined "Northern Neighbors in Real Life."[76] Articles dealt with Soviet experiments in wind and solar power, women's rights, the provision of daycare and opportunities for women outside the home, freedom of religion, human rights and disabled rights, and environmental problems. But the wonder of science, and Soviet science above all, remained a popular theme. For example, in one of its first issues, *Northern Neighbors* showed how "Man's Conquest of Nature Is Taming Siberia" with the help of guest farm workers from across the USSR.[77] Carter published a short article on "Science and Our Future" in the February 1957 issue promising that, once "the Cold War [was] out of the way," a "Climate Alteration Authority of the three northern neighbor countries: USA-Canada-USSR" could be set up to "revolutionize our winters" using atomic power.[78] The same issue featured photographs of massive machines in Soviet construction and industrial projects under the headline "Big Jobs for Heavy Industry."[79] Frequently, articles on Soviet medicine outlined cancer treatments and recommended alternative medicines such as ginseng. Throughout, the idea that Canadians had gone to the USSR and "seen the truth for themselves" was prominent.

The magazine also carried a heavy political message. Until its last issue in 1989, it followed the Soviet line closely—from the events of 1956 in Hungary to the advent of glasnost under Gorbachev. *Northern Neighbors* presented more in-depth political content than did *News-Facts about the USSR*. In January 1957, the magazine ran a long article titled "Our Readers Ask: What Do Soviet People Really Say about Hungary," which essentially outlined the Soviet position on the 1956 Hungarian revolution.[80] Readers were told that the facts of the situation, "rarely noted here" (in the North American mainstream press), were that the Hungarian "rebels" had established a "Reign of Terror" and that the Soviet Army had entered the country to prevent the establishment of a fascist state there.[81] Reading *Northern Neighbors* today, one notices a consistent pattern of about-turns as it followed the lead from Moscow. Khrushchev's famous "secret speech" to the Twentieth Party Congress in 1956 was not mentioned in the magazine's pages until 1989,[82] though from 1957 on Stalin's legacy was referred to as "mixed"—the product of a "personality cult." An explanation of why the Soviets put down the Czech "rebellion" in 1968 was provided,[83] and as the Cold War heated up in the 1980s so did the rhetoric in *Northern Neighbors*: articles defending the Soviet invasion of Afghanistan appeared in 1980,[84] and opinion pieces protesting the boycott of the 1980 Olympic Games in Moscow followed.[85] Articles claiming that the Soviets were winning the space race appeared throughout the 1980s,[86] and photos and speeches of Gorbachev were prominently featured after 1985. In 1986–87, the effects of the nuclear reactor meltdown at Chernobyl were downplayed,[87] and by 1989 perestroika and glasnost were providing the main themes.[88]

Science offered the solutions to technological and industrial dilemmas, Carter argued, and machines brought nature under human control. Many of these articles carried gendered assumptions. In "Big Jobs for Heavy Industry,"[89] the power of mechanical tools was heavily masculinized. Although women were shown to be the partners of Soviet men in bringing the caprice of nature under control, femininity was not sacrificed. Unisex clothing was eschewed in the USSR, Carter told his readers, and women delighted equally in physical work and traditional feminine pursuits such as dancing, teaching, cooking, and childrearing.

The North featured prominently in this pro-Soviet message. Soviet sovereignty in the North, and the technological tools needed to defend it, were the implicit themes of many of Carter's articles, whether the story was about northern cities or icebreakers. During the Cold War, issues related to the North resonated with much greater meaning in Canada than they had previously.[90] The Distant Early Warning (DEW) line, the fear of bombers coming over the North Pole from the USSR, and Prime Minister John Diefenbaker's "Northern Vision" emphasized the link between Canadian sovereignty and the Arctic. Carter's messages played on these themes with a pro-Soviet tune. The USSR was a good friend to Canada, ran the line, and Canadians would do well to expand friendly relations with their northern neighbours in order to learn from them. On the inside cover of the first issue of *Northern Neighbors* in 1956, an image of the North was presented to represent its mission: a map of Canada and the Soviet Union side by side. By 1957, the image depicted the Arctic from above, as if the viewer were looking down on the globe, with the Canadian North on the left and the Soviet North on the right. In 1958, a similar image included a series of human figures holding hands and stretching across the Arctic Ocean from Canada to the Soviet Union. The image was eventually dropped from the inside cover, but the rhetoric of northern links remained. Stories about Soviet icebreakers and skiers reaching the North Pole hinted heavily at Soviet sovereignty in the Arctic.[91]

Carter apparently held a modernist view of what we now call global warming. As a scientist and utopian, he had a strong belief that science could improve the everyday lives of people using techniques that seemed fantastic at times. In addition to an article on how to revolutionize winter using atomic power, Carter frequently referred to Soviet advances in meteorology. In October 1962—in an article entitled "When Will Scientists Change the Weather?"—he informed his readers that

> Soviet scientists believe [that melting the Arctic ice] would have big beneficial effects, and the undesirable effects could be offset by other deliberate actions. Such as: spray the Atlantic Ocean with chemicals to speed up evaporation, and prevent Europe-Soviet drought. Achieve the same end by mounting great solar mirrors on special sputniks, above the Ocean. By the way: both in China and in USSR they are right now trying out a weather-change of immense beneficial possibilities. By spraying cheap carbon-black on high mountain glaciers, vast quantities of solar heat are absorbed (instead of reflected) [;] this melts whole rivers of ice . . . and opens the way to turning some of Asia's worst and biggest deserts into real Gardens of Eden.[92]

But by January 1980 his argument had changed, and under the headline "Ice Work" Carter wrote that the "world is just becoming aware of the fact that our planet's ice is vital to our future. In USSR most elaborate research goes on in many areas." Next to the text were pictures of male scientists taking measurements. Under one photo of snowmobiles, a plane, and an ice tractor, the caption read "Soviet people make greater use of ice than we do. Here they are studying new methods of making landing strips for aircraft. USSR has world's largest fleet of Arctic planes, and nowadays they are increasingly used to carry heavy freight to polar construction sites." On the next page, Carter asked, "what's so fascinating about ICE?" His answer was that, "when you burn down a **jungle** it will re-grow in a couple of years. Damage permafrost, and you've ruined the land for **a century**, maybe forever. Avoiding that tragedy is the goal of hundreds of Soviet researchers. Their aim is no less than preserving one-quarter of our entire planet."[93] Never one to miss an opportunity to criticize the United States, Carter wrote in March 1980 in "Which Way Is Our Weather Going?" that "you'd think, from reports we get in our media, that USA scientists have 'weather theory' pretty well wrapped up. Not so. Recent astonishing discoveries by Soviet researchers show that the Ocean's ice plays a dominant role in weather." Arguing that the world needed cooperation on weather studies, he wrote that "this is the kind of joint world-wide research which the man in the White House is now wiping out. And it may well be that USA needs this most of all. Science for peace, not for profits in bloodshed."[94]

Setting the tone in the earliest issues of *Northern Neighbors*, Carter maintained a commentary on how Soviets had tamed the wild environment of the North, making it fit for human habitation.[95] This rhetoric appears tragically ironic today, knowing as we do that attempts to tame the environment led to extraordinary destruction and suffering. Besides "Man's Conquest of Nature Is Taming Siberia," in which Carter argued that the wilderness of the North was being domesticated by the Soviet state,[96] he wrote "Siberia Has a Winning Combination—Resources for Electric Power, Metallurgy, Chemicals, Agriculture," explaining how machinery and planning were allowing the economic development and exploitation of Siberia.[97] In October 1960, Carter made precise comparisons between Soviet and Canadian experiences: "Mirny, far up near the Arctic Circle[,] is on a parallel with much of Canada that is considered uninhabitable in any big way. Yet look what planners there are doing." He bragged that Mirny had a "hospital, nurseries, kindergartens, schools, movies and clubs, swimming pools, stadiums, centres for skiing and ice-boating," as well as shopping opportunities. Engineers had built a reservoir on a nearby river to supply the town with water, and efficient and low-cost heating techniques were used, and all this amounted to only positive effects on the environment. "Trees?" asked Carter: "A Soviet town just isn't a town without trees. So Experts had to find a way to make them grow in the climate of Yakutia."[98] In February 1962, he claimed that "The Roar of Industry Is the Music of a New Era for the 29 Million People Who Make Their Homes in Siberia."[99] Significantly, he ignored Soviet indifference to the environment, always sacrificed to industry and production. In comparing how government policies affected the lives of people in the North, Carter argued that "we can be proud of Canadian Eskimos and Indians who have achieved professional or trades standing **despite government policies**. But how much more fortunate are their Soviet counterparts who are **not** handpicked—but whose **whole populations** are encouraged and given every opportunity to sweep forward to a full life."[100] The North was well populated, therefore Soviet sovereignty there was secure, Carter seemed to say.

He argued that northern Soviet peoples were better off, more personally developed and happier, than the Inuit of Canada. He emphasized the medical facilities and schools made available to the northern peoples by the "generous" Soviet state, and pictures and text often functioned in a before/after relationship, suggesting how the lives of Soviet people had improved since 1917. Articles were accompanied by pictures of smiling people in northern settings, usually dressed in furs, with signs of progress such as schools and other institutions and industries in the background.

In September 1962, under the headline "A Doomed People Lives Again," photographs of members of the Nivkhi tribe showed them to be modern yet still able to practise their traditions. One photo in particular, of a man dressed in a suit, was accompanied by the caption "Chuner Taxami, (left) of the Nivkhi nationality, a Master of Historical Sciences, recalls: 'My fellow-tribesmen huddled in windowless yourtas and dug-out shelters.' Today the Nivkhi have sound, well-equipped homes. Above, a village kindergarten and nursery."[101] A few months later, in December 1962, an article that asked rhetorically "Soviet 'People of the Deer'—Can They Prosper in the Arctic?" argued that thirty-two years of socialism gave the Evenks new life and new jobs: "They are hunters and reindeer breeders, but also doctors, teachers, writers." Under one photo of a man in traditional dress holding a reindeer was the caption "Vasili Uvachan, Evenki author, has not forgotten how to handle his reindeer team. He travels widely in the taiga (the arctic forest)."[102] In a 1981 article titled "North Country Boom," Carter arranged photos of schoolgirls in classrooms next to adults dressed in furs to show progress made and traditions preserved.[103] The message seemed to be that the Soviet state allowed for progress without usurping the traditional gendered way of life.

Another northern theme that ran through the magazine was the idea that involvement in winter pursuits meant that Soviet people were like their Canadian neighbours. Not surprisingly, this often meant hockey. While noting that it was a rather new sport in the USSR, Carter frequently mentioned hockey as an important game of friendship.[104] Still, the competitive spirit was always present in his writing. For example, following the Summit Series in September 1972, Carter ran an opinion piece under the headline "Truth of the Month: The Russians Didn't Beat Us in Hockey," in which he argued that "Soviet sportsmen took up hockey only 25 years ago" and that "the best system plays the best hockey." That is, the NHL style of hockey was too violent, whereas Soviet players were more sportsmanlike and clearly played for love of the game rather than money.[105] Conveniently, no mention was made of the extraordinary perks to which Soviet hockey players were entitled or the extreme training that they underwent. Carter probably saw himself as combatting the congratulatory rhetoric that pervaded the Canadian press. As the website 1972 SummitSeries.com observes of the winning Canadian goal, "millions of Canadians danced and hugged in a scene that was reminiscent of the celebrations at the end of World War II. Never has a single sporting moment meant so much to so many Canadians." Carter, on the other hand, argued that many Canadians were fed up with the bad behaviour of their players on the ice and that this—rather than the Canadian victory—was the main lesson to be drawn from the series.

Carter used perceptions of the North to persuade Canadian readers, many of whom already admired the Soviet Union, that it was an advanced nation and that friendly relations were possible and desirable. Strangely, what could be considered real and specific advances in northern cooperation, such as the protocols of Canada-USSR cooperation in the North signed in 1984, and Gorbachev's Murmansk speech in October 1987,[106] earned no coverage at all in the magazine. Instead, it was the general message that the North linked Canada to the Soviet Union that predominated: by building bridges of cooperation and goodwill, Canadians could learn from Soviet superiority in the North.

By the late 1980s, it became difficult to maintain this argument. As Aileen Espiritu has shown, with the advent of glasnost, Soviet indigenous people spoke out against the "concealed racism" to which they had been subjected and which had led to cultural decline, environmental damage, and high rates of tuberculosis, poverty, and infant mortality in the Soviet North. Espiritu concludes that the official line was "not congruent with the realities experienced and lived by the indigenous peoples of the Russian North and Siberia."[107] The use of massive machinery throughout the USSR to "tame nature" wreaked havoc with the environment, and technological innovations did not live up to Carter's claims of a "citizen's paradise." The image that Carter created, and that readers had hoped for and believed in, was grotesquely out of sync with the everyday lived experiences of Soviet peoples, especially in the North.

From the archival collections at Library and Archives Canada, we can see how Carter put together his later issues of *Northern Neighbors*. Included among the files in the Carter fonds are pages of news releases published in English summarizing articles from the Soviet press. There are also thick packets of Soviet press agency photos showing smiling Soviet people and enormous machines at work building Soviet socialism. Also included are clippings taken from Western newspapers, underlined and annotated in his red pen, showing how he spliced together scientific reports in the West that coincided with recent reports on Soviet accomplishments. From the VOKS files, we can see that Carter wrote constantly to officials in the USSR asking for further information on particular themes in order to respond to readers' queries and to publish articles on these themes in *Northern Neighbors*. Soviet authorities took his letters seriously and responded to them quickly. Customs forms show that the material sent to Carter included all kinds of books and publications that he used as incentives for subscribers, as well as photos and opinion pieces that he could publish. He did not usually cite his sources, and readers did not always know that he rewrote material found elsewhere.

How was the message produced by Carter received by his readers? They were keenly political, and some were Stalinophiles. In 1980, an Australian reader wrote that "the campaign of vilification of the USSR never lets up for a moment in our press and radio. But in the long run policies of destabilization are not going to destroy the world movement any more than bombs, napalm, etc. were able to do in Vietnam. As you say, peace will win." Accompanying their fifty-dollar donation, a couple from Chilliwack, British Columbia, wrote that they would "gladly send you a donation to help you spread the gospel of truth to many more people." A Toronto reader wrote to thank Carter for the article on Stalin: "Thank you for writing a[n] article on *Stalin* in N.N. as he dissevers [*sic*] to be *honored*. What he did in his lifetime for his country and for the *world*." But a reader in Oregon did not like the article for its reference to the number of people whom Stalin had killed. The American reader wrote that "this [was] without one iota of evidence. This is the cheepest [*sic*] form of Journilism [*sic*] and I want you to know I resent it deeply. It had no place to be used in the *Northern Neighbors*."[108] In 1981, a reader in British Columbia wrote to say that he was "a Christian that believes there is more godliness and Christianity in Soviet Communism than in any Church-centred 'Christian' organization. . . . [In reading scriptures,] it became overwhelmingly clear to me . . . that Soviet Communism would conquer the world, overthrow every imperialist power and wipe out the spirit of imperialism (in some 430 to 540 years) and usher in a reign of peace and righteousness commonly known amongst Bible scholars as the 'millen[n]ium.'"[109]

A specialist on radicalism in the United States, political scientist Michael Barkun, has noted the frequent overlap of radical political messages with information on natural health and the paranormal in right- and left-wing literature.[110] *Northern Neighbors*, too, had its articles on garlic, not to mention onions, ginseng, and other dietary and nutritional advice with titles such as "Garlic Might Cure You" and "Try Beets for Pep."[111] Although the juxtaposition of these dietary and medicinal alternatives might seem odd, they correspond with alternative views on social development and medical care voiced elsewhere in the publication. However, articles on the paranormal and New Age philosophy did not fit quite so well. In the April 1960 issue of *Northern Neighbors*, Carter reported on a Soviet theory that God had been an alien in "Was God a Man from Space?"[112] This story was followed up in June 1964, giving further details on Soviet research on this theme, predictably emphasizing that Westerners were not receiving news of this because of their governments' censorship policies.[113] Particularly in the early 1980s, articles on Soviet sightings of and research on UFOs, sasquatches, aliens, and other "far-out science mysteries" were frequent features of the magazine, always with the underlying premise of "stigmatized knowledge" and the assumption that Soviet scientists would eventually find the answers.[114] These patterns correspond with the observations of Barkun in relation to radical groups in the United States, but how does one begin to understand the relationship between Carter and his readers' political orientation and interest in the paranormal?

One clue might be in the theme of human agency that runs throughout the literature. From the earliest issues of *Northern Neighbors* on, Carter underscored human action in enabling historical change in his excerpts on history makers. For instance, in December 1956, the headline above a series of human interest stories ran "People Are the Makers of History."[115] In 1984, Carter ran an article entitled "God Is Waiting?" arguing that human beings were becoming divine and that "God" then functioned as a collective "in a Communist way."[116] Again, in 1985, Carter suggested that "we are 'super-beings'" in an article entitled "You Boss the Universe."[117] Even when "average" individuals were unable to control their futures, scientists were constantly discovering more about the world that we live in and would eventually solve these dilemmas. For example, in a piece on the "power" of numbers, Carter asked "are numbers part of some general Law of our universe? If we discover it, how can we put it to use?"[118] In his publications, Carter never seemed to waver in the universalist belief that humans would grasp the underlying rules of life when true scientific socialism was reached.[119] Apparently, readers appreciated this optimism, and many letters complimented Carter on this upbeat spirit, and one writer from Mission, British Columbia, said that "my husband and I do enjoy *Northern Neighbours* [*sic*] so much and feel just great when our inner-most feelings about world conditions are confirmed in *N.N.*"[120]

Periodically, Carter asked readers for comments on the photographs published and whether they preferred them to be larger or more plentiful. The response was enthusiastic: more shots of the USSR were better than large ones to allow for a better visual understanding of Soviet life and people. A Waterloo, Ontario, woman wrote to Carter in February 1982 to say that "I enjoy the health articles, science and many pictures," while a reader in White Rock, British Columbia, wrote in September 1981 that *Northern Neighbors* editors "are to be complimented for a spiritual uplift that their writings and pictures give." However, some readers objected to photos of military machines. A woman from Magog, Quebec, wrote in December 1981 that "it makes it difficult to persuade prospective new readers when there are pictures and articles indicating the armnament [*sic*] superiority of the USSR"; a resident of British Columbia suggested that the magazine show "people enjoying themselves in a natural way" since the appeal of military parades is "over except in fascist countries." Stacks of the glossy photos that Carter used for his publications remain in his fonds, including those of Warsaw Pact arms to illustrate a feature entitled "We Must Not Fall for Any Illusions."[121]

The last issue of *Northern Neighbors* appeared in December 1989. Acquaintances of Carter recalled that he observed cynically shortly thereafter that he had spent forty years producing "bull shit,"[122] which they interpreted as disillusionment. But this view was still the Soviet line. The State Committee on Education in the USSR cancelled elementary and high school history exams in June 1988 because, according to *Izvestiia*, the Soviet textbooks were nothing but "lies."[123] The policy of glasnost had been producing almost daily newspaper articles about the inaccurate portrayal of the Soviet past, students had been confronting their history teachers with the gaps between these revelations and their textbooks, and a well-known history professor in the USSR, Yuri Afanasev, was heard to say that "I can give you my assurance that there is not a single page [in the textbook] without a falsification."[124] It appears that Carter, too, had come to this conclusion: "I publicized so many Soviet 'achievements' that were total falsifications . . . that I consider my 'work' an exercise in political pathology."[125] He had an offer to continue publishing *Northern Neighbors* from Moscow, but he decided that it was time to give it up.

How many people read or were influenced by *Northern Neighbors*? In 1985, when Carter celebrated his seventy-fifth birthday, an article in the local press repeated his claim that there were 10,000 subscriptions to *Northern Neighbors* in eighty-one countries, but his ex-wife has said that not all of these were paid subscriptions.[126] Free copies were sent to both public libraries across the country and ethnic organizations on the political left. Readers were encouraged to leave used copies in public places, such as cafés and city buses, for others to read. It is therefore difficult to arrive at an exact number of readers or judge the impact of the publications. Nonetheless, from anecdotal evidence, it appears that Carter's magazines had a large and committed readership on the Canadian left.[127]

Dyson Carter dedicated his career, in fact most of his life, to promoting the Soviet Union. *News-Facts about the USSR* and *Northern Neighbors* represented Soviet propaganda prepared and published by Canadians for a North American audience. In his publications and through his work for the CSFS, Carter tried hard to create a version of the truth that complimented the USSR. Those who travelled there under CSFS auspices and subscribed to *News-Facts about the USSR* and *Northern Neighbors* wanted to believe that the Soviet Union represented an important alternative to Western society. Today we see that this image was highly constructed, consistently ignoring the negative aspects of Soviet reality. In acting out their political views, many CSFS members and readers sincerely hoped that as individuals they could make a difference in Cold War international relations. Carter's efforts were integral to the war of words in that they provided both vehicle and data to the large cross-section of the Canadian left and kept the Soviet "version" in circulation. From the Soviet perspective, this work made Carter an important and valued friend.

CHAPTER 5

Polishing the Soviet Image: The CSFS and Progressive Ethnic Groups

The postwar CSFS, operating in the political climate of the early Cold War, used "friendship" to appeal to Canadians who might have been put off by more politically overt declarations of admiration for the Soviets. This was an extension of the Popular Front appeal undertaken by Communist Parties and communist-front groups during the war, by which they reached out to more mainstream groups and, together with peace and price activism, formed an important part of the radical agenda in Canada after the Second World War. Although superficially appearing non-partisan, political messages were never far below the surface of most CSFS-organized events and publications. The links among radical left-wing communities in Canada have been touched on by other researchers; in the CSFS, this interconnectedness was intentional.[1] In fact, this aspect was probably one of the most attractive features of the CSFS. In this linked community, the USSR was a symbol of progressivism and a shorthand for political and social group identity. For Soviet sympathizers and fellow travellers, being part of a larger community was also comforting since mainstream Canadian public opinion would have been critical of their views and activism.

Judging from both the VOKS archives and the RCMP files, the CSFS saw its mission as liaising with ethnic groups while also attempting to recruit members from the anglophone middle class. Indeed, the archives are full of references to the material shared and the cooperation or conflict between the so-called ethnic leftist groups and the CSFS. Understanding how the self-described "pan-Canadian," Anglo-Saxon[2]-led CSFS interrelated with radical ethnic groups can tell us more about what it meant to be radical in Canada during the early Cold War. Studying the interaction between the CSFS and progressive ethnic groups will provide us with some insight into the effectiveness of the CSFS campaigns to make the Soviet Union look attractive to Canadians, as well as into the experiences of left-wing radicals in Canada.[3]

Before 1945, the task of attracting ethnic and more "Canadian" members to the communist movement was carried out largely within the Communist Party. The so-called language groups had always been more popular than the main body of the CPC and had always raised more money. Members of these "mass organizations" were divided over the political policies that the Comintern wished them to adopt and the linguistic and cultural matters that they thought at least equally important. In 1929, the Comintern decreed that the language groups would no longer be considered officially part of the CPC but "were to be recruiting grounds for party membership."[4] The more ethnically diverse CPC was to be the main link between Canadian communists and the USSR. But after the revelations of Igor Gouzenko in 1946, the Labor-Progressive Party suffered a considerable loss of legitimacy. A decade later the Soviets were still not impressed with the work of the Canadian party. A secret report prepared in 1955 by V. Loginov, a counsellor at the Soviet Embassy, specified the problem: more than half of the LPP membership was composed of "immigrants," the majority of whom were Ukrainian Canadians.[5] Despite this, Loginov argued, the nationalist Ukrainians in Canada still produced stronger propaganda and influenced a larger percentage of Ukrainian Canadians than did the communists.[6] This was disappointing to the Soviets because they wanted to influence mainstream Canadian public opinion, and catering mainly to immigrants (and doing even that poorly) was not considered by them a sign of success. The Soviets were concerned as well that too many Ukrainians in the party would lead to "bourgeois-nationalist tendencies" or admiration of Ukraine rather than the USSR. Marketing Soviet-Canadian friendship to "non-ethnic" Canadians was a strategy supported by VOKS, especially via the CSFS. In reaching out to the general Canadian population—that is, anglophone[7] and middle class—VOKS hoped to make admiration of the USSR and its politics more broadly palatable.

The CSFS was an important element in this strategy because its leaders were Anglo-Saxon or had chosen English-sounding names and because it claimed to be promoting Soviet friendship in a way that appealed to middle-class peace activists, artists, teachers, and others who did not self-identify as communists. For example, John Boyd, an LPP member of Ukrainian origin active in left-wing ethnic communities in the early 1950s, was originally known by the surname Boychuk but was asked by the leadership of the Communist Party to change his name so that he would have greater influence in wider Canadian society.[8] Boyd argued that the Communist Party of Canada skillfully managed the organizations that it supported, such as the CSFS, the Canadian Slav Committee, and various peace groups, to create the illusion of independent, non-partisan progressivism. Dyson Carter was among the best at this, Boyd said, because he was seen to be suitably Canadian. At the time, party insiders were concerned that the ethnic composition of the party was a disadvantage, giving it "a foreign rather than a Canadian image." Many other Ukrainian and Jewish party members changed their names at the request of the party leadership. Among them were John Weir (Vyviursky), Moscow correspondent for the *Canadian Tribune* and later editor of the *Ukrainian Canadian*, and Robert Mendel Laxer (also known as Robert Owen), a leading member of the LPP.[9] Although the cultural events offered by the CSFS attracted Canadians who had arrived from Eastern Europe, and often who had developed socialist ideals, the leaders were invariably chosen for their clear, unaccented speech and Anglo-Saxon names.[10]

The RCMP had been remarking on the ethnic makeup of the Soviet friendship groups for years. It is likely that ethnic origin, from the RCMP point of view, was an indicator of the extent of influence that the groups had gained. When Louis Kon promoted Friends of the Soviet Union at a YMCA meeting in 1934, the RCMP reported that there were "a goodly number of Anglo-Saxons" in attendance, probably worried that the contagion of pro-Soviet communism could spread to wider Canadian society.[11] Later, at a meeting of the Society for the Study of Russia in May 1943, the RCMP reported that "a feature of the meeting as observed by members attending was the unusually large percentage of Anglo-Saxons present."[12] The membership of this society overlapped largely with that of the National Council for Canadian-Soviet Friendship, minus the prominent politicians and businessmen.[13] A month later, at a National Council rally for Soviet troops, the RCMP reported that "at least 80 per cent of the persons present were of foreign extraction and it was noted that many well-known members of the C.P. of C. and the foreign mass language organizations occupied reserved seats in a block of the blue seats on the east side of the Gardens."[14] The same report noted that the UN choir that performed at the rally was made up of the choirs of the AUUC, FRC, and Jewish Labour League, conducted by Emil Gartner.[15] Gartner, a member of the league, and later the United Jewish People's Order (UJPO), continued to be active in the CSFS under Carter, and he travelled to the USSR on a CSFS-sponsored trip in 1951. In 1953, remarking on steadily increasing CSFS activity, the RCMP worried that, by acting as a communist-front organization and a "clearing house" for Soviet materials, the CSFS was "bringing to the fringe of communism groups of people across the Dominion, many of them innocent, who may, in turn, become sympathetic to communist ideology."[16] This was recognition, in RCMP parlance, of the attraction of the CSFS for fellow travellers. The RCMP knew that the LPP was raising funds to send CSFS delegates on Soviet tours but might not have known the extent of the support received from VOKS.[17] This rhetoric was symptomatic of the Cold War. Carter would have taken the RCMP concern as a sign that he was meeting his objectives. Responding to an article in the *Financial Post* in January 1952, he expressed glee with the journalist's consternation over the "friendship front" used by Canadian leftists and boasted that CSFS strategies "have played no small part in changing public opinion in Canada."[18]

Sponsoring events, distributing photographs and films, and organizing trips to the USSR were among the means by which the CSFS attempted to improve the image of the Soviet Union in Canada. The organization also widely publicized the Return to the Homeland campaign launched by Nikita Khrushchev in the 1950s, hoping to persuade ethnic Ukrainians, Finns, Balts, Jews, Hungarians, and other Eastern Europeans that returning to the USSR to live, or at least to visit, would be a positive experience. Key events sponsored by the CSFS included a Canadian-Soviet Friendship Month arranged in November each year, timed to correspond with the anniversary of the Bolshevik Revolution. In addition, through his articles and correspondence, Carter promoted Canadian progressive writers, artists, and activists and became well known in the USSR as a leading Canadian writer.[19]

Sharing human and financial resources among left-wing groups in Canada was an effective way for a marginal movement to maximize its assets. It was also natural in that members of these organizations knew each other personally, frequently attended events organized by other groups, intermarried, and lived and worked in the same areas.[20] Indeed, social and political networking was an important way for these individuals to express and act on their beliefs while lobbying for better work conditions and sheltering themselves from the scathing criticism of Soviet sympathizers in mainstream Canadian society. In this milieu, the USSR itself was a symbolic shorthand for progressive hopes and dreams. In interactions with outside groups, left-wingers with a more "acceptable" name or accent could represent the movement and thereby improve its public face.[21]

The CSFS was set up by the Communist Party of Canada,[22] and its personnel and readership overlapped with those of the "language groups,"[23] and it used left-wing ethnic group halls across Canada for its own meetings. RCMP investigators reading the ethnic press reported to their superiors on CSFS-related events hosted in these premises. Touring the western provinces in 1950 to raise awareness of the CSFS, Dorise Nielsen spoke at the left-wing Ukrainian Hall in Wynyard, Saskatchewan, and at the Doukhobor Dome in Verigin on 28 and 30 November 1950 respectively.[24] In January 1951, CSFS meetings were held at the Ukrainian Labour Temples in Niagara Falls and Welland;[25] in March 1953, the CSFS exhibited Soviet photos and sponsored a talk by Carter in the Niagara Falls Hungarian Hall.[26] In November 1955, a CSFS event was held in the United Jewish People's Order hall in Toronto.[27] In October 1951, the RCMP reported that a "CSF-League evening was to take place at the Hungarian Hall in Niagara Falls, with Emil Gartner, his wife Fagel Gartner, Archie Hamilton, Alek Tichnovich and Dorise Nielsen speaking on their recent trip to USSR."[28] In January 1953, performances of the United Jewish People's Order choir, directed by Emil Gartner,[29] and the AUUC choir, directed by Eugene Dolny, followed speeches by Carter and Nielsen.[30] In 1954, the Russian Canadian newspaper *Vestnik* reported that over 500 people attended a CSFS film screening in Grand Forks, British Columbia, the majority of them Doukhobors and Ukrainians.[31] In a 1955 letter to his Moscow chief, the VOKS representative in Ottawa, Aleksei Tovstogan, reported that the "national committee of CSFS organized and ran 20 Nov. this year a meeting of the Toronto branch of the CSFS dedicated to Canadian Soviet friendship. This meeting took place in one of the big halls belonging to the progressive organization Jewish People's Order."[32] Tovstogan also reported that Carter's speech, "Towards the Further Strengthening of Canadian-Soviet Friendship," was well received and at times "interrupted by applause."[33] In the USSR, this was high praise.

But in addition to sharing space, the CSFS shared information with progressive ethnic groups. In terms of material sent from the USSR, the keystone between the CSFS and these groups was the VOKS representative at the Soviet Embassy in Ottawa. At first, this was Vladimir Burdin, replaced in the mid-1950s by Tovstogan. The VOKS representative collected letters and other materials to send to the VOKS headquarters in Moscow, together with reports on the activities of progressives in Canada and other newsworthy items. In 1953, Burdin forwarded to the VOKS headquarters an "illegal" brochure that he had received from the AUUC, apparently printed in Lviv in 1935–36.[34] He would also receive packages from Moscow and distribute the materials.[35] Frequently, correspondence included information and packages from the VOKS republic branches in the Ukrainian and Belorussian capitals. This material was usually destined for the AUUC and FRC.

In May 1956, the VOKS representative in Ottawa was informed that the Latvian Soviet Socialist Republic had founded a VOKS-affiliated Society for Cultural Ties Abroad, and the Moscow headquarters asked "whether in Canada there exists some kind of progressive organization of Latvian emigrants. If it exists let us know whether it is worth it in your opinion to establish a link and send a short report on it. In the report it is desirable to show the makeup of the organization and its leadership," which activities it planned, and what material was needed.[36] However, the Latvian group was told that "Comrade Tovstogan answered that in Canada for the moment that kind of progressive cultural-enlightening organization amongst emigrants from Latvia does not exist. There does exist amongst that emigration an organization which is nationalistic and diffuses sharp anti-Soviet propaganda."[37]

Sometimes the progressive groups in Canada sent requests via the VOKS representative in Ottawa for particular materials from the USSR. For instance, the director of the Federation of Russian Canadians choir, Alex Tichnovich, requested that a song collection be sent,[38] and in October 1956 Tovstogan wrote that "the leadership of the Federation of Russian Canadians wrote to VOKS with the request to send to its address, if possible, two copies of the *spravochnik* [guide book] by [the] administrative division of the Ukrainian SSR and the Belorussian SSR. These *spravochniks* are quite necessary to the federation, as Russian Canadians often come to the FRC requesting help in finding the address and place of birth according to the new administrative divisions."[39] The AUUC choir director, Eugene Dolny, asked in 1956 for Lithuanian and Latvian folk music to be sent via VOKS.[40]

Packing slips and other correspondence from Moscow note for whom and which groups the materials were destined. From these documents, we can see that hundreds of books were sent to the CSFS via VOKS, and a good number of books were sent to the AUUC, FRC, and others on request. Usually, there were multiple copies, and from the last pages of *News-Facts about the USSR* and later *Northern Neighbors* one can see that these items were for sale. Titles included the works of Lenin, Stalin, Marx, and other theoreticians of the system, as well as classical Russian and Ukrainian literature and Soviet works. Many of the books sent to the CSFS were on topics related to scientific discoveries and health. After the Twentieth Party Congress in 1956, the VOKS representative received 350 copies of a collection of resolutions from the congress in English to be distributed in Canada but not a copy of Khrushchev's speech.[41] One order form filled out by the CSFS secretary, Jim Leech, for books from the Soviet distributor Mezhdunarodnaya Kniga included 100 copies of certain books, with never fewer than twenty-five copies of any book in English or five in French. No mention was made of the CSFS paying for these copies.[42]

Invoices for the customs and excise officials listed books sent from VOKS to the CSFS and showed the value of each book listed in rubles, but the price to be paid by the receiver was listed as "free."[43] From the point of view of VOKS, this was an effective way to disseminate Soviet literature in Canada, while from the perspective of the CSFS it represented an important source of income. The books and other materials were advertised in the bulletins of ethnic groups and their annual picnic souvenir programs.[44] This probably also allowed both groups to avoid customs duties and other taxes. Eventually, the volume of this book-selling business increased to such an extent that Northern Book House was opened in Gravenhurst under Charlotte Carter's name. When first initiated in the CSFS budget as "sales of other literature" in 1952, that income came to $1,879.80, but by 1953 the amount had already doubled, ringing in at $3,005.97.[45] When Carter sold the book house premises in the late 1980s, he received $99,000, which probably represented a profit considering that he had bought it for just $20,000.[46]

Although the VOKS representative in Ottawa sent books and other material directly to the AUUC, the FRC, and sometimes the Lithuanian progressive organization, at other times material was sent to the CSFS to forward. For example, in December 1955, Carter wrote to VOKS requesting material for Armenian progressives, who did not have access to literature elsewhere: "At this time we have a request to make. For the first time, we have succeeded in having a meeting with Canadian-Armenians. It was a fine meeting, and we hope to have more. The people want us to try to get Armenian literature from the Armenian SSR. Will you do your best to get us some literature? I am writing directly to Armenian VOKS, so they will know that at long last we have started some work among the Armenian people here."[47] The VOKS headquarters passed this message on to its branch in the Armenian SSR[48] but received a reply that it had already sent books and a list of further literature available directly to Carter.[49] In 1953, he asked for material in Finnish,[50] and in March 1956 the CSFS requested literature in Lithuanian.[51] Later, however, this proved to be unnecessary, perhaps because Carter could put those who had requested the literature in contact with the Lithuanian progressive organization. In April 1956, Tovstogan wrote to his superiors to say that "the number of periodicals sent by you to the address of the Lithuanian progressive organization is sufficient, and subscribing the CSFS to the same editions is not worthwhile. As regards sending artistic literature in Lithuanian to the CSFS, that will not be necessary."[52]

From time to time, VOKS requested particular kinds of information needed in the USSR. For example, in January 1956, a request came for the AUUC, FRC, CSFS, and other organizations to send to VOKS any newspapers, brochures, books, or other material on the effects of the October Revolution on Canadian political life for possible display in the Museum of the Revolution in Moscow.[53] In addition, VOKS frequently asked Tovstogan to provide information on how the materials being sent from Moscow to the progressive groups were being used.[54]

Files on the Canadian left kept by the RCMP show that cooperation between the CSFS and other groups meant shared space and materials, as well as shared financial support. An RCMP report from November 1957 notes that a CSFS meeting was held at the AUUC hall in Calgary to celebrate the fortieth anniversary of the October Revolution, and sixty people were in attendance.[55] Several speakers spoke enthusiastically about conditions in the USSR, particularly Ukraine, and funds were raised for the Labor-Progressive Party. The reporting officer wrote that "in making an appeal for funds [unnamed person] pointed out that the only political organization that is fighting for the working man with the tradition of Lennin [*sic*] and Marx in the background is the Labor Progressive Party, who have the interest of the working man at heart at all times." He also noted that the CSFS had sponsored the event "in order to deceive the public with the hope that a much larger group would attend. This meeting was actually under the sponsorship of the Labor Progressive Party and the profit derived from same was turned over to the Labor Progressive Party."[56] The CSFS did try to appeal to a broad Canadian audience, but most consistently its readership and financial support came from the LPP and "language groups."

Funds were routinely raised by the various progressive ethnic groups to be donated to the CSFS. In one instance, *Vestnik* published a thank-you note from the CSFS addressed to "all organizations and persons who aided the Society in organizing the trip of the Trade Union delegation to the Soviet Union." Various groups on the Canadian left had raised $1,301.82 for this CSFS-sponsored trade delegation, which toured the USSR in 1952.[57] In 1951, John Weir, editor of the *Ukrainian Canadian*, initiated a campaign to raise money for the CSFS; the FRC also made donations.[58] Carter appealed directly to local clubs of the Federation of Russian Canadians, asking them to read his letters aloud at meetings, to subscribe to at least one copy of his publication, and to contribute financially to the cause of Soviet friendship.[59] Ticket sales also represented income for the CSFS. It sponsored concerts, film screenings, and photo exhibits, and often entry was for ticket holders only.

The society worked hard to convince progressive Canadians, especially Jews, that there was no anti-Semitism in the USSR.[60] An important part of this persuasion was the sponsorship of Reverend Hewlett Johnson, the "Red Dean of Canterbury," on his tour of Canada in February 1953. The RCMP reported that the tour was to counter information given by the anti-communist Canadian Jewish Congress about official state anti-Semitism in the USSR. At the University of Western Ontario, the dean was heckled when he gave a whitewashed version of the Soviet treatment of minority and religious groups, and he avoided speaking on this issue for the rest of his visit.[61] The CSFS literature played the dean's tour as "tear[ing] down the 'velvet curtain' of silence," and it spun the negative reception that the dean received in London as a case of stifling freedom of speech.[62] His appearance in Toronto at Massey Hall was sold out, and more careful attention was paid at the door to allow only ticket holders to enter. Although it was a CSFS-sponsored event, attendees included members of the UJPO, Jewish individuals from the LPP, and members of the larger public. Plainly, the CSFS saw itself as the linchpin between a larger progressive community and the ethnic groups, "Canadianizing" the message.

It is unclear who paid his salary, but Carter definitely received some money from the LPP. When he left the CSFS at the end of the 1950s, John Boyd said, Carter continued to receive support from the LPP because his magazine, *Northern Neighbors*, was so popular, including in the United States.[63] This view fits with the RCMP's notes. In a 1963 report, the RCMP mentioned that the LPP had agreed to continue to subsidize his work because *Northern Neighbors* was "useful."[64] Much later his ex-wife, Sally Nielsen, recalled that party executives asked Carter for a cut of the money that he was making in the book house,[65] and Soviet Embassy personnel brought him cash payments.[66] This direct financing might have begun while he was in charge of the CSFS, but it is certain that Carter received in-kind financial backing from the Soviets as early as 1951 by way of books and other items for sale.[67] When his books and other writings were published in the USSR, he was entitled to royalty payments.[68]

The CSFS requested specific items to be sent from the Soviet Union for exhibition and sale. The sale of these items was noted on the annual financial reports sent back to VOKS. This material represented important Soviet in-kind financial backing for Carter. A three-page list stamped 10 April 1956 and entitled "List of Artistic Handicrafts and Sewn Items Sent to the Embassy of the USSR in Canada for the CSFS" contained close to ninety tablecloths of different sizes and designs, papier-mâché boxes decorated with images from Russian fairy tales, ashtrays, teacups, and glasses.[69] Carter explained the motivation for the request in this way: "We have also been asked (because of the great success of the Slav Handicrafts Exhibit) if it would be possible for us to obtain something of a similar nature; perhaps a small collection of industrial-production consumer goods. We believe that the majority of Canadians still do not know that Soviet consumers can buy a wide range of highest-quality goods, such as photographic equipment, cosmetic articles, etc."[70] The material arrived in the summer, amounting to four boxes of handicrafts, and Tovstogan noted that it was forwarded on to the CSFS for exhibition in the fall of 1956. Shipping costs were covered by VOKS.[71]

But the CSFS did not always reap the financial rewards of the exhibit. To have its exhibit reach mainstream audiences, the CSFS tried to have it hosted by even more "neutral" groups. In 1955, the CSFS organized a series of exhibitions of Soviet children's paintings in Montreal art galleries. Because of the "difficult situation in Quebec" related to the Duplessis government's Padlock Law and discouragement of leftist group meetings, the CSFS could not take public recognition for these exhibitions. Instead, Carter asked Louis Kon to make the arrangements privately.[72] Following what proved to be a success, Carter suggested to VOKS that an exhibition of Soviet dolls be set up.[73] He argued that, "in view of the big success of the Soviet Children's Paintings (which you know have been seen by many thousands of Canadians, in many centers)," a doll exhibit should be sent. Carter pointed out that such displays were "very popular in Canada, and draw wide audiences, not only of the general public and school children, but also intellectuals, artists, teachers, etc." Drawing an audience from the wider Canadian society, and being able to offer this exhibit for non-political groups to show, were important considerations.[74] Carter was disappointed because the exhibit could not be prepared in time for Soviet Friendship Month,[75] but he continued to organize this type of event, which fit well with a genuine interest among Canadians in ethnic handicrafts.

Carter's event promotion was never more apparent than during the annual Soviet Friendship Month. Beginning in 1951, the CSFS organized it every February, but changed to November in 1954 to coincide with the anniversary of the October Revolution.[76] The Friendship Month provided an umbrella for activities in CSFS branches across the country, uniting local, often small, groups in a larger program. The activities were publicized in CSFS publications, and letters sent to specific readers and members were meant to build excitement and, it was hoped, society coffers leading up to November. Such events were often organized in cooperation with local progressive ethnic group branches, and members were encouraged to plan with the local AUUC, FRC, "and all other organizations that support our aims."[77] For instance, in November 1954, Yugoslavian, Macedonian, and Ukrainian groups in Toronto jointly sponsored the screening of a film about a recent visit of Canadians to the USSR, Carter spoke to the Finnish Organization of Canada (FOC) about the need for a trade mission to the USSR, Ted Baxter spoke on the same subject at the Carpatho-Russian Hall, and the Federation of Russian Canadians held a film meeting.[78] All of these events were organized under the auspices of Soviet Friendship Month.

Progressive Canadians received news of and encouragement to attend these events from numerous sources. The CSFS advised all branches to make their activities known via the progressive press, including the *Canadian Tribune*, *Ukrainian Canadian*, FRC journal *Vestnik*, Finnish newspaper *Vapaus*, and *Polish Weekly Chronicle*.[79] In 1953, the Labor-Progressive Party sent a missive to national members encouraging them to support Friendship Month activities,[80] and in announcing the final concert of the 1954 Friendship Month in Vancouver the local LPP branch wrote that "members are asked to fully support this event."[81] The FRC reminded its members that they were obliged to cooperate with all-Slav committees, as well as the CSFS, "whose aim is to throw a correct light on the life of the peoples of the Soviet Union." FRC members were asked to attend Friendship Month activities "but also to aid the Society morally and materially."[82] In January 1953, the editor of *Ukrainske slovo* (Ukrainian Word) urged readers to remember to honour "the late Matthew Shatulsky," "mark the 'month of Slavic unity and friendship,'" and participate in Canadian-Soviet Friendship Month, "held under the auspices of the Canadian-Soviet Friendship Society."[83]

Carter and his assistants began early in the year to send specific requests to VOKS for materials to be used during Friendship Month. Sometimes requests were made for items to be exhibited and sold, including Soviet books, photographs, traditional handicrafts, and household items, and frequently requests were made for films to be shown at these exhibitions. For example, in October 1955, Carter wrote directly to VOKS in Moscow: "On behalf of our National Council I wish to thank VOKS very warmly for the wonderful displays . . . of photographs and works of art, etc., which we have just received. This material has arrived in excellent condition. It has come just in time for Friendship Month, and we shall do our best to make full use of it."[84] The following January Carter wrote to VOKS to say that the $530 raised from the sale of Soviet "household goods" in November had been welcome: "This income played a very important part in keeping the Society alive during November and December."[85] Carter had earlier requested that VOKS send household goods to show Canadians that Soviet people did in fact have a comparably high standard of living, a theme that perhaps foreshadowed the famous "kitchen debate" between Nikita Khrushchev and Richard Nixon in 1959. Carter had suggested that household goods would be a good investment in terms of both image improvement for the USSR and financial improvement for the CSFS.[86] In the same letter, Carter suggested to VOKS that Soviet-made accordions might sell well in Canada. He asked whether it would be possible to send one to test the market: "If it proved saleable, we might be able to arrange for someone here to import Soviet accordions on a commercial basis, for our Society or independently; and the Society would benefit, financially."[87] It appears that VOKS did not take Carter up on this suggestion.

One of the activities organized by Carter during Friendship Month was the collection of greetings to be sent to the Soviet Union on behalf of Canadian individuals and groups. Ahead of November 1955, a form was sent out by the CSFS to 350 organizations and printed in *News-Facts about the USSR*, addressed to "Secretaries of organizations, and Chairmen of meetings! . . . Help to make friends for Canada, in the Soviet Union! In Friendship Month, be one of the thousands who will send greetings to the Soviet people!"[88] Above the form, instructions were given on how to fill it in and which groups or places in the USSR might be appropriate for greetings. Readers were encouraged to enclose a photograph or postcard "as a souvenir" if they wished. Above all, wrote Carter, "remember to send the form back to *News-Facts* and the CSFS, both located at 753 Bathurst St. in Toronto, to be sure your greeting will be forwarded on to the USSR."[89] At the top of the form, readers were given the bonus of a Soviet stamp, with the following caption: "Here you see a real Soviet postage stamp. We suggest you *keep* this souvenir of Friendship Month. If you decide to *visit* the Soviet Union (as thousands of Canadians soon will) you might *use this stamp* to mail a letter back home!"[90]

After the 1955 Friendship Month meeting, Tovstogan reported that "greetings to the Soviet peoples from Canadians living in Toronto" were approved, and that greetings from other Canadian cities would be sent to VOKS at the end of Canadian-Soviet Friendship Month.[91] The list of groups sending greetings, forwarded by Carter to VOKS in December 1955, included AUUC branches in Point Douglas, Transcona, and Winnipeg, Manitoba; Moose Jaw, Saskatchewan; and Port Arthur, Ontario directed to towns in the Ukrainian SSR; FRC branches across the country writing to towns in the Russian and Belorussian republics; UJPO branch greetings for the Birobidjan Autonomous Region; and branches of the FOC sending greetings to the Karelo-Finnish SSR. CSFS branches in Hamilton, Vancouver, Winnipeg, and Welland, Ontario, wrote to cities across the USSR. An LPP club in Vancouver wrote via the CSFS to the denizens of Vladivostok.[92]

Here we can see Carter and the CSFS serving as a liaison between progressive ethnic groups and attempting to present this initiative as a pan-Canadian hand of friendship extended to the peoples of the Soviet Union. He was careful to explain to VOKS that replies to these greetings should be sent to the CSFS and not directly to the organizations that had sponsored them: "I would like to stress that any responses you can get for us, to these greetings, from the various places greeted, would arouse much interest among Friendship Society supporters in Canada, and we would see that the responses were given maximum publicity throughout the entire progressive movement."[93]

In January 1956, Carter sent VOKS another long list of greetings, this time from individuals in Canada and the United States. He repeated that "all replies should be addressed to *our Society*; although, of course, each reply should be directed to the person or persons who sent the particular message. We plan to publish as many of the replies as possible."[94] The list included more than 130 individual greetings from the United States and Canada. The full names of those in Canada sending greetings were listed, and those names appear to be of Anglo-Saxon origin, as well as Ukrainian, Russian, and other ethnic backgrounds. At times, anonymity was preserved by listing the individuals as "friends in Stenen, Sask," or "friends in San Francisco, Calif. USA," and so on. Individual greetings sent from the United States named the sender by initials only. Destinations included particular towns or factories in Ukraine, Moscow, Stalingrad, Azerbaijan, Odessa, Sochi, and elsewhere in the USSR. In February 1956, Carter sent a further list of greetings that included messages from Jim Leech and Ted Baxter, both assistants to Carter who would leave the CSFS later that year as a direct result of the Twentieth Party Congress.[95]

Groups and individuals in the Soviet Union responded to the greetings collected by the CSFS, and these replies were sent via VOKS to Carter. For example, in April 1956, the VOKS representative in Ottawa received copies of the replies from the Kazakh Society for Cultural Ties Abroad and the Stalingrad Committee for the Defense of Peace.[96] In May 1956, the reply from the middle schools in Moscow was sent.[97] In June 1956, workers from the Ternopil region in Ukraine sent return greetings to the Winnipeg branch of the AUUC, written in Ukrainian, wishing the peoples of the world peace.[98] The responding message to the AUUC in Moose Jaw from the Kostelnyky village in Ternopil region, also sent in June 1956, ended with the wish "may 1956 bring heightened friendship between our peoples."[99] In each case, VOKS noted that the original letters had been sent directly to the CSFS. The CSFS published these letters and made much of forwarding them.

These greeting campaigns were not restricted to Friendship Month, though. Probably encouraged by the success of the 1955 campaign, Carter organized another one the next year. In March 1956, the CSFS collected messages for a telegram to be sent to the Bratsk Hydroelectric Station. When the names were all collected, the telegram was to be sent to VOKS in Moscow, with the request to forward it on to Bratsk.[100] In a letter to CSFS members, Carter asked them to send in the attached card plus twenty-five cents to greet and congratulate Bratsk Hydroelectric Station construction workers: "Men and women have left comfortable homes all over the U.S.S.R., to carry out this remarkable job of peaceful construction. And some of your fellow-members of the Society want to greet them, to send them *a word of encouragement and friendship from Canada*. . . . And remember: The people at Bratsk are 'the finest.'"[101] It is difficult to judge the effect of these greetings. Most likely they did not persuade people to change their minds about the USSR, but the CSFS did offer those already sympathetic to the Soviet Union a chance to express themselves. In the greetings, we can see the CSFS as a means for individuals to articulate alternative views of Cold War international affairs. Many of these Canadians might not have been aware of the degree to which this exercise was orchestrated by Carter and VOKS in the Soviet Union.

The CSFS participated in other events organized by progressive groups. For example, in November 1955, the Canadian Peace Congress organized a meeting of 1,725 delegates at Massey Hall in Toronto, among whom were CSFS representatives, as well as well-known peace activists such as James D. Endicott and Reverend D.S. Kendy, women's rights activist (and LPP member) Mrs. Rae Luckock, labour leaders, members of the CCF and LPP, and John Boyd, secretary of the Canadian Slav Committee. This meeting, and the presence of individuals sympathetic to the Soviet Union and to the progressive movement in Canada, was duly reported on by the VOKS representative in Ottawa.[102] Carter also advertised his magazine and the book house in souvenir brochures issued by the AUUC and other progressive groups at special events, labour picnics, and anniversaries.[103]

Photographs and films were central to most CSFS events. As mentioned previously, Carter began to use photos in *News-Facts about the USSR* in the first few years of publication, and from then on the photo pages multiplied, photo exhibits became part of the CSFS repertoire, and delegates fresh from touring the USSR showed their own pictures. Curious Canadians who might not otherwise have attended CSFS events were attracted by the opportunity to see behind the Iron Curtain "for themselves" via the photos. Some might have viewed these photos with nostalgia for their ancestral homes. Most of the photos came directly from Moscow via VOKS, but after 1961 some came from the Novosti Press Agency office in Ottawa.[104] Carter asked for photos "showing different sides of life of the Soviet people" to be used in *News-Facts about the USSR*.[105] Of course, Canadians who visited the USSR, especially those on CSFS-sponsored trips, were encouraged to take photos and send them and a report on their visits to Carter. These photos made it into CSFS publications and were shown at their speaking engagements upon return.

The Soviets monitored which groups used their materials. In March 1956, VOKS reported that "on D. Carter's request we are sending 28 photographs of Soviet sportsmen and 13 photographs of artists of the theatre, ballet and cinema," and in 1955 VOKS had sent to Canada four photo exhibits, entitled *Soviet Uzbekistan*; *At the Soviet Textile Makers'*; *VSKhV* (the All-Soviet Agricultural Exhibition in Moscow); *Sport in the USSR*.[106] The VOKS representative in Ottawa was asked to report back to Moscow "about the use of these materials by CSFS, AUUC, FRC and other organizations."[107]

Films were also of interest because, according to Marxist-Leninist theory, art was meant to "'picture life as it is.'"[108] As proof of the usefulness of films, Tovstogan wrote to his chief that there had been a showing of the Soviet film *Sources of Life*, at which Carter had also given a speech on "The Problems of Long-Life" and which the CSFS had advertised through the local Toronto press. Tovstogan reported that, "in the words of D. Carter, this event was successful and showed that [these events] attracted not only the progressive circles. . . . By far the majority of the audience was made up of those far from the progressive movement, but interested in the achievements and life of the Soviet Union."[109] Apparently, for this event, there was standing-room only in a hall meant for 250 people, and some had to be turned away. Tovstogan wrote that the audience responded to the film and Carter's speech "very warmly." Repeating Carter's words, Tovstogan argued that this "shows once more that the Canadian public is interested in the life of the Soviet people, willingly attends suitable events[,] and the Society [CSFS], because of this ready co-operative desire, is able to find the necessary audience amongst Canadians."[110]

Sometime in 1955, a firm called New World Films was set up in Toronto to show and sell Soviet films in Canada. The founding members were in fact CSFS members, as a letter from 1956 detailing how Sovexportfilm would send between ten and fifteen films to New World Films and the CSFS shows.[111] The list of films, in both English and French, included *Romeo and Juliet*, *VSKhV*, *Ostrov Sakhalin*, *A Portrayal of the Art of China*, *Peter I*, *State Hermitage*, and *Vietnam*.[112] In March 1956, Tovstogan received a list of "16mm films produced in the USSR and available to the CSFS."[113] VOKS asked that this list be sent to the CSFS for its use and to Artkino, a CSFS club, and New World Films.

Films and photographs represented a budgetary consideration for the CSFS, but the amounts were rather small. In 1952, the CSFS finances listed "films" as accounting for $269.75; in 1953, "receipts from films" came to $123.00; "receipts from records," $30.00; "receipts from exhibition," $662.50; and "sale of donated picture," $102.50.[114] Probably, more than amounting to income per se, the films and photos were used to draw both subscribers to the publications and audiences to the events. Even when the CSFS did not host the showing itself, the income raised from selling tickets was given to it. One example was in Sudbury, where the "red" Finnish organization ordered Soviet films from the CSFS, showed them during Friendship Month, and gave the proceeds to the CSFS.[115]

The sensitivities of particular ethnic groups were considered in ordering films for use in Canada. A letter written by Tovstogan on behalf of New World Films in December 1956 requested that films sent in Ukrainian and Latvian languages to Canada have English subtitles (not Russian) because the clients, members of the progressive organizations specifically listed as "Russians, Ukrainians, Latvians, etc." found the Russian subtitles displeasing. Indeed, he suggested that the subtitles allowed Ukrainian Canadian nationalists to publish anti-Soviet propaganda about the Russification of the USSR.[116] In forwarding this letter on to the Ukrainian cultural organization, the request was made that action be taken "in alleviating the uncomfortable situation for Ukrainian-Canadian progressive organizations."[117]

Although the political message was ever present at CSFS events, some people likely attended them to socialize with friends and converse in their native languages. For instance, though some elderly Armenian women who attended a film about Soviet Armenia in Brantford might have been politically motivated, others might have attended because of nostalgia. These women had come to Canada forty or more years earlier. At that event, Kate Bader, a recent CSFS delegate, spoke about her impressions of the USSR.[118] For some of the women in the audience, the motivation to attend might have been entertainment as much as politics, but in this ethnically interlinked leftist community social and political networking overlapped.

One of the most tangible ways that the CSFS tried to make the USSR attractive was by endorsing Khrushchev's Return to the Homeland project. As Glenna Roberts and Serge Cipko have argued, this sophisticated campaign was deliberately promoted among refugees who left the USSR after the Second World War, some of whom were convinced to emigrate back to the Soviet Union. Unfortunately, many of these individuals later regretted their decision, but only a small number were able to leave the USSR.[119] As an editor, Carter featured stories that supported Soviet efforts to entice some Canadians to return to the homeland. In March 1956, *News-Facts about the USSR* reproduced some of their stories under the headline "Thousands of Soviet 'DP's' Return to Find Sympathy, Friendship, and Jobs."[120] For example, Arkady Berishvili, who had worked for a German intelligence agency, "repented, took advantage of the Soviet Union's pardon offer, and returned home. He has completed his college education, is a Master of Architecture, and now lectures in university." Carter also cited Andrei Mikhailichenko, quoting him as saying that "'any returning Soviet citizen . . . who wants to work honestly, will find good work, and sympathy and friendship.'"[121] In June 1956, Carter published photographs of repatriates getting off ships in a Soviet harbour, all smiling and being welcomed with open arms.[122] None of these individuals appears to have come from Canada. In contrast to the CSFS view, the Return to the Homeland campaign caused trauma in the lives of Canadians convinced to go back. The fact that the CSFS helped to lure Canadian families back to the USSR, where their Canadian passports were taken and destroyed, highlights the repercussions of pro-Soviet apologia.

Apart from these articles written specifically on the Return to the Homeland initiative, those considering such a move would have found plenty of encouragement in the pages of Carter's publication. For example, Frank Park, director of the friendship organization during the Second World War, wrote an article entitled "How to Get a Place to Live" in the Soviet Union, published in March 1950. His wife and partner, Libbie Park, wrote an article in the same issue headlined "Canadian Social Worker Visits Moscow . . . Gets First-Hand Information: 'I Was Inside Soviet Hospitals.'"[123] Carter tried to make Canadian-Soviet friendship appear as non-political admiration of everyday socialism, and he included material targeted at certain groups. In 1951, Dyson and Charlotte Carter's account of their visit to the USSR, *We Saw Socialism*, presented a more in-depth view of everyday life in the Ukrainian SSR:

> Is the Ukrainian Soviet Socialist Republic a free nation, or are its 40 million people "enslaved" by the Russians, and seeking "independence"? This was a matter we looked into carefully during our trip. We observed, we asked questions everywhere. And this is what we two "Anglo-Saxons" say: anyone who actually goes to the Ukraine and lives there, in the cities and out in the countryside, as we did, will discover two warm, passionate "loves" in the hearts of all the people there. First comes their love for their Socialist

> Ukraine. With it, inseparable, is their love for all the other Soviet Republics, above all for the Russian people.[124]

The Association of United Ukrainian Canadians sent a letter to all "English-speaking branch executives" in November 1951 praising the book,[125] published by Eveready Printers. In 1957, readers of the newspaper the *Ukrainian Canadian* ordered 1,000 copies of Charlotte and Dyson Carter's book *Cancer, Smoking, Heart Disease, Alcohol*, which compared the health situations in capitalist and socialist countries.[126]

Carter also worked hard to counteract any negative publicity of the Soviet Ukraine in other publications. When an employee of the Massey-Harris plant, Harry Colegate, distributed CSFS leaflets at the entrance to the plant, explaining that he was off to see the USSR for himself, and asking his fellow workers if they had any particular questions they wanted him to look into, the incident made it into the *Globe and Mail*. The article presented him as a seeker of the truth about the USSR and his co-worker, Nicholas Prychodko, as a counter-witness with true knowledge of Soviet life.[127] Prychodko wrote to the editor, arguing that visitors to the Soviet Union were exposed to propaganda tours over which they "enthused" when they returned home, so he asked them fifteen pointed questions about what was "true" for Soviet workers. At the end of the letter, he identified his own group as the anti-Soviet Ukrainian Association of Victims of Russian Communist Terrorism and asked "in whose interests does the Canadian Soviet Friendship Society operate, Canadian or Russian?"[128]

Prychodko presented himself as someone who could see through the policy of misinformation presented by Soviet authorities. The Carters mocked witnesses who argued against their more idealistic view of Soviet reality. In putting quotation marks around Prychodko's self-identification as a "living witness" and arguing that his description of life in Soviet labour camps was exaggerated, the Carters implied that Prychodko was a liar intent on self-promotion, that the *Globe and Mail* was biased since it published his story but not the Carters' rebuttal, and finally that their perspective was more scientifically and logically sensible.[129] We can only assume that, at the time, Carter believed what he was saying, ignoring the opinion of an eyewitness to negative Soviet realities.

Apart from his own publications, Carter also encouraged Canadian progressives to subscribe to Soviet publications. For example, he announced in *News-Facts about the USSR* that any reader who joined the CSFS would be able to receive the *VOKS Bulletin* magazine for fifty cents a year.[130] During the 1954 Soviet Friendship Month, a free subscription to the *VOKS Bulletin* was given to paid-up members and new members of the CSFS.[131] This money might have gone directly into CSFS coffers since Carter claimed in a 1954

Your Delegation Will Report Back To You

Harry Colegate
Machinist, Massey - Harris, Member Local 439, U.A.W., Plant Committeeman and delegate to the District Council, U.A.W. Was President of Acme Screw and Gear local when it was first organized.

Dave Biderman
Cloakmaker, member of the International Ladies' Garment Workers Union. Former Business Agent I.L.G.W.U., Toronto, Ont. President United Jewish Peoples Order, Toronto.

Marg Popoff
Finisher, Secretary of her Local, International Fur and Leather Workers Union. Former Executive member U. A. W. Local, Massey - Harris Aircraft Division, Weston.

Dewar Ferguson
Seaman, Vice - President Canadian Seamen's Union. Former Labor Alderman, Ward Six, Toronto, Ont.

HOW WERE THE DELEGATES CHOSEN?

They were nominated by the labor committee of the Canadian-Soviet Friendship Society, composed of a large number of prominent Toronto trade unionists. They were nominated because they are representative of Canadian trade unionists, capable of making an unbiased and objective study of conditions in the Soviet Union and other European countries.

SEND IN YOUR QUESTIONS

If you have any questions you would like the delegates to look into while in the Soviet Union, write them out and send them to

DEWAR FERGUSON, Secretary, Labor Committee,
Canadian-Soviet Friendship Society,
95 Springhurst Ave., Toronto, Ont.

Or speak to one of the delegates personally.

000249

Figure 14. CSFS flyer detailing the upcoming visit of trade unionists Harry Colegate, Dave Biderman, Marg Popoff, and Dewar Ferguson to the USSR, 1951.

letter to VOKS that, "as you probably know, our Society receives a number of copies of the periodicals: *Soviet Union, Soviet Woman, Soviet Literature, News, New Times*. We have received these for a long time, without any invoices, and we distribute them for free."[132] Lists of new *VOKS Bulletin* subscribers were regularly sent by the CSFS to VOKS in Moscow. One activist in Montreal leftist circles wrote that the *VOKS Bulletin* was "a source of joy and comfort . . . in times when reaction seems to be firm in the saddle."[133] When VOKS first launched the *Bulletin*, Carter was among the first people solicited for constructive criticism,[134] and when VOKS stopped publishing the *Bulletin* in favour of *Culture and Life* the CSFS was asked to "propagandize the journal along their channels."[135] Lists of individuals interested in receiving the new journal were duly sent along.[136]

There were other perks to membership. In 1955, CSFS members were offered a course book in the Russian language for $1.00, or they could receive the course plus a year's subscription to *News-Facts about the USSR* for $1.25.[137] VOKS handled shipping of the textbook. Carter also came up with an idea to increase Canadian subscriptions to the Soviet English-language paper *Moscow News*. The response to his January 1956 letter to the main VOKS office in Moscow[138] was that not enough Canadian subscriptions to *Moscow News* were being taken. The

VOKS headquarters indicated a strong need to increase subscriptions to the English version of *Moscow News* and to ensure that it was "distributed widely" in Canada.[139] In April 1956, Tovstogan passed on Carter's idea that *Moscow News* subscriptions be linked to *News-Facts about the USSR*, but by June the decision to do so had been made in Moscow. Subscribers to the latter would receive a discount on subscriptions to the former.[140]

In addition to being translated in the USSR and appearing in Soviet newspapers, Carter's own writing was frequently featured in the Canadian progressive ethnic press. For instance, in February 1954, his article arguing that there was growing interest in the USSR in Canada, and that joining the CSFS was one way that Canadians could satisfy their curiosity, was carried in both the *Ukrainian Canadian* and the Hungarian *Kanadai magyar munkas* (Canadian Hungarian Worker). In the Ukrainian paper, the headline was "Trade, Jobs, Peace in Friendship with USSR," and in the Hungarian paper the article appeared under the title "Millions Are Awakening to the Fact that Friendship with the Soviet Is for Our Own Sake, for Canada." In both cases, Carter's byline was "President, Canadian-Soviet Friendship Society."[141] The photograph captions suggested to readers that Soviet-Hungarian friendship had a long history, as did Ukrainian-Russian cooperation within the USSR; there were the usual pictures of the Lenin Mausoleum in Red Square and ballet stars.[142] Carter claimed that "already big sections of our population are beginning to see a great, historic truth. Friendly relations between Canada and our neighbour to the north are what we Canadians urgently need to make sure of a peaceful, prosperous, independent future of our country."[143] He urged all Canadians to read CSFS publications to get the "eye-witness story" published by the CSFS, to read a brochure entitled *Canadians Visit Our Northern Neighbours*, to listen to radio broadcasts from Moscow, and to attend CSFS events. "It's our responsibility to see that we and all our friends show the people of Canada, and the people of the Soviet Union, just where we stand," Carter argued.[144] His pro-Stalin stance, still the official Soviet position at that time, was clear in the caption to a photo of a statue of Sergei Kirov, now known to have been assassinated by Stalin's agents. Carter claimed that Kirov was "killed by agents of foreign imperialists."[145]

CSFS branches placed ads in the left-wing press looking for volunteers to host Friendship Month activities in their homes, CSFS publications were reviewed in the left-wing press, and the times, dates, and frequencies of Soviet radio programs were published there.[146] Biographies of the Carters were run in newspapers such as the *Canadian Jewish Weekly* promoting the couple as "a Canadian man and his wife" who admired the USSR and were admired by

Soviet people.[147] An essential part of this message was that the Carters had been to the USSR, proven by the picture of them in front of Moscow State University, and they encouraged other Canadians to see the Soviet Union for themselves.

That was the ultimate dream for many Soviet sympathizers, not to mention other curious Canadians. The CSFS regularly offered Canadian progressives subsidized trips to the USSR. Analysts of the Soviet reaction to the Gouzenko Affair have concluded that the idea of sending selected Canadians to the USSR, so that they "could deliver the 'truth' about the Soviet Union" to their fellow Canadians, had been in the works since 1946 and "would soon be the new Soviet approach" to the management of perceptions.[148] A trip of a few weeks was a tempting option for members of progressive groups interested in the Soviet Union, and talks given by returnees drew large audiences. It was especially tempting because most of the expenses were covered by VOKS. Only the airfare needed to be paid by delegates, and the money for that was raised locally by the LPP and progressive ethnic groups.[149] Dyson and Charlotte Carter first went in 1950 and then again in 1953. Subsequently, Dyson was a frequent visitor to the USSR. The Carters used the experiences of their first trip to write their book *We Saw Socialism* and to proclaim in other publications that their view of the USSR was truthful because they had been there and seen it for themselves. Their trips also provided material for articles in *New Times*, the English-language Soviet newspaper for foreign readers. They might not have been aware that their questions were sent in advance of their visits to various Soviet organizations.[150]

After their return in 1950, Carter began to organize follow-up tours for other individuals. In his letters to VOKS suggesting possible delegates, we can see him attempting to reach out to the wider progressive community, to reward those who had been active, and to encourage others to contribute on their return. The main requirement was always that delegates would participate in speaking tours on behalf of the CSFS once they returned. Lectures were often accompanied by exhibitions of personal photographs or photos and films sent by VOKS. The number of public lectures given by each delegate, the venues, and the approximate number of people in attendance at each were sent in reports back to VOKS, which maintained contact with delegates after their trips, and effusive letters of friendship remain in the VOKS archival collection.

So who went on these trips? The trip of Frank and Libbie Park in December 1949 gave them the material to write *Moscow: As Two Canadians Saw It.*[151] Their travel file reveals that they attended a large list of cultural events, including Bolshoi Ballet performances, and were invited to an official gala in Moscow celebrating Stalin's seventieth birthday. The invitation came directly from the

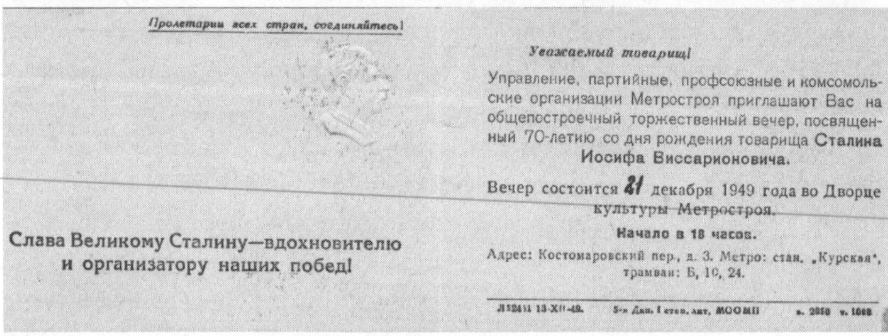

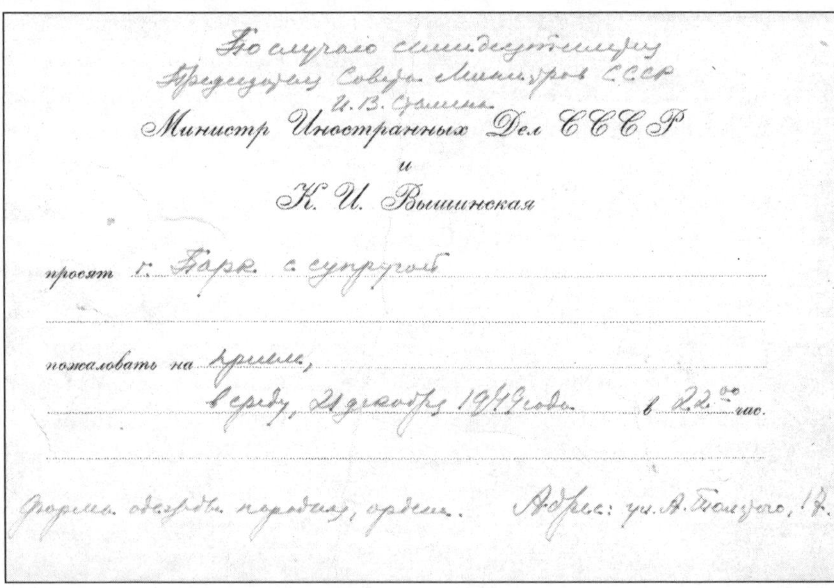

Figures 15–17. In 1949, Frank and Libbie Park visited the Soviet Union on an all-expense-paid research trip, about which the CSFS published a book, Moscow: As Two Canadians Saw It, *in 1951. During their visit, the Parks were invited to attend the seventieth birthday party of Josef Stalin. Pictured here are invitations to Kremlin parties for Stalin addressed to Frank Park and spouse, 21 December 1949.*

office of Soviet Foreign Minister Andrei Vyshinsky.[152] It is not clear why the Parks were rewarded with such a high-level invitation, but it is a sign of Soviet authorities' recognition of the importance of the visit. Other delegates might not have received invitations from such a high-ranking individual, but they nonetheless established good contacts with VOKS personnel in Moscow.

In February–March 1955, the CSFS delegation was comprised of Morris Biderman from the UJPO in Toronto; Louis Kon from Montreal; Mrs. Anna Sochasky, an AUUC member in Vancouver; K. Rankin, a CSFS member from Vancouver; Kate Bader from Toronto; R. Patriquen from Saskatchewan; and Dorothy Johnson from Manitoba. On her return, Sochasky wrote a letter to VOKS addressed to "Dear Soviet Friends" describing the Ukrainian Canadian left:

> As a Canadian I want to tell you how some of us spend our spare time in the evenings in Canada. I belong to a club called the Society of United Ukrainian Canadians. Across the whole of Canada we have 125 such clubs, some larger, some smaller. There are about 115 Ukrainian halls that belong to us. The workers have built them with their own money. I will tell you about such a club in Vancouver British Columbia. We have a separate men's club and a separate women's club. We have about 80 women in our club. There is also a large youth club. We have private teachers that teach our children the Ukrainian language in the evening. Ukrainian dancing is also tought [*sic*]. We have about 150 children that dance. We have a youth mandolin orchestra, and a mixed choir of young and old of 50 people. We give concerts in our hall with these groups once a month. Every Sunday we have a Soviet film showing. Three hundred people can be seated in our hall. Our women's club has a sewing circle, and we embroider Ukrainian shirts, aprons, and other articles. Our members take an active part in peace campaigns.[153]

Sochasky's letter reflects the gendered realities of the progressive movement,[154] also reflected in the eyewitness stories brought back by delegates.

Details of the delegates' presentations were reported back to VOKS. In a letter to his boss, the VOKS representative in Ottawa, Vladimir Burdin, noted the dates and venues for each event, as well as the number of people in the audience and what else was on offer at that meeting. Sometimes this included an FRC choir concert, the playing of Soviet records or screening of Soviet films, or special speeches given, for example in honour of the tenth anniversary of the Warsaw uprising.[155]

VOKS and the CSFS had company keeping track of attendance figures; the RCMP also counted speaking engagements and individuals attending them. For instance, a report noted that, on their return from the USSR, Anna Sochasky and Kay Rankin spoke in Natal, British Columbia, to an audience of forty-five people, where funds were raised for the local FRC branch. Sochasky was said to have spoken poorly, but Rankin was "impressive."[156] Another RCMP report from April 1955 notes that Sochasky and Rankin spoke on 30 March in Nelson, British Columbia, where there were about eighty-five people present, 90 percent of whom were Doukhobors.[157] After two films were shown, the women "described conditions in the Soviet Union including modern bakeries, meals throughout the trip, and Technical Institutes and other general living conditions."[158] At some meetings, Sochasky spoke in Ukrainian, and at others she spoke in English.[159] The RCMP included in their reports reviews and publicity from the local press, in which the women said that there was plenty of meat to eat in the USSR, that Soviet television sets did suffer from interference, and that bread produced in modern, efficient factories was "not handled by human hands."[160] The Potemkin village tours provided to Rankin and Sochasky were meant to give them a picture invariably rosier than the reality experienced by most Soviet families. They, in turn, painted a rosy picture for CSFS audiences.

The overlap of progressive personnel on this delegation was not coincidental—it was an important characteristic of the CSFS. Delegates and CSFS executive members were carefully selected for their ability to interact with diasporic groups and the LPP and attract new members. William Teresio, executive member of the AUUC, was also on the national council of the CSFS.[161] When he died in 1954, the CSFS made this connection explicit in a eulogy sent to all CSFS branches: "His death is a grievous loss to the cause of Canadian-Soviet friendship, and will be deeply felt by all members of our Society."[162] Members of progressive groups were asked to help finance trips to the USSR made by local individuals, whether or not they belonged to the same ethnic group. For instance, a fundraiser was held at the Ukrainian Labour Temple in Moose Jaw, Saskatchewan, in November 1954 to raise funds for R.L. Patriquen's trip to the USSR. A form letter was sent out to local progressives, addressed to "Dear Friend," suggesting that the remaining funds "can be secured through contributions from men and women who are aware of the need for goodwill and friendship between nations."[163] Signatures on the attached form show that eight individuals gave between five and ten dollars each. Later Carter sent out thank-you notes published in the pages of the leftist ethnic press. Returned CSFS delegates had their stories published in the progressive press in Canada, and the RCMP in turn clipped the articles and put them in files. In one, a Jewish delegate noted that Soviet Jews had told him that they had all the money and comfort they needed: "'All Jews should feel as free as we do.'"[164] This was just a few years before Khrushchev admitted in his speech at the Twentieth Party Congress that Jews had been among the most repressed minority groups under Stalin.

In March 1955, Carter wrote to the VOKS headquarters in Moscow to suggest a Soviet "professors" tour of Canadian universities and CSFS branches in Canada. In regard to whether public meetings or Society events would take precedence, he wrote, "of course, what we actually do will be in the sole interest of this delegation having greatest impact and influence for Friendship."[165] He was also planning another CSFS delegation to be made up of Dr. Howard Lowrie, who had been an important financial contributor to the CSFS; the Canadian artist Tom Thompson's sister, Margaret Tweedale, "a long-time worker for Friendship, [with] a wide circle of friends in CCF and Church groups";[166] and her husband, William, who sat on the CSFS Administration Committee after 1956, when his views on events in Hungary were judged by VOKS to be "correct."[167] But the events in Hungary and Poland in 1956[168] threw a wrench into Carter's plans. In 1957, the Soviet Embassy decided not to support the visit, possibly because the delegates were on the "wrong side" of the policy shake-up, and the tour did not go ahead.[169] VOKS did organize, however, a Soviet tour for members of the CCF in 1956, but this tour was not sponsored by the CSFS.[170]

Significant aspects of CSFS work changed in 1956 after news of Khrushchev's secret speech at the Twentieth Party Congress in February slowly reached international communist groups.[171] Key CSFS staff members left the society over it, and membership shrank. As previously mentioned, in the summer of 1956, Ted Baxter, the national secretary, cancelled his subscription to *VOKS Bulletin*[172] and left the society.[173] Next to leave was Jim Leech, the organizing secretary, whom VOKS had congratulated for managing much of the everyday work of the CSFS and the publication of *News-Facts about the USSR*.[174] In September 1957, Tovstogan informed the VOKS head office that Leech had asked the CSFS leadership to relieve him of his duties. "Considering his request, and also his incorrect behaviour following the Twentieth Congress of the CPSU," the CSFS leadership agreed, Tovstogan wrote.[175] In late 1956, Louis Kon died.[176] In May 1957, Charlotte Carter's comments that the Twentieth Party Congress had "made the idea of Canadian-Soviet friendship unpopular in Canada (especially amongst the Jewish members)" were reported to VOKS in Moscow.[177] Apparently, only half of the CSFS executive members turned up for a meeting to discuss the CSFS plan for 1957.

A few months later the Carters moved north from Toronto to Gravenhurst,[178] taking their new journal *Northern Neighbors* with them. John Boyd suggested that Carter had a falling out with the Canadian party leadership, and, though "the party tried to get the Soviet Embassy to loosen its ties with Carter, the embassy found him more of an asset than what the party could offer."[179] The Carters remained in touch with VOKS for materials and continued to visit the USSR from time to time. After the CPC-LPP changed the name of the CSFS to the Canada-USSR Association and put Les Hunt[180] in charge, links between progressive ethnic groups and the more Anglo-Saxon association remained. Many of Carter's readers continued to be of Ukrainian, Russian, Finnish, Polish, and Baltic backgrounds.[181]

Reorganization of the CSFS after the events of 1956 shows flexibility in the persuasive strategies used by its Soviet sponsors and leaders of the Canadian left. The relative success of CSFS initiatives can be seen in the number of people attending the events and subscribing to the journals, some of which would have been read by individuals outside left-wing communities. Convinced that anti-Soviet feeling was being constructed by the Western press and governments, Carter and other CSFS leaders consciously constructed an alternative, progressive, warmer image of the USSR. This image often turned on definitions of ethnicity, some of which were intentionally constructed to make the message more attractive. To CSFS readers and members, the USSR represented a hope and a dream, and evidence to the contrary was either not available or ignored. How this dream was articulated by and for Canadian women is discussed in the following chapter.

CHAPTER 6

The "Pink Tea Circuit" or "Dreams of Equality"? Women and the CSFS

The *Financial Post* published an article in 1951 under the headline "The Reds' Pink Tea Circuit: The Communist Front Fools a Lot of Women."[1] Claiming that there were hidden connections among Moscow, the Labor-Progressive Party, and women activists in Canada who protested expensive daycare and visited communist countries, the article suggested that communist-inspired protests were recognizably "belligerent, abusive in a well-organized way."[2] The journalist hinted that, as a "pink tea circuit," the women were involved for superficial reasons, were not real communists, and were being manipulated by other forces. He argued that, since two of the women cited, both from Toronto, were not known to be Communist Party members, they must have been "duped" into activism on behalf of leftist groups such as the Canadian Congress of Women and the CSFS. In hindsight, the *Financial Post* article invites us to ponder the role of gender in CSFS activities.

To what extent were women in the CSFS fooled into activism? To what extent did gender impel their activism? The LPP in postwar years used methods tested during the 1930s to attract socialists of all brands, and the "woman question" was one of these methods. Joan Sangster explained that the Popular (or People's) Front was an attempt by the Communist Party of Canada to increase its membership base and its profile by appealing to progressives outside the party, emphasizing issues that had broad support rather than criticizing other "brands" of socialism and activism. For women, Sangster noted, this policy "generated new opportunities for activism and inspired innovative organizing techniques," allowing women to have more active roles in organizing campaigns against fascism and for progressive ideals.[3] Studying women's roles within the CSFS and how the society played up rhetoric about women's equality in the USSR demonstrates that members were drawn to activism through idealism. They were not duped into activism.

The Soviet Union was held up as a concrete example of a state where equality of the sexes had been achieved, and no matter how inaccurate the message was it was repeated in CSFS literature and speeches. The Canadian women who put voices to this message were convinced that equality was both desirable and achievable in Canada, and in turn they convinced other women to attend CSFS-sponsored events on that basis. Rather than being "fooled" into activism, these women chose their roles, for they thought that their participation would further their idealistic cause. In understanding this, we can better understand how the CSFS appealed to its members. Yet the perception of an egalitarian and progressive environment for women in the Soviet Union promoted by the CSFS were sadly mistaken, and CSFS persuasion was built upon this lie.

In her work on Canadian women on the left, Sangster identified the opportunities that Popular Front strategies offered women in the 1930s and 1940s.[4] The Communist Party appealed directly to progressive women outside the Party to improve the political profile of the CPC, but most of these women were far from passive dupes.[5] Encouraged to join mainstream groups to educate working-class housewives about political issues, communist women found the "apolitical" nature of this task more suited to their interests than high party positions. Some women hesitated to take up leadership roles and instead chose tasks related to fundraising and administrative and general support, tasks important enough to make them the party's "foot soldiers" but not bring them into the limelight. This reluctance was partly the result of class and cultural norms about what women should do, but it was also related to the material conditions of everyday life. Most of these women had domestic childcare responsibilities, and many, particularly those in Finnish, Ukrainian, and Jewish communities, brought in income by keeping boarders or working outside the home.[6] Limited free time meant that women did not always achieve the degree of theoretical knowledge that their male counterparts considered necessary for leadership positions, though they were important actors when it came to maternal policy campaigns, such as better schools, access to daycare, and reproductive rights. However, the CPC never took feminism seriously, and class interests, and in some groups ethnic identity, took precedence over campaigns for women's equality.[7] Despite rhetoric to the contrary, deep-seated convictions about male privilege were as prevalent in leftist groups as they were in the wider Canadian society at that time, and mainstream notions of femininity and a woman's place percolated into the CSFS.[8]

This predicament also drew to some extent on the situation in the Soviet Union. There Vladimir Lenin and the Communist Party of the Soviet Union had considered the woman question a factional interest, and overt consideration of it was banned by the CPSU from 1921 on as part of left-wing opposition challenging party unity. Indeed, Marxist-Leninists held that consideration of feminism as a theoretical issue separate from class interests was bourgeois. For Alexandra Kollontai, an "Old Bolshevik" most well known as an advocate of women's rights in the USSR, issues of women's equality were deeply connected to class inequality, and attempts to address women's rights had to challenge the class-based nature of capitalism. However, just as Kollontai was shunted aside from main decision making in the CPSU in the 1920s, so too were women's issues gradually subjugated to the struggle for survival. Most female Bolsheviks supported Lenin's approach to party unity, and "factionalism" was no small matter.[9] Although the representation of women in political bodies was often trumpeted by Soviet leaders, their numbers were based largely upon quotas, and women were rarely in positions to affect decisions. The fact that "several educated and talented women [were] in the Russian socialist movement, but, like [Nadezhda] Krupskaya, they concentrated on secretarial or technical work and did not participate much in editorial boards or policy-making discussions,"[10] became more significant once Stalin closed all the women's departments of the CPSU in 1930. In the CPC, the precedence given to class (and the energy spent arguing about ethnic issues) over questions of women's place in society was defined by Marxist-Leninist theory and the Soviet example. This was put in practice in the CPC-supported CSFS, in which women played key organizational roles but always as helpmates to their male counterparts.

Following the Gouzenko revelations and the debut of the Cold War, the Communist Party (or LPP) was under pressure, and, watching the arrests and public hearings both in Canada and in the United States, its members were worried and fearful. Once again the party resorted to Popular Front strategies to shore up its membership and to boost its support within the larger Canadian society. The CSFS was a big part of this campaign. The promotion of women to high positions never really took hold in the CSFS despite constant lip service to the ideal of gender equality. Still, of the fifty people listed as members of the National Council for Canadian-Soviet Friendship in 1951, eleven were women, proportionally not insignificant.[11] In addition, it is clear from the documents left by the CSFS on its activities that frequently the wives of husbands who belonged to the CSFS performed important organizational tasks for the group, though they were not always listed as members.

The main leadership positions were held by men except for Dorise Nielsen, who as executive secretary was the only woman ever in a position to become a CSFS leader. She was not offered the position that she wanted and stepped aside.[12] Yet, as her biographer has pointed out, "Nielsen's low profile may have suited her in some ways."[13] With news of the pronouncements of Joseph McCarthy in the United States, and attempts by the RCMP to curtail radical political activities in Canada, Nielsen worried about arrest. On a personal level, she also worried about her health and that of her children.[14] Charlotte Carter, at times listed as a simple member, later handled the CSFS finances and often took up her husband's responsibilities when Dyson was physically unable to do so, yet she was never officially in a leading position. Perhaps she did not wish to be. The Northern Book House, through which Carter sold Soviet books sent to him by VOKS, was set up in her name in Gravenhurst in 1957.[15] Helen Burpee, a chartered accountant and member of the CPC, did end-of-year accounting for the CSFS.[16]

Many other women whose names did not appear on event banners or letterheads actively participated in CSFS activities. Although not often in the limelight, these women played important roles at the membership level. They attended events, subscribed to newsletters, wrote letters to editors, went on delegations, organized fundraising campaigns, and provided administrative support to the CSFS. It is difficult to accurately quantify their numbers, but anecdotally the women whose names appear in these capacities outnumber those listed as CSFS members or executive members, and it is therefore worth exploring how and why they were active. Their reasons for choosing these activities over more high-profile leadership positions might have been similar to Nielsen's.

In her work on the Housewives' Consumers Association (HCA), another communist-backed group in Canada that took up the cause of price activism immediately following the war, Julie Guard explains how radical Canadian women expressed their opinions on public policy in ways that fit with their conceptions of class, ethnicity, and femininity.[17] Through this group, women were able to express their disagreement with the status quo, and voice their conception of "the state in familial terms,"[18] without challenging their own positions in the home and the community. Ethnicity was also a consideration. Guard notes that women with Anglo-Saxon names, not known to be openly associated with the Communist Party, were chosen to speak on behalf of the housewives' campaign to minimize the negative association between "foreigners" and communism that many Canadians perceived. Guard notes that they were also portrayed in the press as having been duped into activism. Although "politicians and the press publicly dismissed the Housewives as a political force," because of their communist affiliation and status as women, their ideas did generate support,[19] and an alternative, elite-driven group, the Canadian Association of Consumers, eventually took on the campaign for fairly priced consumer goods.

The patterns of women's activism noted by Guard and Sangster are similar to those of women involved in the CSFS. There was even an overlap in personnel. Dorise Nielsen and Rae Luckock (both of whom usually signed their names with the prefix *Mrs.*) were involved with the HCA, as well as the CSFS. Like the HCA, the CSFS drew its overlapping members from many of the progressive ethnic groups, such as the United Jewish People's Order, Association of United Ukrainian Canadians, Finnish Organization of Canada, and Federation of Russian Canadians, and the CPC-LPP itself.[20] Most likely the RCMP were referring to Dorise when they reported in 1935 that "a Mrs. Neilsen [*sic*]" was working as an assistant at a CPC children's camp at Sylvan Lake, Alberta.[21] Mary Kardash, a prominent member of the AUUC and Congress of Canadian Women, and a school board trustee, subscribed to CSFS literature and wrote to the USSR using CSFS channels. So did Beatrice Ferneyhough, once pulled from the stage in Montreal when she spoke in favour of the CPC.[22] Kay Hladiy, who joined the Ukrainian Labour Farmer Temple Association (ULFTA) in 1932 and served on the executive of the AUUC for years, was a CSFS subscriber and delegate to the USSR in 1952.[23] Many of the most active women in the CSFS were married to executive members and supported the organization by handling administration. I have already noted that Charlotte Carter took over important duties when Dyson was incapacitated because of illness and dealt with financial matters.[24] Like their male counterparts, many of the women chosen as CSFS delegates and speakers had Anglo-Saxon names, which might have increased the appeal of their messages.

From the founding of the Soviet friendship movement in 1949, Dyson Carter played down its political aspect, repeating that Canadians of all ideological and political orientations should recognize that a policy of good relations with the USSR was beneficial to Canada and Canadians. But few would have missed the strong message favouring socialism that ran through all CSFS publications and events. Women who spoke on behalf of the CSFS said that they were attracted to the group because they saw the Soviet Union as an example of fairer state treatment of women, which included institutionalized and subsidized daycare, extracurricular education, and opportunities for women to advance in the workplace. In other words, they hoped that the USSR represented a state that operated in familial terms.

Women involved in the rigidly hierarchical Labor-Progressive Party often found the experience stifling and were frustrated by their failure to advance in the male-dominated executive.[25] The friendship society offered them more opportunities to be active in organizing, hosting, and speaking at left-wing events while maintaining lower profiles than many of their male counterparts. Handling the secretarial and financial duties of the national CSFS, as well as the branch groups, allowed women to play essential roles. Their perceived expertise in educating children and running everyday matters of the home were capitalized on by CSFS leaders, who often asked female delegates to write and speak about these issues when they returned from the USSR. A few leading women, including Dorise Nielsen, Charlotte Carter, and—after the group was renamed the Canada-USSR Association—Helen Lucas, played active roles in the society, but delegates also used their special position as women to articulate admiration of the Soviet system to progressive Canadians.

The use of women's issues for pro-Soviet propaganda in Canada was encouraged by Soviet authorities. For instance, during the Canadian-Soviet Friendship Month in 1952, a letter to Canadian mothers written by the mother of one of the youngest Soviet women partisans to die in the Second World War, Lyubov Kosmodemyanskaya, was published in the *Canadian Tribune*.[26] This could only have been done with official Soviet encouragement, probably via the Soviet Information Bureau or VOKS. The image of a Soviet mother reaching out to Canadian mothers was powerful. As she argued, "I believe that the peace won at the cost of the lives of our children, at the cost of the tears of mothers, widows and orphans, will not be violated again at the will of a handful of imperialists gone mad: we will not permit it." She quoted Stalin, whom she called the "great standard-bearer of peace," and concluded by saying that "I press your hands, dear friends, the hands of the working folk of Canada. From the bottom of my heart I want this month of friendship to make still stronger the fraternal ties between our two peoples."[27] This message, couched in the language of maternal feminism, touched on issues of peace and friendship, the raison d'être of several CPC-supported groups but also concepts with appeal in the greater Canadian society.

Dramatic style, combined with good speaking skills, gave some women an edge on the stage, as evidenced from reports of earlier Soviet friendship meetings. For instance, in 1945 the RCMP reported that speeches given by Margaret Gould and Soviet Military Attaché Nikolai Zabotin at an NCCSF event in Toronto were humdrum but called the guest speaker, Nila Magidoff, the "*pièce de résistance*."[28] The RCMP officer reported that Magidoff "is described in publicity as a Soviet writer and stylist, whatever that is. In any event, she would make a dramatic actress. She has been perfectly schooled probably both in the Soviet Union and America. In a 20-minute speech, using only meager notes, she did not once make a mistake in Soviet party line or in conventional Soviet emotional appeal." He wrote further that her performance "was too perfect, but to an unsophisticated audience, very effective," and he concluded that, "whatever her ability, which may be considerable, the dramatic perfection of her performance indicated undoubted training as a propagandist."[29] The "unsophisticated audience" of about 1,550 was largely Slavic, the officer reported. This fact, he suggested, made her performance so "effective" and might explain why a second RCMP report noted that it was "not outstanding in any way."[30] The *Toronto Star* noted that Magidoff had returned to speak in Toronto because of "popular request," and she would continue to tour the country.[31]

Nielsen, too, was known as a colourful speaker who could make a strong impression on her audience. With experience speaking in small auditoriums to local constituents, in the House of Commons, and later on behalf of the party for peace, civil liberties, and women's equality, she knew how to tweak her message to suit her audience. In 1950 in Winnipeg, Nielsen drew a crowd of more than 1,000 to hear her speak about her impressions of the USSR and the newly reconstituted CSFS.[32] In Drumheller, Alberta, she spoke about how the USSR "had made great progress in conquering poverty, insufficiency and want." She gendered this argument to appeal to women in the audience, explaining that "styles in women's clothes . . . did not change as often in Russia as in Canada, United States or England. Materials and cuts, however, were serviceable and equal to other markets."[33] Nielsen had been to the USSR to attend the Soviet-backed Women's International Democratic Federation conference in Moscow. In Lethbridge, she told her audience that "over 3000 women delegates representing 62 countries attended the Congress in Russia and that the Russian delegates asked that visitors from all [over] the world come to Russia providing they were of the working class. Bank Managers and such were not welcome there."[34] After speaking "very glowingly" of conditions in the USSR, Nielsen showed pictures of what she had seen and informed her audience that the CSFS was planning to send "as many delegates as possible," to be chosen from the Canadian working class, to the USSR.[35] Her tasks on this tour were to promote the newly founded CSFS and to gain subscribers for *News-Facts about the USSR*. At each event, she went out of her way to credit Carter for bringing the "truth" to Canadians, with the help of friendly diplomats in the Soviet Embassy in Ottawa.

Nielsen was also ready to make excuses for the USSR if negative comments arose from the audience. In Manitoba, challenged by an elderly gentleman to explain the Soviet policy on Jews, she dodged the question: "I don't profess to know everything about Russian policy, some questions will have to be sent to Dyson Carter."[36] But she supplemented this response by saying that clearly the USSR couldn't let just anyone leave because then these individuals "might give an undesirable misconception of the USSR which would be exploited by the Americans or British, or even engage in the disgracefull [*sic*] business of spying."[37] For the same reason, she said, "Russia doesn't welcome certain Canadian or American visitors."[38] The "seeing is believing" approach was typical of CSFS events and meant to build enthusiasm in the audience, but the CSFS only wanted individuals who would declare the positive version of the truth about the Soviets.

Her flair for public speaking could backfire, however, and Nielsen was at times dismissed by male party comrades as a populist. Despite efforts to improve her knowledge of Marxist theory, the LPP continued to limit the tasks that Nielsen was given to publicity and behind-the-scenes organization (rather than real leadership).[39] It is hard to tell whether her lack of theoretical knowledge was the only reason that she was not chosen to lead any party-supported group. Probably, this was the official reason, but the party's preference for male leaders, and her own choices and responsibilities, were also influential. This situation reflected the broad gender patterns elsewhere in Canadian society.

In her role as CSFS executive secretary, Nielsen encouraged and even prodded female members to publicly articulate their experiences in the USSR. In 1952, for example, she wrote to Carole Laurie in Vancouver, who had recently returned from a CSFS-sponsored trip to the Soviet Union, asking her to write down six typical questions that she was being asked at various meetings about life in the USSR, especially from a woman's perspective. If Laurie could not remember the questions, Nielsen advised her, she should make them up, along with plausible answers, and send them "RIGHT AWAY" to the Toronto office.[40] Questions and answers gathered from recent delegates would be made into a pamphlet published by *News-Facts about the USSR*, she explained.

A common pattern for CSFS events, especially under the leadership of Carter, was for women to speak about the everyday concerns of Soviet people, particularly those seen to affect women and children. This says as much about the Canadian context in which the CSFS events took place as it does about their observations of the USSR. Likely, curiosity about everyday socialism was high in Canada, where reports on the lives of individuals were difficult to obtain. In covering the "overflow meeting" in Vancouver where 300 people heard Nielsen speak, the *Canadian Tribune* wrote that "questions on free health, educational services and general welfare in the U.S.S.R. come thick and fast, placed by teachers, normal school students and professional people."[41] From Moscow, a CSFS-sponsored delegation in 1951 sent a statement home to Canada via VOKS, rhapsodizing about what they had seen. While the men on the trip spoke about Soviet music and art, both Fagel Gartner and Jeannette Pratte were quoted on the position of Soviet women: "Jeannette Pratte, a housewife, and the well-known Canadian pianist Fagel Gartner, spoke of the impressions produced on them by the position of the woman and children in the Soviet Union. The nurseries, kindergartens, schools and Young Pioneer Houses, they said[,] are real palaces where the Soviet children receive a versatile education, culture and physical training. . . . The difference between the education of the children in the Soviet Union and in Canada . . . is as great as the difference between day and night, said Jeannette Pratte."[42] The *Soviet Monitor* published Gartner's comments that

> in Ukraine we had unforgettable meetings with Soviet women employed in different branches of industry, agriculture and culture. Everywhere we witnessed happy motherhood. Soviet children are surrounded with the solicitude of the State. Marvellous medical institutions have been set up for Soviet women who, on an equal footing with men, have every opportunity to master knowledge and various specialities and to be useful members of society. The women collective farmers whom we met at the Komintern Collective Farm in the Korsun-Shevchenkovski District . . . seem to be the happiest women in the world. They are proud of their work and do it with joy and energy, being confident that their labour serves the cause of peace.[43]

There is no evidence to suggest that Canadian visitors were aware that great care was taken by Soviet authorities to show only the best. At any rate, it is clear that visitors missed, avoided, or were isolated from the realities. Women in the Soviet Union would not have recognized these experiences as their own. Rather, recent research has shown that Soviet women's experiences of motherhood were anything but ideal, and certainly the "solicitude of the State" in their regard has been questioned.[44]

Still, the CSFS women seemed to see their homegrown ideals in practice in the distant USSR: that is, they saw what they wanted to see. The 1952 CSFS trade delegation told the Soviet press that they were impressed to see that "women receive without exception good pay equal to that of men and suffer no discrimination. The social welfare and care for the health of the workers and their families are unique."[45] On paper, this might have been true, but in practice skilled workers, managers, CPSU leaders, and military scientists were better paid and usually men. On reaching Odessa, CSFS National Secretary Jim Leech and his wife, Constance, "recorded statements giving their impressions of industrial relations, welfare and construction work and of the benefits enjoyed by Soviet women. Both stressed that the Soviet people were building for peace, not war."[46] The equality of women and the high standard of children's education were directly related, in this message, to the peaceful nature of Soviet society. They contrasted this message of Soviet peace with what they saw as the hawkish rhetoric in the North American press, the influence of which, they said, was apparent even in the toys given to children. On their return, Pearl Wedro was among those who gave public speeches, concluding with "an appeal for support of the Canadian-Soviet Friendship Council."[47] Mary Kardash, secretary of the local CSFS, collected $78.80 from the audience "to help defray expenses of the Trade Union delegates."[48]

The reports given by these Canadians in the USSR were meant for a domestic Soviet audience, showing them that foreigners supported their system. Usually, the reports also made it back to Canada, appearing in the progressive press. Rosalind McCutcheon, a CSFS delegate to the USSR in 1953, was interviewed about her impressions on Radio Moscow, and she spoke particularly about the place of women and children in Soviet society. In Uzbekistan, McCutcheon said, she had been especially impressed that the minister of culture and an honoured artist who greeted her were "two wonderful women."[49] Rather than being veiled, these Muslim women were "two modern cultured women who were the equals of men." She continued, saying that "two phenomena particularly surprised me—the new Uzbek woman and the maternal care of the Soviet state for the children. I saw these remarkable women and children, warmed by nation-wide kindness, on the streets of Tashkent and Samarkand, in factories and in theatres, in an excellent kindergarten in Samarkand and the Pioneers' Palace here, in Tashkent. Concern for the children is a most striking example of how your society is devoting all efforts to the welfare of the people."[50] McCutcheon was particularly pleased to see women in the higher echelons of Uzbek society: "To meet these women who today are deputies, scientists, honoured artists, will always be for me one of the highlights of my visit to the Soviet Union." She thought that speaking about how women and children in the USSR were cared for by the state would encourage Canadian women in particular to become friends of the Soviet Union.[51] In fact, the Soviet example was related specifically to Canadian homes and the children in them, the delegation told a press conference that it gave at the VOKS offices in Moscow: "More and more Canadians are coming to realize that the struggle for friendship with our great northern neighbour is at the same time a struggle for the peace of our own homes, for our children and our country's growth and independence."[52]

Another delegate on the same CSFS tour, Margaret Spaulding, commented that geriatric care in the Soviet Union was much more advanced than that in Canada: "After three weeks in the USSR, I feel like dropping the term 'old age' from my vocabulary altogether. It does not seem to have any of the usual meaning here at all. People in the USSR live a long time, but it is a ripe old age, full of energy, of usefulness and of happiness." This, she argued, was because of the "provision of pensions, the absence of compulsory retirement and the fact that they 'are an important part of every community.'"[53]

After returning to Canada, CSFS women continued spreading the message about how fortunate Soviet women were. Whether in public speeches or in written reports sold to CSFS members and subscribers, they invariably put a positive spin on news of the condition of Soviet women. In 1950, Nielsen told an audience in The Pas, Manitoba, that children in their town "spent their time window shopping, windows that are full of toy guns," while Soviet children read and engaged in cultural activities.[54] One statement from the trade union delegation included the point that "even [Soviet] children's toys reflect the desire to teach youth the art of peaceful construction." The direct relationship between the provisions of the state for women and children was noted: "When visiting industrial enterprises the equitable position of women produced a deep impression on us. We met many women working as directors of huge industrial enterprises, engineers and doctors. They all, without exception, receive equal pay with men for their work and have equal opportunities for promotion to more responsible work. . . . Everywhere there are crèches and kindergartens. A woman worker can leave her children there while she is at work. Children are surrounded with attention and affection. An insignificant fee is taken for the upkeep of the child in such children's institutions."[55]

The trade union story was sold by the CSFS as "we were there!" The delegates on the 1953 trip to the USSR wrote about their impressions as well, and the CSFS published these essays in a pamphlet entitled *Canadians Visit Their Northern Neighbours: Picture-Report of a Trip to the Soviet Union*. This report was sold to CSFS members and other progressives for twenty-five cents. McCutcheon's essay was called "Children Come First," and her biography listed her as being a married woman from Montreal, "bookkeeper and office worker. Mother of one child. Secretary, Montreal branch, C.S.F.S.: member of National Council, Chairman of the delegation."[56] McCutcheon dealt with the schooling of Soviet children, which she praised, but she also claimed that

Figure 18. In 1953, the CSFS published this brochure titled "Canadians Visit Our Northern Neighbours." The delegates pictured here are (L–R) Eleanor Ashworth, Major R.T. Lafond, Florence Dorland, Rosalind McCutcheon, Margaret Spaulding, Paul Pauk, and Leo Clavir.

women who chose to stay home with their children, or have them at home with a relative, were not stigmatized.[57] Florence Dorland's essay, entitled "Out of the Darkness," described how Uzbek women were liberated since the Soviets had taken power. Dorland, described as a worker in the trades and the secretary of the Vancouver CSFS branch, wrote her essay as a letter home to her son, describing the wonderful sights of the Uzbek SR.

Most of the pictures accompanying her text show Uzbek women, and the captions under the photos depict a "before and after effect" of the Bolshevik Revolution. For instance, the captions mention that one girl's "mother was a chattel slave" in the pre-Soviet days, that a group of women now serving in the Uzbek Supreme Soviet were once slaves, and that another woman, following dictates of thirty years earlier, "could eat only the leftovers on her husband's plate."[58] Dorland was impressed by the children: "Little girl whose mother was a slave—little Uzbek girl whom life itself has brought out from behind the veil of darkness."[59] In the same publication, Margaret Spaulding wrote about the health care available to all Soviet citizens, Eleanor Ashworth about the housing of Central Asian farmers, and Paul Pauk about the condition of workers, including women. Other contributors addressed the rights of minority groups in the USSR, arts, and university education. Dorland concluded the pamphlet with a short piece about consumer goods available to Soviet shoppers. She said that Soviet consumers were presented with only one problem: how to get the products that they want before someone else buys them. Nevertheless, she claimed, the shelves were quickly restocked.[60]

An all-expense-paid trip to the USSR usually came with the condition that delegates would travel widely on speaking tours after their return to Canada. These were well-planned events. Ida Kovalevich (Edith Kowalewich), described in *Ukrainske slovo* as a "young activist among the Slav progressive youth," spoke about her trip to the USSR and China at a CSFS-sponsored event at the Winnipeg Playhouse Theatre on 7 November 1954.[61] She said that, as a delegate to the World Federation of Youth, she found that the Chinese and "Soviet people recognize the Canadian delegation as messengers of peace."[62] After their trip to the USSR in 1954, Anna Sochasky and Kay Rankin described their impressions in words that would appeal to women. They spoke particularly about the quantity and quality of bread available to Soviet families at a low price.[63] In the immediate postwar years, rations and prices concerned many Canadian women, and to suggest that the USSR was producing such basic foods at reasonable prices, despite the hardships of its people during the war, was to give the impression that the socialist system was superior to the capitalist system in Canada.

Sochasky and Rankin continued speaking tours in British Columbia through 1955 and 1956. Sochasky frequently spoke in Ukrainian, and Rankin often showed Soviet films. The RCMP took Rankin's appearances seriously enough to advise local detachments in April 1956 that "continued reports received indicate that Kay RANKIN of Vancouver is again touring British Columbia and showing Soviet films. . . . Should the appearance of this woman become known to your Special Branch, it is suggested that some coverage be given the meetings which she will be holding."[64] In May 1956, the inspector of the Victoria RCMP Special Branch noted that "more urgent duties" had kept his officers from covering Rankin's entire Vancouver Island tour but mentioned that her stops had also included Cumberland, Port Alberni, Nanaimo, Duncan, Lake Cowichan, and Sidney.[65] The RCMP interest in Rankin was not new. It was reported twenty years earlier that she toured southern Alberta publicizing the CPC policy on unemployment insurance and ran as the CPC candidate for the Calgary School Board.[66]

On her return from the USSR, a report to be given by Katherine (Kay) Hladiy, employed in the Toronto needle trade industry, was advertised directly to needle trade workers in Port Douglas. The ad noted that she had "made it a point to visit a number of Needle Trades Shops—Cloaks, Garment, Fur, Shoe, etc.," and the questions that she would deal with in her presentation were listed.[67] It was signed by the Needle Trades Committee of the CSFS. It was also noted that, "while the speaker will devote considerable time to the above subjects, Mrs. Hladiy will also refer to other features of Soviet life. This is your opportunity to hear the facts from first hand information." Those who received the notice were asked to "pass this invitation along to your shop-mates."[68] Yet the RCMP reported that "her main topic of discussion was the welfare of a mother and child." To wit, "in the USSR the women are on the same level as the men are and they receive the same pay. Every woman that become[s] pregnant receives a special security from the Soviet Government. During a certain time of her pregnancy she receives one half of her wages until she is able to work again and her place in the factory is secure. After the birth of her baby she can place the child in a nursery provided by the factory and return to her same employment."[69]

Hladiy's enthusiasm probably stemmed from her sincere desire to see such conditions in Canada. But whereas de jure these conditions might have existed in the USSR, de facto the lived experiences of women, particularly mothers, was far from this idealized depiction. The reports that CSFS members gave supported the message carried in Carter's publications that because of the socialist state Soviet women could handle the "double burden" of work outside the home and childrearing. From these speeches, there appeared to be no contradiction in Soviet women's increasing autonomy, and even pre-eminence, in the workforce and their continuing traditional roles in the family. Production line factories and common kitchens helped to ease the burden for women, it was claimed. Yet more recent research has shown that, despite Soviet claims to the contrary, the position of women in the USSR was nowhere near egalitarian. After leaving work, they often had to stand in long lineups to purchase essentials for the family, goods were not always readily available, housing was cramped and several generations lived in small apartments, the divorce rate and rate of single motherhood were high, access to birth control and abortion was difficult, pay was not equal, and neither was political representation. In fact, officially, "feminism" had been co-opted by the state, and the problem solved, while women continued to experience gender and sexual discrimination in their everyday lives. As journalist and social commentator Slavenka Drakulic has written, the communist system in Eastern Europe and the Soviet Union was utterly unable to satisfy the fundamental needs and wishes of women, who represented more than half of the population.[70] Once Drakulic dared to stand before a conference of American leftists and made this declaration more dramatic by insisting that basic feminine hygiene products had never been available in Eastern Europe, proving that the system, with its exaggerated claims to superiority, was in fact a failure. Those at the conference did not believe her and treated her as a "right-wing freak," not because they lacked knowledge of the communist system, but because they had no "experience of living under such conditions."[71]

The lives of Soviet and Eastern European women were not what leftists in North America believed—or wanted—them to be. Perhaps the declarations of Canadians can be better understood in relation to their idealistic hopes for their own lives. In Winnipeg in October 1952, Kay Hladiy spoke to an audience of 200 in the Hebrew Sick Benefit Hall on women and medical care in the USSR. She described the facilities available to Soviet workers in the factory, and she said that "the wages for men and women are equal and the state provides free nursery for working women." She liked the youth camp that delegates visited near Leningrad, where boys were active, disciplined, well fed, and well supervised. She appreciated the fact that, if a working man is killed on the job, "his beneficiary receives his full wages monthly. Pregnant women are not discharged, but 2 months before and after the birth they receive holidays with pay and are cared for by the state. Their pay is half their monthly salary. 2 months after the birth of the child they return to work and the child is cared for in a state nursery while the mother works."[72] Concluding the meeting, Mary Kardash said that more delegations to the USSR were necessary if Canadians were to know the truth about Soviet conditions, including the Soviet approach to the woman question, and she urged the audience to read Soviet publications.

The political message was ever-present at these events, but probably the desire to socialize with friends and the chance to converse in native languages were also important to the audience. For instance, one November evening in 1955 several elderly Armenian Canadian women attended a CSFS showing of the film *Soviet Armenia* at the Armenian Hall in Brantford. These women had come to Canada forty years or more earlier. In addition to the film, Kate Bader, a recent CSFS delegate, spoke about her impressions of the USSR.[73]

Not every CSFS woman could afford time away from her family or job to travel to the USSR on a delegation or was given to public speaking. Some of the tasks that women performed in their local groups were more behind the scenes. Of the four friendship society secretaries listed for the western provinces in 1952, three were women: Eleanor Ashworth, Edmonton; Wilma Williams, Saskatoon; and Mary Kardash, Winnipeg.[74] By 1953, Pearl Wedro, a delegate on the trade union tour who had subsequently spoken in public halls on behalf of the CSFS, had moved to Toronto to serve as the helm of the CSFS branch there. The Toronto branch and the main CSFS office worked hand in hand in organizing events in the provincial capital, as shown by a 1953 circular signed by both Nielsen and Wedro inviting area members and subscribers to a film screening and a presentation by Carter.[75]

Carter and Nielsen called on readers of *News-Facts about the USSR* in towns where there was no CSFS branch to get together and, with help from the central office, plan local events. In 1952, Carter noted that there were readers in Windsor, Port Arthur, Fort William, St. Catharines, Timmins, Trail, Kimberley, Kamloops, Crowsnest, Medicine Hat, Brandon, Swift Current, The Pas, Sydney, Glace Bay, and St. John's but no CSFS branches there. Nielsen asked readers in these places to consider hosting small events. Earlier she had sent out a circular letter asking them directly "can you invite a number of friends and neighbors to someone's home and have a 'Friendship' evening together? We will send you some Soviet pictures, literature, or even a Movie."[76] Organizing a home meeting was an activity that some women might have found easier than arranging big meetings in halls. For instance, Louise Harvey and Margaret Russell hosted an informal, question-and-answer discussion of Soviet life in their living room. They invited two recent delegates to the USSR to their home to tell guests "how the people live there, what kind of homes, jobs and recreation they have."[77] Casual evenings in the homes of CSFS members were part of the appeal of joining these groups and discussing Canadian-Soviet friendship.

The CSFS also encouraged active members to attend conferences at the head office in Toronto and to organize events afterward to report on developments. Eleanor Ashworth travelled from Edmonton to the convention in Toronto and then spoke at a meeting in the Ukrainian Labor Temple Hall in Newcastle, Alberta, in March 1952. According to an RCMP officer, she said that in the USSR "women . . . had equal rights with the men and were able to compete with them in every phase of industry and science." She compared the number of female pilots in the USSR to the number in Canada, where "not a single woman pilot [is] employed," and after reading extracts from the Constitution of the United Nations she apparently accused Canadian newspapers of ignoring Soviet attempts to broker world peace.[78]

There were other tasks that women stepped forward to do, even if they were not actually the leaders of local CSFS branches. For the Winnipeg

CSFS, Mary Kardash handled correspondence and logistics for speakers at various meetings, and she did the introductions, but Chester King was in fact the chairman.[79] In 1950, Kardash spoke about the good living conditions for workers in the Soviet Ukraine and mentioned that farmers had electricity in their homes, whereas some Canadian farmers did not yet.[80] Canadians who had been convinced to return to the homeland would have disagreed with her about superior Soviet living conditions. Like Ashworth, Kardash was a delegate to the CSFS convention in Toronto in late January 1952.[81] Earlier that month she appeared on stage in Winnipeg before an audience of about 350[82] to speak about the position of women in the USSR. She shared the stage with Alderman Jacob Penner, who argued that the "level of the Soviet democracy is much higher than in Canada," and with Nikolai Hrynchyshin, who worked for the Canadian Ukrainian newspaper *Ukrainske slovo* and spoke on the freedom of the press in the Soviet Union.[83] If Hrynchyshin knew about the role of the Soviet authorities in censoring and controlling the Soviet press, he did not mention it. In March 1952, Kardash introduced a Soviet film at a Winnipeg CSFS meeting and explained the purpose of the CSFS, defined in the words of an RCMP investigator as "to promote friendship with the USSR and to counteract alleged anti-Russian 'propaganda' in the Canadian press." She also solicited new members and readers.[84]

Much of the financial side of CSFS work was handled by women. At the CSFS-sponsored performance of the new Shostakovich oratorio in Toronto by the Jewish Folk Choir in 1951, Marge Ferguson sold books and VOKS literature in the Massey Hall lobby. The RCMP reported that she and other women did this "despite the protests of Massey Hall officials" and identified them as "LPP women members."[85] Ferguson's husband, Dewar, was on the CSFS executive at the time.[86] Hazel Currie, an activist in Port Arthur, handled the letter writing and fundraising needed to send Bruce Magnuson to the USSR with the CSFS trade delegation in 1952. Her letter, addressed to "all Labor Unions, Workers, Farmers and Citizens of Northwestern Ontario," asked for contributions to support not only his travel but also his family while he was away.[87]

Indeed, from 1949 on, the women closest to CSFS leaders played crucial supporting roles, particularly in handling the business end of the work. Charlotte Carter was Dyson Carter's business manager and often compensated for his absences or injuries. Later, after the Carters moved to Gravenhurst, the Northern Book House, through which they sold the books that they received from VOKS, was under her name. Charlotte co-authored many books with Dyson, and as a nurse and mother her focus in these publications was often on public health standards and conditions for women and children in the USSR. After her death in 1972, Dyson set up the Charlotte Carter Memorial Fund, to which readers of *Northern Neighbors* could contribute.[88] Some years later Irja Paul,[89] who had been friends with the Carters for years, took over some of Charlotte's tasks. She also lived with Dyson. Officially, she was termed "executive secretary" on the editorial page of *Northern Neighbors*, but she said that her work dealt mostly with "looking after Dyson," whose health was deteriorating.[90] Paul and her daughter Irene Kuusela have fond memories of both Dyson and Charlotte and recall with pleasure trips to the USSR when Irja accompanied Dyson. They enjoyed receiving *Northern Neighbors*, and Irja in particular spoke about the significance of being a member of a progressive community and family circle. Being born into a progressive Finnish family in Sudbury meant that she had been familiar with Carter, CSFS-sponsored movie nights, and other such events from childhood.[91] She said that he had investments on the stock exchange, built with royalty payments that allowed him to charge minimal rates for the magazine subscriptions. In his memoirs, Carter also refers to investments on Bay Street and how during the Depression he had learned to play the markets.

When his relationship with Paul ended in 1980, Carter employed Sally Nielsen as his secretary, and they were married in 1981. Sally had known Dyson and his family for years but was not sure that her mother, Dorise, who had passed away, would have been pleased to know that she had married her friend-turned-rival.[92] She recalled with sadness the tragic effects of the Depression in Canada, and she spoke with pride of the efforts of her mother and Dyson to find a better solution through the progressive movement. In the 1980s, Sally ran the office for Dyson, did the banking,[93] and occasionally wrote pieces for *Northern Neighbors*. She recalled that he would periodically receive cash payments brought to Gravenhurst in briefcases when Soviet Embassy personnel visited. On these occasions, Dyson always went into the office and closed the door. The Soviets once asked Sally whether she would like to become more involved in the work that he was doing, but she refused, saying that she had enough to do in keeping house for him, looking after him, and managing the secretarial duties for *Northern Neighbors*. Some of her memories of Dyson might be coloured by difficulties in their marriage. Today she remembers him as an angry, stubborn man who would simply turn off the lights to win an argument, an effective way for him, as a lip reader, to refuse to listen. Dyson and Sally were divorced in 1988 on acrimonious terms because, according to her, he refused to share his unofficial income with her.[94] After she left him, his name remained alone on the editorial page of *Northern Neighbors* until its last issue in December 1989.

For forty years, Carter's publications, *News-Facts about the USSR* and *Northern Neighbors,* carried the message that because of the socialist state Soviet women were able to handle the double burden of work outside the home and childrearing. Today we know that this message was false. Soviet women struggled with their workload, and their efforts to free themselves from this predicament were actually frustrated by the official claim that the issue had long ago been solved.[95] But readers were told that there was no contradiction between Soviet women's increasing autonomy, and even pre-eminence, in the workforce and their continuing traditional roles in the family. The undertone of all articles on youth and school systems in the USSR was that the socialist system allowed children to learn while remaining true to their traditional, gendered identities. Often Carter transmitted this message using photographs and captions. For instance, the message that work did not interfere with nurturing was apparent in the photo of two adult women, one working at the daycare centre, the other dropping her child off there. Both women are smiling and inclined toward the child, who appears to be pleased to spend the day there. The caption reads "Mrs. Baranova, a young nurse, brings her daughter to kindergarten in a section of Stalingrad . . . (Russian Republic)."[96] That this photo is placed in Stalingrad is not entirely coincidental. Soviet publicity, and hence Carter's, often showed how Stalingrad had recovered from its devastating battle with the Nazi Army during the Second World War and how life had returned to "normal." Describing his visit to Stalingrad, Carter wrote that he found "laughter" there: "Along the Volga there is singing and laughing today." This, he argued, was the best memorial to the fallen—"human joy."[97]

In its first issue in December 1956, *Northern Neighbours*[98] had Soviet ballerina Galina Ulanova on the cover, and inside was a picture story of the International Seminar on the Equality of Rights of Women, held in Moscow. Photographs showed women from around the world smiling at one another while touring Soviet industries and speaking at a Kremlin reception.[99] Twelve years later an article entitled "Where Else?" claimed that "all advanced countries have women who are outstanding. But in our world of Capitalism, such women are written about and interviewed as if they were inhabitants of a distant planet. In the Soviet Republics, in Socialism, no one is surprised to hear of women in high places."[100] The accompanying photos show the female foreign affairs minister of Kirghizia, a dairymaid who was also a district councillor, chief justice, symphony orchestra conductor, teacher, and head of a state farm.

Interestingly, considering Carter's claim, no reference was made to the lack of women in the CPSU leadership or Politburo, where policy was made.

Mothering and professional skills went hand in hand, wrote Carter. An article on Soviet vaccinations of babies for smallpox shows a photograph of a female doctor administering the shot.[101] The fact that so many women in the USSR were doctors, whereas in Canada most women in the medical profession were nurses, was cited frequently to show the advanced nature of women's rights in the Soviet Union. On the cover of the June 1973 issue, a photo shows a mother coming home from a business trip and kissing her children. Readers are referred to the article "Soviet Women Are Overtaking Their Men," which details why women in the USSR were not seeking liberation: they already had it, Carter claimed.[102] Photos of prominent women in Ukraine are on the facing page, in an issue appearing just after Mother's Day in Canada.[103] But, in fact, science and medicine neglected Soviet women. Carter made no mention of the high rates of maternal death in childbirth and infant mortality in the USSR. Nor did the subject of high divorce rates or abortion as the main Soviet method of birth control warrant any mention.[104]

Women's "liberation" did not come at a cost to femininity, according to Carter. In a 1974 article entitled "Why They Want NO UNISEX in Socialism," he claimed that the Western women's liberation movement had "done much fine work" but also "much damage by taking the unscientific position that equality means identity."[105] Instead, Carter pointed out, the Soviets thought that differentiating between the sexes was not only healthy but also important for building the future: "Sex difference created human beings and all our magnificent cultural heritage . . . and will lead us into our great awaiting future."[106] In 1978, he wrote that "There Are No Homely Women" in the USSR.[107] Advancing the views of a Moscow hairstylist on why it was essential that a woman "always look nice," Carter argued that "in Socialism all girls and women are encouraged to make themselves attractive. They don't buy the current notion [in the West] that this is 'sexism.'"[108] Instead, readers of his publications were sold the theory that the position of Soviet women was superior to that of Western women.

Women might not have served at the head of the CSFS, but they did take on important roles in its administration and publicity and were political activists. They led branch groups, monitored finances and correspondence, sold tickets, and were the target audience for many CSFS public speaking events and published articles. Motivated by the message that conditions for women were better in the USSR under socialism than in Western countries under capitalism, women on the Canadian left played important organizational roles for the CSFS. They were not fooled into activism but clearly chose to participate, albeit usually in supporting roles. In local branches from Vancouver to Montreal, women were active not only in "traditional" roles such as preparing food for buffet dinners but also in soliciting funds, writing articles, and speaking at meetings. Many probably hoped to redefine gender roles at a time when Canadian society seemed to put more value on women's domestic identities.

But these women did believe Soviet claims and tried to convince others to do so. Although their activism did help some progressive Canadian women to leverage a sense of political engagement and agency, this engagement was part of a larger *mise-en-scène*. All the rhetoric about women's position in society aside, their activism was not different from that of their male counterparts. CSFS women operated under a series of false perceptions of women in the USSR and tried to persuade others that their version was the truth. Soviet women did not experience anything like the CPSU and Soviet leadership claimed they did. In defending claims that the woman question had been solved by the Soviets, CSFS delegates suspended their critical faculties and believed what they heard in the USSR. In transmitting this erroneous message, the CSFS contributed to the smokescreen that hid great divisions and inequalities in the USSR. And in attempting to persuade their fellow Canadians to believe these declarations as the truth, CSFS activists cast themselves as apologists for the Soviet Union.

CHAPTER 7

Culture as Political Persuasion: Performing Soviet Friendship

"There is no other country where art remains on such a high level as in the USSR," proclaimed Dyson Carter in 1951.[1] During the Cold War, culture and ideological competition were linked.[2] For Carter and executives of the CSFS, culture provided the main stage on which Canadian-Soviet friendship could be enacted, and it was a political performance. The exchange of information on art; displays and sales of representative cultural artifacts, paintings, and books; and CSFS-sponsored tours of the USSR and Canada by artists promoted cross-cultural friendship with overt political implications. Within the CSFS and other progressive groups, admiration of Soviet culture was a symbol of a subculture[3] in which members shared ideological, political, and social values and dreamed of radically changing Canadian society. Art was perceived as an international language that tied Canadians of different ethnic backgrounds together and connected them to Soviet sympathizers in other countries. In singing, reading, and attending film screenings and lectures, CSFS members thought and lived "otherwise,"[4] defining the world in opposition to the mainstream. For the CSFS, Soviet culture also represented an avenue to reach out to the wider Canadian public, because many Canadians were genuinely interested in Soviet cultural and artistic figures, given the storied reputation of Russian literature, art, and music. High-profile Soviet artists, writers, composers, and performers knew that they were playing a political role, and they were aware that the Soviet state, particularly under Josef Stalin, "had a superlative appreciation of the propaganda potential of art."[5] VOKS actively encouraged cultural exchange in Canada via Carter, the CSFS, *News-Facts about the USSR*, and later *Northern Neighbors*.

The CSFS was supported by other progressive organizations in promoting Soviet culture to the wider Canadian public. In 1952, the *Canadian Tribune* proclaimed that "sports and culture are vital avenues for friendship among nations," and it congratulated the CSFS "for its initiative in developing friendship with our neighbors to the north."[6] The *Ukrainian Canadian* enthused over a "number of exciting cultural events [sponsored by the CSFS] to celebrate the increasing desire for friendship between the Canadian and Soviet peoples."[7] Soviet culture was the USSR's best tool for propaganda and one of the hardest for Canadian authorities to counter. Carter was aware of this and promoted Soviet culture and cultural actors with all his energy and publishing ability. His message unfailingly emphasized that the social and political system that produced these artistic works should be admired. Carter never remarked on the stifling restrictions put on artistic development by the Soviet state or on the periodic official criticisms of high-profile Soviet artists for failing to live up to these dictates.

In his authoritative book on cultural exchange and propaganda during the Cold War, David Caute writes that, in addition to being a "traditional political-military confrontation," this period was characterized by "an ideological and cultural contest on a global scale and without historical precedent."[8] The prize, according to Caute, was the ability to declare one's own side the legitimate inheritor of Enlightenment ideals, so the conflictual rhetoric drew on definitions of culture, modernity, progress, "facts," and reason.[9] In Canada, the identification of culture as one of the Soviet Union's greatest exports, which had considerable value as propaganda, was also recognized by the RCMP and Department of External Affairs.

In the USSR, the term "propaganda" coincided almost exactly with the Soviet concept of social and political education, and it was exploited to the maximum. Carter sent VOKS material to Canadians prominent in cultural associations and promoted lesser-known Canadian artists whose messages fit nicely with Soviet philosophy.[10] Painter Frederick Taylor, writers such as Wilson Macdonald and Ted Allan, and Fagel and Emil Gartner,[11] musicians well known in Jewish progressive groups, were promoted by Carter at CSFS events. He tried to encourage VOKS to view artists who were seen as mainstream, such as Frederick Philip Grove, favourably. The CSFS had the same role models as many other progressive organizations. Among the models was Paul Robeson, the Afro-American peace activist and singer, featured frequently in Carter's magazine as in other Soviet promotional material and progressive publications.[12]

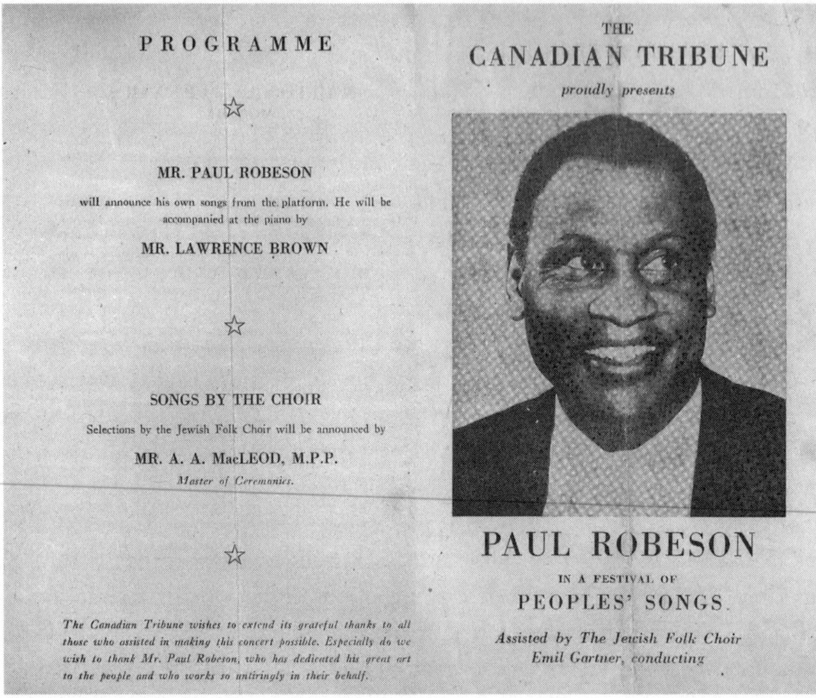

PROGRAMME

☆

MR. PAUL ROBESON

will announce his own songs from the platform. He will be accompanied at the piano by

MR. LAWRENCE BROWN

☆

SONGS BY THE CHOIR

Selections by the Jewish Folk Choir will be announced by

MR. A. A. MacLEOD, M.P.P.

— *Master of Ceremonies.*

☆

The Canadian Tribune wishes to extend its grateful thanks to all those who assisted in making this concert possible. Especially do we wish to thank Mr. Paul Robeson, who has dedicated his great art to the people and who works so untiringly in their behalf.

THE

CANADIAN TRIBUNE

proudly presents

PAUL ROBESON

IN A FESTIVAL OF

PEOPLES' SONGS.

Assisted by The Jewish Folk Choir

Emil Gartner, conducting

Figure 19. Paul Robeson's concerts had long been sponsored by left-wing publications like the Canadian Tribune *and* National Affairs Monthly, *and were featured in Dyson Carter's* Northern Neighbors *magazine. This concert program is from 1946.*

Culture had been an important feature of the older National Council for Canadian-Soviet Friendship, and soon after it was founded in 1943 the Arts Committee included poet E.J. Pratt, painter A.Y. Jackson, writer (and LPP member) Ted Allan, and NFB founder John Grierson. But the atmosphere changed, and by the 1950s most of these artists no longer chose to be actively involved. Nevertheless, the use of culture as a vehicle for Soviet friendship was stepped up while high-level negotiations over cultural contacts were under way. Carter and the CSFS called for more cultural exchanges with the USSR, echoing the official Soviet emphasis on increasing cultural exchanges between the USSR and the West. In the late 1950s, VOKS pursued a policy of encouraging Canadian impresarios to bring performers to Moscow. Jack Bowdrie, Glenn Gould, and Lois Marshall took VOKS up on the invitation and allowed their impresario, Walter Homburger, to make arrangements for Soviet tours in 1957 and 1958. The fact that the VOKS representative in the Soviet Embassy in Ottawa negotiated these contracts as a "cultural attaché" made for an overlap between cultural promotion and persuasion. In the late 1950s, there was a large increase in general exchanges between the USSR, under Nikita Khrushchev's leadership, and Canada, studying agriculture, forestry, and other trade-related domains. The Department of External Affairs (DEA) also advocated increased cultural exchange at this time, suggesting that it was the best way to counteract overly positive views of the USSR.[13] The DEA considered that the more often Soviets visited the West, and the more frequently Westerners saw the USSR for themselves, the harder it would be to convince foreigners that the Soviet Union was in fact a socialist ideal. The Soviets thought just the opposite. In the cultural field, the international stakes were high.

When the *VOKS Bulletin* was replaced with *Culture and Life* in 1957, Carter was asked to promote it in Canada and to send a list of people who should receive free issues. On the list that the VOKS representative in Ottawa sent to Moscow were Celia Franca, director of the National Ballet School of Canada; M.P. Beique, head of the Montreal Symphony Orchestra; Walter Susskind, conductor of the Toronto Symphony Orchestra; plus directors of the Stratford Shakespearean Festival, directors of theatres in Montreal and Ottawa, impresarios, journalists, and editors of large newspapers and scholarly journals.[14] Editors of left-wing publications also received free copies. It is unclear whether all of these individuals asked to be put on the VOKS mailing list. Canadian poet Joe Wallace, who received VOKS literature, was known to admire the USSR. Since Homburger was dealing with the USSR on cultural matters, he was probably pleased to have the journal. In any case, there is no record in the VOKS documents of anyone complaining about receiving it. Of course, that does not suggest that its line was fully accepted by readers.

CSFS events were made more colourful by the addition of cultural performances, but they were always understood by performers and audiences alike to be acts of political significance. Concerts often set the stage and were possibly the main attraction for CSFS-organized speeches and discussions. The choir of the Federation of Russian Canadians and the Jewish Folk Choir led by Emil Gartner were frequently featured at large CSFS gatherings. Often mini-concerts were followed by lectures or discussions of life and politics in the USSR. For example, in November 1954, between 700 and 900 people attended a concert organized in honour of Friendship Month by the CSFS at the Playhouse Theatre in Winnipeg.[15] The evening opened with renditions of the Canadian and Soviet national anthems.[16] Choirs from local AUUC and FRC branches, as well as the United Jewish People's Order choir and the Winnipeg Folk Singers, performed folk songs in several languages, as well as songs about peace. The head of the Winnipeg CSFS branch, Fred Chester King, was the master of ceremonies. He insisted that the success of the recent Soviet artists' delegation showed that friendship with the USSR was a popular idea in Canada. Ida Kovalevich (Edith Kowalewich) from Winnipeg spoke about her recent trip to the USSR and China. Two films shown at the event depicted a Canadian delegation visiting the USSR and the celebration of Friendship Month in Moscow.[17]

The *Vochenblatt* (Canadian Jewish Weekly) advertised this concert and similar events in Vancouver, Brandon, and Port Arthur organized by the CSFS for Friendship Month.[18] To mark the Canadian-Soviet Friendship Month and the forty-first anniversary of the Bolshevik Revolution, the Winnipeg branch of the CSFS organized a concert at the Playhouse Theatre on 9 November 1958. There were 400 people in the audience, including Alexei Tovstogan, the VOKS representative at the Soviet Embassy in Ottawa. He spoke on "Science and Education in the USSR," but because of his poor English and the faulty public address system,[19] few people in the audience understood what he said, so the text of his address was later printed in full in *Ukrainske slovo*.[20] The women's AUUC choir, the women's FRC choir, and the Winnipeg Folk Singers performed.[21] By bringing in popular performers, Carter attracted and retained the attention of individuals interested not only in the music, singing, and socializing but also in the political message that the CSFS wanted to convey. As one UJPO member recalled, the cultural aspect was integral to the progressive movement in Canada: "It was an ideology and a way of life." Another participant said that "the political was cultural and the cultural was political."[22]

Mainstream commentators at the time noted that, though peace was an important part of this rhetoric, it took the backstage to culture. A writer for the *Financial Post*, Ronald Williams, suggested in January 1952 that this was a new tactic used by the Canadian left to attract a broad spectrum of Canadians to view the USSR more favourably. Comparing the big names that the friendship society had during the war with the relatively little information available on the postwar financial backers, Williams suggested that the real message of the CSFS was neither about Soviet achievements nor about increased trade and cultural exchange with the USSR but about a consolidated attempt to counter the negative publicity that the USSR had been getting since 1946. He cited comments made by Beckie Buhay, one of the top CPC leaders. Her comments about "unmasking the foul Big Lie that the USSR menaces Canada and Peace" sound remarkably similar to speeches made by Dorise Nielsen and Dyson Carter on behalf of the CSFS.[23] Williams pointed to the printed *Photo-Facts* cards, which CSFS members were urged to send to members of Parliament and leave in public spaces as "weapons of truth," and to the expensive delegations to the USSR as a left-wing effort to replace the relatively unpopular peace campaign as a unifier in leftist Canada. Williams concluded that

> all this expense and trouble is taken to be an admission that the "peace" offensive isn't going so well in Canada and that something had to be done not only outside the party, but inside as well. It is no secret that the various peace petitions have been received by many party workers with something less than wild enthusiasm. The rough time they had trying to get people to sign petitions didn't help either. The Reds hope the "friendship front" will smooth out some of the roughest spots, and perhaps again lure some big non-Communist names in the Communist bear trap.[24]

There was not much discovery here, for this was precisely what Carter and Nielsen had been saying for some time. Progressive Canadians would not have denied the basic argument that cross-cultural friendship was meant to draw in more supporters from beyond traditional party constituencies. Carter loved the publicity that Williams unwittingly gave the CSFS. In his president's speech at the January 1952 convention, Carter laughed at the anger of Williams over *Photo-Facts*: "Mr. Williams, watch your blood pressure! You're going to blow a valve. By the way, in this 'Financial Post' piece, Mr. Williams manages to come out with one piece of truth. He says: 'The friendship front is going ahead like a house afire.'" Carter agreed that this was the case, and the CSFS and its *Photo-Facts* "have played no small part in changing public opinion in Canada."[25]

Meanwhile, Carter continued to put forward progressive Canadians as delegates to the USSR and to send their manuscripts and biographical information to VOKS for possible publication in Moscow. He believed that "cultural workers," by engaging in these exchanges, could use culture as a political tool to improve society. This idea fit nicely with the official Soviet view that artists were servants of the (Soviet) state who gave their art for state use and were rewarded for doing so. Of course, Carter never acknowledged that in theory Soviet artists were to mirror the interests of a class, not those of the state, probably because he accepted the claim that the Soviet state and the working class were synonymous. In his letters to VOKS, he emphasized the contributions of certain Canadian artists to the labour movement over and above their artistic work. Highest praise was reserved for members of the Labor-Progressive Party. Some of the artists, such as Frederick Taylor and Avrom Yanovsky, wrote directly to VOKS. Apparently blissfully unaware of the tragic circumstances under which many Soviet artists lived, Taylor assured VOKS that the artist in the USSR was in a superior position to that of artists under capitalism because of the social values and responsibilities that the work entailed.[26] Echoes of bitterness about how he believed he had been treated in Canada can be heard between the lines of his letter. In his opinion, his work received little acknowledgement from the mainstream Canadian art community because he refused to leave the LPP.[27] Yanovsky wrote to VOKS in June 1951 to introduce himself as the new chairman of the CSFS Arts Committee, noting that he had "set myself the task of establishing to the best of my ability friendly relations and exchange of information . . . between art workers of our two countries."[28] Art exchanges, he argued, encouraged international truth telling and were thus an important path to peace.

Hoping to shape Canadian public opinion, Carter wrote to VOKS constantly about the need to reach out to all types of Canadians to convince them that information about the USSR in mainstream newspapers in Canada was false. Names of prominent Canadians who supported his cause, and names of people abroad who did so, were dropped as reminders that respected citizens elsewhere had already become convinced of this argument. Most of these individuals were writers, actors, or artists. An article in the *Pacific Tribune* in 1952, for example, proclaimed that delegates' reports were leading more Canadians to be attracted to the CSFS and its cause: "A number of Canadian trade union and cultural delegations visited the Soviet Union in 1951 and brought back impressions which diverge widely from the stock cold war anti-Soviet propaganda . . . the Canadian people are fed daily. Thus an interest in getting at the real truth, instead of the usual propaganda, is also a factor in the growth of friendship sentiment."[29] In November 1951, a *Canadian Tribune* article reported that "the people of Canada are showing such an interest in learning the truth about the Soviet Union that the Canadian Soviet Friendship Society cannot keep pace with the demand."[30] However, Carter was reported to have said "but please don't give Tribune readers the idea we are too busy to look after their orders. Tell them to step up the demand."[31]

In 1952, the British-Soviet Friendship Society sent greetings to its Canadian counterpart via a group of British artists. In addition to Hewlett Johnson, not an artist but the "red" dean of Canterbury, this group included a professor, an author, two actors, and a composer. Their message to Carter read thus: "Best wishes for the success of Canadian-Soviet Friendship Month, which we hope will lead to that mutual understanding and toleration on which the peace of the world depends."[32] Three years later the LPP jumped onto the bandwagon. At the LPP Cultural Conference, it was proclaimed that the CSFS has

> always stressed cultural relations between the peoples of the Soviet Union and Canada and that this was a positive feature of the CSFS' work. The truth is that our Party cannot, in a full fashion, pick up and carry forward the banner of the nation unless we vigorously enter into the cultural struggle and do everything we can to encourage, cultivate and aid the work of the cultural forces of our movement and the entire labor movement. Everything that defends Canada is good! We are for the uniting of all, the encouragement of all who resist the Yankee assault.... Our Party must vigorously get into the cultural battle. We must seize every opportunity to get into public debate on all cultural issues.[33]

In demonstrating the propaganda value of promoting Soviet culture, the CSFS had provided a model for the LPP. This was one of its most significant contributions to the progressive movement in Canada.

Culture and the prestige that went with it were part of the message, but it was also inextricably linked to the cause of peace. The general secretary of the British-Soviet Friendship Society, Pat Sloan, greeted delegates to the convention organized by the CSFS by saying that "the British and Canadian peoples have everything to gain from friendly peaceful co-operation and trade with the Soviet Union and everything to lose from a new international conflict."[34] The opening ceremonies of the convention were held in Bathurst United Church, where Carter spoke and the Soviet film *The Childhood of Maxim Gorki* had "its Canadian premiere."[35] Each reference to cultural exchange was followed by a reference to the peaceful intentions of the USSR: "How can one believe that the Soviet people are preparing for war against us when they are reading millions of copies of the works of Maxim Gorki whose every word cries out against war, against oppression and slavery?"[36] To cite an example, during the 1952 Soviet Friendship Month, Canadians were able to receive Soviet radio programs on short-wave radios every day. The programs included concerts given by Dmitri Shostakovich and Sergei Prokofiev, reviews and readings of Stephen Leacock's work, and lectures on Soviet agriculture and science,[37] as well as recent CSFS publications.[38]

Just as friendship and peace were linked in this narrative, so too was the work of the CSFS linked to the Canadian Peace Congress. In the context of the Korean War, peace resonated. A January 1952 editorial in *Vestnik* stated that a "plan for an energetic campaign" would see the CSFS cooperate with the congress to promote friendship and trade with the USSR. In particular, the contention that "Canada could play a decisive role in regulating the relations between the Soviet Union and the U.S." was hauled out as a motivating factor in promoting Soviet-Canadian friendship.[39] Ahead of the showing, Carter announced that in "'combining as it does great Soviet film art and the story of a world-renowned Russian literary figure . . . the presentation of this film symbolizes one of the functions of our society, namely the building of friendship with the Soviet people through the interchange of cultural media and the presentation to Canadians of the truth about the influences that mould Soviet thinking.'"[40]

In May 1951, a delegation of Canadians went to the USSR to observe this cultural superiority for themselves. The delegation, composed of Winnipeg Alderman Jacob Penner, Emil and Fagel (Fanny) Gartner, artist Frederick Taylor, and Jeannette Brunelle-Pratte, was reported by TASS to have "acquainted themselves with cultural, educational and scientific institutions in Kiev, [and] made a trip to the town of Kanev, where they visited the grave and the museum of the great Ukrainian poet, Taras Shevchenko."[41] Penner was quoted enthusiastically describing the quality of these institutions, especially the university, rebuilt after having been destroyed by the Nazis. Penner had come to Canada in his twenties, and it was natural that he was pleased to visit these places. He admired the equipment at the university, as well as the machines at the Komintern Collective Farm, which they also visited. "We saw with our own eyes that the members of this collective farm lead happy, prosperous and cultured lives," he said.[42] According to the delegation, this culture lent itself to peaceful living, which in turn inspired more creativity. Taylor was quoted by TASS as saying that "the arts serving the people are developed in the Soviet Union as nowhere else in the world. The peaceful labour of the Soviet people, their devotion to their Motherland, their patriotism are sources of inspiration for artists, sculptors and designers."[43] The *Soviet Monitor* reported Taylor saying that "the paintings of Soviet artists . . . are the most vital and life-asserting of all now produced in the world."[44] It was emphasized that "conductor Emil Gartner particularly stressed the high level of musical culture in the land of the Soviets and the perfect organization of musical education in schools for children."[45] The delegation told Soviet journalists that they would take this message home to Canada: "In our speeches at meetings, and over the radio and in the press, we shall tell our fellow countrymen the truth about the Soviet Union and shall assist in consolidating Canadian-Soviet friendship."[46] The *Soviet Monitor* quoted Penner as saying that "on our return home we shall spare no effort to prevent our country from being involved in an aggressive war against the USSR."[47] The Canadian artists' impressions were encapsulated here for Soviet domestic consumption more than for foreign progressive audiences.

But the main purpose of the trip, at least according to Taylor, was to witness the May Day celebrations as official guests atop the reviewing stand in Red Square. Presenting its foreign supporters at the event had special significance that year since the USSR now belonged to the atomic club. For Taylor, the emotional impact of being in the centre of Moscow, not far from the Soviet leadership, viewing the military hardware and rapturous crowds on parade was intense. His biographer wrote that, "despite the downpour, Fred later said that he could feel the power emanating from the Soviet premier [Stalin], 150 feet distant."[48] In his reminiscences, Taylor enthused over the "philosophy" of culture articulated by Soviet ideological chief Andrei Zhdanov, the clean cities, the efficient public transportation, and the energetic Soviet people.[49] He was also impressed by the respect that the Canadian delegation received from other international delegates because they were from the same country as Norman Bethune, and apparently he spoke with great effect of his personal friendship with Paul Robeson.[50] This "mileage" paid off for him on his return to Canada since he was put "on the party's lecture circuit," and the *Financial Post* called him the "darling of the Communist artistic crowd," but a few years later, when his family threatened to cut off his financial backing, Taylor quit the LPP.[51]

On their return, the Canadian delegates did their best to live up to Penner's promises to "spare no effort" in their speaking tours. The ethnic left press carried interviews with Penner and touted his speaking tour.[52] Groups interested in having one or more of the delegates speak were asked to contact the CSFS.[53] On 20 May, Frank and Libbie Park held a discussion of their book *Moscow as Two Canadians Saw It*, followed by a performance of the United Jewish Folk Choir, led by the Gartners. The *Canadian Tribune* noted that "the concert will mark the first public appearance of EMIL and FAGEL Gartner following their return from a visit to the Soviet Union."[54] A few days later the choir performed again, followed by a speech by Carter on Soviet musical developments.[55]

On 29 May, a CSFS meeting held in the AUUC hall in Toronto opened with Emil Gartner directing the approximately 500 people in the audience in singing "O Canada." Fanny Gartner accompanied the singing on the piano. She was then introduced by Carter as "the beloved pianist of the famous United Jewish People's Folk Choir." She spoke about the availability of cultural education to all Soviet young people, which allowed them to pursue careers in the fine arts.[56] Introduced as "almost as popular as his wife," Emil also chose to speak about the high cultural development of the Soviet people. He pointed to the forty-six opera houses in Moscow, the numerous Soviet composers, and the schools and theatres that supported them as proof. In particular, he noted that "the theatres were always jammed with people, and the people who attended these lavish performances were the common working class, since the admission price was well within the reach of all classes (2 rubels) [*sic*]."[57] All of this was true, and for Canadians accustomed to the elite nature of high culture it was a real marvel. A system that allowed people such access to theatre appeared to be as enlightened as the citizens. Jacob Penner was the main speaker that evening, and he spoke for close to an hour about the living conditions of average Soviet working people and their desire for peace. Dorise Nielsen took up the collection, raising $160 for the CSFS, and urged the audience to ask the speakers questions.[58] CSFS literature was distributed, and attendees were asked to sign a petition for peace.

An important consideration here is that the itineraries for delegations were determined by the Soviet authorities, not by the visitors, and highly organized. No random or chance encounter was permitted. The controlled Soviet repertoire, vetted by the responsible state institutions, was a safe choice for foreign tourists' entertainment. At the same time, the more culture they saw, the less time there was to inspect other aspects of Soviet life. In this way, cultural visits were double performances: one stage was set up inside the theatre, while the theatre itself was part of an elaborate display put on to dazzle and impress the foreign visitors. *Pokazukha*,[59] or the "Potemkin village" approach, is an effective technique, and the CSFS reports were part of the show. The post-visit speaking tours extended the performance.

On 1 June 1951, an account of Penner's impressions was published in the *Winnipeg Free Press*. Penner noted the number of cultural events that he had attended while in the USSR, and his wife "held out a handful of programmes from operas, ballets and similar events" that he had presumably brought home.[60] A few weeks later the scene at a talk by Penner in Winnipeg was not so peaceful. On 6 June, a meeting at which he was due to speak was cancelled because of a bomb threat in the hall.[61] The case was taken to the Winnipeg City Council, where Penner argued that "'a small group' had come to his meeting with the deliberate purpose of disrupting it. They were overheard 'plotting in a Main street hall' prior to the meeting."[62] He asked for groups holding meetings in the Playhouse Theatre to be authorized to prevent anyone from attending if it was determined that he or she would disturb the proceedings. Apparently, what the RCMP called a "security squad" of LPP members had been in the habit of patrolling the entrances to meeting places to keep out those expected to break up the meeting. The RCMP said that these people were often displaced persons (DPs), implying that they were recent immigrants. The authorization was denied by council, and the meeting was rescheduled to 18 June. A CSFS ad urged Winnipeggers to come and "hear the speech which illegal elements endeavoured to suppress."[63] The left press blamed Ukrainian nationalists for the "fascist hoax" and headlined the rescheduled meeting, proving that the "trick" had failed.[64]

In November 1951, Frederick Taylor wrote to the *Montreal Gazette* to dispute the claim of another reader that anti-Semitism existed in the USSR. He wrote that he drew on first-hand knowledge gained by being a member of the CSFS delegation. "I met a great many people including many Jews, among them several outstanding artists," wrote Taylor.

> There is no discussion of a "Jewish question" or anti-Semitism there. Everything which I saw and heard substantiates quite the opposite status quo referred to by Mrs. Marshall. In fact, the Constitution of the Soviet Union specifically bans anti-Semitism and its laws make it a criminal offence. Two members of the Canadian delegation attended services in one of the principal synagogues in Moscow and talked to the rabbi and members of the congregation. In the Soviet Union a Jew is simply as anyone else, a person, and as all other citizens. His lot is his own making as is that of all other individuals.[65]

Taylor was whitewashing the Soviet reality for Canadian readers. Five years later, with the revelations of Khrushchev's "secret speech," Jewish members of the progressive movement were shocked by the degree to which they had been fooled into believing this rubbish, and many abandoned the left as a result.

In January 1952, Pearl Wedro spoke about her recent visit to the USSR at a CSFS meeting held at the Pender Auditorium in Vancouver. She "emphasized that the people of Russia are very interested in Canadian culture and working conditions." She advocated setting up student exchange programs between the countries that would promote peace and friendly relations.[66] The provincial secretary for the BC branch of the CSFS, George Palmer, complained that when he had approached the Vancouver Art Gallery about exhibiting the photographs of Soviet industry and culture, displayed at this meeting, he had been told that there was "not enough space available."[67] Palmer was probably right in his suggestion that this was just an excuse to avoid acquiring propagandistic photos.[68] It was decided that a hall should be rented to display the photos to a larger public.

The rhetoric surrounding CSFS discussions of art was not without a strong hint in Canada of national pride and self-congratulation for breaking down Cold War cultural barriers. In April 1951, a Dmitri Shostakovich oratorio was performed in Toronto in Massey Hall by the Jewish Folk Choir, directed by Emil Gartner and sponsored by the CSFS.[69] The choir appealed to the audience by including a prelude that featured French Canadian, Jewish, "Negro," and

Figure 20. The cover (front and back) of a concert program hosted by the Canadian-Soviet Friendship Society at Massey Hall in April 1951, with a word from Dyson Carter.

Newfoundland folk songs. At the end of the program, a message from Carter appeared under the title "Canadian-Soviet Friendship": "Today we are very fortunate. We are the first people outside the Soviet Union to hear an inspiring work by a world-famous composer. As Canadians, let us all congratulate each other! We have drowned out the roar of hateful propaganda with a splendid song of peace and love and life."[70] During the intermission, Dorise Nielsen read a telegram from Shostakovich in which the Soviet composer referred to the "peaceful pursuits of the Soviet people."[71] The Quebec Special Branch of the RCMP saw the event quite differently. It reported that "it was no co-incidence that the Canadian-Soviet Friendship Society chose the time of the National Assembly of Peace to hold this concert."[72] In fact, the officer reported, "all the top LPPers were to be seen in Massey Hall as well as the music-lovers amongst the delegates to the National Assembly of Peace. All in all, it was a very successful evening for the stooges of VOKS in Canada."[73]

By this time, Shostakovich was making public statements credited to him but drafted by Soviet officials. He was obliged to make "occasional mandatory public appearances, hurriedly and with visible revulsion reading confessions or pathos-filled pronouncements he had not written."[74] His music was periodically attacked by Soviet authorities, as was the case in 1948 when the CPSU passed a resolution condemning "formalism" in music, a meaningless term that nevertheless had serious consequences for Soviet composers. As his friends and colleagues in the artistic world were arrested, executed, and silenced, Shostakovich managed to escape bodily harm, though the negative and pseudo-positive attention that he received from the authorities had severe psychological effects. Obliged by Stalin to travel abroad, he complained of being a "mock celebrity."[75] Members of Canadian left-wing groups saw him as a real celebrity, and Jewish progressives in particular admired his use of Yiddish folk songs as sources for some of his work.[76] Truthfully, Shostakovich took pride in his Jewish-themed compositions because they challenged, however subtly, the Soviet system's rampant anti-Semitism. His music was banned in the USSR, his life was in jeopardy, yet Soviet authorities shamelessly used his image abroad for their own purposes.[77] For example, congratulations were heaped on him in the *VOKS Bulletin*, reminding foreign readers that he had "repudiated" those works that Soviet authorities had criticized.[78] Undoubtedly, Shostakovich would have thought the CSFS lauding of the Soviet Union and his oratorio as "humiliating" as his command performances and official Soviet pronouncements on his work.[79]

The CSFS program from 1952 contained phrases attributed to Shostakovich that were most likely exaggerations for political purposes. In writing "Song of the Forests," the program explained, Shostakovich "was inspired by the Stalin master plan for the transformation of nature in the Soviet Union, and by the composer's love for the forests of the north." The program quoted him as saying that it was his "desire to create a poetic song of the woods in which the strong voice of man, subduing and transforming his natural environment, would ring out loudest of all." The poem written by Eugene Dolmatovsky to accompany the oratorio deals with the reconstruction of the USSR following the Second World War.[80] Following the performance, Carter sent a telegram to Shostakovich: "This was [a] historic cultural event demonstrating to our people the immense benefits of free cultural exchanges between our countries. . . . In [the] universal language of music your oratorio and our singers spoke powerfully of glories of peace." He sent a similar cable on behalf of the CSFS to the VOKS headquarters in Moscow.[81] There is no record of a reply from Shostakovich.

In January 1952, publicity carried in the *Canadian Tribune* and other left-wing publications by the CSFS encouraged readers to celebrate Soviet Friendship Month by attending the 1952 CSFS convention in Toronto, "bring[ing] the family to the exhibit of Soviet displays, photos, films, etc." at the offices of the United Jewish People's Order (83 Christie Street), arranging a film showing locally, joining a "listening group" to tune in to Moscow radio, or "help[ing to] build up the collection of typical Canadian art and handicrafts which the Convention will send as a gift to the Soviet people."[82] One of the Soviet radio programs made available in Canada during the 1952 Friendship Month was the *This Is Canada* pageant presented by the Canadian Youth Friendship League at the World Youth Festival in Berlin in 1951.[83] The left-wing press, including the *Canadian Tribune* and *Canadian Jewish Weekly*, publicized a campaign to donate a collection of Canadian cultural artifacts to the USSR and specified that they could be "books about Canada, especially on history, politics, economics, art and literature together with distinctive Canadian handicrafts, paintings, music, photograph records or stamps."[84] Gifts were to be brought to the convention in Toronto or sent to the address of the CSFS newspaper *News-Facts about the USSR*.

Leonid F. Teplov, the Soviet chargé d'affaires, delivered the closing address in Massey Hall at the CSFS annual convention in January 1952. Because no ranking Soviet diplomat had made a public appearance in Canada since the Gouzenko revelations in 1946, the CSFS took the address as a sign of its importance to Moscow.[85] The *Ottawa Journal* headlined its coverage of the speech as "Top Soviet Diplomat to Canada Charges 'Big 3' Preparing War," and it noted that "it was the first major address by a Soviet diplomat in this country since 1945, when the RCMP cracked a spy ring funneling top-secret information behind the Iron Curtain."[86] James McCook elaborated: "Since the spy trials the Soviet representatives here have kept much to themselves.... They have stayed away from gatherings where they would be expected to speak in public and have done little to develop personal friendships among Ottawa citizens. The indications of a change were seen in the visit of L.F. Teplov, USSR chargé d'affaires, in Toronto where he addressed the annual convention of the Canadian-Soviet Friendship Society."[87]

Accompanied by Vladimir Burdin, the first secretary at the embassy and the VOKS representative in Canada, Teplov also called briefly on the mayor of Toronto. Constable David Balfour of the Toronto Board of Control told the *Toronto Telegram* that he thought "'they are in the city to visit the Art Gallery,'" but of course they had come to attend the CSFS convention.[88] Before Teplov spoke to the audience of 2,200 in Massey Hall, greetings from friendship societies in Britain, Czechoslovakia, Poland, the United States, and across Canada were read by Dorise Nielsen and Ross Russell, chairman of the convention. Teplov presented the CSFS with a Prokofiev oratorio, *On Guard for Peace*, while Emil Gartner, director of the Jewish Folk Choir, presented Teplov with an oratorio written by Canadians Sam Dolan and Louis Model.[89]

The text of the speech by Teplov, in which he called the CSFS delegates "ambassadors for peace" and claimed that Britain, the United States, and France were thwarting Soviet peace gestures in the United Nations, was published in the *Canadian Tribune*.[90] The RCMP made sure that a copy of the text was sent to George Glazebrook, head of the Defence Liaison division of the Department of External Affairs.[91] In the CSFS literature promoting the speech, Carter claimed that this exchange was purely cultural, that the majority of CSFS supporters were in favour of capitalism, and that the claim that the CSFS was a communist front was untrue. However, people entering the hall were carefully checked and had to be holding an invitation or be known by those at the door.[92] Highlights of the convention, which included speeches by John Boyd and Dorise Nielsen, and crowds visiting the cultural exhibitions and performances, were listed in the *Canadian Tribune* with photographs.[93]

In the spring of 1954, a group of Soviet concert artists visited Canada on a CSFS-sponsored tour. Sophie Golovkina and Leonid Zhdanov, ballet dancers; Leonid Kogan, violinist; Elizaveta Chavdar, soprano; Arturs Frindbergs, tenor; and Pavel Serebryakov, pianist, were welcomed by Carter when they arrived in Toronto.[94] The concerts were popular: 3,000 were in attendance at the first concert in Massey Hall, and 7,000 crowded into Varsity Arena to hear them at the end of their tour. More than 4,000 were reported to have attended the concert in Winnipeg, over 1,000 in Sudbury, and 2,500 in Ottawa at the Capitol Theatre.[95] At one performance in Toronto, the RCMP reported that "there were numerous known local communists in attendance."[96] As head of the Slav Committee and something of an impresario, John Boyd was asked by the CPC to be master of ceremonies.[97] On behalf of the CSFS, he also conducted the delegation as it played in Vancouver, Edmonton, Saskatoon, Winnipeg, Fort William–Port Arthur, Sudbury, Ottawa, Hamilton, and once more in Toronto. The schedule for the concerts was printed in *Ukrainske slovo* and other left-wing publications, with information about where to buy tickets.[98]

Both the mainstream and the left-wing press carried generally enthusiastic reports of the performances and the Soviet artists' impressions of Canada, but the tone differed. The progressive ethnic press stressed what the *Ukrainian Canadian* called "a Spring thaw in the icy barrier the Western cold-war diplomats have tried to set up between the Canadian and Soviet people during the past few years."[99] The unwelcoming attitude of the Duplessis "regime" was blamed for not allowing a performance in Montreal, and stress was laid on the incongruity of Western stereotypes of the Soviet people in contrast to the wonderful performances. "The Soviet cultural delegation made a tremendous impression on the Canadian people and the greetings of friendship and peace they brought with them were sincerely welcomed," wrote Rose Mickoluk for the *Ukrainian Canadian*. She continued: "They have taken back with them many favourable impressions of Canada and the Canadian people also. They loved the city of Vancouver, where they visited Stanley Park and the native Indians. They marveled at the beauty of Niagara Falls, as does the whole world. They were deeply moved by the warm reception of the Canadian people everywhere they went and will convey to their people the sincere desire of the Canadian people for still closer bonds of friendship between our two countries."[100] The *Canadian Tribune* proclaimed that the Soviet artists "Fell in Love with Canada" and that it was "A Triumphant Tour."[101] Interviewed by the paper, Boyd said that the audiences everywhere were large and that ads taken out by anti-communist Ukrainian groups did little to deflate enthusiasm. He mentioned that at one of Leonid Kogan's performances Wilson Macdonald, whom Boyd called "one of Canada's leading poets," presented Kogan with an illuminated scroll calling him "the new king of the violin."[102] At the end of May, Carter reported to the VOKS chief of the British Section, Konstantin Perevoschikov, that "we are still receiving wonderful letters and calls about the visit of the Soviet concert artists." He promised that a full report on the tour would be sent soon, and he wondered whether Macdonald might be allowed to visit the USSR to see the Volga River, about which he had written a poem.[103] It is not clear from the archives whether Macdonald got his wish.

A *Montreal Gazette* article was more critical, noting that the impressions of the Soviet artists on their return to the USSR were that "Canada could be a nice enough place if Canadians would only listen to their 'progressive people' and 'throw off the yoke of that phony low-class culture from the United States that is strangling the country.'"[104] The article noted that the artists had praised Canadians of Eastern European background for "keeping alive their culture with choruses and dancing groups, and that the music of Shostakovich, Khatchaturian and other Russian composers is very popular in these circles."[105] Apparently, Canadians, and especially the audience in Winnipeg, had poor "concert manners": they moved about in the aisles during the performances and were noisy.[106] In April 1955, a few articles appeared in the Canadian press reporting that Kogan had issued a statement saying that he and other artists would be pleased to welcome Canadian musicians to the USSR on a return visit.[107]

In terms of the inability to find a concert hall for the Soviet performers in Quebec, the *Montreal Gazette* suggested that perhaps the Quebec government had missed an opportunity to use culture as a political tool. In an editorial on

29 April 1954, the *Gazette* pointed out that, rather than fearing the impact of Soviet culture on Quebec society, "more would be gained by showing the Party the benefits of life in Canada and sending them back to Russia as missionaries. . . . They would have taken back to others, it is argued, word of life on this side of the Iron Curtain."[108] The editors wondered, however, whether this would have worked, since clearly individuals chosen for a foreign delegation were trusted by Soviet authorities, and it would probably be difficult to persuade them to view the West favourably. Moreover, their families were still at home, "hostages" of the system. The idea of culture as a political lever in the Cold War was not restricted to the Soviets.

The same day that the Soviet concert stars arrived in Canada a group of Canadian artists left for Moscow. This delegation included one of the painters from the Group of Seven, F.H. Varley; Eric Aldwinkle, a Toronto muralist and writer; Micheline Legendre, a Montreal puppeteer; Wilfred Lemoyne, whom Carter called a "Montreal poet and literary critic"; Pierre St. Germaine, also a journalist from Montreal; and Madeleine Perron-St. Germain, not an artist but a Montreal social worker, formerly associated with the Red Cross.[109] The CSFS press release noted that, while the Soviet artists were being hosted by the CSFS, the Canadian artists would "spend three weeks as the guests of the USSR [All-Union] Society for Cultural Relations with Foreign Countries."[110] A photograph of the delegation at the Dorval International Airport appeared in the *Montreal Gazette* on 10 April 1954.[111] Except for Varley, the travellers seem to be young, smiling in presumed anticipation of their trip. Varley appears to be nonchalant, not looking at the camera, with his hands in the pockets of his overcoat.

The *Gazette* quoted Aldwinkle as saying that "this is the first time the U.S.S.R. has invited any group who are not associated in any way with their party or political ideas."[112] He also commented on the motivation of the artists in going, saying that they wanted "to see what's going on in the cultural field in Russia."[113] Varley said that he was sure they would be able to travel freely and that, "whatever we especially want to see, they will let us see."[114] The RCMP had doubts about this being an apolitical trip, and their correspondence on the delegation was copious.[115] The *Canadian Tribune* claimed that a "press and radio campaign in Montreal attempting to witchhunt the delegation has . . . failed to intimidate most of the delegates," but it noted that Fraser MacDonald, a Toronto composer employed by the CBC, had changed his mind about making the trip.[116]

Louis Kon made the passport arrangements for the Canadian delegation and saw them off at the airport. The *Montréal Matin* could not resist reporting the rumour that Kon was "un agent rélévant directement de Moscou" but was sure that he was "une espèce d'attaché culturel officieux pour le compte de l'URSS à Montréal," who was "bien connu à Montréal pour ses sympathies communistes."[117] The paper further noted that Secretary of State for External Affairs Lester B. Pearson had no objection to the delegation making the trip.[118] In each report, it was repeated that the delegation had been invited by VOKS, which would foot the bill, and sponsored by the CSFS.

A year later Kon wrote to VOKS about Varley and this delegation. With the letter, he forwarded an "account of [the] life of F.H. Varley and reproductions of some of his paintings" and indicated that he had visited Moscow.[119] In an awkward statement, Kon commented that Varley, "like others of that delegation, gained a lot from the visit to the USSR, though too intimidated and afraid to tell the truth publicly, though doing so in their own fashion in personal conversations, and like Walter Duranty, to my recollections, resent and refute the lies maliciously circulated."[120] This might have meant that Varley had refused to speak at public events after his return. It is likely that his refusal to give voice to fawning descriptions of the USSR had resulted in his censure within progressive circles. Kon explained that Varley was "unfortunately addicted to drink and an ultra-individualist," but he noted that he "undoubtedly is one of our foremost painters."[121] From the Soviet point of view, this was damning. An artist, no matter how talented, was not useful to the (Soviet) state if he or she would not defend its interests in public; nor could an artist of any kind be an "ultra-individualist" in the USSR.

The VOKS representative at the Soviet Embassy was tasked with bringing forward Canadian writers whose work fit with Soviet literary ideals. Dyson Carter made this job easier. He took seriously not only the promotion of cultural delegations but also that of Canadian progressive writers. Such writers were not necessarily well known to their fellow Canadians, but they were of great interest to Soviet authorities and often had their work published in the USSR. Carter promoted their work through CSFS events and routinely sent reports to VOKS on their performances and publications. In 1951, he was already lobbying on behalf of Canadian playwright Melville Taylor.[122] Certainly, any artist who had been a delegate to the USSR and spoke publicly afterward remained of interest to VOKS. Officials at the VOKS headquarters in Moscow corresponded with Frederick Taylor after his return to Canada and sent him publications at his request. They also asked for material that he had written, including the article describing his tour of the USSR, which appeared in *Canadian Art* in December 1951.[123]

In January 1954, Carter sent a long letter to the Soviet Writers' Union via Vladimir Burdin describing the work of Frederick Philip Grove, a

German-born Canadian writer who Carter claimed wrongly had been born in Russia.[124] He called Grove "the leading Canadian novelist" and mentioned that he had discussed his career with members of the Writers' Union the previous year. One reason that Carter recommended Grove to Soviet experts was that he had come in later life to hold anti-American views. Similar views, Carter wrote, were held by "Canadian people today" who understand that "the 'American ideal' is only an empty dream, an historical legend, perpetuated by ... their [America's] propagandists and even by 'progressives' in the USA who are fond of portraying their country as only 'diverted' from its 'ideal course' by a handful of reactionaries."[125] The fact that Grove's book *The Master of the Mill* (1944) was critical of capitalism would also have appealed to Carter.[126] In addition, he found it significant that the only book Grove ever translated was a biography of Sun Yat Sen telling the story of the Chinese revolution. This letter was duly sent to the VOKS headquarters and forwarded to the Soviet Writers' Union, together with Grove's autobiography, *In Search of Myself*, and a biography of the writer by Desmond Pacey, all of which had been sent by Carter.[127] Presumably, they were placed in the Lenin Library.

Carter was not completely submissive in his correspondence with Moscow. In March 1954, he wrote to VOKS to complain about a Soviet book review that called Barker Fairley, a professor at the University of Toronto, an "exponent of fascist ideologies."[128] The review was written by Marietta Shaginyan, the Soviet author of a book on Goethe, at a time when Fairley was known in the West as one of the foremost experts on the German poet. Carter pointed out that the aspersions rankled most because Fairley was an executive member of the CSFS and had long been a peace activist. Proof, according to Carter, was the fact that he was banned from entering the United States.[129] In fact, his wife, Margaret, was a long-time member of the Labor-Progressive Party, a writer and critic for *New Frontiers*. In 1949, when Margaret and Barker attended the Cultural and Scientific Conference for World Peace at the Waldorf Hotel in New York, they were arrested for associating with leftists and subsequently refused entry into the United States. Together with his letter of complaint, Carter sent VOKS Fairley's well-respected book on Goethe.[130] Both letter and book were sent to the VOKS headquarters and later forwarded to the Writers' Union for Shaginyan,[131] but no further reply is recorded. Members of the Writers' Union were not famous for changing their minds.

Carter wrote several times to VOKS recommending the poetry of Wilson Macdonald, who "personifies the tragic condition of Canadian culture: his genius has been recognized by great men in many countries, yet he is officially treated almost with silence in Canada."[132] Although Carter noted with regret that Macdonald was "not a Marxist," he wrote that he had been a "tireless supporter of peace and a friend of the Soviet Union from the days of the Intervention."[133] Carter almost apologized for the liberal Christian beliefs held by Macdonald, and the fact that the poet's father was a clergyman, but brushed these issues aside, saying that "his father was a clergyman who abandoned the church because of its hypocrisy. . . . In university he [Macdonald] became known as a rebel against convention[al] ideas and hypocrisy, and to this day he is a 'persona non grata' at most of the leading Canadian Universities. . . . For the last 15 years or so his sharp attacks on various reactionary forces have greatly restricted his engagements."[134] The disdain shown by E.J. Pratt and "his breed" was evidence enough, according to Carter, that Macdonald was deserving of Soviet support. What is more, Carter wrote, the poetry of the "greatest living Canadian poet" included no glorification of "sexual deviations" so prevalent in other modern poetry, and he is a "poet of healthy, normal love relationships."[135] In this case, at least, Carter's praise was enough for VOKS. Macdonald's books were immediately sent on to the Foreign Language Press in Moscow for consideration, and Macdonald received official congratulations from VOKS on his seventy-fifth birthday in 1955.[136] In the USSR, this signalled official approval.

Apparently, Macdonald first became interested in VOKS in 1954 when he read the lecture given by the chairman of VOKS, Professor A.I. Denisov, on Canadian culture.[137] The lecture in honour of Canadian-Soviet Friendship Month had criticized an article written by history professor Arthur Lower in *New Liberty*,[138] claiming that Lower did not recognize that Canada had its own culture independent of England and France. Lower heard about this lecture and wrote a scathing letter to Denisov.[139] Lower had no idea where Denisov had got his information, but clearly he did not know what he was talking about. Contrary to what Denisov had suggested, Lower said that Stephen Leacock would not have been friendly toward the Soviet Union but "was a reactionary capitalist if ever there was one."[140] Lower concluded by saying that "even your friends here will no doubt be embarrassed" by the lecture. The source of most of Denisov's comments was probably Carter/the CSFS. The VOKS headquarters sent its Ottawa representative a copy of the letter from the Canadian historian but told Burdin that "it is not considered worthwhile to answer Lower."[141]

Carter was not always successful in promoting Canadian writers. Collections by working-class poet Joe Wallace were sent several times to Moscow and forwarded on to the Writers' Union, but in 1955 Wallace complained bitterly that the USSR was ignoring him.[142] This despite recommendations from Dyson Carter, Wilson Macdonald, and even Tim Buck, leader of the LPP. Wallace referred to his long service to the Canadian left as justification for publication of his work in the USSR: "Because of my writings and because of my activities in strikes, unemployed demonstrations, I was driven out of my business, lost my home, and was imprisoned for 18 months. My work in the movement extends beyond 36 years: Tim Buck refers to me as one of the founders of the Party in Canada in one of his books."[143] The VOKS files contain no reply to Wallace's letter, possibly because there was none.

In 1952, when Carter sent VOKS a radio play called *Coloured Buttons* by Ted Allan, he wrote that "all progressive people were enthusiastic about it. The importance of the play was shown by the vicious attacks on the author and the C.B.C. by certain reactionary elements who heard the broadcast."[144] Allan, Carter explained, was worthy of Soviet consideration because he was "a progressive, although his views are not known by the C.B.C."[145] A year later, when Carter recommended the book just released by Ted Allan and Sydney Gordon on Norman Bethune entitled *The Scalpel and the Sword*, the VOKS representative in Ottawa wrote to his superiors to say that "Carter considers it desirable to place a reference or review of this book in a Soviet periodical."[146] In 1954, another play by Allan, entitled *The Money Makers*, was sent to VOKS, this time with Burdin's comment that "T. Allan himself sympathizes with the progressive movement, but out of fear he will lose his job (he is a radio commentator), it is necessary to conceal his views and therefore he does not himself participate in the progressive movement."[147]

In 1957, an active CSFS executive member in Montreal, Romeo Lafond, wrote to VOKS to recommend a play by D.S. Daniels entitled *The Witching Hour*, but his efforts were unsuccessful. VOKS communicated to the Writers' Union the credentials of Daniels, which included having worked for an LPP newspaper for years, being from a poor working family, and being a member of the communist-led Canadian Seamen's Union.[148] The Writers' Union concluded that, though the playwright's profile was correct, the play itself had "serious artistic deficiencies,"[149] which meant that it failed to meet the doctrinaire requirements.

Of all the progressive authors in whom VOKS took interest, Carter was the most prolific. When he was first selected as president of the reorganized National Council for Canadian-Soviet Friendship, VOKS wrote a page-long description of his work, praising him for being "very well known as a friend of the Soviet Union."[150] VOKS was especially pleased that in the books that Carter had published about the USSR since the Second World War he had argued that the Soviet socialist system was superior to other forms of government. The facts that he was a member of the Labor-Progressive Party, and had written for the *Canadian Tribune*, were also noted, and underlined was the fact that with the help of LPP leaders Carter had been chosen to rejuvenate the practically defunct wartime friendship society.[151] In 1953, the head of the VOKS British Countries division, Konstantin Perevoschikov, reviewed Carter's 1943 book *Stalin's Life*. The reviewer noted that, though the book described "correctly" Stalin's actions and the historical events that took place in Russia and the Soviet Union during his lifetime, a reader would be able to tell that Carter had not yet been to the USSR.[152] By 1950, he had, and he would continue to visit the USSR regularly. The books that he subsequently published about what he had seen in the USSR,[153] as well as articles and books on the Canadian social and economic system, made him even more popular with Soviet authorities and Canadian progressive groups. Copies of his work were always sent to Moscow for review and possible publication there,[154] and materials for publication in his *Northern Neighbors* magazine were shipped in return. Carter took great initiative in encouraging this, sending his books with progressive reviewers' comments to the VOKS representative,[155] as well as constant requests for information for his future projects. In 1957, the Soviet ambassador, Dmitri Chuvakhin, helped Carter to receive payment in Canadian funds for the publication of *Tomorrow Is With Us* in Ukrainian. The royalty came to $3,086.09.

Staff at the VOKS headquarters in Moscow, as well as the VOKS representative in Ottawa, took seriously the opportunities for propaganda offered by cultural exchanges. This attitude also informed dialogue between the Canadian DEA and Moscow in the 1960s and 1970s. When Soviet poet Andrei Voznesensky visited Canada in 1971, the VOKS representative at the Soviet Embassy in Ottawa spoke of the trip as being successful in both artistic and propagandistic terms. VOKS was still well pleased with its investment in the CSFS and its leader, Carter, both convinced that socialism provided artists with an environment favourable to cultural development and willing to inform Canadians of this. He benefited personally by receiving materials, enjoying a large readership in the USSR, and having VOKS vouch for his political "correctness," but the relationship was mutually beneficial.

The CSFS performed an important function for VOKS, and through their interaction VOKS could argue that a politically important void was being filled in Canada. The CSFS played its role by cooperating with the Soviet Union in its export of cultural geniuses, with their images and speeches retooled for the purpose of propaganda, and by providing the Soviets with access to Canadian artists in sympathy with the USSR. For the CSFS, culture represented its most effective influence over Canadian perceptions of the USSR. It was a "soft" reality better suited to persuasion than the "hard" reality of politics, and in this it had real appeal in Canada. The Soviets had used this technique of "agitation and propaganda" domestically for years, and as a result many Soviet denizens had developed the habit of deciphering official "Aesopian" language and using "doublethink." Canadian fellow travellers and committed communists who were members of the CSFS did not appear to distance themselves from the often greatly exaggerated Soviet claims to superiority.

Canadians of all political stripes had been fascinated for years by Russia and its cultural products. In offering information and exchanges on ballet, literature, and music, the CSFS had real appeal in Canada. Undoubtedly, its members were sincere in their admiration and enjoyment of Soviet culture. Cultural diplomacy was an effective way to increase international understanding and not one with which diplomats and officials at the DEA were unfamiliar. However, in commenting on the freedom of Soviet artists, the CSFS seems to have been unaware that the officially sanctioned content of Soviet art was limited. The experiences of many famous and less famous Soviet performers demonstrate the vicissitudes of official Soviet policy on art.[156] Gushing CSFS descriptions of life in the USSR published in the Soviet press assured foreign sympathizers and Soviet readers that Westerners thought the official claims accurate. The CSFS was an actor in an elaborate show, with Carter playing the role of agent, providing information for all sides and facilitating contacts.

Conclusion

We wrote [this book] because we believe Canadians want to know the truth, the real facts about the Soviet Union as it is today.

—Charlotte Carter and Dyson Carter,
We Saw Socialism (Toronto: CSFS, 1951), 10.

This is the truth. And you can be absolutely sure that the truth will win out.

—Dyson Carter, "About This Book," in *Moscow: As Two Canadians Saw It*, by Libbie Park and Frank Park (Toronto: CSFS, 1951), 12.

To a certain extent, the Cold War was an information war fought between opponents who used the rhetoric of the "truth" as a weapon to make powerfully emotional claims of superiority. In striving to define their ideological approaches as the most "truthful," players on all sides aimed to legitimize their beliefs and actions. Particularly after Igor Gouzenko's defection in Ottawa in 1945, the Soviet press argued that Canadians were being targeted by an orchestrated anti-Soviet propaganda campaign.[1] As David Caute has pointed out, besides being a "traditional political military confrontation between empires," the Cold War was "an ideological and cultural contest on a global scale and without historical precedent."[2] The history of the CSFS, and its relationship with the Soviet organization VOKS, should be seen as part of this larger ideological/cultural conflict.

Accessibility and use of archives have been at the centre of debate over the historiography of the postwar period in North America. The stakes in these arguments were raised as archival collections from the former Soviet Union became more accessible to Western scholars. Long limited in their access to sources available for study in the USSR, academics such as John Lewis Gaddis went so far as to declare that, on the basis of this new archival information, "we now know" how ideology affected Cold War politics, and he refuted some of his own earlier conclusions.[3] Melvyn Leffler, who reviewed the book by Gaddis, argued that we must consider ideology beyond the highest echelons of power, or we simply contribute to the creation of a new version of an old master narrative. He argued that "we now do know that ideas, beliefs, culture and ideology count, but that we have to continue to study the average person, not only high politics."[4] If, as Canadian historian Nancy Partner quipped, "archives contain many interesting things, but Truth is not among them,"[5] then previously restricted documents at least allow us to better understand the context of the period.

RCMP documents, as well as those from other Canadian government departments and the VOKS archive, are neither neutral nor infallible. The gaps and frustrations inherent in working with RCMP documents have been described by other scholars. Yet together these sources corroborate basic assumptions made by the RCMP at the time: the CSFS was a communist-front organization, its leaders were Communist Party members, Dyson Carter provided the Soviets with a lot of (publicly known) information on Canada and Canadians, and he widely published the Soviet versions of current events. The close ties among the Soviet foreign ministry, VOKS, and later the Union of Soviet Societies for Friendship and Cultural Relations with Foreign Countries, or SSOD,[6] the Labor-Progressive Party (Communist Party of Canada), and the CSFS are demonstrable now, but they were less clear before Soviet archives were opened to the public in the 1980s. The appeal of the CSFS was precisely in playing down these connections, and most members probably did not know the extent of Soviet and LPP support for their organization. This was intentional.

As an extension of his earlier work for the CPC-LPP, Carter aimed to influence Canadian public opinion in favour of the Soviet Union. He drew on all kinds of material, most of it sent to him from the USSR, articles and ideas sent to him by readers, or items in the mainstream North American press that he adapted. His message, always optimistic, was that Canadians were gradually coming around to his way of seeing things. In the larger Canadian society, this was not the case, but among those who self-identified as "progressive" Canadians, for whom the USSR was a symbol of their political hopes and dreams, his claims were believed, and his efforts were celebrated. The popularity of his magazine *Northern Neighbors*, and the refusal of the Soviets to let him go after he was replaced as head of the CSFS in 1960, are proof of his importance to the left in Canada and as a propagandist to Moscow.

The RCMP attention to Carter was reasonable considering the literature that he was publishing. Taken separately, some of his articles appear to be benignly naive, but read over long stretches their anti-American and at times militaristic support for the USSR was strident in tone and content. Carter was successful in appealing to Canadians already looking for this type of radicalism, couched in positive images of the USSR and the Soviet system, and the promotion of peace. Judging from letters to the editor preserved in the Library and Archives Canada collection, at times his message fit well with the messages that individuals received from other pro-Soviet organizations in Canada, and at other times readers were interested in the opportunities to contradict more mainstream views published in the larger Canadian dailies. They were no doubt motivated by a sincere desire to see a different kind of international climate make headlines.

Carter was clever and a skilled writer. At one of the earliest postwar CSFS conventions, he bragged that, "in the last 12 months, millions of Canadian men and women have learned the truth. According to the Gallup Poll early this month, 5 million Canadian adults believe the Soviet Union does not want war. A tremendous change, a complete reversal of public opinion[,] has taken place in our country. A year ago a big majority of people felt that war was facing us. Today, a very large majority no longer believe this."[7] Besides citing a Gallup Poll to back up his claims, Carter referred to an editorial from the *Globe and Mail*, purposely choosing a conservative business paper, to support his argument that Canadians wanted to see the USSR as a peaceful nation.[8] He immodestly claimed credit for these attitudes: "It is correct to say that 'NEWS-FACTS' has played a part in changing public opinion in Canada."[9]

The CSFS did enlarge its membership. If in 1949, when the CSFS was founded, there were only about sixty delegates, at the 1952 convention in Toronto Carter announced that there were 259 registered delegates, with 118 corresponding delegates from the United States, Yukon, and Newfoundland, and thirty-five observers.[10] From a few readers in 1950, Carter could boast in 1952 readers in every province and territory, as well as in fourteen other countries, including the United States.[11] A poll in 1965 confirmed that *Northern Neighbors* was one of the most popular magazines among youth of the Association of United Ukrainian Canadians,[12] and anecdotal evidence suggests that progressives of all ethnic backgrounds found Carter's magazine inspirational.

The Mounties were correct in 1953 when they reported that, "as a communist front organization, the CSFS fulfill[ed] two functions in Canada. First as a clearing house for invitations for visits to the Soviet Union, and for the distribution of films, books, and propaganda literature produced in the USSR. Second, by directing or making available the cultural products of communist

Russia."[13] The CSFS probably had some limited success in "bringing to the fringe of communism groups of people across the Dominion . . . who may, in turn, become sympathetic to communist ideology,"[14] but more likely the CSFS appealed to those already sympathetic to the cause. In 1963, the RCMP suggested that the Canada-USSR Association was similarly "designed to act as an instrument of the Soviet Government controlled through the apparatus of the CP of C." Once more they were correct that the SSOD had a central role, for it functioned "in part [as] a propaganda department whose purpose it [was] to encourage foreigners to think of the Soviet Union as a friendly and peace-loving country."[15] In the context of the times, the CSFS and its successors did represent a considerable worry for the Mounties. Archives also show that External Affairs carefully positioned itself vis-à-vis the Canadian-Soviet "friends," so as to neither enflame accusations of anti-Soviet propaganda, nor prevent the useful flow of information about life in the USSR. In the end, the sympathy that the CSFS claimed to have generated for the USSR was of limited tangible consequence.

There was continuity between Carter's CSFS and the Canada-USSR Association that replaced it in 1960. Although the Communist Party of Canada, in consultation with authorities in Moscow, changed the leadership and renamed the organization,[16] its goals and activities remained remarkably similar. But the success of the group continued to depend to a large extent on the personalities of the leaders, and by 1969 the association was again faltering under Les Hunt. It appears that it was practically defunct between 1969 and 1972, when it was reorganized under the leadership of Michael Lucas. He later complained that he had had to repurchase all of the necessities for the association's work because "what was accumulated by Leslie Hunt . . . had gone with very few exceptions."[17] Lucas continued to head the association until 1991, when it was renamed once more, and he still leads a Toronto-based group that advocates the re-establishment of the Soviet Union and friendly relations with Soviet peoples.

A report in the VOKS collection written in Russian, probably intended for the main office of the SSOD in Moscow, explained that the association "Canada-USSR" was founded in 1960 in Toronto and could, around 1974, claim 2,500 members.[18] An RCMP report also placed the official launch of the revised friendship group at the King Edward Hotel in Toronto in December 1960.[19] The RCMP noted that William Irvine was the honorary chairman of the new group, with Les Hunt as secretary and Clarence Richard Claus as treasurer. The Mounties also suspected that CPC members who had been involved in Canadian-Soviet friendship organizations were members of the new group as well.[20] A list specifying members of the "Canada-USSR Association, Canadian Council," included the names of Toronto bookseller Robert Kenny, Michael Lucas, Helen Lucas, John Wigdor, and Guelph herbalist Dr. A.J. Thut.[21] A Quebec variant called the Quebec-USSR Association was led by André Maire, whom the RCMP identified as a communist from Richelieu.[22] Initial funding for the association was to come from the CPC, and individual members were asked for donations to ensure sustainability.[23] Thut was apparently among its most generous financial backers.[24] Not unlike the CSFS, with its links to progressive ethnic groups supported by the CPC, the association maintained "traditional ties with progressive organizations of emigrants from Soviet republics, for instance, the Canadian Ukrainians, Russians, Carpatho-Russians."[25] Some Canadian Doukhobors also found attractive the association's message of peaceful coexistence and cultural exchange with the Soviet Union.[26] Members of these groups actively participated in the association and its events.

One remarkable difference between Carter's CSFS and its successor is that from 1958 on a separate francophone association existed in Quebec. It is not clear what became of the group led by André Maire, but documents from the VOKS/SSOD collection show that in 1969 a Montreal-based organization called the Société culturelle Québec-URSS was active with a dentist, Adélard Paquin, described as "popular" by the authorities in Moscow, at its head. This group apparently had lawyers, doctors, and journalists as members and boasted of good ties with Montreal University and the press. Like its Toronto affiliate, the society organized professional meetings with Soviet individuals visiting Canada, held exhibitions of Soviet art and objects, and offered Russian-language courses and Soviet film screenings. In the early 1970s, it claimed to have 4,500 members.[27] A major event planned by the Montreal group in 1973 was a large party on board the Soviet ship *Aleksandr Pushkin*, docked in the harbour. Three hundred people were guests of the society that night, and Paquin and Soviet Ambassador to Canada B.P. Miroshinchenko gave speeches. E. Gusarov, of the General Consulate of the USSR in Montreal, was also present.[28] Documents from the Laurence Nowry fonds at the Canadian Museum of History clearly demonstrate the link between the Montreal-based Soviet friendship society and the Parti communiste du Québec.[29] In 1973, Paquin refused categorically to be united with the group led by Lucas because, he said, it "would be a brake" on the Quebec society, but he did agree to cooperate when necessary with Toronto.[30] Paquin did not like how the Toronto-based association was run and, undoubtedly for political reasons, preferred to keep the groups separate.

Like its predecessor, the association claimed to have a pan-Canadian membership. A list of the branches in the VOKS collection noted that there were active groups in Halifax, Winnipeg (led by Mary Kardash), Regina, Toronto, Edmonton, Hamilton, Vancouver, London, Grand Forks (led by Doukhobor leader John J. Verigin), Windsor, Vernon, Sudbury, Saskatoon, Brantford, Montreal, Thunder Bay, Guelph (led by herbalist A.J. Thut), Calgary and the province of New Brunswick.[31] The Montreal-based society was listed as a partner group. Paquin complained that, except for the groups in Toronto, Montreal, and Vancouver, none of these association branches was really working.[32] Koozma J. Tarasoff has nonetheless described the Ottawa branch as having been active in hosting discussion groups.[33] Organized Canadian-Soviet friendship had less appeal in the Maritimes, perhaps because the CPC-LPP had never gained much popularity there. Lucas and Paquin remained, for all intents and purposes, the Canadian voices of Soviet friendship through the 1980s. In 1988, they published separate reports in the SSOD journal *Culture and Life* celebrating Mikhail Gorbachev's policy of glasnost and declaring that it made it easier for all Canadians to admire the USSR.[34] In tone, these articles were reminiscent of Carter's unceasingly optimistic pandering to the USSR and its leadership.

The Vancouver branch of the Canada-USSR Association was established with lawyer Harold Dean as president in 1960. George Legebokoff also took a leading interest in organizing events and writing to SSOD in Moscow. A Russian document in the VOKS collection reports that in the 1970s the Vancouver group claimed to have 2,000 members and was "engaged in active propaganda work about the achievements of the Soviet Union" and organizing Canadians to tour the USSR. The group claimed to have established good contacts in the past two years within science circles, universities, and technical colleges.[35] In 1973, the Vancouver branch got the go-ahead from Moscow to begin planning a concert tour of the Vancouver Kitsilano Boys' Band to the USSR.[36]

The SSOD representative in Ottawa continued to serve as a liaison between these groups in Canada and the main SSOD office in Moscow. In 1974, a document accounting for the work of the Moscow-based society USSR-Canada said that it engaged with "Dr. Paquin, Michael Lucas, Dyson Carter, the AUUC, the FRC, and the anti-Soviet Ukrainian population in Canada."[37] When an SSOD delegation came to Canada and the United States in October that year, various progressive groups organized their visit, with meetings arranged for the press and other individuals.[38] In April 1973, the SSOD representative in Ottawa, Valentin Mayorov, attended the Festival of Soviet Lithuania, as did the deputy chair of the Novosti Press Agency, A.Y. Chekuolis.[39]

Figure 21. Carter continued to maintain close contacts with the Soviet authorities. This photograph, presumably taken in Moscow, is captioned "Cosmonaut Alexi Leonov (left) shows his painting to Canadian writer Dyson Carter (right), 15 October 1980."

Sometimes the task of liaising was more difficult than others. In May 1974, Mayorov reported a clash between Lucas's association and the AUUC. Lucas complained that the AUUC had been trying to make all the arrangements for the visit of a Ukrainian SSR delegation to Canada in 1973. At issue was who was in charge. Mayorov had earlier reported to the SSOD office in Moscow that, when the delegation came to Toronto, none of the association leaders was available. Lucas was in the USSR, and Robert Kenny was in England, so the AUUC organized almost everything. Mayorov concluded that more accountability was needed from Lucas[40] and later pointed out that "here, clearly, a big role is played by the personal interrelationship of Lucas with the AUUC leadership."[41] As far as the SSOD was concerned, Mayorov was to ensure coordination between the pro-Soviet groups in Canada.

The SSOD maintained close contact with Carter after he left the friendship society. Carter's popularity among Canadian progressives, and his willingness and ability to rework Soviet news into a popular left-wing magazine, were important to the Soviets, and, though *Northern Neighbors* was not to be a Canada-USSR Association publication, the CPC agreed to continue to subsidize it.[42] John Boyd suggested that Soviet support for Carter was real, and amid LPP-CPC disputes it made him "untouchable."[43] The relationship had tangible results for the Soviets. In spring 1973, the Novosti Press Agency office wrote to the VOKS secretary-general in Moscow to explain that Carter, "well-known Canadian writer, publicist, and Society member," had asked readers of *Northern Neighbors* to collect books for Soviet youth on Canada during A.N. Kosygin's visit to Canada in autumn 1971. The Novosti representative in Ottawa suggested that the SSOD take the forty sets of books collected and distribute them to its members and associates in the USSR.[44] In 1974, Carter wrote to Igor Zabrodin in Moscow about his idea of organizing a tour of Soviet battlefields. Carter had apparently already had a discussion in SSOD Deputy Chairman Andrei Ledovski's Moscow office about the idea. Irja Paul was with Carter in Moscow at that time.[45] Zabrodin in Moscow and Mayorov in Ottawa routinely asked Carter about his family, and in 1973, having recently taken up his post, Zabrodin wrote to Carter with condolences on the passing of Charlotte the year before.[46] Soviet authorities liked Carter and ensured that the SSOD representative in Canada would continue to deal with him.

Known as cultural attachés, and at times as first or second secretary at the Soviet Embassy in Ottawa, the representatives of VOKS, and later the SSOD, were probably also liaising with the KGB. Here the archival record fails us, yet internal logic is strong. In the context of the times, it could not have been any different. Working in a foreign country, performing daily tasks that required the individual to reach out to highly placed Canadian politicians and figures, as well as to contact "average" individuals, attempting at all times to encourage a more positive view of the USSR, these diplomats would have had to pass the highest degree of KGB-approved security. The primary goal for the VOKS representatives was to influence Canadian public opinion in favour of the Soviet Union. In the context of the times, the interest taken by the RCMP in surveillance of Vladimir Burdin's and Alexei Tovstogan's contacts in Canada is understandable.

From their correspondence and reports of their activities, it is plain that CSFS members believed themselves to be committed to ideals of social, political, and economic equality and the promotion of Soviet ideas abroad—ideas known to be contradicted by practices in the USSR. Canada was situated, geographically and culturally, between the United States and Great Britain, and even after the Second World War Soviet ideologues still predicted that the capitalist, imperialist powers would eventually take up arms against one another. As J.L. Black has written, "whenever the foreign-policy elite in the Soviet Union took up a position on the United States or Britain, they found Canada bobbing up in front of them."[47] Canada was important to the Soviets.

If they needed friends in Canada after the Gouzenko allegations made politically active Canadian communists taboo, it is natural that the friendship society was taken up as a viable—and maybe the only—alternative.[48] Yet these friends lived and worked in an environment frequently hostile to Soviet or communist sympathizers. Attendees at public rallies were keenly aware that they were making political statements. How and why did they choose to speak publicly about Soviet successes, to visit the Soviet Union, and to receive Soviet publications? What motivated a Canadian to become a friend of the USSR?

In reference to the era of McCarthyism in the United States, American journalist Edward R. Murrow said that "we must not confuse dissent with disloyalty."[49] Most CSFS members were dissenters, but some passed information intentionally to the Soviets. It has been mentioned that Burdin, the first secretary and VOKS representative at the Soviet Embassy in Ottawa, through whom most of the CSFS requests and correspondence were channelled in the early 1950s, was accused by Vasili Mitrokhin in the well-known Mitrokhin archive of being an operator for the KGB.[50] Mitrokhin also alleged that a member of the CSFS passed passports through Burdin to be used by illegals in Canada and the United States.[51] Via VOKS, the CSFS was indirectly funded and closely monitored by Soviet authorities.[52] Clearly, those who associated with Burdin or his successors ran the risk that they would be put under surveillance themselves.

Although charges of espionage were rarely proven, many Canadian leftists felt vulnerable through the postwar period.[53] The times were such that communists and other progressives were fearful that allegations would lead to loss of employment or worse. Labour activist Jack Scott's memoirs refer to the effect of the Gouzenko Affair on the Canadian left: "The middle class elements that had flocked into the Party during the war years, they just cut and ran. Disappeared. Working-class elements may have stuck around. They might have raised hell about the policies that were being pursued and that seemed wrong. But the middle class types weren't about to chance it. They had too much to lose. Who's to blame them. You're gonna save what you can from the goddamn wreckage and you certainly weren't willing to confront going to jail."[54] This fear and the "ideological prejudice of the early Cold War" might explain why, until recently, former CSFS members have not spoken publicly about their involvement or links to the Communist Party of Canada.[55] Former CSFS members attest to RCMP surveillance and even harassment. Post–Cold War studies give insight into how people could find themselves accused of having passed along sensitive information and the security issues represented by Soviet attempts to repair the image of the USSR in North America. Historians J.L. Granatstein and

David Stafford have said that, not only did Gouzenko's information warrant serious investigation, but also some Canadian spy rings escaped detection.[56] Information passed on to the USSR by CSFS leaders, while not representing our usual conception of cloak-and-dagger spying, was nevertheless deemed useful by Soviet authorities.

Fellow travellers found shelter in the close-knit, overlapping communities that formed the Canadian left.[57] The CSFS was part of this network, but so were the "ethnic" groups, the peace groups, and to some extent the Communist Party itself. The oral histories and other testimonies left by CSFS members supplement the archival record and allow the personal dimensions of their activism to be recorded. They show that, immediately after 1956, several changes were made to the CSFS and *Northern Neighbors*, the Carters relocated, and more emphasis was placed on appealing to a broad base of progressive supporters in Canada. The VOKS documents refer to a decline in attendance at CSFS events and to the removal of an executive member who did not take the proper (i.e., Soviet) stance on these issues,[58] but the society did not die out, and Carter continued to publish a pro-Soviet magazine. Eventually, he was replaced, and the CPC renamed the CSFS on the suggestion of authorities in Moscow. Formed after the Gouzenko revelations of 1946 and reorganized after the events of 1956, the CSFS was one facet of a larger Soviet-inspired strategy to manage perceptions.

The CSFS was sponsored and guided by the USSR for specific reasons. To appeal to a broader membership, the CSFS generally denied this link publicly, but since the Berlin Wall came down in 1989 Carter himself and many of his associates openly admitted that the Soviets supported the group. Historians have largely ignored the CSFS and, in fact, have paid little attention to the communist-front organizations and the role of fellow travellers in Cold War Canada. Most likely this has been because access to the documentation and oral history has been difficult. But documents from the collections of the RCMP, Canadian Department of External Affairs, and Moscow-based VOKS and later SSOD are now available for research, and some former participants have come forward to supplement the historical narrative. We can query the underlying assumptions in the collection of this information, but the material does allow us to understand more about this period.

The RCMP's concern that in the event of a Third World War CSFS members might be on the wrong side[59] did not materialize, but their assumption that the CSFS represented an extension of Soviet foreign policy making was correct. The archival documentation is heavily redacted, however, and does not allow the historian to ascertain RCMP responses to their surveillance reports.

Carter claimed that he had been beaten up at least once by police, Romeo T. Lafond complained that the police had stolen his photographs of the USSR,[60] and others worried that authorities were interfering in their personal affairs, but it has been impossible to prove or disprove many of these claims based upon documentary evidence. Although not the only motivating factor, intimidation by the RCMP was influential in Ted Baxter's decision to change jobs and ultimately leave the CSFS.

The story of the CSFS adds to our knowledge of Cold War Canada and to our understanding of how some Canadians chose to negotiate their personal political beliefs. It is a story of propaganda and persuasion, of soft-power foreign influence in Canada, and of individual Canadians' responses to that influence. As a mechanism for the dissemination of Soviet propaganda, the CSFS was effective among the believers in its narrow membership base, where the unwaveringly pro-Soviet message fell on sympathetic ears. In terms of persuasion, the CSFS was somewhat more effective in giving a public forum to those who would soften the hard edges of the Cold War, especially through cultural exchanges. From the Soviet perspective, it was a cost-effective method of perception management, not unlike the Soviet friendship societies supported by Moscow in the United States, Britain, Belgium, France, New Zealand, Switzerland, and elsewhere.[61] Apart from the VOKS representative's time, divided among other tasks, the cost of producing and shipping materials, and the periodic hospitality provided to delegates, most of the work was done by Carter and other key Canadian members.

CSFS publications served to carry false ideals about the USSR and to build a sense of community among readers who felt isolated and marginalized. Unfailingly upbeat, Carter aimed to convince readers that they were part of a larger global movement, while access to information not readily available to North Americans about their Soviet counterparts drew interest. Conveniently, Carter was not so naively idealistic that the twists in Soviet policy bothered him, and he took the required policy turns in 1956, 1968, and 1985 in step with Soviet authorities. He also gladly supplied the Soviets with information that might otherwise have been difficult for a Soviet diplomat to garner himself. This is not to suggest that Carter had any particular access to secret information, but his prolific reports and letters show that he forwarded copious amounts of publicly available information on Canadian living conditions, public opinion, and the political situation to VOKS. The RCMP were likely unsure how to handle such a character. In retrospect, the CSFS and Carter himself do not appear especially dangerous, but in the context of the times, in dealing with cultural exchange, intelligence gathering and foreign influence, they were active agents in the Cold War interplay.

CSFS members hoped for a place where there were no gender, class, and ethnic inequalities; in the end, the USSR did not prove to be this place, but for a time it was, for some, an attractive illusion. The CSFS story suggests to historians the importance of not only considering class, gender, ethnicity, and generation as categories of analysis but also paying serious attention to ideology and perception. The story is also one of individuals re-evaluating their beliefs and actions in light of another age: the Soviet Union is gone and, with it, the Cold War. Individual memories and perceptions have since changed, and oral history interviews have revealed elements of this change.

Dyson Carter worked to persuade Canadians that the USSR was a friendly, peaceful neighbour, and Canadians who joined the group or subscribed to his journals did so because they found this message appealing. This is a complex, multi-faceted story of political persuasion and propaganda in the Cold War. It deals with a real attempt by Soviet authorities to influence Canadians to view the USSR sympathetically. It deals with the close links among the Communist Party of Canada, "front" organizations such as the CSFS, and Moscow authorities. And it deals with narratives (and counter-narratives) of "truth" in Cold War Canada.

Notes

Introduction

1 Len Scher, *The Un-Canadians: True Stories from the Blacklist Era* (Toronto: Lester Publishing, 1992); also see Merrily Weisbord, *The Strangest Dream: Canadian Communists, the Spy Trials, and the Cold War* (Montreal: Véhicule Press, 1994).

2 "Let Ottawa Act, Conant Ordered, Inquiry is Told," *Toronto Daily Star*, 5 July 1945, 2. Also in Libbie and Frank Park fonds, LAC, MG31K9, vol. 8, File "Gestapo Affair, 1945."

3 LAC, RG146, ATIP request A-2006-00105, RCMP report, Prince Albert, Sask., 31 May 1946, 11 and *passim* in this file.

4 Ivan Avakumovic, *The Communist Party in Canada: A History* (Toronto: McClelland and Stewart, 1975), 175.

5 See J.L. Black, "Soviet Tactics and Targets in Canada before and after the Gouzenko Defection," in *The Gouzenko Affair: Canada and the Beginnings of Cold War Counter-Espionage*, ed. J.L. Black and Martin Rudner, 108–29 (Manotick, ON: Penumbra Press, 2006).

6 Avakumovic, *The Communist Party in Canada*, 232–34.

7 Weisbord, *The Strangest Dream*, 177.

8 Dyson Carter to John Boyd, 28 February 1990, personal collection of Boyd.

Chapter I: Who's Who of the Canadian-Soviet Friendship Society

1 For a history of VOKS activities in Switzerland, see Jean-François Fayet, *VOKS: Le laboratoire helvétique: Histoire de la diplomatie culturelle soviétique durant l'entre-deux-guerres* (Chêne-Bourg: Georg éditeur, 2014).

2 I use the term "fellow traveller" defined by David Caute as signifying individuals who were not necessarily communists but enamoured with the Soviet socialist experiment. Their imaginations, as Caute suggests, were "captivated" by "the primitive aspects of Russia and later China ... but only in so far as dramatic underdevelopment provided a *tabula rasa* for planned construction and rational experimentation." They did not always join Communist Parties because their "disillusionment with Western society [was] less radical, less total, less uncompromising" than that of those who became

party members. They were admirers of Enlightenment values articulated by the Soviets and others, but they also had respect for the same values in the Western context, according to Caute. This idea is similar to James C. Scott's concept of the "high modernist," who had faith in scientific rationalism and wished to see it embodied by the state, and to the term "progressive" used by many of the activists themselves. David Caute, *The Fellow Travellers: Intellectual Friends of Communism*, rev. ed. (New Haven, CT: Yale University Press, 1988), 3–10; James C. Scott, *Seeing like a State: How Certain Schemes to Improve the Human Condition Have Failed* (New Haven, CT: Yale University Press, 1998).

3 This is the term that the Soviets used to describe fellow travellers. I discovered that my interviewees preferred the word *progressive* over that of *communist* and even *fellow traveller* to describe themselves, particularly when they were not members of the Communist Party of Canada and even though their political views aligned at times with CPC policy. The term applies to individuals whose leftist notions led them to become involved in left-wing organizations or subscribe to left-wing publications of all types. In some cases, the word *progressive* can be used interchangeably with *fellow traveller*. In this, they are following, perhaps unconsciously, the contention made in 1952 by CPC member and literary critic Margaret Fairley that Canada's "progressive culture" is defined as the "energetic expression of our life of social struggle, directed to positive, creative, fruitful ends." Margaret Fairley, "Our Cultural Heritage," *New Frontiers* 1 (1952), 2. Drawing on her definition, James Doyle also chose this term for his book *Progressive Heritage: The Evolution of a Politically Radical Literary Tradition in Canada* (Waterloo: Wilfrid Laurier University Press, 2002).

4 Propaganda, in the Soviet sense, as articulated by Vladimir Lenin, was related to the dissemination of agitational information and ideas to small groups in an effort to persuade them about a particular viewpoint. See, for instance, Barry Crowe, *The Concise Dictionary of Soviet Terminology, Institutions, and Abbreviations* (Oxford: Pergamon Press, 1969), 117.

5 LAC, RG146, ATIP request A-2006-00091, RCMP report, "The Canadian Soviet Friendship Society, February 1951 to March 1953," dated 15 April 1953, 116.

6 Dyson Carter, *This Story Fierce and Tender* (Gravenhurst, ON: Northern Book House, 1986). This is an unusual autobiography because Carter splits his biographical details between two protagonists: "Dyson Carter" and "Elgin Morley." Doyle, *Progressive Heritage*, 260, argues that this narrative technique allowed an older Carter to re-examine his youth.

7 LAC, RG146, ATIP request A-2006-00091, RCMP report "The Canadian-Soviet Friendship Society, February 1951 to March 1953. Addendum to Brief Ending February 1951," biographical notes, dated 15 April 1953, 117.

8 Ibid.

9 The RCMP might have made this mistake because Carter belonged to one of the secret (closed) party clubs. Ibid.; Dyson Carter to John Boyd, 28 February 1990, in Boyd's private collection; John Boyd, interview with the author, 2 August 2006.

10 Dyson Carter, *Russia's Secret Weapon* (New York: Contemporary Publishers, 1942).

11 Dyson Carter, *Sea of Destiny: The Story of Hudson Bay, Our Undefended Back Door* (New York: Greenberg, 1940).

12 Doyle, *Progressive Heritage*, 104, 105.

13 Faith Johnston, *A Great Restlessness: The Life and Politics of Dorise Nielsen* (Winnipeg: University of Manitoba Press, 2006), 203.

14 LAC, RG146, ATIP request A-2006-00091, 117.

15 Andrée Lévesque, *Red Travellers: Jeanne Corbin and Her Comrades*, trans. Yvonne M. Klein (Montreal: McGill-Queen's University Press, 2006), 168.

16 James Laxer, *Red Diaper Baby: A Boyhood in the Age of McCarthyism* (Vancouver: Douglas and McIntyre, 2004), 25. Laxer's father was on the executive of the Labor-Progressive Party until 1956.

17 References to his books being sent to the USSR, and their publication and review there, are frequent in the VOKS documents. Carter received royalties for these Soviet-published books. VOKS 6:55:107, D. Carter to A. Tovstogan, 18 February 1957. A journalist for Canadian Press, G.W. Boss, once sarcastically commented to VOKS that there were other Canadian writers besides Carter and asked whether there was any plan to publish their work in the USSR. VOKS 6:45:99–105, G.W. Boss to K. Perevoschikov, with responses from A. Denisov, head of VOKS, 24 February 1954. An interview with Carter appeared in the Moscow English-language newspaper the *New Times* 41 (1983): 27.

18 Carter did this by writing an open letter to party leader Tim Buck, entitled "Dyson Carter Explains: Why I've Joined the LPP," published in the *Canadian Tribune* on 15 December 1945; see Doyle, *Progressive Heritage*, 224.

19 Dyson Carter, "How *Not* to Be Afraid of Your Heart," *New Liberty*, August 1952, 22–23, 62–63.

20 Carter, *This Story Fierce and Tender*, frontispiece.

21 Johnston, *A Great Restlessness*, 225–26.

22 LAC, RG146, ATIP request A-2006-00101, RCMP excerpt of the *Telegram*, 24 March 1952, 92.

23 VOKS 5:3:31:206–11, biography and itinerary of Carter trip to USSR, April 1950; LAC, RG146, ATIP request A-2006-00101, translation of Vladimirov and Erde, "Exposed Provocation," *Ogonyok* 37 (1952): 125; VOKS 6:41:5–8, K. Perevoschikov, review of Carter's 1943 biography of Stalin, 13 April 1953.

24 Carter, *This Story Fierce and Tender*, 46.

25 Ibid., 541.

26 Ibid., 471–73.

27 Ibid., 472–94.

28 Louis Kon to "Dyson and Lina—Lina and Dyson," 3 April 1944, Louis and Irene Kon Collection, Osler Library, McGill University, P162, Folder 1.19. In his "autobiography," Carter appears to refer to this woman as "Eleanor." Carter, *This Story Fierce and Tender*, 555–56.

29 Sally Nielsen, correspondence with Jennifer Anderson, 23 June 2008.

30 In 1957, Charlotte took over the editorial work for *Northern Neighbors* since Dyson was in the hospital. VOKS 6:55:150–51, A. Tovstogan to G. Ioanisyan, 31 May 1957. Previously, much of this work might have been done by Jim Leech and Ted Baxter, CSFS secretaries, but both left the CSFS in 1956 following the announcement of the Twentieth Party Congress speech by Nikita Khrushchev and other international events of that year.

31 VOKS, 6:47:76, D. Carter to K. Perevoschikov, 20 October 1954; VOKS 6:50:111, Carter to Perevoschikov, 12 November 1954.

32 Michael Lucas, interview with the author, 27 July 2006.

33 Sally (Thelma) Nielsen, interview with the author, 28 November 2006.

34 LAC, RG146, ATIP request A-2006-00091, RCMP report "The Canadian-Soviet Friendship Society, February 1951 to March 1953. Addendum to Brief Ending February 1951," biographical notes, dated 15 April 1953, 121.

35 Ibid.

36 Johnston, *A Great Restlessness*, 47. Irja Paul was married to Bob Paul before she became Carter's partner.

37 LAC, RG146, ATIP request A-2006-00091, 121.

38 Ibid.

39 Ibid.

40 Johnston, *A Great Restlessness*, 231.

41 Ibid., 230–31.

42 Interviews conducted by Faith Johnston with Norman Penner and William Kashtan in 1988, cited in ibid., 229.

43 Ibid.

44 Ibid., 262.

45 Ibid.

46 LAC, RG146, ATIP request A-2006-00091, RCMP report "The Canadian-Soviet Friendship Society, February 1951 to March 1953. Addendum to Brief Ending February 1951," biographical notes, dated 15 April 1953, 118–20.

47 Gérard Fortin and Boyce Richardson give some details on Lafond's political activities in *Life of the Party* (Montreal: Véhicule Press, 1984), 200–04, 219, 235.

48 J.E. (Ted) Baxter, interview with the author, 8 December 2006. Nielsen resigned from the CSFS in the summer of 1953, in 1955 went to England for some time, and in 1957 went to China. She died in 1980 in China. Johnston, *A Great Restlessness*, 231–37.

49 VOKS 6:45:109–14, Ted Baxter, text of talk given on 6 November 1953.

50 Baxter, interview.

51 Ibid.

52 Ibid.

53 Ibid.

54 Ibid.

55 Ibid.

56 Ibid.

57 VOKS 6:49:232–37, list of *VOKS Bulletin* subscribers, August 1956.

58 Baxter, interview.

59 The list includes twenty-nine names in Ontario, six in Saskatchewan, five in British Columbia, only three in Quebec, two each in Alberta and Nova Scotia, one each in Manitoba, New Brunswick, and Newfoundland, and none in Prince Edward Island. VOKS 6:1:36:23, "National Council of the C.-S.F.S.," 1951. Names on this list include those of prominent members of other left-wing organizations, including Emil and Fagel Gartner, John Weir, Harry Colegate, Mary Kardash, and Mary Popoff. John Boyd, whose name appears on this list, said that he was never, in fact, a CSFS member. John Boyd, comments on the manuscript by Jennifer Anderson, April 2008.

60 VOKS 6:1:36:53–54, Dorise Nielsen, "Report on Organization," CSFS convention, 26 January 1952. She noted that 4,500 people had been reached in British Columbia,

900–1,000 in Alberta, 200 in Saskatchewan, 7,000 in Manitoba, and about 4,500 in Ontario. The Padlock Law (or La loi du cadenas in French), in effect under the leadership of Premier Maurice Duplessis, was so called because it allowed for owners to be locked out of their properties if material that promoted communism was found there. The material was confiscated, and individuals could serve time in jail. It was actually called the Act to Protect the Province against Communistic Propaganda and was struck down by the Supreme Court of Canada in 1957. Jacques Rouillard, *Le syndicalisme québécois : Deux siecles d'histoire* (Montréal: Éditions Boréal, 2004), 68.

61 Besides Major Lafond, R. McCutcheon and Irving Meyers are listed as members in Quebec. Oddly, Louis Kon is not listed as a member even though he was clearly active in Montreal on behalf of the CSFS.

Chapter 2: Setting the Stage: The Soviet Friendship Phenomenon, 1917–49

1 J.L. Black, *Canada in the Soviet Mirror: Ideology and Perception in Soviet Foreign Affairs, 1917–1991* (Ottawa: Carleton University Press, 1998).

2 On Canadian fears of communism being imported together with immigrants from Eastern Europe, and the particular "fear of aliens" engendered by the Winnipeg General Strike, see Donald H. Avery, *Reluctant Host: Canada's Response to Immigrant Workers, 1896–1994* (Toronto: McClelland and Stewart, 1995), especially 75–79.

3 Black, *Canada in the Soviet Mirror*, 42. Immigrants were selected based upon their abilities to work in agriculture, and Russian Jews were discouraged from coming to Canada because it was thought that they would be too urban. Although some immigrants from Russia prior to 1917 had socialist sensibilities, many of those who arrived immediately following the revolution were White Army refugees. Their perceptions of the Bolshevik government would clash. The Doukhobor belief system was essentially pacifist but also emphasized communal living and farming. Later the Soviets would attempt to convince Doukhobors and other left-wing ethnic groups to return to the homeland. All of these ideological differences brought the conflict from Russia closer to home for many Canadians. On the Return to the Homeland campaign, see Glenna Roberts and Serge Cipko, *One-Way Ticket: The Soviet Return-to-the-Homeland Campaign, 1955–1960* (Manotick, ON: Penumbra Press, 2008).

4 Black, *Canada in the Soviet Mirror*, 37–46, 69–70; CRCR collection, previously at University Partnership Centre, Georgian College, Barrie, ON, now at Cameron Library, University of Alberta, copied from GARF, fonds 5283, opis 3, delo 74, 82–85.

5 These included famine relief committees run by Canadian communist groups, the more mainstream Canadian Committee for Russian Relief, and Save the Children Fund, also headed by Herbert Mackie. See A. Balawyder, "Canada and the Famine in Soviet Russia and the Ukraine (1921–23)," *New Review*, December 1964, 1–10; Black, *Canada in the Soviet Mirror*, 44–46.

6 Black, *Canada in the Soviet Mirror*, 44–45.

7 GARF, fonds 5283, opis 3, delo 74, 82–85, report prepared by I. Amdur, head, VOKS British Countries division, 30 December 1930.

8 LAC, RG146, ATIP request A-2006-00091, RCMP "Brief: The Canadian Soviet Friendship Society," February 1951, attached to RCMP report dated April 1953, 126.

9 LAC, RG146, ATIP request A-2006-00124, RCMP report "The National Council for Canadian Soviet Friendship—Origin and Growth," dated 1945 by hand in the margin, 179. Vadim Kukushkin also referred to this society and its influence

in convincing Ukrainians in Canada to return to the USSR in the 1920s. Vadim Kukushkin, "Back in the USSR," *Beaver* 86, 4 (2006): 33–36.

10 This event took place in a hall on West 27th Street, New York City, on 24 January 1999. See Angelo D'Angelo, "80th Anniversary of Hands off Russia Committee," *Northstar Compass* (journal of the International Council for Friendship and Solidarity with Soviet People, editor Michael Lucas, based in Toronto), http://www.northstarcompass.org/usfsp/anniv.htm. The invitation to this event also appeared in the *Northstar Compass*, http://www.northstarcompass.org/usfsp/flyer98.htm.

11 Information in this paragraph comes from Irene Kon, "Remembering Louis Kon," 7 November 1983, Louis and Irene Kon Collection, Osler Library, McGill University, P162, Folder 1.9.

12 Kon was the author of four of the twelve papers in the commission's seventy-seven-page final report, published in 1919. Along with J.S. Dennis, chairman, Kon signed the report as secretary. Canada, Department of Trade and Commerce, *Report of the Canadian Economic Commission (Siberia)* (Ottawa: Labroquerie Taché, 1919).

13 Letter written by L.D. Wilgress, Canadian Trade Commissioner to Royal North-West Mounted Police (RNWMP), 7 May 1919, obtained through an ATIP request by Irene Kon and released into the Louis and Irene Kon Collection, Osler Library, McGill University, P162, Folder 1.1.

14 RNWMP reports, 22 August 1919, 30 August 1919, 5 September 1919, 9 September 1919, all found in the Louis and Irene Kon Collection, Osler Library, McGill University, P162, Folder 1.1.

15 Letter from the Civil Service Commission to the Royal North-West Mounted Police, 29 August 1919, Louis and Irene Kon Collection, Osler Library, McGill University, P162, Folder 1.1.

16 Irene Kon, "Remembering Louis Kon," 7 November 1983, Louis and Irene Kon Collection, Osler Library, McGill University, P162, Folder 1.9.

17 "RCMP Weekly Summary Reports on Revolutionary Organizations and Agitators in Canada," no. 772, 11 September 1935, and no. 778, 23 October 1935, in *The R.C.M.P. Security Bulletins: The Depression Years, pt. II, 1935*, ed. Gregory S. Kealey and Reginald Whitaker (St. John's: Canadian Committee on Labour History, 1993), 485, 551.

18 Ibid., 344, 485.

19 Irene Kon said that Norman Bethune did not at first accept communism, but after Louis Kon lent him some books and made arrangements for him to attend a medical conference in Moscow in 1935 he changed his mind. Interestingly, though Frederick Banting travelled with Bethune on this trip to the USSR, he came back to Canada opposed to the Soviet Union. Irene Kon to Professors Yang and Chen, China, 15 June 1986, Louis and Irene Kon Collection, Osler Library, McGill University, P162, Folder 1.5; Black, *Canada in the Soviet Mirror*, 102.

20 Louis Kon to Dyson Carter, 7 November 1943, Louis and Irene Kon Collection, Osler Library, McGill University, P162, Folder 1.9.

21 Letter of sympathy from Louis Kon to the National Council, Canadian-Soviet Friendship Society, 6 March 1953, Louis and Irene Kon Collection, Osler Library, McGill University, P162, Folder 1.19.

22 Letter from Tim Buck to Louis Kon on LPP letterhead, 28 September 1955, wishing him to get well soon, Louis and Irene Kon Collection, Osler Library, McGill University, P162, Folder 1.9.

23 Irene Kon, "Remembering Louis Kon," 7 November 1983, Louis and Irene Kon Collection, Osler Library, McGill University, P162, Folder 1.9.

24 Libbie Park, "Bethune as I Knew Him," in *Bethune: The Montreal Years: An Informal Portrait*, ed. Wendell MacLeod, Libbie Park, and Stanley Ryerson (Toronto: James Lorimer and Company Publishers, 1978), 78.

25 Irene Kon to Louis Kon, 9 July 1937 or 1938, Louis and Irene Kon Collection, Osler Library, McGill University, P162, Folder 1.4. Park has written that Kon was "never, as far as I knew, a member of the Communist Party of Canada," but he was well known by friends and newspaper editors for his pro-Soviet views. Park, "Bethune as I Knew Him," 77. According to the RCMP, Kon arranged for the Montreal Stadium to be used for a CPC meeting in 1935 and attended a CPC election rally, but more often he spoke and organized events for more (at least officially) non-partisan organizations such as the Friends of the Soviet Union, the YMCA, and a tenants' league in Montreal. Kealey and Whitaker, *The R.C.M.P. Security Bulletins: The Depression Years, pt. I, 1933–1934*, 102, 146; *pt. II, 1935*, 6, 230, 344, 551.

26 For the program of meetings at the 1935 conference, see "Report of Proceedings, National Conference of Friendship with the USSR, June 28–29–30, 1935, Odd Fellows' Temple, Toronto, issued by Friends of the Soviet Union, Canadian Section," LAC, RG146, ATIP request A-2006-00091, 54–96. A 1965 memorandum on the RCMP file says that the 1935 FSU program, together with material on the Young Communist League, Canadian Youth Congress, Civil Rights Union, Workers Unity League, and fascist organizations in Canada, was seized from the Canadian Labor Defense League in 1940. LAC, RG146, ATIP request A-2006-00091, 51–52.

27 LAC, RG146, ATIP request A-2006-00091, 56.

28 Ibid., 58.

29 Park, "Bethune as I Knew Him," 78.

30 Ibid.

31 LAC, RG146, ATIP request A-2006-00091, 65.

32 A rally in Maple Leaf Gardens was held in 1943 on the second anniversary of the Soviet entry as an ally into the Second World War.

33 Kealey and Whitaker, *The R.C.M.P. Security Bulletins: The Depression Years, pt. I, 1933–1934*, 146–47.

34 LAC, RG146, ATIP request A-2006-00091, 66.

35 Ibid., 67.

36 Ibid., 59.

37 Ibid., 61.

38 Ibid., 65.

39 Black, *Canada in the Soviet Mirror*, 102–04.

40 LAC, RG146, ATIP request A-2006-00091, 68.

41 LAC, RG146, ATIP request A-2006-00091, 78.

42 Ibid.

43 Ibid.

44 Dyson Carter and Charlotte Carter, *We Saw Socialism* (Toronto: CSFS, 1951).

45 LAC, RG146, ATIP request A-2006-00091, "Conference Resolution on the Journal 'Soviet Russia To-Day,'" 95.

46 *Soviet Russia Today* 1, 1 (1933): 15.

47 Alexei Stakhanov, "How We Work," *Soviet Russia Today* 3, 27 (1936): 3, 13.

48 "The Truth about the Soviet Union," *Soviet Russia Today* 1, 1 (1933): 16.

49 LAC, RG146, ATIP request A-2006-00091, "Conference Resolution on the Journal 'Soviet Russia To-Day,'" 95.

50 Ibid., 92, 93.

51 Ibid., 94.

52 Black, *Canada in the Soviet Mirror*, 104.

53 On the attraction of reading groups concerned with the USSR and concern over the Depression, see, for example, Duncan McDowall, "The Trial and Tribulations of Miss Agatha Chapman: Statistics in a Cold War Climate," *Queen's Quarterly* 114, 3 (2007): 357–69.

54 The Communist Party of Canada, banned in 1941, called itself the Labor-Progressive Party from 1941 to 1959.

55 LAC, RG146, ATIP request A-2006-00124, RCMP brief "National Council for Canadian Soviet Friendship—Origin and Growth," handwritten date in margin, 8 February 1945, 179.

56 Joan Beaumont, *Comrades in Arms: British Aid to Russia, 1941–1945* (London: Davis-Poynter, 1980), 97.

57 BBC, *Mindbenders: Propaganda with Facts: Our Soviet Friends*, 1980.

58 LAC, RG146, ATIP request A-2006-00124, RCMP report "The National Council for Canadian Soviet Friendship—Origin and Growth," dated 1945 by hand in the margin, 179–90. This report also appears in Gregory S. Kealey and Reginald Whitaker, eds., *R.C.M.P. Security Bulletins: The War Series, pt. 2, 1942–1945* (St. John's: Canadian Committee on Labour History, 1993), 251–59.

59 Ibid.

60 Joseph H. Davies, *Mission to Moscow* (New York: Simon and Schuster, 1941).

61 LAC, RG146, ATIP request A-2006-00124, RCMP report "The National Council for Canadian Soviet Friendship—Origin and Growth," dated 1945 by hand in the margin, 179–90.

62 Ibid.

63 Kealey and Whitaker, *The R.C.M.P. Security Bulletins: The War Series, pt. 2, 1942–1945*, 18.

64 Dyson Carter to Louis Kon, 28 November 1942, Louis and Irene Kon Collection, Osler Library, McGill University, P162, Folder 1.19.

65 Ibid.

66 LAC, RG25, file 2727-V-40, vols. 2923, 4186, 2923, references *passim*.

67 LAC, RG25, file 2727-V-40.1, vol. 2923, Malcolm Ross to N.A. Robertson, 13 July 1943.

68 LAC, RG25, file 2727-V-40.2, vol. 2923, D. Wilgress to Secretary of State for External Affairs, 16 October 1944, with attached speeches made at VOKS, 13 October 1944. The art was donated to Leningrad in honour of its defence under Nazi siege, and some dealt directly with this theme.

69 Public support for this organization during the war was likely a key reason that post-1949 the CSFS chose to keep the National Council moniker for its first few years.

70 LAC, RG146, ATIP request A-2006-00124, RCMP memorandum from Officer J. Leopold to the Deputy Commissioner, 7 August 1943, 26.

71 LAC, RG146, ATIP request A-2006-00124, RCMP report "The National Council for Canadian Soviet Friendship—Origin and Growth," dated 1945 by hand in the margin, 179–90.

72 A CSFS and *News-Facts about the USSR* leaflet, undated but probably from 1950, in the RCMP collection, "Questions People Ask about the Canadian-Soviet Friendship Society," LAC, RG146, ATIP request A-2006-00091, 53.

73 The reporting officer wrote that the "exact year [of the list was] unknown, but probably 1943." LAC, RG146, ATIP request A-2006-00097, RCMP report, Toronto Special Section, 10 January 1951, 97.

74 Reference here to the Toronto lawyer who defended members of the Communist Party and other leftists before the courts in the 1930s and 1940s. Laurel Sefton MacDowell, *Renegade Lawyer: The Life of J.L. Cohen* (Toronto: University of Toronto Press, 2001).

75 The RCMP noted that until June 1944 Flavelle was chair of the National Council of the Civil Liberties Association, which had supported lifting the ban on the CPC-LPP and returning property confiscated from the left-wing Ukrainian Labour Farmer Temple Association. This apparently made the RCMP suspicious of Flavelle. Kealey and Whitaker, *R.C.M.P. Security Bulletins: The War Series, pt. 2, 1942–1945*, 255.

76 LAC, RG146, ATIP request A-2006-00097, list "National Executive," attached to the RCMP report, Toronto Special Section, 10 January 1951, 99–101.

77 John Grierson, called the "father of the documentary film," was still serving as the first film commissioner of the National Film Board.

78 Nat Taylor, Canadian film mogul, was the first in the world to open a multiplex cinema in 1957. It was the Elgin, in Ottawa.

79 Allan had recently moved to Toronto to serve as head of radio drama at the main office of the CBC.

80 The Allen family had the controlling interest in the Hollywood production company Columbia Pictures. Herbert Allen's address is listed c/o Columbia Pictures, Hermant Building, Toronto, the same address given by Nat Taylor.

81 LAC, RG146, ATIP request A-2006-00097, List "Arts Committee," attached to RCMP report, Toronto Special Section, 10 January 1951, 102. Next to the names of some members of the committee is the handwritten word *films*, denoting their particular interest.

82 LAC, RG146, ATIP request A-200-600097, List "Science Committee," attached to RCMP report, Toronto Special Section, 10 January 1951, 103.

83 LAC, RG146, ATIP request A-2006-00097, List "Educational Committee," attached to RCMP report, Toronto Special Section, 10 January 1951, 104.

84 LAC, RG146, ATIP request A-2006-00097, List "National Agricultural Committee," attached to RCMP report, Toronto Special Section, 10 January 1951, 106.

85 LAC, RG146, ATIP request A-2006-00097, List "National Labor Committee Elected at 1943 Congress of Canadian-Soviet Friendship," attached to RCMP report, Toronto Special Section, 10 January 1951, 107.

86 LAC, RG146, ATIP request A-2006-00097, RCMP report, Toronto Special Section, 10 January 1951, 97.

87 Beaumont has noted that in Britain thousands of ordinary citizens were also turning out for rallies and contributing financially to support the USSR in the war. Beaumont, *Comrades in Arms*, 97–99.

88 LAC, RG146, ATIP request A-2006-00097, "Abstracts of Addresses Delivered at Congress for Canadian-Soviet Friendship, November 12, 13 and 14, 1943, Toronto," "Address by Leonard W. Brockington at Maple Leaf Gardens, Sunday Nov. 14, 1943," 170.

89 Ibid., 172. The Russian spelling of the Ukrainian cities (e.g., Kharkov not Kharkiv) was used in this report and at the time in most Soviet references.

90 LAC, RG146, ATIP request A-2006-00097, "Abstracts of Addresses Delivered at Congress for Canadian-Soviet Friendship, November 12, 13 and 14, 1943, Toronto," "Address by Edgar Snow, Maple Leaf Gardens, Sunday, November 14, 1943," 182. Snow had published *Red Star over China* in 1937, bringing some of the earliest and most in-depth accounts of the Chinese Red Army and Mao Zedong to the West.

91 Dyson Carter, *Stalin's Life: At Last the True Story* (Winnipeg: Contemporary Publishers, 1943).

92 "We Apologize to Dyson Carter," letter from Dyson Carter to the editor of *Canadian Tribune*, and "Ed. Note," Louis and Irene Kon Collection, Osler Library, McGill University, P162, Folder 1.19.

93 Louis Kon to Dyson Carter, 7 November 1943, Louis and Irene Kon Collection, Osler Library, McGill University, P162, Folder 1.19.

94 LAC, RG146, ATIP request A-2006-00097, "National Council for Canadian-Soviet Friendship, Proceedings of National Executive Meeting, Thursday, January 6, 1944, 4:30–6:00 p.m.," attached to RCMP report, Toronto Special Section, 10 January 1951, 109–11.

95 Ibid., 110.

96 Ibid., 109–11.

97 LAC, RG146, ATIP request A-2006-00097, "Minutes of the National Council for Canadian-Soviet Friendship Executive Meeting—Friday, February 18, 1944 in the Conference Room of the Star Bld., 80 King St. W., Toronto," attached to RCMP report, Toronto Special Section, 10 January 1951, 113.

98 Ibid., 113–14.

99 *Council Bulletin* 1, 8 (1944), published by the National Council for Canadian-Soviet Friendship, in ibid., 118–22.

100 Ibid., 119.

101 Ibid., 121.

102 LAC, RG146, ATIP request A-2006-00097, "Meeting of Agricultural Committee, National Council for Canadian-Soviet Friendship," 10 August 1944, King Edward Hotel, Toronto, 124.

103 LAC, RG146, ATIP request A-2006-00097, "Meeting of the Agricultural Committee, National Council for Canadian-Soviet Friendship, Held at 409 Huron Street, Toronto, Oct. 30, 1944," 128.

104 Ibid.; also LAC, RG146, ATIP request A-2006-00097, "Minutes of the National Executive Meeting, Held on Monday, October 2, 1944," 131–34.

105 Ibid., 128, "Meeting of the Agricultural Committee."

106 LAC, RG146, ATIP request A-2006-00097, minutes of the meeting "Congress Committee—August 24, 1944," 143.

107 LAC, RG146, ATIP request A-2006-00097, "Dear Friends" letter accompanying invitation to the Second Annual Congress for Canadian-Soviet Friendship, 27 October 1944, signed by Margaret Cooke, Congress Manager, and attached list "Patrons," 146–47.

108 "Programme, Second Annual Congress for Canadian-Soviet Friendship, Friday, Saturday, and Sunday, Nov. 17, 18, 19, 1944," article in press "Friendship Congress Film Warns against Soft Peace," copied from the private collection of Larissa Stavroff, Toronto.

109 Ibid.

110 LAC, RG146, ATIP request A-2006-00124, RCMP report, Intelligence Branch, Toronto, dated 21 November 1944, 201–02.

111 R.H. Davies, *Canada and Russia: Neighbors and Friends* (Toronto: Progress Books, 1944).

112 Wallace favoured trade with the USSR and resigned from Truman's cabinet in 1946 over disagreements on development of the Cold War military apparatus. He ran unsuccessfully for president as a Progressive Party candidate in 1948. Wallace House Foundation, "The Wallace Family," http://www.wallace.org/wallacefamily.html.

113 "Programme, Second Annual Congress for Canadian-Soviet Friendship, Friday, Saturday, and Sunday, Nov. 17, 18, 19, 1944," copied from the private collection of Larissa Stavroff, Toronto.

114 See, for example, the editorial "Enriching Political and Social Life," *Toronto Star*, 20 November 1944, 6, which said that the congress "has performed a signal public service" in bringing news of the USSR to Canada. The Nazi invasion of the USSR had been thwarted. "Thus the rest of the world will gain the benefit of the vast and humanitarian experiments of the Soviet Union, which has celebrated its 27th anniversary this month, and will be able voluntarily to profit from its achievements and its high social purposes without having to ward off attempts by Russia itself to force its political institutions and system on other lands. The world as a whole, its political and social life, will be enriched by the Russian accomplishments."

115 Ibid. Zabotin was recalled to Moscow after the Gouzenko revelations came to light in 1946 and identified him as the main contact for Canadians who passed along sensitive information to the Soviet Embassy.

116 "War Correspondent with Russian Friends" and "Russia Saved Mankind at Stalingrad—Snow," *Globe and Mail*, November 1944 (no precise date noted), from the private collection of Larissa Stavroff, Toronto.

117 Articles from the *Globe and Mail* entitled "Lesson Seen in Soviet Aims," "Calls U.S.S.R. Pioneer in Free Education," and "Soviet Shines in Medicine," all held in the private collection of Larissa Stavroff, Toronto.

118 "The Complete Letters of E.J. Pratt: A Hypertext Edition," E.J. Pratt to Carl F. Klinck, 7 January 1946, and attached notes, http://www.trentu.ca/faculty/pratt/letters/frletters.html. In this letter, Pratt mentions that he hosted Soviet Embassy personnel at his home in Toronto in 1944 and 1945 and suggested that his biography (Carl F. Klinck and H.W. Wells, *Edwin J. Pratt: The Man and His Poetry* [Toronto: Ryerson, 1947]) include "a paragraph or two" about his involvement with the CSFS.

119 "Board of Control Approves Friendship for Russia Week," *Toronto Daily Star*, 19 July 1945, in LAC, RG146, ATIP request A-2006-00124, 165.

120 "Let Ottawa Act, Conant Ordered, Inquiry Is Told," *Toronto Daily Star*, 5 July 1945, 2. Also in Libbie and Frank Park fonds, LAC, MG31K9, vol. 8, file "Gestapo Affair, 1945." For more on this scandal and the Lebel Commission inquiry, see the *Toronto Star*, *Globe and Mail*, *Toronto Telegram*, and other newspapers late June–July 1945. Clippings of these articles can also be found in the Park fonds.

121 LAC, RG146, ATIP request A-2006-00124, "Memorandum to Inspector Parsons re: National Council for Canadian Soviet Friendship, Toronto, Ontario," 15 December 1945, 112–13.

122 "Groundless Story," *Ottawa Citizen*, 6 July 1945, clipping in Libbie and Frank Park fonds, LAC, MG31K9, vol. 8, file "Gestapo Affair, 1945."

123 LAC, RG146, ATIP request A-2006-00124, "Memorandum for File Re: National Council for Canadian Soviet Friendship, Toronto, Ontario," RCMP report dated 11 October 1945, 154. The RCMP got this information from a letter sent out by the Toronto Council for Canadian-Soviet Friendship on 24 September 1945 advertising a Soviet film available via the firm Artkino. This letter is attached to the RCMP report, ibid., 160.

124 LAC, RG146, ATIP request A-2006-00124, "Memorandum for Intelligence Bulletin re: Toronto Council for Canadian-Soviet Friendship," handwritten date in margin 24 October 1945, RCMP report quoting newsletter sent out by the Toronto Council for Canadian-Soviet Friendship, 152.

125 LAC, RG146, ATIP request A-2006-00124, "National Council for Canadian Soviet Friendship re: Memorandum to Inspector Leopold, Ukrainian-Canadian Association, Toronto, Ontario," RCMP report dated 12 June 1945, 163.

126 LAC, RG146, ATIP request A-2006-00124, RCMP report "C.P. Activities in National Council for Canadian-Soviet Friendship," Toronto Special Section, 26 November 1945, 116.

127 LAC, RG146, ATIP request A-2006-00124, program of the Congress on Canadian-Soviet Friendship, Royal York Hotel, Toronto, November 23, 24, 25, 1945, attached to RCMP report dated November 1945, 115.

128 Louis Kon to Dyson Carter, 21 December 1945, Louis and Irene Kon Collection, Osler Library, McGill University, P162, Folder 1.19.

129 Carter made this declaration in an open letter to party leader Tim Buck entitled "Dyson Carter Explains: Why I've Joined the LPP," published in *Canadian Tribune* on 15 December 1945.

130 Louis Kon to Dyson Carter, 21 December 1945, Louis and Irene Kon Collection, Osler Library, McGill University, P162, Folder 1.19.

131 See J.L. Black and Martin Rudner, eds., *The Gouzenko Affair: Canada and the Beginnings of Cold War Counter-Espionage* (Manotick, ON: Penumbra Press, 2006); Amy Knight, *How the Cold War Began: The Gouzenko Affair and the Hunt for Soviet Spies* (Toronto: McClelland and Stewart, 2005); I.A. Ageeva, "Kanada i nachalo kholodnoi voinyi: Delo Gouzenko v Sovetsko-Kanadskix otnoshenyax [Canada and the Start of the Cold War: The Gouzenko Affair in Soviet-Canadian Relations]," in *Kholodnaia Voina, 1945–1963* [*The Cold War, 1945–1963*], ed. N.I. Yegorova and A.O. Chubaryan (Moscow: Olma-Press, 2003), 369-405; Black, *Canada in the Soviet Mirror*, 171–72; Merrily Weisbord, *The Strangest Dream: Canada's Communists, the Spy Trials, and the Cold War* (Montreal: Véhicule Press, 1994), 145; Reg Whitaker and Gary Marcuse, *Cold War Canada: The Making of a National Insecurity State, 1945–1957* (Toronto: University of Toronto Press, 1994); Len Scher, ed., *The Un-*

Canadians: True Stories from the Blacklist Era (Toronto: Lester Publishing, 1992); J.L. Granatstein and David Stafford, *Spy Wars: Espionage and Canada from Gouzenko to Glasnost* (Toronto: Key Porter Books, 1990); J.L. Black, "Canada and the Soviet Union in 1945: The View from Moscow," in *Uncertain Horizons: Canadians and Their World in 1945*, ed. Greg Donaghy (Ottawa: Canadian Committee for the History of the Second World War, 1996), 285–302; J.L. Black and Norman Hillmer, eds., *Nearly Neighbours: Canada and the Soviet Union from Cold War to Détente and Beyond* (Kingston: Ronald P. Frye and Company, 1988); and Robert Bothwell and J.L. Granatstein, eds., *The Gouzenko Transcripts: The Evidence Presented to the Kellock-Taschereau Royal Commission of 1946* (Ottawa: Deneau Publishers, 1982).

132 The full title of the report was *The Report of the Royal Commission to Investigate the Facts Relating to and the Circumstances Surrounding the Communication by Public Officials and Other Persons in Positions of Trust of Secret and Confidential Information to Agents of a Foreign Power*, Honourable Mr. Justice Robert Taschereau and Honourable Mr. Justice R.L. Kellock, Commissioners (Ottawa: Edmond Cloutier, 1946).

133 See Weisbord, *The Strangest Dream*; June Callwood, *Emma* (Toronto: Stoddart, 1984); Scher, *The Un-Canadians*; and McDowall, "The Trial and Tribulations of Miss Agatha Chapman."

134 Denis Smith, *Diplomacy of Fear: Canada and the Cold War, 1941–1948* (Toronto: University of Toronto Press, 1988), 5. For the similar American experience, see Elaine Tyler May, *Homeward Bound: American Families in the Cold War Era* (New York: Basic Books, 1988), and Alan Nadel, *Containment Culture: American Narratives, Postmodernism, and the Atomic Age* (Durham, NC: Duke University Press, 1995).

135 Ageeva, "Kanada i nachalo kholodnoi voinyi"; Black and Rudner, *The Gouzenko Affair*.

136 This development, the changing role of VOKS, and the reasons that Moscow thought the CSFS could present a more positive image of the USSR than the discredited LPP will be discussed in detail in subsequent chapters.

137 Soviet Ambassador G.N. Zarubin was reported to have extended an open invitation to groups of Canadian journalists, "businessmen, artists or churchmen" to visit the USSR. This was announced at an Ottawa victory meeting of the NCCSF and published in the press. LAC, RG146, ATIP request A-2006-00105, RCMP memorandum to Inspector Parsons, 17 November 1945, 95; "May See Russia," *Ottawa Journal*, n.d. 1945; "Russia Invites Canadian Visits," *Standard*, 24 November 1945, clippings in LAC, RG146, ATIP request A-2006-00105, 85, 94. The LPP and NCCSF were apparently publicizing a possible trip for summer 1946 among members and "foreign-born Canadians." Investigators across Canada were advised to stay "alert" for signs of Canadians interested in going on these tours. LAC, RG146, ATIP request A-2006-00105, RCMP "confidential" memorandum, signed by A.B. Persons, S/Inspector, Special Section, 5 December 1945, 92.

138 Invited in 1945 to tour the USSR, members of progressive groups initially showed an enthusiastic response, and the RCMP warned that "foreign groups" (i.e., progressive ethnic groups in Canada) might be inclined to go, but then no report of any such visits was recorded, and it was observed that this loss of interest might have been because of "spy trials" in 1946. LAC, RG146, ATIP request A-2006-00105, RCMP report, Prince Albert, SK, 31 May 1946, 11. Reports from RCMP branches saying that no interest was recorded are *passim* in RG146, ATIP request A-2006-00105; one report stated that interest remained high "among the Doukhobor element."

LAC, RG146, ATIP request A-2006-00105, RCMP report, Yorkton Subdivision, Kamsack Detachment, 8 February 1946, 68.

139 LAC, RG146, ATIP request A-2006-00091, RCMP "Brief—The Canadian Soviet Friendship Society," 129.

140 Ibid., 130.

141 In doing research for her book on Emma Woikin, Callwood interviewed Kay and Brough Macpherson, well acquainted with Frank Park, and others detained by the RCMP after the Gouzenko defection. The Macphersons suggested that, since Park knew the others and had participated in many of the same study groups as those detained, he might have "escaped arrest" in those worrisome days because he was in Toronto for an extended period then. LAC, MG31K24, June Callwood fonds, vol. 20, file 20-18, "Interview with Kay and Brough Macpherson, 8 November 1982."

142 Frank Park, letter to the editor, and rejoinder of the *Toronto Telegram*, 15 March 1948, in Libbie and Frank Park fonds, LAC, MG31K9, vol. 13, file 226.

143 From "Questions People Ask about the Canadian-Soviet Friendship Society," in LAC, RG146, ATIP request A-2006-00091, 102.

144 LAC, RG146, ATIP request A-2006-00091, RCMP "Brief—The Canadian Soviet Friendship Society," 130.

145 In February 1947, the National Council for Canadian-Soviet Friendship issued a newsletter entitled *Northern Neighbours*, which specifically outlined its postwar aims. The newsletter was sent to Pearson, and on an attached memo he asked "who are these people?" LAC, RG25, ATIP request A-2007-00336, 99–107, copies of *Northern Neighbours* dated 15 February 1947, addressed to Pearson and P. Heeney, Clerk of the Privy Council, and memorandum from Heeney to Pearson, 25 February 1947, with Pearson's marginal note. The title of this publication would later be taken up by Carter when he replaced the CSFS newsletter *News-Facts about the USSR* (1950–56) with a magazine dealing with similar issues called *Northern Neighbours* (1956–89).

146 LAC, RG25, ATIP request A-2007-00336, exchanges between Pearson and Leslie Roberts and related memoranda, August–September 1947, 812–28; RG25, ATIP request A-2007-00336, exchanges between Department of External Affairs and Canadian Embassy in Moscow, spring 1948, 651–73. Roberts was referred to as a "misguided fellow traveller but not repeat not so far as we know a member of the Communist party" in RG25, ATIP request A-2007-00336, telegram from Secretary of State for External Affairs to J.B.C. Watkins, Canadian Charge d'Affaires, Moscow, cipher no. 93, 22 April 1948, 672.

147 LAC, RG25, ATIP request A-2007-00336, "Memorandum for Mr. Pearson," prepared by G.G. Crean, 27 February 1947, 97–98, referring to an earlier memo by H. Wrong, 27 November 1946.

148 LAC, RG146, ATIP request A-2006-00091, RCMP "Brief—The Canadian Soviet Friendship Society," 130.

149 Ibid., 130–31. On Stefansson's activism in communist-front organizations, see Henry F. Srebrnik, "The Radical 'Second Life' of Vilhjalmur Stefansson," *Arctic* 51, 1 (1998): 58–60, http://pubs.aina.ucalgary.ca/arctic/Arctic51-1-58.pdf.

150 LAC, RG146, ATIP request A-2006-00091, RCMP "Brief—The Canadian Soviet Friendship Society," 131.

151 Igor Gouzenko, *This Was My Choice: Gouzenko's Story* (Toronto: J.M. Dent and Sons, 1948). It has been argued that this book was ghost-written by Andy O'Brien since, he says, "they wanted to jazz it up." John Sawatsky, *Gouzenko: The Untold*

Story (Toronto: Macmillan, 1984), 99. Gouzenko also wrote a Governor General's Literary Award–winning novel entitled *Fall of a Titan* (New York: Norton, 1954), and Svetlana Gouzenko published *Before Igor: Memories of My Soviet Youth* (New York: Norton, 1960).

152 Gouzenko, *This Was My Choice*, 285.

153 Ibid., 321.

154 Ibid., 323.

155 Gouzenko's wife's name was, in fact, Svetlana.

156 The continued use of this name was likely to attract broad popularity.

157 LAC, RG146, ATIP request A-2006-00091, RCMP "Brief—Canadian-Soviet Friendship Society," 131.

158 Ibid.

159 Ibid.

160 "Otchet o rabote VOKS v Kanade za 1946" [Report on the Work of VOKS in Canada in 1946], VOKS, Cold War file 2, Cameron Library, University of Alberta, 5.

161 Ibid.

162 LAC, RG146, ATIP request A-2006-00096, RCMP report "Extract re: National Council for Canadian Soviet Friendship," dated 28 February 1949, marked "By Hand" and "Secret," 133. Pearson's letter does not appear in this file, but the RCMP response begins "with reference to your letter of February 1, 1949, and your request in paragraph two for information concerning current developments in the National Council for Canadian Soviet Friendship."

163 LAC, RG146, ATIP request A-2006-00096, RCMP report, Toronto Special Section, 15 February 1949, 135–36.

164 LAC, RG146, ATIP request A-2006-00096, RCMP Toronto division, extract dated 18 November 1949 from the Lithuanian newspaper *Liaudies balsas* (People's Voice) of 11 November 1949, 107. The article said that "the Society for Canadian-*Soviet Friendship*, conducted by Dr. Endicott, asked the Canadian government to resume friendly relations with the Soviet Union. The Society also demands the recognition of the new government of China and to begin trade with it."

165 LAC, RG146, ATIP request A-2006-00096, RCMP report "Re: National Council for Canadian Soviet Friendship—Canada General," dated 4 April 1949, 129.

166 Ibid.

167 LAC, RG146, ATIP request A-2006-00096, RCMP report, Hamilton detachment, 28 March 1949, 127–28.

168 "Trade, Friendship with USSR Is Call," *Canadian Tribune*, 7 November 1949, front page. Also found in RG146, ATIP request A-2006-00096, 115.

169 The press releases are dated 11 and 17 November 1949. LAC, RG146, ATIP request A-2006-00096, 96–97.

170 The announcement appeared in *Ludove zvesti*, *Ukrainian Life*, *Canadian Jewish Weekly*, *Pacific Tribune*, and *Novo vreme*. See LAC, RG146, ATIP request A-2006-00096, 50, 105, 109, 110, 115.

171 See LAC, RG146, ATIP request A-2006-00096, 108, where RCMP officers commanding are informed of the conference on 26 November 1949 in Toronto and asked to send all relevant information. Responses are *passim* in LAC, RG146, ATIP request A-2006-00096, mostly reporting that no locals were known to be attending. In the end, most attendees were from Toronto.

172 LAC, RG146, ATIP request A-2006-00096, RCMP report, Toronto Special Branch, 9 November 1949, 112.

173 LAC, RG146, ATIP request A-2006-00096, from Dyson Carter's notes, "Speech for C.S.F. Meeting Nov 26 49," 81–94. Throughout, Carter's notes to himself show the highly choreographed enthusiasm in the speech (e.g., "PAUSE, AND SOFTLY!," "EMPHASIS," "SLOW").

174 Ibid., 82, 83.

175 Ibid., 83.

176 Jennison was listed as national secretary for the Canadian Peace Congress, "World Peace Congress," *Canadian Tribune*, 10 July 1950, in RCMP report also dated 10 July 1950, LAC, RG146, ATIP request A-2006-00096, 200.

177 LAC, RG146, ATIP request A-2006-00096, 44, 61–79.

178 "'End Cold War Madness' Canadians Want Amity," *Ukrainian Canadian*, 1 December 1949, in LAC, RG146, ATIP request A-2006-00096, 55. Reports also appeared in the *Vestnik*, *Canadian Tribune*, and *Canadian Jewish Weekly*. See LAC, RG146, ATIP request A-2006-00096, 49, 53–54.

179 From the CSFS publication "Questions People Ask about the Canadian-Soviet Friendship Society," in LAC, RG146, ATIP request A-2006-00091, 53.

180 A CSFS and *News-Facts* leaflet, undated but probably from 1950, found in the RCMP collection, from "Questions People Ask about the Canadian-Soviet Friendship Society" in RCMP files. LAC, RG-146, ATIP request A-2006-00091, 53.

181 On Nielsen's reaction to this reassignment, see Johnston, *A Great Restlessness*, 225–27.

182 VOKS 5:3:31:206–11, biography and itinerary of Dyson Carter trip to the USSR, April 1950; VOKS 6:41:5–8, K. Perevoschikov, review of Carter's 1943 biography of Stalin, 13 April 1953.

183 LAC, RG146, ATIP request A-2007-00336, RCMP Research Section report "The Canada-USSR Association," 27 March 1963, 835–37; Les Hunt, interview with the author, 2 January 2007.

Chapter 3: Institutionalizing Friendship: The All-Union Society for Cultural Relations with Foreign Countries

1 Olga Davidova Kameneva, "Cultural Rapprochement: The U.S.S.R. Society for Cultural Relations with Foreign Countries," *Pacific Affairs* 1, 5 (1928): 6.

2 This information comes from British sources, and it might not be exact. In 1928, the same source said that VOKS was linked to eleven friendship societies abroad, while Kameneva, head of VOKS, said that there were twenty such groups. LAC, RG25, vol. 7117, file 9055-40, part 3.1, document apparently prepared by UK Embassy in the USSR, examined by the Canadian Embassy to the USSR, 21 October 1955, signed by "Soviet Section F.O.R.D."

3 These activities were described in 1955 by British observers as being common to all Soviet friendship societies in contact with VOKS. LAC, RG25, vol. 7117, file 9055-40, part 3.1, 21 October 1955, signed by "Soviet Section F.O.R.D."

4 Fernand Jacquemotte, "Belgian-Soviet Friendship," *VOKS Bulletin* 9, 104 (1956): 32–34.

5 In Department of External Affairs exchanges dealing with Burdin at the time of the ambassadorial exchange negotiations, he was invariably referred to as "Bourdine

of the Soviet Embassy" or as first secretary. Although the links between VOKS and the CSFS were known to DEA officials, they might not have realized that the link was Burdin himself. In 1963, the RCMP informed the undersecretary of state for external affairs that the renamed Soviet organization did have an individual with past experience as a KGB official placed at the Soviet Embassy in Ottawa, responsible for corresponding with the Soviet friendship society in Canada. LAC, RG25, ATIP request A-2007-00336, RCMP memorandum to Undersecretary of State for External Affairs J.J. McCardle, 2 April 1963, 833. As mentioned in the previous chapter, the archive published by Vasili Mitrokhin with notes on documents from the KGB collection suggests that Burdin was a KGB operator. Christopher Andrew and Vasili Mitrokhin, *The Mitrokhin Archive: The KGB in Europe and the West* (New York: Penguin Press, 1999), 181, 220, 227–28, 532.

6 See "Vsesoyuznoe obshchestvo kul'turnoi svyazi s zagranitsei (VOKS)," in *Bolshaya sovetskaya entsiklopediya*, 3rd ed., vol. 5 (Moskva: Izdatel'stvo 'Sovetskaya Entsiklopediya,' 1971), 464. Also available in English translation as "All-Union Society for Cultural Exchange (VOKS)," in *Great Soviet Encyclopedia*, vol. 5 (New York: Macmillan, 1970). On the SSOD, see "Union of Soviet Friendship Societies and Cultural Relations with Foreign Countries," in *Great Soviet Encyclopedia*, vol. 24 (New York: Macmillan, 1979), 637, and "Public, Social, and Arts Organizations," in *Great Soviet Encyclopedia*, vol. 31 (New York: Macmillan, 1979), 538.

7 In 1928, Lev Kamenev and Leon Trotsky fell out of favour with Stalin. Kameneva was executed on Stalin's orders in 1941, a few years after her two sons and ex-husband were also executed.

8 Kameneva, "Cultural Rapprochement," 6.

9 Ibid., 7, 8.

10 This is made clear by reports on the work of VOKS, the Communist Party of Canada (called the Labor-Progressive Party from 1943 to 1959), and other Soviet interests in Canada, forwarded to the ministry and ID. Copies from the Russian State Archives are now part of the VOKS collection, Cameron Library, University of Alberta. For instance, see "Otchet o rabote VOKS v Kanade za 1946 god" (Report on the Work of VOKS in Canada from 1946), VOKS collection, Cold War Documents, from the Russian State Archives of Social and Political History, Moscow, file 2, number 6. V. Loginov sent to the Soviet Ministry of Foreign Affairs and N. Slavin, deputy director of the European Section, ID, CPSU, a report on the LPP, April 1955, VOKS 6:3:98:5–20. See also Black, "Soviet Tactics and Targets in Canada before and after the Gouzenko Defection."

11 LAC, RG25, vol. 7117, file 9055-40, part 3.1, 21 October 1955.

12 Ibid.

13 Ibid.

14 "Vsesoyuznoe obshchestvo kul'turnoi svyazi s zagranitsei (VOKS)," in *Bolshaya sovetskaya entsiklopediya*, 3rd ed., vol. 5 (Moskva: Izdatel'stvo 'Sovetskaya Entsiklopediya,' 1971), 464.

15 LAC, RG25, vol. 7117, file 9055-40, part 3.1, 21 October 1955.

16 Ibid., part 3.2, memorandum from the Canadian Embassy in the USSR, "USSR Establishes New Cultural Relations Committee," n.d. 1957, marked "Canadian Eyes Only—Secret."

17 For the suspension of these planned agreements, and the reconsideration of this suspension, see "Memorandum from Under-Secretary of State for External

Affairs [Jules Léger] to Secretary of State for External Affairs [L.B. Pearson]," 20 December 1956, "Exchange of Visits with the Soviet Union," marked secret, no. 518, DEA/12230–40; and "Memorandum from Under-Secretary of State for External Affairs to Secretary of State for External Affairs," 17 April 1957, "Exchange of Visits with the U.S.S.R. and the Satellites," no. 519, DEA/12230–40; both in *Documents on Canadian External Relations* (hereafter *DCER*), vol. 23, 1956–57, part 2, ed. Greg Donaghy (Ottawa: Foreign Affairs and International Trade Canada, 2002), 845–48.

18 Not to be confused with VOKS, officially a non-governmental organization, on 21 May 1957 a State Committee for Cultural Relations with Foreign Countries was established, led by former deputy director of *Pravda*, Yury Zhukhov, reporting to the Soviet Ministry of Culture. Canadian diplomats argued that the establishment of this committee, which preceded the reorganization of VOKS, and subsequently the CSFS in Canada, was "the most recent indication of Moscow's desire to break out of the isolation imposed by its actions in Hungary and the Suez Crisis. The USSR has been conducting a vigorous campaign to restore contacts at all levels with the West." LAC, RG25, vol. 7117, file 9055-40, part 3.2, memorandum from the Canadian Embassy in the USSR, "USSR Establishes New Cultural Relations Committee," n.d. 1957. This campaign might also have been related to a desire to signal change as a result of the Twentieth Party Congress, which took place in 1956 and in which Khrushchev broke with the past actions of Stalin. The reorganization of VOKS in 1958 and the CSFS in 1960 will be discussed further below.

19 Mark Kramer, "The Role of the CPSU International Department in Soviet Foreign Relations and National Security Policy," *Soviet Studies* 42, 3 (1990): 429–46 (see, especially, 429–30).

20 Black, *Canada in the Soviet Mirror*, 295.

21 Herbert Romerstein, "History of the ID," in *The International Department of the CC CPSU under Dobrynin*, by Foreign Service Institute (Washington, DC: US Department of State, Center for the Study of Foreign Affairs, 1989), 111–38. See also J.L. Black, "Introduction," in *The Canadian Soviet Friendship Society: Useful Liaison, Harmless Dupe, or Source of Subversion? Documents from Russia Held at CRCR: Annotated with Name Index, 1945–1957*, ed. Jennifer Anderson, David Hood, and Lindsay Kent, Bibliographic Series No. 17/Occasional Paper No. 11 (Ottawa: Carleton University, Centre for Research on Canadian-Russian Relations, 2005), n.pag. This last reference is the finding aid to the VOKS collection, currently held at the Centre for Research on Canadian-Russian Relations at Georgian College, Barrie, Ontario. The collection contains copies of files from the British Countries division of VOKS, kept at the Russian State Archives.

22 Kramer, "The Role of the CPSU International Department in Soviet Foreign Relations and National Security Policy," 429–30. Carter had articles and interviews appear in both of these publications.

23 TASS is the Soviet news service—literally it means *Telegrafnoye agentstvo svazi i soobshcheniya* but it was less about telegraphs than about the distribution of information outside the USSR.

24 VOKS 6:3:97:36–47, V. Kachanov, Deputy Director of the Soviet Information Bureau in Canada, report of the mission of the Soviet Information Bureau in Canada in 1954.

25 The Sovinformburo reported in 1954 that materials that it had distributed were published in the *Canadian Tribune* and *Pacific Tribune* (LPP newspapers); *Vestnik* (Messenger, FRC newspaper); *Ukrainske zhyttia'* (Ukrainian Life), *Ukrainske slovo* (Ukrainian Word), and *Ukrainian Canadian* (AUUC newspapers); *Vapaus* (Freedom,

Finnish progressive newspaper); *Kanadai magyar munkas* (Worker, Hungarian progressive newspaper); *Liaudies balsas* (Lithuanian progressive newspaper); *Novo vreme* (New Time, Bulgarian-Macedonian); *Ludovy zvesti* (People's News, Slovenian); *Chempion* (Albanian); *Vochenblatt* (UJPO newspaper); *Kronika tygodniowa* (Weekly Chronicle, Polish); and *News-Facts about the USSR* (CSFS newsletter). Kachanov suggested ways to improve the distribution of this material. VOKS 6:3:97:37–47, Kachanov, report of the mission of the Soviet Information Bureau in Canada in 1954.

26 Evidence can be found in the documents relating to VOKS and the CSFS released under the Access to Information and Privacy Act, as well as to exchanges within the Department of External Affairs, and between the DEA and RCMP, LAC, RG25.

27 See Black, *Canada in the Soviet Mirror* 179–80.

28 Ibid., 180.

29 See Ageeva, "Kanada i nachalo kholodnoi voinyi"; Black, *Canada in the Soviet Mirror*, 171–72; Weisbord, *The Strangest Dream*, 145; Whitaker and Marcuse, *Cold War Canada*; Scher, *The Un-Canadians*; Black, "Canada and the Soviet Union in 1945"; and Black and Hillmer, *Nearly Neighbours*.

30 See, for example, discussions of Soviet insecurity in Vojtech Mastny, *The Cold War and Soviet Insecurity: The Stalin Years* (New York: Oxford University Press, 1996), and Vladislav Zubok and Constantine Pleshakov, *Inside the Kremlin's Cold War: From Stalin to Khrushchev* (Cambridge, MA: Harvard University Press, 1996).

31 See, especially, Robert Mann, *The Petrov Affair: Politics and Espionage* (Sydney: Pergamon, 1987), and Aleksei P. Makarov, "Living with the KGB and GRU: A 'Clean' Diplomat Recalls His Experiences inside Soviet Embassies," in Black and Rudner, *The Gouzenko Affair*, 158–60.

32 Ageeva, "Kanada i nachalo kholodnoi voinyi."

33 Black, *Canada in the Soviet Mirror*, 180.

34 Ibid., 180–81; V.I. Lenin, *Imperialism: The Highest Stage of Capitalism*, trans. Communist Party of Britain (London: Communist Party of Britain, 1924).

35 Vladimir O. Pechatnov, "The Big Three after World War II: New Documents on Soviet Thinking about Post War Relations with the United States and Great Britain," Working Paper No. 13, 1995, Cold War International History Project, Woodrow Wilson Centre; G.F. Aleksandrov, "The Pattern of Soviet Democracy" ("O sovetskoy demokratii," speech delivered in 1946), trans. Leo Gruliow (Washington, DC: Public Affairs Press, 1948).

36 VOKS 6:3:98:5–20, V. Loginov, Adviser, Soviet Embassy in Ottawa, "Short Report on the 5th Congress of the Labor-Progressive Party of Canada and Its Post-Congress Work with the Masses," 19 March 1955. In 1961, Loginov was expelled from Canada for having attempted to pay for information from Canadians whose friendship he had cultivated. Department of External Affairs, *Canadian Weekly Bulletin*, 20 December 1961, 5.

37 VOKS 7:2:6, Belokhvostikov to Molotov, Minister of Foreign Affairs, USSR, 21 October 1948. The Roberts book was criticized in a review in the LPP newspaper *Canadian Tribune* for not being pro-Soviet enough. LAC, RG25, ATIP request A-2007-00336, Frank Williams, "Confusion, Contradiction, Mar Roberts' Reportage of 'Cold War,' *Canadian Tribune*, 8 November 1948, 628–29. In 1954, Roberts published an article criticizing McCarthy-like attitudes in Canada: "McCarthyism—It's Spreading in Canada—Now," *New Liberty* 31 (1954): 15–17, 78–83.

38 McDowall has written about the unfortunate effects of this climate on the career of national statistician Agatha Chapman, active in the wartime National Council for Canadian-Soviet Friendship. McDowall, "The Trials and Tribulations of Miss Agatha Chapman." On how Canadian communists experienced this change, see Weisbord, *The Strangest Dream*.

39 See LAC, RG25, ATIP request A-2007-00336, Mackenzie King's approved response from Pearson to Roberts's letter, 8 August 1947; memorandum to the Secretary of State for External Affairs from Escott Reid, 26 August 1947; and letters from Roberts, 4–30. Roberts had been sending memoranda on Canadian-Soviet postwar relations to Pearson, Mackenzie King, and St. Laurent.

40 Leslie Roberts, *Home from the Cold Wars* (Toronto: S.J. Saunders, 1948), 57.

41 LAC, RG25, ATIP request A-2007-00336, telegram no. 93 to Canadian Chargé d'Affaires, Moscow, from Pearson, 22 April 1948, 672.

42 LAC, RG25, ATIP request A-2007-00336, John Holmes to L.B. Pearson, 28 April 1948, 667–71.

43 Reid was assistant undersecretary of state for external affairs at this time.

44 LAC, RG25, ATIP request A-2007-00336, Escott Reid, Undersecretary of State for External Affairs, to John Holmes, 11 May 1948, 657.

45 LAC, RG25, ATIP request A-2007-00336, John Holmes to L.B. Pearson, 28 April 1948; R.M. Macdonnell, Chargé d'Affaires, Prague, to John Holmes (copied to Norman Robertson and Lester Pearson), 13 May 1948, 656, 667–71.

46 VOKS 2:2:5, "Otchet o rabote VOKS v Kanade za 1946" (Report on the Work of VOKS in Canada from 1946), appears to have been written in 1949.

47 As mentioned in Chapter 1, VOKS had maintained contact with Colonel Herbert Mackie, head of the Society for Cultural Relations with the USSR in the late 1920s, as well as Friends of the Soviet Union, in the 1930s.

48 VOKS 6:3:98:5–20, V. Loginov, Counsellor, Soviet Embassy in Ottawa, "Short Report on the 5th Congress of the Labor-Progressive Party of Canada and Its Post-Congress Work with the Masses," 19 March 1955.

49 Ibid.

50 The first letter in the VOKS collection that refers to Burdin by name is dated December 1950, and he was present at the meeting in November 1949 at which Carter was elected as president of the CSFS. Before this, requests from Canadians were addressed to N.D. Belokhvostikov, Soviet attaché. VOKS 6:35:25, 27, 28–29; LAC, RG146, ATIP request A-2006-00096, 49, 53–54. But another document places Burdin in Canada earlier in 1949. See VOKS 6:40:34–37.

51 VOKS 6:31:206–11, dated April 1950. The biography says that Carter is a member of the "kommunisticheskoi partii," even though at that time the Communist Party of Canada was using the name Labor-Progressive Party.

52 VOKS 6:33:111, V. Burdin to N. Gorshkov, 11 November 1951. Burdin had been in Canada for some time before this date, however. The VOKS records show correspondence dealing with the fact that his four-year-old son, Sergei, had been killed in a car accident in Montreal in 1949. VOKS 6:40:34–37. It is not known what Burdin was doing in Montreal at that time.

53 VOKS 6:53:12, Carter to Perevoschikov, Chief, British Countries, VOKS, Moscow, 5 December 1955.

54 VOKS 6:53:29–34a, VOKS to Central Committee of the CPSU, 1956; VOKS 6:55:122, A. Tovstogan to G. Ioanisyan, 20 June 1957.

55 Makarov, "Living with the KGB and GRU," 150–89.

56 John Holmes, "Memorandum by Assistant Under-Secretary of State for External Affairs," 29 September 1953, "Discussion with Mr. Bourdine of the Soviet Embassy," in *DCER*, vol. 19, 1953, ed. Donald Barry (Ottawa: Foreign Affairs and International Trade Canada, 1991), 1011.

57 Jules Léger, "Memorandum by Assistant Under-Secretary of State for External Affairs," 23 June 1953, marked "Secret," in *DCER*, vol. 19, 1006.

58 The USSR suggested Dmitri Sergeyvich Chuvakhin as Soviet ambassador to Canada in August 1953. Canada reciprocated in December 1953 by suggesting John Watkins as Canadian ambassador to the USSR, and the Soviets agreed in January 1954. The diplomatic rupture over the Gouzenko Affair in 1946 meant that the Soviet ambassador to Canada, G. Zarubin, did not return to Ottawa, and External Affairs transferred the Canadian ambassador to the USSR, L.D. Wilgress, to Switzerland and did not replace him. From 1946 to 1953, the embassies in the two countries were run by chargés d'affaires. In 1953, they were R.A.D. Ford in Moscow and L. Teplov in Ottawa. See correspondence in *DCER*, vol. 19, 1007, 1009, 1012, 1014. Also see Hector Mackenzie, "Canada's International Relations in the Early Cold War: The Impact and Implications of the Gouzenko Affair," in Black and Rudner, *The Gouzenko Affair*, 25.

59 Léger, "Memorandum by Assistant Under-Secretary of State for External Affairs," 1006.

60 Holmes, "Memorandum by Assistant Under-Secretary of State for External Affairs," 1011.

61 Ibid.

62 LAC, RG25, vol. 8225, file 2.2, R.A.D. Ford to External Affairs, "Meetings with Vladimir Bourdine," 12 November 1952.

63 Andrew and Mitrokhin, *The Mitrokhin Archive*, 181, 220, 227–28, 532. Boyd, as a long-time member of the CPC, an acquaintance of Carter, and active in other CPC-supported groups, had inside knowledge and agreed that Burdin and his successor, Tovstogan, were known to be with the KGB. John Boyd, comments on the manuscript by Jennifer Anderson, April 2008.

64 VOKS 6:47:18–19, V. Burdin to K. Perevoschikov, 10 August 1954.

65 Baxter, interview.

66 VOKS 6:47:143–44, V. Burdin to V. Bogatyrev, February 1953, and V. Bogatyrev to V. Yakovlev, Deputy Chief, VOKS, 30 March 1953.

67 VOKS 6:47:157, K. Perevoschikov to V. Burdin, 3 April 1954.

68 VOKS 6:40:34–37, N. Gorshkov (VOKS administration) to A. Antisishkin, Director, Moscow Crematorium, 5 April 1952; V. Burdin to A. Denisov, Chief, British Countries, VOKS, 12 April 1952; Perevoschikov to Burdin, 21 May 1952.

69 LAC, RG25, vol. 8225, file 2.2, Ford to External Affairs, 12 November 1952.

70 In February 1955, Bulganin became Soviet premier, and Khrushchev was at that time first secretary of the CPSU. In 1958, Khrushchev became leader of both party and state. VOKS 6:53:114, Dyson Carter to Svetlana Kolmakova, Secretary, British Countries, VOKS, 6 June 1956. John Boyd said that Burdin was also serving in this capacity in India as Khrushchev's translator and guard. John Boyd, comments on the manuscript by Jennifer Anderson, April 2008.

71 VOKS 6:55:120–21, 144, 175, A. Tovstogan to G. Ioanisyan, 17 May 1957; A. Tovstogan to G. Kalishyan, 18 June 1957; A. Tovstogan to G. Ioanisyan, 29 October 1957.

72 VOKS 6:49:32, A. Tovstogan to V. Yakovlev, 10 January 1956. This fire, which raged out of control despite the efforts of embassy staff to put it out themselves, resulted in a conflict with Mayor Charlotte Whitton, who insisted that the Soviet personnel allow Ottawa firefighters to enter the building. Once staff thought that as much as possible was saved from the flames, firefighters were allowed in, but it was necessary to demolish and rebuild the building. Harold Kalman and John Roaf, *Exploring Ottawa: An Architectural Guide to the Nation's Capital* (Toronto: University of Toronto Press, 1983), 72. This naturally made headlines across Canada. See, for instance, "Embassy in Ottawa Burned as Russians Impede Firemen: Documents Taken out by Carload," *Globe and Mail*, 2 January 1956, 1; and Harvey Hickey, "Russians Fought Blaze Alone as Firemen Kept out for 2 ½ Hours," *Globe and Mail*, 3 January 1956, 7.

73 LAC, RG146, ATIP request A-2006-00114, Winnipeg Security and Intelligence Section report, F.S. Spalding, Superintendent, 19 November 1958, 289–99. The RCMP also recorded an audio version of the proceedings and reported that on the stage with Tovstogan were Chester King, head of the local CSFS branch, Mary Kardash, and other CSFS members. Approximately 450 people were in attendance.

74 Unfortunately, an RCMP report dedicated to analyzing the background of Alexei Tovstogan, dated 18 November 1958, was completely blacked out by ATIP staff, so the details were unavailable to me. LAC, RG146, ATIP request A-2006-00114, 290–91. Only the title and date are visible on the document. It was signed by Superintendent F.S. Spalding on 24 November 1958 at Winnipeg.

75 VOKS 6:34:40, V. Bogatyrev to Y. Brusnichkin, Head, Soviet Culture, VOKS, 7 April 1952; VOKS 6:40:7–8, Bogatyrev to Brusnichkin, 5–6 June 1952; VOKS 6:38:129, 135, Perevoschikov-Brusnichkin-Bogatyrev, April–June 1952. These materials and requests were largely sent to VOKS by Carter.

76 VOKS 6:38:134, K. Perevoschikov to K. Chugunov, 3 May 1952; VOKS 6:49:46, I. Kulakovskaya to K. Chugunov, 8 March 1956; VOKS 6:40:153–54, memos forwarding letter from American citizen J.M. MacDonald (noting that he had tried to become a Soviet citizen in 1945–46), 30 December 1951. This correspondence dealt with Americans subscribing to Soviet magazines or asking for information on the USSR.

77 A separate chapter on this interaction follows.

78 VOKS 6:55:27–29, A. Tovstogan to V.V. Abramov, Sovexportfilm, 11 December 1956; VOKS 6:55:27–29, G. Ioanisyan to K. Litvin, UkrOKS (VOKS branch in Ukrainian SSR), 9 January 1957.

79 VOKS 6:54:2–3, A. Hill to G. Chesnokov, 1 January 1956, sending New Year's greetings and a request; Chesnokov's reply, 31 January 1956.

80 VOKS 6:47:98, K. Perevoschikov to N. Shenko, Head, Book Exchange, VOKS, 10 August 1954.

81 The correspondence among Ferneyhough, Burdin, the VOKS headquarters, and Dr. R.M. Samarin of the Institute of World Literature, Academy of Sciences, is in VOKS 6:47:4–6, 53–54, 167, 168–70; 50:108–11. Ferneyhough was a *VOKS Bulletin* subscriber. VOKS 6:47:34.

82 VOKS 6:55:19, 94–95, L. Starikov, VOKS, to G. Besedin, 26 September 1956, and Dewhurst's thank-you, referenced in A. Tovstogan to A. Vertogradov, 24 August 1956.

83 VOKS 6:54:21–23, 53, 54, 67–69, 85–90, correspondence among Mr. Burney at the Victory Bookshop in Montreal, known to stock progressive literature; D. Rome, director of the Jewish Public Library in Montreal; and VOKS, February–August 1956.

84 The FRC's request sent to the VOKS headquarters is in VOKS 6:55:60–62, A. Tovstogan to I. Kulakovskaya, 3 December 1956, forwarded (VOKS 6:55:13) by I. Kulakovskaya to A. Chikin, International Sport Ties, Committee on Physical Culture and Sport, Council of Ministers, USSR), 28 January 1957.

85 Dorland was a CSFS delegate to the USSR in 1953, and she passed Ferneyhough's MA thesis to VOKS for evaluation. VOKS 6:47:167. Correspondence between Dorland and VOKS on the theme of children's letter exchanges during the spring of 1954 is in VOKS 6:47:4–6, 10–13, 60, 161.

86 VOKS 6:55:183, A. Tovstogan to G. Ioanisyan, 25 September 1957.

87 VOKS 6:55:41–43, P. Strunnikov, Temporary Chargé d'Affaires, Soviet Embassy, Ottawa, to S. Romanovsky, Preparatory Committee for Worldwide Festival of Youth and Students, 4 February 1957.

88 VOKS 6:44:37–41, 42–49, D. Carter, March 1953; A. Yanovsky, 31 March 1953.

89 On pen pals, see VOKS 6:54:138–40; 57:28–30, 33–36, 44–46, 58–59; on requests for coins and stamps, see VOKS 6:54:51–52, 59, 128–29; 57:40–42; on requests for photos, postcards, and other souvenirs, see VOKS 6:55:24, 118–19; on requests for scientific and medical information (not including Carter's), see VOKS 6:54:43–50; 55:68–69, 57:60–62.

90 For correspondence among G. Kingsford, D. Chuvakhin, VOKS Moscow, and S. Golubovich, Acting Head, Leningrad branch of VOKS, November 1954–May 1955, see VOKS 6:48:155–56, 159–61, 192–96.

91 For correspondence among N. English, VOKS, and N. Tsitsin, Director of Main Botanical Gardens, Academy of Sciences, USSR, November–December 1956, see VOKS 6:48:7–10, 28, 34–35, 38–39, 40, 42.

92 Davies, *Canada and Russia*. He also wrote (with Andrew J. Steiger) *Soviet Asia: Democracy's First Line of Defense* (New York: Dial Press, 1942) and *This Is Our Land: Ukrainian Canadians against Hitler* (Toronto: Progress Books, 1943).

93 This exchange among Davies, VOKS, and the Ministry of Foreign Affairs of the USSR, April 1956, is in VOKS 6:54:112–18.

94 The correspondence between E.W. Mulaney and Jane Banfield of the World University Service of Canada and VOKS is in VOKS 6:57:2–4, 37.

95 These requests occur throughout the collection.

96 VOKS 6:51:51–52, K. Sidora to VOKS, July 1955; VOKS 6:47:49, K. Perevoschikov to A. Chikin, 22 October 1954, forwarding a letter from B. Freedman, Editor, *Chess Life*.

97 VOKS 6:47:114, V. Burdin to V. Bogatyrev, 25 March 1954.

98 VOKS 6:35:14–16, 30––31, 32–33, ; Samuel Gibson letter about cosmos, 29 December 1950; Mr. H.H. Jacobson to VOKS on nursery schools, 1 February 1951, reply on 13 April 1951; Mr. W. Schacter to VOKS on cinema design, 2 February 1951, reply 13 April 1951.

99 VOKS 6:32:153, D. Carter cable to K. Perevoschikov and A. Denisov, 8 April 1951.

100 VOKS 6:34:1–3, N. Gorshkov cable to D. Carter, 1952.

101 Written in May 1951, these letters and other testimonials prepared by the delegates about their experiences appear in VOKS 6:32:130–51.

102 VOKS 6:54:74–83, B.F. Tanner, Harold Bronson, Dorothy Johnson, and William Irvine letters to VOKS and responses, August–September 1956. Irvine published a book on his impressions of the USSR entitled *Live or Die with Russia* (Edmonton: self-published, 1958), in the foreword to which the USSR was hailed as "a great laboratory of social experimentation." Alexander Calhoun, "Foreword," in ibid., 3. The book was translated by V.V. Isakovich and published in Moscow as *Zhit' vmeste s Rossiyei* (Live with Russia) (Moscow: Inostrannoi izdatel'stvo literature, 1958).

103 VOKS 6:54:74–83. *New Times* was overseen by the International Department of the Central Committee of the CPSU.

104 LAC, RG25, ATIP request A-2007-00336, RCMP Research Section report, "The Canada-USSR Association," 27 March 1963, 834–45.

105 VOKS 6:57:14–19, correspondence between Otto Wobick and VOKS, December 1956–February 1957.

106 VOKS 6:57:5–7, 58:52, R.T. Lafond to "Helen" (Korolkova), February 1957, and her reply of 28 February 1957; Lafond to Perevoschikov, 19 April 1954.

107 VOKS 6:57:20, Cysz family New Year's greeting, 10 January 1957. Dorothy Johnson, who had recently visited the USSR with the CCF delegation, also sent a New Year's card to VOKS. VOKS 6:57:13–13a, Dwight and Dorothy Johnson, 2 February 1957.

108 VOKS 6:51:26–27, Louise Harvey to VOKS, 12 October 1955; G. Chesnokov to L. Kon, 13 November 1955.

109 VOKS 6:55:2, A. Tovstogan to I. Kulakovskaya, 11 December 1956.

110 VOKS 6:32:59, Carter to Denisov, 4 October 1951.

111 VOKS 6:58:23, Carter to Denisov, 24 November 1954.

112 VOKS 6:57:64–65, W.E. Ricker letter, 14 June 1957.

113 VOKS 6:32:161–62.

114 Correspondence among Denisov, Bogatyrev, Pskrebyshev, Brusnichkin (Head, Soviet Culture, VOKS), and Riggs (an American CSFS member), April–June 1952, in VOKS 6:40:3–5, 7–8. The poem appears to have been written by Riggs.

115 VOKS 6:55:138, A. Tovstogan to G. Ioanisyan, 11 July 1957.

116 Including books by Carter, *passim* in the VOKS collection, VOKS 6:55:21, 103–04, 204. Carter frequently forwarded plays and novels that he thought would interest VOKS. They will be discussed further in the chapter on the CSFS and culture.

117 VOKS 6:55:63–65, 70–77, A. Tovstogan to A. Vertogradov, 1 February 1957; A. Tovstogan to G. Ioanisyan, 22 February 1957.

118 VOKS 6:39:180, 189, K. Perevoschikov to A. Tushunov, Director, Institute of Marx-Engels-Lenin-Stalin, 7 December 1953. One brochure dealt with a speech given by Stalin in 1945 at Lviv (Lvov), Ukrainian SSR, and came from the AUUC. Others dealt with resolutions of the Comintern Congress, also held in 1945 in Lviv.

119 Correspondence between Kulakovskaya and these journals, as well as her letters to the editors who did not answer, are in VOKS 6:54:103–10, 134–37, 144–46; 57:7–12.

120 Khrushchev's declarations were not made fully public in the USSR until Gorbachev's glasnost allowed for their complete release.

121 VOKS 6:49:264–67, A. Tovstogan to A. Vertogradov, 20 September 1956. Probably, "incorrect behaviour" meant that Leech became disillusioned with the USSR over the revelations and change of policy.

122 Baxter, interview.

123 VOKS 6:49:232–37, A. Tovstogan to A. Vertogradov, 17 August 1956.

124 VOKS 6:55:150–51, A. Tovstogan to G. Ioanisyan, 31 May 1957.

125 VOKS 6:55:145, G. Ioanisyan to N. Shenko, Chief, Book Exchange, VOKS, August 1957.

126 See Kate Bader, "Let Us Be Friends!," *VOKS Bulletin* 2, 91 (1955), n.pag.; Louis Kon, "A Letter from Moscow," *VOKS Bulletin* 3, 92 (1955), 66–68. LAC has sporadic issues of the *VOKS Bulletin* in its collection and a fairly complete run of *Culture and Life* from 1985 to 1990. LAC is currently unable to locate issues of *Culture and Life* from 1957 to 1984.

127 VOKS 6:53:11, I. Kulakovskaya to D. Carter, 17 November 1956.

128 VOKS 6:55:199–202, A. Tovstogan, "Notes on Interview with Director of Canadian Firm 'International Artists,' Walter Homburger," 28 March 1957.

129 VOKS 6:55:199–202.

130 "Memorandum from Under-Secretary of State for External Affairs to Secretary of State for External Affairs," 17 April 1957, "Exchange of Visits with the U.S.S.R. and the Satellites," no. 519, DEA/12230–40, in *DCER*, vol. 23, part 2.

131 Ibid. On the other hand, Léger noted that the Soviets had yet to place an order for Canadian wheat in 1957.

132 "Memorandum from Assistant Under-Secretary of State for External Affairs to Acting Secretary of State for External Affairs," 6 June 1957, "Exchange of Visits with Communist Countries," no. 500, DEA/12230–40, in *DCER*, vol. 25, ed. Michael Stevenson. Pearson was away from Ottawa at this time, campaigning for the election, which took place on 10 June 1957.

133 "Memorandum from Assistant Under-Secretary of State for External Affairs to Under-Secretary of State for External Affairs," 7 February 1958, no. 501, DEA/12230–40, and "Extract from Cabinet Conclusions," 19 June 1958, no. 503, in *DCER*, vol. 25. Sydney Smith was the minister of external affairs at this time.

134 DEA note no. 35, dated 19 August 1958, attached to "Memorandum from Under-Secretary of State for External Affairs [Jules Léger] to Secretary of State for External Affairs," 22 August 1958, no. 504, DEA/12230–40, in *DCER*, vol. 25.

135 VOKS 6:55:153–57, A. Tovstogan, "Notes on Interview with President of the Company, 'Canadian Concerts and Artists,' N.F. Koudriavtsev."

136 VOKS 6:55:153–57.

137 VOKS 6:55:209–14, A. Tovstogan, "Notes on the Interview with Canadian Composer L.A. Applebaum, 22 October 1957," dated 12 November 1957.

138 VOKS 6:55:216–18, D. Chuvakhin to G. Zhukov, 13 December 1957.

139 VOKS 6:55:170–72, A. Tovstogan to V. Bony, 29 October 1957.

140 VOKS 6:55:186–88, A. Tovstogan to G. Ioanisyan, 29 October 1957.

141 Kramer, "The Role of the CPSU International Department in Soviet Foreign Relations and National Security Policy," 430.

142 Ibid.

143 Roberts and Cipko, *One Way Ticket*. See also Peter Roberts and Serge Cipko, "Canada and the Khrushchev Government's 'Return to the Homeland' Campaign," Occasional Paper No. 8, Centre for Research on Canadian-Russian Relations, Carleton University, 2000.

144 LAC, RG25, vol. 3704, file 5496-40, part 2, "New Organization to Control 'Friendship,'" April 1958, attached to memorandum from Defence Liaison (2) to Information Liaison, DEA, 15 January 1959.

145 LAC, RG25, vol. 7117, file 9055-40, part 3.2, memorandum from the Canadian Embassy in the USSR, 1957, "USSR Establishes New Cultural Relations Committee," marked "Canadian Eyes Only—Secret." Establishment of the State Committee was announced in *Sovetskaya kultura* on 21 May 1957. LAC, RG25, vol. 7117, file 9055-40, part 3.2, David M. Johnson, Canadian Ambassador, to Undersecretary of State for External Affairs, 23 May 1957.

146 LAC, RG25, vol. 7117, file 9055-40, part 3.2, memorandum from the Canadian Embassy in the USSR, 1957, "USSR Establishes New Cultural Relations Committee," marked "Canadian Eyes Only—Secret."

147 LAC, RG25, ATIP request A-2007-00336, memorandum entitled "New Organization to Control 'Friendship,'" April 1958, 510–11.

148 Ibid.

149 Ibid.

150 LAC, RG25, ATIP request A-2007-00336, memorandum from Defence Liaison (2) to Information Division, DEA, 15 January 1959, 494–95.

151 On the overlap of diplomatic duties and KGB interests, see Makarov, "Living with the KGB and GRU."

152 This information had become available after the Australian Royal Commission on Espionage of 1955. LAC, RG25, ATIP request A-2007-00336, memorandum from Defence Liaison (2) to Information Division, DEA, 15 January 1959, 494–95.

153 These names are confusing. VOKS had a British Countries division that corresponded with the CSFS in Canada until 1957, after which the SSOD established a Moscow-based USSR-Canada Society, and after 1960 the CSFS became the Canada-USSR Association, with its main office in Toronto.

154 LAC, RG25, ATIP request A-2007-00336, David Johnson, Canadian Ambassador to the USSR, to the Undersecretary of State for External Affairs, Ottawa, no. 275, 27 February 1958, 519–21.

155 LAC, RG25, ATIP request A-2007-00336, telegram from Ottawa to NATO, Paris, 328/518, 15 February 1958, copied to Moscow, 535.

156 LAC, RG25, ATIP request A-2007-00336, David Johnson, Canadian Ambassador to the USSR, to Undersecretary of State for External Affairs, Ottawa, 29 December 1959, with a translated excerpt from the *Pravda* article "To Strengthen Soviet-Canadian Friendship" attached, 451–55; LAC, RG25, ATIP request A-2007-00336, RCMP Research Section report "The Canada-USSR Association," 27 March 1963, 834–45.

157 The inaugural meeting was held on 28 December 1959 at the "House of Friendship" in Moscow. LAC, RG25, ATIP request A-2007-00336, David Johnson, Canadian Ambassador to the USSR, to Undersecretary of State for External Affairs, Ottawa, no. 1425, 29 December 1959, 451–55; LAC, RG25, ATIP request A-2007-00336, "Letter from Moscow to the Under-Secretary of State for External Affairs, Ottawa," no. 415, 15 May 1962, 850–51.

158 LAC, RG25, ATIP request A-2007-00336, "Letter from Moscow to the Under-Secretary of State for External Affairs, Ottawa," no. 415, 15 May 1962, 850–51.

159 LAC, RG25, ATIP request A-2007-00336, M. Cadieux, Undersecretary of State for External Affairs, Ottawa, to Canadian Embassy, Moscow, no. S34, 20 January 1960, 442–43.

160 LAC, RG25, vol. 3704, file 5496-40, part 2, David Johnson, Canadian Ambassador to the USSR, to Undersecretary of State for External Affairs, Ottawa, no. 1425, 29 December 1959, 451–55.

161 LAC, RG25, ATIP request A-2007-00336, RCMP Research Section report "The Canada-USSR Association," 27 March 1963, 834–45; Hunt, interview.

162 LAC, RG25, ATIP request A-2007-00336, RCMP Research Section report "The Canada-USSR Association," 27 March 1963, 834–45.

163 Baxter, interview; Boyd, interview; LAC, RG25, ATIP request A-2007-00336, RCMP Research Section report "The Canada-USSR Association," 27 March 1963, 834–45; LAC, RG25, ATIP request A-2007-00336, "Letter from Moscow to the Under-Secretary of State for External Affairs, Ottawa," no. 415, 15 May 1962, 850–51.

164 John Boyd, a party insider, said that the CPC tried to convince the Soviets to distance themselves from Carter but was unsuccessful. Carter and his prolific, pro-Soviet writing were just too valuable to the Soviet cause. John Boyd, comments on the manuscript by Jennifer Anderson, April 2008.

165 LAC, RG25, ATIP request A-2007-00336, letter delivered by hand from J.R.W. Bordeleau, Assistant Commissioner, Director, Security and Intelligence, RCMP, to Mr. J.J. McCardle, Undersecretary of State for External Affairs, 2 April 1963, 833. ATIP officers have deleted the name of this Soviet official and his position at the Soviet Embassy in Ottawa.

166 Details on the activities and makeup of the Canada-USSR Association will be given in the epilogue.

167 VOKS 6:1:55:99, Carter letter, no date (probably autumn 1956).

Chapter 4: The Pro-Soviet Message: Dyson Carter and the CSFS Literature and Photographs

1 For an unpublished biography of Carter, see Mary Eleanor Barber Watson, "Study of Dyson Carter's Life and Works" (undergraduate paper, Carleton University, 1974). His role in promoting the USSR and socialism has been discussed in J.L. Black and Norman Hillmer, "Canada and the Soviet Union as Neighbours," in *Nearly Neighbours: Canada and the Soviet Union from Cold War to Détente and Beyond*, ed. J.L. Black and Norman Hillmer (Kingston: Frye, 1989), 6, 7; Black, *Canada in the Soviet Mirror*; Black, "Soviet Tactics and Targets in Canada before and after the Gouzenko Defection"; Doyle, *Progressive Heritage*; and Johnston, *A Great Restlessness*.

2 This claim appeared on the banner of *Northern Neighbors*. See also *Gravenhurst News*, 6 December 1985.

3 Literature on Soviet propaganda in the West has at times been polemical and defensive, but there have also been more balanced attempts to understand the role of ideology and perception in creating political propaganda. The word *propaganda* in Russian is not pejorative and derives, as in English, from the verb to *propagate* or *diffuse* information. In this sense, it is close to the Soviet understanding of "political education," thus the Bolshevik acronym "agitprop" (agitation and propaganda). Consider, for instance, Ian Greig, *The Assault on the West* (Peterham, UK: Foreign Affairs Publishing, 1968); Mark W. Hopkins, *Mass Media in the Soviet Union* (New

York: Pegasus, 1970); Anatoliy Golitsyn, *New Lies for Old: The Communist Strategy of Deception and Disinformation* (New York: Dodd and Mead, 1984); Jean Delmas and Jean Kessler, eds., *Renseignement et propagande pendant la guerre froide, 1947–1953* (Bruxelles: Éditions Complexe, 1999); Black, *Canada in the Soviet Mirror*; David Caute, *The Dancer Defects: The Struggle for Cultural Supremacy during the Cold War* (Oxford: Oxford University Press, 2003).

4 See, for instance, Catherine Vance, *Not by Gods but by People: The Story of Bella Hall Gauld* (Toronto: Progress Books, 1968); Avakumovic, *The Communist Party in Canada*; Louise Watson, *She Never Was Afraid: The Biography of Annie Buller* (Toronto: Progress Books, 1976); Norman Penner, *The Canadian Left: A Critical Analysis* (Scarborough: Prentice-Hall of Canada, 1977); Stephen Endicott, *James G. Endicott: Rebel out of China* (Toronto: University of Toronto Press, 1980); Ian Angus, *Canadian Bolsheviks: The Early Years of the Communist Party of Canada* (Montreal: Vanguard, 1981); Weisbord, *The Strangest Dream*; Peter Hunter, *Which Side Are You On Boys . . . Canadian Life on the Left* (Toronto: Lugus, 1988); Bryan D. Palmer, ed., *A Communist Life: Jack Scott and the Canadian Workers Movement, 1927–1985* (St. John's: Committee on Canadian Labour History, 1988); Norman Penner, *Canadian Communism: The Stalin Years and Beyond* (Toronto: Methuen, 1988); Joan Sangster, *Dreams of Equality: Women on the Canadian Left, 1920–1950* (Toronto: McClelland and Stewart, 1989); Andrée Lévesque, *Scènes de la vie en rouge: L'époque de Jeanne Corbin, 1906–1944* (Montréal: Éditions de Remue-Ménage, 1999); Maurice Rush, *We Have a Glowing Dream: Recollections of Working-Class and People's Struggles in B.C., 1935–1995* (Vancouver: Centre for Socialist Education, 1996); Cy Gonick, *A Very Red Life: The Story of Bill Walsh* (St. John's: Canadian Committee on Labour History, 2001); Julie Guard, "Canadian Citizens or Dangerous Foreign Women? Canada's Radical Consumer Movement, 1947–1950," in *Sisters or Strangers? Immigrant, Ethnic, and Racialized Women in Canadian History*, ed. Marlene Epp, Franca Iacovetta, and Frances Swyripa (Toronto: University of Toronto Press, 2004), 161–89; and Johnston, *A Great Restlessness*.

5 John Boyd, private collection (hereafter Boyd collection), Carter to Boyd, 28 February 1990.

6 On fellow travellers in the United States, Britain, and Western Europe, see Caute, *The Fellow-Travellers*, and Julia L. Mickenberg, *Learning from the Left: Children's Literature, the Cold War, and Radical Politics in the United States* (Oxford: Oxford University Press, 2006).

7 A growing literature has challenged the distinction between political and social history, showing that Cold War rhetoric shaped North American culture in the 1950s. Coming out of cultural studies, this scholarship has analyzed trends in popular culture and pointed to how these trends were influenced by political considerations. This work has led, in turn, to a rethinking of what it has meant to be a "radical" in the United States and Canada. Implicit in this work is an explication of how individuals challenged the prevailing discourse of "normalcy" and the significance of ideology. See Melvyn P. Leffler, "The Cold War: What Do 'We Now Know'?," review of *We Now Know: Rethinking Cold War History*, by John Lewis Gaddis, *American Historical Review* 104, 2 (1999): 501–24; Stephen J. Whitfield, *The Culture of the Cold War* (Baltimore: Johns Hopkins University Press, 1991); Joel Foreman, ed., *The Other Fifties: Interrogating Midcentury American Icons* (Urbana: University of Illinois Press, 1997); May, *Homeward Bound*; Smith, *Diplomacy of Fear*; Wini Breines, *Young, White, and Miserable: Growing Up Female in the Fifties* (Chicago: University of Chicago

Press, 1992); Nadel, *Containment Culture*; Mary Louise Adams, *The Trouble with Normal: Postwar Youth and the Making of Heterosexuality* (Toronto: University of Toronto Press, 1997); Valerie Joyce Korinek, *Roughing It in the Suburbs: Reading* Chatelaine *Magazine in the Fifties and Sixties* (Toronto: University of Toronto Press, 2000); Lizabeth Cohen, *A Consumer's Republic: The Politics of Mass Consumption in Postwar America* (New York: Knopf, 2003); Caren Irr, *The Suburb of Dissent: Cultural Politics in the United States and Canada during the 1930s* (Durham, NC: Duke University Press, 1998); Joanne Meyerowitz, ed., *Not June Cleaver: Women and Gender in Postwar America, 1945–1960* (Philadelphia: Temple University Press, 1994); Joy Parr, ed., *A Diversity of Women: Ontario, 1945–1980* (Toronto: University of Toronto Press, 1995); Caute, *The Dancer Defects*; and Richard Cavell, ed., *Love, Hate, and Fear in Canada's Cold War* (Toronto: University of Toronto Press, 2004).

8 Ian McKay, *Rebels, Reds, Radicals: Rethinking Canada's Left History* (Toronto: Between the Lines, 2005), 35.

9 On the link between fellow travellers and the language and ideals of the Enlightenment, as well as how the USSR was seen to embody these ideals, see Caute, *The Fellow-Travellers*, especially 250–66.

10 Scott, *Seeing like a State*. Scott argued that "high modernism" was a "faith" or "ideology" based upon the idea that scientific and technological progress could be used by a state to create an improved social order and to champion nature (see 4–6).

11 Adapted from the term "everyday Stalinism" used by Sheila Fitzpatrick in *Everyday Stalinism: Ordinary Life in Extraordinary Times: Soviet Russia in the 1930s* (New York: Oxford University Press, 1999).

12 "Potemkin village" is an expression derived from Grigory Potemkin's efforts to present Catherine the Great with an ideal village in Ukraine by putting false fronts on the buildings.

13 Doyle, *Progressive Heritage*, 174–79; Carter, *This Story Fierce and Tender*.

14 Unfortunately, we know little about Charlotte. Their son Breck was not available for oral interviews. Some additional comments on her role in the CSFS and as Dyson's partner occur in the chapter on the role of women in the CSFS.

15 A discussion of the concept of "rejected knowledge" prevalent in radical literature can be found in Michael Barkun, *A Culture of Conspiracy: Apocalyptic Visions in Contemporary America* (Berkeley: University of California Press, 2003), 23–24.

16 See Weisbord, *The Strangest Dream*. A similar experience of communism is described by Laxer in *Red Diaper Baby*. In the American context, Kim Chernin describes how and why communists and Soviet sympathizers admired the USSR and how narrative is constantly reformulated by the storyteller, the reader, and the circumstance. Kim Chernin, *In My Mother's House: A Daughter's Story* (New York: HarperCollins, 1983).

17 See, for instance, Frances Swyripa, *Wedded to the Cause: Ukrainian-Canadian Women and Ethnic Identity, 1891–1991* (Toronto: University of Toronto Press, 1993); Varpu Lindstrom-Best, *The Finns in Canada* (Ottawa: Canadian Historical Association, 1985); and Varpu Lindstrom, *Defiant Sisters: A Social History of Finnish Immigrant Women in Canada* (Toronto: Multicultural History Society of Ontario, 1992). The path-breaking work on radicalism in Canada and ethnicity is Avery, *Reluctant Host*, a reworking and expansion of his earlier *"Dangerous Foreigners": European Immigrant Workers and Labour Radicalism in Canada, 1896–1932* (Toronto: McClelland and Stewart, 1979). On Canadian responses to immigrants in Cold War Canada, see also Franca Iacovetta, *Gatekeepers: Reshaping Immigrant Lives in Cold War Canada*

(Toronto: Between the Lines, 2006). On how leaders with Anglo-Saxon names were chosen to head up the radical consumers' movement in the late 1940s, in order to avoid being seen as communist, see Guard, "Canadian Citizens or Dangerous Foreign Women?," 161–89.

18 Boyd, interview; John Boyd, "A Noble Cause Betrayed . . . But Hope Lives On: Pages from a Political Life," originally published as Canadian Institute of Ukrainian Studies Report No. 64, 1999; Socialist History Project, http://www.socialisthistory.ca/Remember/Reminiscences/Boyd/B1.htm; Nielsen, interview; Hunt, interview.

19 There are references throughout the VOKS collection to products and books shipped to Carter for sale. He wrote frequently to VOKS asking for material on particular subjects for publication. A report sent from the Soviet Information Bureau representative in Canada in 1954 specified the number of articles and partial articles that the office had supplied that year to the progressive press in Canada, including *News-Facts about the USSR*. VOKS 6:3:97:36–47, V. Kachanov, Deputy Director of the Soviet Information Bureau in Canada, top secret report of the mission of the Soviet Information Bureau in Canada in 1954. Documents originally in Russian have been translated by the author.

20 Nielsen interview; Boyd interview. The RCMP confirmed in 1960 that the CPC would carry on subsidizing Carter's publication of *Northern Neighbors* because it was popular and considered "useful." LAC, RG25, ATIP request A-2007-00336, RCMP Research Section report "The Canada-USSR Association," 27 March 1963, 834–45. Boyd commented that the party tried to convince the Soviet Embassy to distance itself from Carter after 1960, but embassy personnel maintained close contact with him for the same reasons. John Boyd, comments on manuscript by Jennifer Anderson, April 2008.

21 Nielsen interview.

22 VOKS 5:3:31:202, "Kharakteristika prezidenta Obshestvo Kanado-Sovetskoi druzhbi Daisona Cartera" (Biography of the President of the Canadian-Soviet Friendship Society, Dyson Carter), 1950.

23 LAC, RG146, ATIP request A-2006-00101 RCMP translation of G. Vladimirov and D. Erde, "Exposed Provocation," *Ogonyok* 37 (1952), dated 27 September 1952, 124; VOKS 6:1:41:5–8, K. Perevoschikov, review of Carter's 1943 biography of Stalin, 13 April 1953. Perevoschikov said that Carter "correctly" described Stalin's activities and events in the USSR.

24 LAC, RG146, ATIP request A-2006-00101, RCMP translation of Vladimirov and Erde, "Exposed Provocation," 125.

25 Letters from American readers can be found in the VOKS collection, as well as in the Carter fonds at LAC (MG31-D182).

26 See Doyle's commentary on Carter's literary work in *Progressive Heritage*, 105–06, 174–79, 224–30, 258–62.

27 Carter, *Stalin's Life*.

28 This declaration was published as Dyson Carter, "Dyson Carter Explains: Why I've Joined the LPP," *Canadian Tribune*, 15 December 1945, but Carter said elsewhere that he had been a party member since 1931. Carter and Boyd were in the same closed party group in Winnipeg at that time. Boyd collection, Carter to Boyd, 28 February 1990; Boyd interview.

29 Other published books by Carter include *Men, Machines, and Microbes* (Winnipeg: Contemporary Publishers, 1942); *Night of Flame* (1942; reprinted, London:

Chapman, 1946); *Atomic Dollars* (Winnipeg: Frontier Books, 1946); *Sin and Science* (New York: Heck-Cattell, 1946); *Fatherless Sons* (Toronto: Progress Books, 1955); with Charlotte Carter, *Science of Health and Long Life in the U.S.S.R.* (Sydney: Current Book Distributors, 1956); with Charlotte Carter, *Cancer, Smoking, Heart-Disease, Drinking in Our Two World Systems Today* (Toronto: Northern Book House, 1957); *The Big Brainwash* (Toronto: Northern Book House, 1958); *Future of Freedom* (Gravenhurst, ON: Northern Book House, 1961); *Worker Power: Dare We Win?* (Gravenhurst, ON: Northern Book House, 1970); and his semi-autobiography, *This Story Fierce and Tender*. An interview with Carter appeared in the Moscow English-language *New Times* 41 (1983): 27. His article on new treatments for heart disease, "How Not to Be Afraid of Your Heart," was published in *New Liberty* 29 (1952): 22–23, 62–63, but no mention was made of the USSR or CSFS. For a list of his publications in the USSR, showing that Carter was published there almost every year between 1956 and 1983, see J.L. Black, *Soviet Perception of Canada: An Annotated Bibliographic Guide*, vol. 1 (Ottawa: Carleton University Press, 1987), 231.

30 Laxer, *Red Diaper Baby*, 25.

31 Hunt interview; Boyd interview.

32 VOKS 6:1:36:19, "Canadian-Soviet Friendship Society, Draft Constitution," January 1952.

33 Ibid.

34 VOKS 6:1:36:60, "President's Speech, January 27, 1952."

35 During the Second World War, the NCCSF enjoyed broad support, and many prominent Canadians were honorary members, including Prime Minister Mackenzie King. However, soon after Igor Gouzenko defected from the Soviet Embassy in the fall of 1945, an event that most historians agree signalled the beginning of the Cold War in Canada, the National Council membership dropped off sharply, and in February 1949 the RCMP told Undersecretary of State for External Affairs Lester Pearson that it was "inactive." VOKS suggested that the council's trouble was an "absence of leadership," a lack of funds, and an anti-Soviet campaign. In November 1949, the National Council was reorganized, under the leadership of Carter, who claimed that council members who "withdrew their support" had done so "(many with sincere regrets) due to anti-Soviet hysteria." See Knight, *How the Cold War Began*; LAC, RG146, ATIP request A-2006-00096, RCMP report "Extract re: National Council for Canadian Soviet Friendship," 28 February 1949, 133; VOKS 6:3:2:5, "Otchet o rabote VOKS v Kanade za 1946" (Report on the Work of VOKS in Canada in 1946); LAC, RG146, ATIP request A-2006-00091, from "Questions People Ask about the Canadian-Soviet Friendship Society," n.d., 53.

36 VOKS 6:1:36:65–66.

37 VOKS 6:1:32:165, draft of article by Carter for *New Times* on Canadian-Soviet Friendship Month entitled "A Demonstration of Friendship," 1951.

38 Ibid., 166.

39 VOKS 6:1:32:1, D. Carter to V. Bogatyrev, Head, British Countries, VOKS, October 1951, 34.

40 VOKS 6:1:36:29, "The President's Recommendations to the Convention," n.d.

41 Ibid.

42 LAC, RG146, ATIP request A-2006-00091, from "Questions People Ask about the Canadian-Soviet Friendship Society," 53.

43 The *Photo-Facts* cards are copied in LAC, RG146, ATIP request A-2006-00101, 11–12, 95–102.

44 Allan Kent and Clem Shields, "Red Menace Real if War with Russ or Slump Comes," *Toronto Telegram*, 1 April 1952.

45 "Communist Posters Shown to Women's PC Association," *Globe and Mail*, 20 February 1952, 8.

46 VOKS 6:1:32:51, D. Carter to V. Bogatyrev, 10 October 1951. If the CSFS gained from distribution of the cards, then it was mostly in terms of publicity. The financial statements from 1951 indicate that only $100 were made from sale of the cards. LAC, MG28-V-154, vol. 25, file 11, CSFS income statement, 1 November 1950–1 November 1951.

47 VOKS 5:3:31:206–11, biography and itinerary of Carter trip to the USSR, April 1950.

48 Carter and Carter, *We Saw Socialism*, 25, 65, 59, 368, 225.

49 Ibid., 62–65.

50 LAC, RG146, ATIP request A-2006-00114, RCMP Special Section report, 9 November 1950, on an event at the Winnipeg Playhouse Theatre on 5 November 1950, 210.

51 Boyd interview.

52 *News-Facts about the USSR* 1 (1950): 4.

53 *News-Facts about the USSR* 62 (1956): 3; 65 (1956): 7.

54 Johnston, *A Great Restlessness*, 226–27.

55 VOKS 6:1:50:29, V.G. Yakovlev to P.A. Pozdeev, 17 December 1955.

56 *News-Facts about the USSR* 36 (1953): 7.

57 Ibid.

58 *News-Facts about the USSR* 43 (1954): 7, 10.

59 *News-Facts about the USSR* 55 (1955): 8.

60 VOKS 6:1:32:74–75, "Report on Activities of Society Delegation to USSR" in May 1951, 20 July 1951.

61 VOKS 6:1:36:57, "Report on Organization," 26 January 1952.

62 Ibid., 58.

63 Ibid.

64 VOKS 6:1:55:186–88, G. Ioanisyan to A. Tovstogan, 29 October 1957.

65 LAC, RG146, ATIP request A-2006-00091, RCMP report "The Canadian Soviet Friendship Society, February 1951 to March 1953. Addendum to Brief Ending February 1951," 15 April 1953, 113–44.

66 VOKS 6:1:49:74, A. Tovstogan to I. Kulakovskaya, 9 March 1956.

67 VOKS 6:1:55:27–28, A. Tovstogan to V.V. Abramov, Sovexportfilm, 11 December 1956.

68 VOKS 6:1:55:29, G. Ioanisyan to K. Litvin (UkrOKS), 9 January 1956.

69 VOKS 6:1:32:32–37, D. Carter to V. Bogatyrev, 1 October 1951.

70 VOKS 6:1:49:150–53, A. Vertogradov to A. Tovstogan, 17 April 1956.

71 VOKS 6:1:49:217, A. Tovstogan to V.G. Yakovlev, 16 October 1956.

72 LAC, RG146, ATIP request A-2006-00102, RCMP summary of a Hungarian-language newspaper, 72, title blacked out but probably *Kanadai magyar munkas* (Canadian Hungarian Worker), 8 January 1953, 10.

73 *News-Facts about the USSR* was published from 1950 to 1956 and *Northern Neighbors* from the end of 1956 to 1989. The former was the official journal of the CSFS. Carter's magazines and many of his books, though published by the CSFS or *Northern Neighbors*, were printed by Eveready Printers of Toronto. This continued to be the case after he moved to Gravenhurst in 1957. Eveready was the printer used most often by the LPP-CPC, and many of the employees were in fact LPP members. Nielsen interview; Boyd, "A Noble Cause Betrayed."

74 *Northern Neighbours*, December 1956, title page.

75 Hunt interview. The year 1956 was a watershed for many communists and fellow travellers. Khrushchev's "secret speech" to the Twentieth Party Congress in Moscow, officially distancing the CPSU from the legacy of Stalin, plus the Suez Canal affair and the invasion of Hungary, created a crisis in the international communist movement. Charlotte Carter commented that the congress had "made the idea of Canadian-Soviet friendship 'unpopular' in Canada." VOKS 6:55:150–53, A. Tovstogan to G. Ioanisyan, 31 May 1957. An executive member of the CSFS was "freed from his duties" because of his "incorrect behaviour" following the congress. VOKS 6:49:264–67, A. Tovstogan to A. Vertogradov, 20 September 1956. The new magazine was probably an attempt to respond to this crisis. For more on the response in Canadian leftist circles, see Weisbord, *The Strangest Dream*.

76 *Northern Neighbours*, December 1956, 5, 12, 13. The Canadian spelling was used in the first issue only, after which the magazine was called *Northern Neighbors*.

77 Ibid., 13.

78 Ibid., February 1957, 3.

79 Ibid., 12–13.

80 Ibid., January 1957, 7.

81 Ibid.

82 Ibid., May–June 1989, 4–5.

83 Ibid., March 1957, 16; February 1980, 11; "Student Rebels—Czech Liberals," September 1968, 3.

84 Ibid., February 1980, 4–5, and special supplement; March 1980, 6; October 1980, 13; cover story in November 1986 issue as Soviets left Afghanistan in "friendship."

85 Ibid., March 1980, 4, 17.

86 See, for example, ibid., November 1982.

87 See, for example, "Real 'Chernobyl' Disaster Was in West," ibid., June 1986, 4; "How Many Will Die from Chernobyl?," ibid., January 1987, 3. In the last article is the claim that "no informed scientist . . . can state that this fall out *will in any significant way change the future cancer death rate*."

88 See, especially, the final issue, December 1989.

89 Ibid., February 1957, 12–13.

90 There has been a good deal of work in Canadian historiography on the links between Canadian (self-) identity and the North. See, for instance, Janice Cavell, "The Second Frontier: The North in English-Canadian Historical Writing," *Canadian Historical Review* 83, 3 (2002): 364–89, and Kerry Abel and Ken S. Coates, eds., *Northern Visions: New Perspectives on the North in Canadian History* (Peterborough: Broadview Press, 2001). Soviet writers, such as A. Cherkassov, had made the northern link a theme for years.

91 An article on the Soviet atomic icebreaker *Lenin* appeared in *Northern Neighbors*, July–August 1961, 19; "How to Ski to the Pole," ibid., February 1980, 20.

92 Ibid., October 1962, 8.

93 Ibid., January 1980, 20, 21.

94 Ibid., March 1980, 10.

95 It is worth noting here how winter, technology, and ideas about national exceptionalism in Canada are also linked. Newcomers to the North often had the attitude that, rather than adapt to winter, they should "conquer" the North. Ken S. Coates and William R. Morrison, "Winter and the Shaping of Northern History: Reflections from the Canadian North," in *Northern Visions: New Perspectives on the North in Canadian History*, ed. Kerry Abel and Ken S. Coates (Peterborough: Broadview Press, 2001), 23–35.

96 *Northern Neighbors*, December 1956, 13.

97 Ibid., June 1960, 18–19.

98 "New Siberian Town Has No Chimneys," ibid., October 1960, 16.

99 Ibid., February 1962, 14.

100 "Arctic Socialism: Full Education, Full Employment among Rights of Northern Peoples," ibid., May 1962, 12–13.

101 Ibid., September 1962, 17.

102 Ibid., December 1962, 14–15.

103 "North Country Boom," ibid., February 1981, 14–15.

104 See, for example, "World-Wide Hockey," ibid., January 1958, 12–13.

105 Ibid., October 1972, 4.

106 For a discussion of these developments, see the special edition of *Northern Perspectives* 16, 4 (1988), published by the Canadian Arctic Resources Committee, http://www.carc.org/pubs/v16no4/index.html. From this issue, particularly useful are Dan Hayward's "Gorbachev's Murmansk Initiative: New Prospects for Arms Control in the Arctic?"; Carl Macmillan's "Joint Ventures in Arctic Resource Development"; and J.L. Black's "The Soviet Perspective on Canada's North: An Overview of the Literature, 1947–1988," n.pag. Also see Walter Slipchenko, "Co-Operation in Arctic Science," *Northern Perspectives* 15, 2 (1987), n.pag., published by the Canadian Arctic Resources Committee, http://www.carc.org/pubs/v15no2/6.htm.

107 Aileen Espiritu, "Whither the Northern Natives in Russian History?," in *Northern Visions: New Perspectives on the North in Canadian History*, ed. Kerry Abel and Ken S. Coates (Peterborough: Broadview Press, 2001), 170–71.

108 LAC, MG31-D182, vol. 2, file 10, Alf and Kay Watt, New South Wales, Australia, to Dyson Carter, 2 January 1980; vol. 1, file 2, Signie and Henry Traeger, Chilliwack, BC, to Dyson Carter, n.d. (probably December 1978); vol. 4, file 5, Anna Hintsa, Toronto, to Dyson Carter, 29 February 1980; vol. 3, file 7, Norman Haaland, Portland, to Dyson Carter, 27 February 1980.

109 LAC, MG31-D182, vol. 5, file 7, Paul Mann, Telegraph Creek, BC, to Dyson Carter, 13 March 1981. The broken English apparent in many of these letters hints that many readers were not native speakers. Indeed, it is clear from the VOKS files that members of the progressive ethnic organizations were among the most faithful subscribers.

110 Barkun, *A Culture of Conspiracy*.

111 See, for example, "Garlic Might Cure You," *Northern Neighbors*, March 1984, 11; "Onions Might Cure You," ibid., April 1985, 16; "Soviet Views on Eating Meat," ibid., May 1982, 16; "Try Beets for Pep," ibid., June–July 1980, 13; and "What You May Not Know about Vegetables," ibid., September 1980, 19.

112 "Was God a Man from Space?," ibid., April 1961, 21.

113 "Gods Are Space-Men?," ibid., June 1964, 9.

114 See, for example, "Bermuda Triangle Exposed," ibid., October 1980, 3; "Abominable Snowman Walks Again," ibid., December 1980, 5; "Seen Any UFOs Lately?," ibid., September 1982, 3; "Four Far-Out Science Mysteries," ibid., March 1983, 12; and "Astonishing New Mysteries Are Upsetting Astronomers Today," ibid., March 1985, 3.

115 "People Are the Makers of History," ibid., December 1956, 16.

116 "God Is Waiting?," ibid., May 1984, 3.

117 "You Boss the Universe," ibid., June 1985, 7.

118 From "Unbelievable 'Power' of Numbers" in "Four Far-Out Science Mysteries," ibid., March 1983, 12.

119 This theme is elaborated in *This Story Fierce and Tender*. In the "autobiography," a character named Dyson Carter writes a book on a man named Elgin Morley, who closely resembles Carter himself. It is purported to be the first of two volumes, but apparently the second volume was never published.

120 LAC, MG31-D182, vol. 3, file 7, Frank and Irene Horsford, Mission , BC, to Dyson Carter, 5 February 1980.

121 LAC, MG31-D182, vol. 7, file 7, Mrs. Olive Cooper to Dyson Carter, February 1982; vol. 10, file 2, Lynn K. Sully to Dyson Carter, 28 September 1981; vol. 6, file 12, Florence Petrie to Dyson Carter, 4 December 1981; vol. 7, file 10, Belly Farmer, Tofino, BC, to Dyson Carter, March 1982. These photos are in LAC, MG31-D182, vol. 11, file 9.

122 Hunt interview; Boyd interview; Baxter, interview; Boyd collection, Carter to Boyd, 28 February 1990.

123 I. Ovchinnikova, "Na temi dnya: Ekzamen otmenen, istoriya ostaetsya!," *Izvestiia*, 10 June 1988, 1; Esther B. Fein, "Moscow Summit: Unmaking History and Debating Rights; Soviet Pupils Spared Exams while History Is Rewritten," *New York Times*, 31 May 1988; David Remnick, "Soviets Cancel History Tests over Text," *Washington Post*, 11 June 1988, A1.

124 Quoted in Tatyana Volodina, "Teaching History in Russia after the Collapse of the USSR," *History Teacher*, February 2005, paragraph 5, http://www.historycooperative.org/journals/ht/38.2/volodina.html.

125 Boyd collection, Carter to Boyd, 28 February 1990.

126 Reg Watson, "Controversial Pro-Soviet Publisher Turns 75," *Gravenhurst News*, 6 December 1985; Nielsen interview. The magazine was distributed in the United States; friends of the USSR in other countries also received it. This international character was promoted by Carter as further proof of the popularity of interpretations in the magazine.

127 A survey of young members of the AUUC in 1965 found that many of them read *Northern Neighbors*. LAC, MG28-V-154, vol. 27, file 14–18, "Poll of Participants of the AUUC National Youth Conference, July 9–11, 1965, Ukrainian Camp Palermo," Toronto.

Chapter 5: Polishing the Soviet Image: The CSFS and Progressive Ethnic Groups

1 On this, Ester Reiter's work on the Jewish radical left in Toronto has been most useful. Ester Reiter, "Secular *Yiddishkait*: Left Politics, Culture, and Community," *Labour/Le travail*, spring 2002, http://www.historycooperative.org/journals/llt/49/05reiter.html.

2 In using this term, I am following my sources. Although the term is unwieldly, and possibly inaccurate, "Anglo-Saxon" is used here to refer to anglophone Canadians of white, Protestant, middle-class, British ancestry. Some of the sources suggested that these people were more "Canadian" than individuals with Ukrainian, Russian, or other "ethnic" last names. Francophones did not have prominence in the CSFS under Carter, but a separate chapter did exist after 1960. This fact, and the Quebec francophone Soviet friendship group, are discussed in the conclusion.

3 On admiration of the USSR among ethnic groups on the Canadian left, see Swyripa, *Wedded to the Cause*; Lindstrom-Best, *The Finns in Canada*; Lindstrom, *Defiant Sisters*; *Letters from Karelia*, dir. Kelly Saxberg, prod. Joe MacDonald (NFB, 2005); and Reiter, "Secular *Yiddishkait*." For admiration of the USSR by the CPC, see Weisbord, *The Strangest Dream*, and Laxer, *Red Diaper Baby*.

4 Reiter, "Secular *Yiddishkait*," paragraph 14; Penner, *Canadian Communism*, 273–74; Peter Krawchuk, *Our History: The Ukrainian Labour-Farmer Movement in Canada, 1907–1991* (Toronto: Lugus Publications, 1996), 154–85.

5 VOKS 6:3:98:5–20, V. Loginov, Counsellor, Soviet Embassy, Ottawa, "Short Report on the 5th Congress of the Labor Progressive Party of Canada and Its Post-Congress Work with the Masses," 19 March 1955. Another Loginov, A.F. Loginov, a military attaché at the Soviet Embassy, was expelled from Canada in 1961 for attempting to pay Canadians for information. Department of External Affairs, *Canadian Weekly Bulletin*, 20 December 1961, 5. John Boyd, an active LPP organizer until 1968, also wrote about "the LPP's inability to effectively reach Anglo-Saxon Canadians." Boyd, "A Noble Cause Betrayed."

6 VOKS 6:3:98:5–20.

7 The leadership of the CSFS was almost exclusively English speaking, and correspondence with authorities in Moscow was almost exclusively in English, even with members from Quebec, until the 1960s, when a Canada-URSS Society was founded in Montreal. It is no coincidence that the francophone friendship group was founded at the same time as the Parti communiste du Québec. These developments were a response to changes taking place in Quebec through the 1960s.

8 Boyd, interview. Boyd said that he was never a member of the CSFS, but Carter claimed that he was a National Council executive member in 1951. VOKS 6:1:36:22–23. Boyd was secretary of the Canadian Slav Committee in the late 1940s and 1950s.

9 Boyd interview; Boyd, "A Noble Cause Betrayed"; Laxer, *Red Diaper Baby*, 25, 54. Other CPC-LPP supporters who changed their names were Fred Rose (Alfred Rosenberg), Sam and Bill Walsh (Saul and Mo Wolofsky), and Louis Kon (Koniatski).

10 On how this was also attempted in the Housewives' Consumers Association, see Guard, "Canadian Citizens or Dangerous Foreign Women?," 161–89.

11 Kealey and Whitaker, *The R.C.M.P. Security Bulletins: The Depression Years, pt. I, 1933–1934*, 102.

12 LAC, RG146, ATIP request A-2006-00124, RCMP Intelligence Branch, Toronto, report on Society for the Study of Russia, Toronto, 31 May 1943, 96.

13 Besides Gartner, R.A. Davies and Margaret Gould attended events run by both organizations. The Montreal-based group led by Kon in the 1930s called itself Friends of the Soviet Union, and Kon became more involved again with the CSFS under Carter. In November 1949, at the founding meeting of the new CSFS, Carter said, "Ladies and Gentl[e]men . . . GONE ARE THE DAYS, FOREVER, when we have to APOLOGIZE for friendship with the Land of Socialism! Never again do we have to go, hat-in-hand, to people in high places, and ask them: 'Please won't you allow your name to be used for the sake of friendship. . . . Important names will make people think the Russians are important!'" LAC, RG146, ATIP request A-2006-00096, Carter's notes for "Speech for C.S.F. Meeting Nov 26 49," 81–94.

14 LAC, RG146, ATIP request A-2006-00124, RCMP Intelligence Branch, Toronto, "Re: Rally—Maple Leaf Gardens, Toronto, Ont. June 22nd. 1943," 25 June 1943, 49.

15 Ibid.

16 LAC, RG146, ATIP request A-2006-00091, RCMP report "The Canadian Soviet Friendship Society, February 1951 to March 1953. Addendum to Brief Ending February 1951," 15 April 1953, 116.

17 Ibid., 113, 116.

18 Ronald Williams, "Reds at Work on 'Friendship': Now Start Photo Propaganda Deluge," *Financial Post*, 5 January 1952, LAC, RG146, ATIP request A-2006-00099, 114; LAC, RG146, ATIP request A-2006-00100, Dyson Carter, "President's Speech, January 25, 1952," 67–76; also in VOKS 6:1:36:43–52.

19 In 1954, a Canadian journalist posted to Moscow, G.W. Boss, went to see A. Denisov, chief of VOKS, at its headquarters. He mentioned to Denisov that there were contemporary Canadian writers besides Carter, and he asked whether there were any plans to publish their work in the USSR. Denisov's notes on this interview were forwarded to M.A. Suslov, of the International Department of the CPSU. VOKS 6:1:45:99–105, G.W. Boss to K. Perevoschikov, with questions for upcoming interview with A. Denisov, 24 February 1954; VOKS 6:3:96:19–21, A. Denisov to M.A. Suslov, 3 March 1954.

20 This interaction, which deserves more study, has been noted by Reiter, "Secular *Yiddishkait*."

21 In oral interviews, former CSFS members and acquaintances frequently referred to this inside/outside relationship, particularly in arranging events. At times, it might have been in response to nastier circumstances. Reiter, ibid., paragraph 28, has noted that in 1925, when the Jewish Labour League wanted to buy land from the Canadian National Railway to be used for Camp Kindervelt, a "Ukrainian sympathizer" had to be asked to front the sale, because the CNR would not sell to Jews.

22 For an interesting discussion of how Nielsen and Carter were asked by the party to travel across Canada to do damage control following the Gouzenko revelations of 1946, and their work to reorganize the CSFS, see Johnston, *A Great Restlessness*, 197, 225–31.

23 There are numerous examples of personnel being asked to serve on committees for the language groups, the LPP, and the CSFS. They include Nadia Savich, asked in 1955 by the FRC national executive , to represent the FRC in the CSFS. LAC, RG146, ATIP request A-2006-00104, "Minutes of Proceedings N. 25 of the Meeting of the National Executive of the FRC of September 27, 1955," 30.

24 LAC, RG146, ATIP request A-2006-00097, RCMP, Yorkton Special Branch, report of 21 December 1950, 20.

25 LAC, RG146, ATIP request A-2006-00117, RCMP Headquarters, report of information in *Ludove zvesti* (Slovak for People's News), 20 January 1951, 11.

26 From the Sudbury Finnish-language newspaper *Vapaus*, 21 March 1953, 8.

27 VOKS 6:1:49:17, A. Tovstogan to I. Kulakovskaya, 26 November 1955.

28 LAC, RG146, ATIP request A-2006-00117, "RCMP Report, 19-10-51 source *Ukrainian Life* 18-10-51," 10.

29 On the Jewish left generally, and its links to other leftist ethnic groups in Canada, see Reiter, "Secular *Yiddishkait*." For more on the Jewish Folk Choir's mission and appeal, see Benita Wolters-Fredlund, "'We Shall Go Forward with Our Songs into the Fight for Better Life': Identity and Musical Meaning in the History of the Toronto Jewish Folk Choir, 1925–1959" (PhD diss., University of Toronto, 2005).

30 LAC, RG146, ATIP request A-2006-00091, RCMP report "The Canadian Soviet Friendship Society, February 1951 to March 1953. Addendum to Brief Ending February 1951," dated 15 April 1953, 115.

31 M.I. Gritzak, "Meeting of Canadian Soviet Friendship in Grand Forks," *Vestnik*, 27 February 1954, RCMP summary in LAC, RG146, ATIP request A-2006-00121, 20.

32 VOKS 6:1:49:17, A. Tovstogan to I. Kulakovskaya, 26 November 1955.

33 Ibid.

34 No other details of this brochure are given, but considering the date of printing it might have dealt with issues of Ukrainian nationhood and identity. VOKS 6:1:39:188–89, V. Burdin to V. Bogatyrev, 25 June 1953.

35 VOKS 6:1:49:272, A. Tovstogan to I. Kulakovskaya, 12 October 1956.

36 VOKS 6:1:49:115, A. Vertogradov to A. Tovstogan, 12 May 1956.

37 VOKS 6:1:49:181, I. Kulakovskaya to L.V. Rimyans, 19 September 1956.

38 VOKS 6:1:49:125–27, A. Tovstogan to I. Kulakovskaya, 7 April 1956. Tichnovich's name had been anglicized from Tsekhanovich.

39 *Spravochnik* is the Russian word for "guide" or "reference book." In this case, they probably meant a type of address book. VOKS 6:1:49:272, A. Tovstogan to I. Kulakovskaya, 12 October 1956.

40 The choirs of the AUUC and FRC would frequently sing folk songs from other Eastern European traditions, particularly if they knew that these ethnic groups were represented in the audience. VOKS 6:1:49:227, I. Kulakovskaya to P. Valeskeln, Chairman, Latvian OKS, 3 July 1956; VOKS 6:1:49:228, I. Kulakovskaya to P. Ratomskis, Lithuanian OKS, 3 July 1956.

41 VOKS 6:1:49:59, A. Vertogradov to A. Tovstogan, 13 April 1956.

42 VOKS 6:1:49:210–12, dated 18 June 1956.

43 VOKS 6:1:53:19–25, dated 3 March 1956; 53:81, dated 23 May 1956.

44 Examples can be found in the Robert S. Kenny Collection, Thomas Fisher Rare Book Library, University of Toronto.

45 VOKS 6:1:50:116, "Canadian Soviet Friendship Society, Receipts and Payments—13 Months to December 31 1952"; VOKS 6:1:50:117, "Canadian Soviet Friendship Society, Receipts and Payments—Year to December 31 1953." These are among the few documents reporting CSFS income. Carter's second wife, Sally Nielsen, has said that thousands of dollars were kept in the house, and periodically CPC leaders would come to ask Dyson for a share. She said that book sales accounted for a large share of this income, and Dyson received cash from Soviet Embassy officials who visited their home in Gravenhurst. Nielsen, interview.

46 Nielsen interview. Certainly, real estate costs and taxes would have eaten up some of the profit.

47 VOKS 6:1:53:12, D. Carter to K. Perevoschikov, 5 December 1955.

48 VOKS 6:1:53:13, I. Kulakovskaya to B.A. Astvatsaturyan, 26 January 1956.

49 VOKS 6:1:53:14, B.A. Astvatsaturyan to I. Kulakovskaya, 3 February 1956.

50 This request was forwarded by VOKS in Moscow to the Karelo-Finnish SSR. VOKS 6:1:44:79–81; 89–90; 96–97, D. Carter to V. Bogatyrev, 1 March 1953; N. Gorshkov, VOKS, to I. Tsvetkov, 16 April 1953; D. Carter to V. Bogatyrev, 12 June 1953.

51 VOKS 6:1:49:47, I V. Yakovlev to L. Smilgebichius, 6 March 1956.

52 VOKS 6:1:49:125, A. Tovstogan to I. Kulakovskaya, 7 April 1956.

53 VOKS 6:1:49:28, I. Kulakovskaya to A. Tovstogan, 26 January 1956.

54 VOKS 6:1:49:52, A. Vertogradov to A. Tovstogan, 23 March 1956.

55 LAC, RG146, ATIP request A-2006-00091, RCMP Security and Intelligence Section, Calgary, report, 20 November 1957, 7.

56 Ibid., 9.

57 "Account of Bruce Magnusson's Trip to the Soviet Union," *Vestnik*, 31 December 1952, in LAC, RG146, ATIP request A-2006-00102, RCMP report, 5 January 1953, 77.

58 "'If People Know Truth about Us—No More War' Stalingrad Woman," *Canadian Tribune*, n.d., in LAC, RG146, ATIP request A-2006-00105, 129; LAC, RG146, ATIP request A-2006-00103, "Circular Letter N. 2," from the National Executive of the FRC, signed by J. Kurban, Secretary, Toronto, 27 November 1953, 86.

59 LAC, RG146, ATIP request A-2006-00096, Carter to "Dear Friends of the Federation of Russian Canadians," 24 March 1950, 234–35.

60 After Khrushchev's speech in 1956 documenting Soviet abuses under Stalin, including systemic anti-Semitism, many Jews left the LPP and associated groups. Hints of this situation appeared earlier in the 1950s, however, and LPP-supported clubs had been working for some time on damage control. The CSFS was no exception, and articles in its journal celebrated the Soviet treatment of Jews. Revelations by Khrushchev and others regarding the real injustice caused deep disillusionment for many leftists.

61 LAC, RG146, ATIP request A-2006-00091, RCMP report "The Canadian Soviet Friendship Society, February 1951 to March 1953. Addendum to Brief Ending February 1951," dated 15 April 1953, 115.

62 *News-Facts about the USSR* 35 (1953): 1.

63 Boyd interview.

64 LAC, RG25, ATIP request A-2007-00336, RCMP Research Section report "The Canada-USSR Association," 27 March 1963, 834–45.

65 Nielsen interview.

66 Ibid. Boyd did not believe that the money came from Moscow, arguing instead that the CPC had clever ways of financing its supported organizations. He pointed out that the RCMP and the Bank of Commerce knew about these strategies all along. Boyd interview.

67 Much of this came as books and objects, as discussed earlier and in the next section.

68 A letter from Carter to Tovstogan dated 18 February 1957, thanking him and Ambassador Chuvakhin for their help in making sure that $3,086.09 in royalty fees for *Tomorrow Is with Us* were received by Carter from "Goslitigat Ukrainy," seems

to suggest that he was not always able to get his royalty payments. VOKS 6:1:55:107. The Soviets always took interest in his books published in Canada, and he usually forwarded them via VOKS to the Writers' Union and others in the USSR. In 1956, when Carter complained about a Soviet review of his book *Fatherless Sons*, his letter was forwarded to the Central Committee of the CPC. VOKS 6:1:53:28–36. The VOKS headquarters informed the Ottawa representative that this book was to be published in the USSR in 1957. VOKS 6:1:49:55. In 1957, two copies of Charlotte and Dyson Carter's book *Cancer, Smoking, Heart Disease, and Alcohol in Two World Systems* were sent to the Soviet Ministry of Foreign Affairs. VOKS 6:1:55:122. In February 1957, VOKS discussed the fact that their *Science of Health and Long Life in the U.S.S.R.* was published in Australia and reviewed in the Soviet press. VOKS 6:1:55:63–65.

69 VOKS 6:1:49:61–63, dated 10 April 1956.

70 VOKS 6:1:50:71–72, D. Carter to V. Bourdine, 12 January 1955.

71 VOKS 6:1:49:173, A. Tovstogan to A. Vertogradov, 13 August 1956.

72 VOKS 6:1:50:81, D. Carter to K. Perevoschikov, 22 March 1955. There is also a reference to this in the Louis and Irene Kon Collection at Osler Library, McGill University, Montreal. Kon had organized Soviet art exhibitions for the prewar Friends of the Soviet Union. Kealey and Whitaker, *The R.C.M.P. Security Bulletins: The Depression Years, pt. II, 1935*, 344.

73 VOKS 6:1:50:49, V.G. Yakovlev to A.E. Petrushev, Chief of Tsentropromsovet, 28 July 1955.

74 VOKS 6:1:50:47–48, D. Carter to K. Perevoschikov, 3 July 1955.

75 VOKS 6:1:50:50, V.G. Yakovlev to A. Goryachkin, 11 August 1955.

76 LAC, RG146, ATIP request A-2006-00091, Ted Baxter to CSFS branches, 1954, 25.

77 Ibid., 29 September 1954, 23.

78 A list of these Soviet Friendship Month events was published in the *Canadian Tribune*, 9 November 1954, LAC, RG146, ATIP request A-2006-00104, 100; also published in *Vestnik*, 3 November 1954; *Jedinstvo* (Unity), 2 November 1954; *Laudis balsas* (People's Voice), 29 October 1954; summaries in RCMP files, LAC, RG146, ATIP request A-2006-00104, 107, 108, 110.

79 LAC, RG146, ATIP request A-2006-00091, memo from Ted Baxter, Secretary, CSFS, to "All Society Branches on Publicity," 19 October 1954, 16.

80 VOKS 6:1:45:123–24, letter from LPP, 19 November 1953.

81 LAC, RG146, ATIP request A-2006-00103, "Club Letter," signed by Maurice Rush, Secretary, City of Vancouver, dated 23 February 1954, recorded in RCMP Vancouver Subdivision, Special Branch, memo "RE: Labor Progressive Party—British Columbia," dated 4 March 1954, 241.

82 LAC, RG146, ATIP request A-2006-00103, "Circular Letter N. 2," from the National Executive of the FRC, signed by J. Kurban, Secretary, Toronto, 27 November 1953, 86.

83 Editorial "Fulfill These Tasks in January," *Ukrainske slovo* (Ukrainian Word), 7 January 1953, 10, LAC, RG146, ATIP request A-2006-00102, RCMP summary, dated 9 January 1953, 71.

84 VOKS 6:1:49:24, D. Carter to K. Perevozchikov [*sic*], 15 October 1955.

85 VOKS 6:1:53:27, D. Carter to I. Kulakovskaya, 3 January 1956.

86 VOKS 6:1:50:71–72, D. Carter to V. Burdin, 12 January 1955.

87 Ibid.

88 VOKS 6:1:49:6, A. Tovstogan to I. Kulakovskaya, 26 November 1955. The greeting form is found in VOKS 49:22.

89 VOKS 6:1:49:22, 23. The form destined for groups listed the name of the CSFS above the Bathurst address, and the one printed in *News-Facts about the USSR* used the name of the journal, with the same address.

90 VOKS 6:1:49:22.

91 VOKS 6:1:49:17, A. Tovstogan to I. Kulakovskaya, 26 November 1955.

92 VOKS 6:1:53:42–44, D. Carter to I. Kulakovskaya, 28 December 1955.

93 Ibid.

94 VOKS 6:1:53:45–52, D. Carter to I. Kulakovskaya, 2 January 1956.

95 VOKS 6:1:49:88, dated February 1956.

96 VOKS 6:1:49:5, A. Vertogradov to A. Tovstogan, 3 April 1956.

97 VOKS 6:1:49:117, A. Vertogradov to A. Tovstogan, 12 May 1956.

98 VOKS 6:1:53:87–89, forwarding letter L.E. Kiz to I. Kulakovskaya, 22 June 1956, and "Greetings to the AUUC in Winnipeg, Manitoba, Canada."

99 VOKS 6:1:53:90.

100 VOKS 6:1:49:126, A. Tovstogan to I. Kulakovskaya, 7 April 1956.

101 VOKS 6:1:49:127b, Dyson Carter to CSFS members, dated 29 February 1956.

102 VOKS 6:1:49:5–6, A. Tovstogan to I. Kulakovskaya, 26 November 1955.

103 Numerous examples of these brochures, and the Carter advertisements, can be found in the Robert S. Kenny Collection, MS Collection 179, Thomas Fisher Rare Book Library, University of Toronto, box 62.

104 The Novosti Press Agency Office photograph archives are located in Special Collections at Carleton University.

105 VOKS 6:1:50:29, V.G. Yakovlev to P.A. Pozdeev, 17 December 1955.

106 VOKS 6:1:49:52, A. Vertogradov to A. Tovstogan, 25 March 1956.

107 Ibid.

108 Hanno Hardt, *In the Company of Media: Cultural Constructions of Communication, 1920s–1930s* (Boulder, CO: Westview Press, 2000), 38. This quotation is from Leon Trotsky, but though Carter would have agreed with the notion he would never have acknowledged Trotsky for having made the comment. Trotsky had been declared an "enemy of the people" by Stalin in the late 1920s, exiled, and assassinated in 1940. He was never rehabilitated, and Carter followed the official Soviet line unfailingly in his publications.

109 Most likely the attendees were not, as Carter claimed, "far from the progressive movement" but left-leaning individuals who were not party members.

110 VOKS 6:1:49:74, A. Tovstogan to I. Kulakovskaya, 9 March 1956.

111 VOKS 6:1:49:116, A. Vertogradov to A. Tovstogan, 12 May 1956.

112 VOKS 6:1:49:117–120, lists of films in French and English, colour and black-and-white.

113 VOKS 6:1:49:74a–75, I. Kulakovskaya to A. Tovstogan, 5 March 1956.

114 VOKS 6:1:50:116, 1952 finances; 6:1:50:117, 1953 finances.

115 LAC, RG146, ATIP request A-2006-00103, RCMP review, dated 24 February 1953, of *Vapaus*, 21 February 1953, 251.

116 VOKS 6:1:55:27–28, A. Tovstogan to V.V. Abramov, Sovexportfilm, 11 December 1956.

117 VOKS 6:1:55:29, G. Ioanisyan to K. Litvin (UkrOKS), 9 January 1956.

118 *Ukrainske zhittia*, 12 January 1956, summarized by the RCMP, LAC, RG146, ATIP request A-2006-00104, 17.

119 Roberts and Cipko, *One Way Ticket*. See also Roberts and Cipko, "Canada and the Khrushchev Government's 'Return to the Homeland' Campaign." Cipko has also studied the campaign in relation to the Ukrainian diaspora in Argentina. Some Finnish Canadians were encouraged earlier to return to the Karelo-Finnish Soviet Socialist Republic, and this movement was generally tragic for them. See, especially, Lindstrom's work and the NFB-produced film *Letters from Karelia*, for which Lindstrom was consulted. On propaganda used to convince Canadians to return to the USSR, and their subsequent desire to return to Canada, see also memos exchanged among the Department of External Affairs, the prime minister, and the Canadian Embassy in Moscow in 1960, in *Documents on Canadian External Affairs*, vol. 27 (1960), ed. Janice Cavell (Ottawa: Foreign Affairs and International Trade Canada, 2007), 1009–13.

120 *News-Facts about the USSR* 63 (1956): 3.

121 Ibid.

122 Ibid., 65 (1956): 7.

123 Ibid., 3 (1950).

124 Carter and Carter, *We Saw Socialism*, 100.

125 VOKS 6:1:35:2, letter from M. Korol, 10 November 1951.

126 VOKS 6:1:55:123–25, A. Tovstogan to G. Ioanisyan, 4 June 1957.

127 Ralph Hyman, "What's behind the Curtain? One Fled, Knows; One Sails to Learn," *Globe and Mail*, 5 September 1951, 15.

128 N. Prychodko, letter to the editor, "Questions of Victims Challenge the Iron Curtain," *Globe and Mail*, 8 September 1951, 6. Clipping also in LAC, RG146, ATIP request A-2006-00198, 79.

129 Carter and Carter, *We Saw Socialism*, 271–73. This section is subtitled "'But I Was There!'"

130 *News-Facts about the USSR* 61 (1955–56): 16.

131 "Society Offering Sub to Members," *Pacific Tribune*, 25 November 1955, in LAC, RG146, ATIP request A-2006-00104, 26; LAC, RG146, ATIP request A-2006-00104, CSFS circular letter signed by Carter, 19 October 1955, 35–36. CSFS yearly membership cost fifty cents.

132 VOKS 6:1:50:84, D. Carter to K. Perevozchikov [*sic*], 17 August 1954. It seems that there is a contradiction—Carter told VOKS he was distributing the periodicals for free, but did charge at least a nominal fee for a subscription—where did that money go? Maybe it paid postage. Sadly, no evidence of bank transactions exists.

133 VOKS 6:1:57:60, Louise Harvey to VOKS, 1 April 1957.

134 VOKS 6:1:39:23, V.G. Yakovlev to V. Burdin, 23 February 1953.

135 VOKS 6:1:49:217, Yakovlev to A. Tovstogan, 16 October 1956.

136 See, for example, VOKS 6:1:55:55, 56–59.

137 "At Last! You Can Learn the Russian Language," ad in *News-Facts about the USSR*, dated 27 March 1955, LAC, RG146, vol. 3349, part 20, 50.

138 VOKS 6:1:49:37–38, A. Tovstogan to I. Kulakovskaya, 10 January 1956.

139 VOKS 6:1:49:49, V.G. Yakovlev to A. Tovstogan, 5 March 1956.

140 VOKS 6:1:49:157, Kulikov, Deputy Director of Publication at *Moscow News*, to L. Starikov, VOKS, 15 June 1956; 6:1:49:165, I. Kulakovskaya to A. Tovstogan, 19 June 1956.

141 Dyson Carter, "Millions Are Awakening to the Fact that Friendship with the Soviet Is for Our Own Sake, for Canada," *Kanadai magyar munkas*, 18 February 1954; Dyson Carter, "Trade, Jobs, Peace in Friendship with USSR," *Ukrainian Canadian*, 15 February 1954; both articles in LAC, RG146, ATIP request A-2006-00103, 5–10.

142 LAC, RG146, ATIP request A-2006-00103, 5–10.

143 Ibid.

144 Ibid.

145 Ibid., 5. Claiming that Kirov had been murdered by a foreign agent gave Stalin the necessary justification to arrest and execute hundreds of party members in the purges of the 1930s.

146 See, for instance, clippings from the *Pacific Tribune*, *Canadian Jewish Weekly*, *Ukrainian Canadian*, and *Kanadai magyar munkas*, in LAC, RG146, ATIP request A-2006-00103, 11, 20, 23, 33.

147 Bobbie Marsden, "A Name to Remember," *Canadian Jewish Weekly*, n.d., LAC, RG146, ATIP request A-2006-00103, 21.

148 Black, "Soviet Tactics and Targets in Canada before and after the Gouzenko Defection," 109.

149 See, for instance, the record of a "collection card issued to raise funds to send X on a trip to the Soviet Union under the auspices of the Canadian Soviet Friendship Society," issued by the BC branch of the LPP, recorded by the RCMP in a memo from the Vancouver Subdivision, Special Branch, 9 November 1953, LAC, RG146, ATIP request A-2006-00103, 95. The delegate's name has been erased from the document by ATIP. He/she was the secretary of the BC CSFS branch.

150 The biography and itinerary of the trip are in VOKS 6:31:206–11. See also Black, "Soviet Tactics and Targets in Canada before and after the Gouzenko Defection," 117.

151 Ibid., 118. Also see Libbie and Frank Park, *Moscow: As Two Canadians Saw It* (Toronto: CSFS, 1951).

152 Canadian Museum of History Archives, Jennifer Anderson fonds 2016-H0036, "Frank and Libbie Park Trip to USSR."

153 VOKS 6:1:50:107, Sochasky to VOKS, 12 March 1955 handwritten in the margin. Her name was variously transliterated in VOKS documents as Suchasky, Suchaski, and Sokhatsky, but each time she was listed as Mrs. Anna/Anne from Vancouver, CSFS delegate, *VOKS Bulletin* reader, AUUC and/or CSFS member.

154 On this see, especially, Swyripa, *Wedded to the Cause*.

155 VOKS 6:1:48:135, V. Burdin to K. Perevoschikov, 25 May 1955.

156 LAC, RG146, ATIP request A-2006-00092, RCMP report from Cranbrook Special Branch, Nelson, BC, "Canadian-Soviet Friendship Society, Delegation to the U.S.S.R., December 1954," 13 April 1955, 7–8.

157 LAC, RG146, ATIP request A-2006-00092, RCMP report from the Special Branch, Nelson, BC, "Canadian-Soviet Friendship Society, Delegation to the U.S.S.R.—December 1954," 4 April 1955, 11.

158 Ibid.

159 LAC, RG146, ATIP request A-2006-00104, RCMP report dated 14 April 1955, 53.

160 LAC, RG146, ATIP request A-2006-00092, "Soviet Life Described Here," *Nelson Daily News*, 31 March 1955, attached as part of the RCMP report "Canadian-Soviet Friendship Society, Delegation to the U.S.S.R.—December 1954," 4 April 1955, 14.

161 An RCMP report from 1950 noted emphatically that "the AUUC is a part of the *CANADIAN SOVIET FRIENDSHIP SOCIETY*, and that Mr. WM. TERESIO, president of the AUUC[,] is on the executive of the *CANADIAN SOVIET FRIENDSHIP SOCIETY*." LAC, RG146, ATIP request A-2006-00096, RCMP report dated 6 March 1950, 248.

162 LAC, RG146, ATIP request A-2006-00091, "Memo to All Society Branches" from Ted Baxter, 15 January 1954, 38. Teresio died on 6 January 1954.

163 LAC, RG146, ATIP request A-2006-00092, "Dear Friend" letter and form from John Flatt, Joe Kossick, and Jack Bingley, calling themselves jokingly the "Committee for 'Pat,'" Moose Jaw, SK, 8 November 1954, attached to RCMP report, 24, 26. A postscript to this letter announced that "this month is Soviet Friendship Month."

164 For instance, Morris Biderman, himself a CSFS delegate, published an article on Louis Benzvy's trip to the USSR in 1955. LAC, RG146, ATIP request A-2006-00092, Morris Biderman, "A Warm Reunion in Moscow," *Vochenblatt*, stamped 30 April 1955, attached to RCMP report, 46. For more on Biderman's activism, see his autobiography, *A Life on the Jewish Left: An Immigrant's Experience* (Toronto: Onward Publishing, 2000).

165 VOKS 6:1:50:52–54, D. Carter to K. Perevoschikov, 31 March 1955.

166 VOKS 49:268, D. Carter to A. Tovstogan, 12 September 1956.

167 VOKS 49:264–67, letter from A. Tovstogan to A. Vertogradov, 20 September 1956; VOKS 55:70–77, A. Tovstogan to G. Ioanisyan, 22 February 1957.

168 Khrushchev's so-called secret speech was given to a closed session of the party at the Twentieth Party Congress on 25 February 1956. It became public in March and was influential in giving impetus to uprisings in the Soviet satellite countries later that year. When the revolt in Hungary was put down forcibly by the Soviets in November, international critics of all political orientations expressed alarm at this response. Many leftists worldwide trace their disillusionment with the USSR back to this moment.

169 VOKS 50:203, D. Chuvakhin, Soviet Ambassador to Canada, to G. Ioanisyan, 8 April 1957.

170 William Irvine, Dorothy Johnson, Harold Bronson, and B.F. Tanner participated on this tour, and their thank-you letters to VOKS personnel (August–September 1956) are in VOKS 6:1:54:72–83.

171 On the crisis in the Canadian LPP, and the strong feelings of disillusionment and disappointment among members, caused by the events of 1956, see Weisbord, *The Strangest Dream*.

172 VOKS 49:232–37, list of *VOKS Bulletin* subscribers and one cancellation, attached to a letter from A. Tovstogan to A. Vertogradov, 17 August 1956.

173 Baxter, interview. Baxter said that RCMP officers repeatedly visited his workplace and spoke with his boss about his political activities.

174 VOKS 49:13, A. Tovstogan to I. Kulakovskaya, 16 December 1955.

175 VOKS 49:264, A. Tovstogan to A. Vertogradov, 20 September 1956.

176 VOKS 55:2, A. Tovstogan to I. Kulakovskaya, 11 December 1956.

177 VOKS 55:150–51, A. Tovstogan to G. Ioanisyan, 31 May 1957.

178 VOKS 6:1:56:24–25, D. Carter to S.G. Kolmakova, 10 September 1957. The move might have been necessary partly because of his health. An accident in 1957 led to time in the hospital and might have kept him from walking again. See VOKS 6:1:55:150–51, 161–63, A. Tovstogan to G. Ioanisyan, 31 May 1957; A. Tovstogan to G. Ioanisyan, 13 September 1957; VOKS 6:1:56:18–19, 24–25, C. Carter to S.G. Kolmakova, 11 June 1957; S.G. Kolmakova to C. Carter, 21 June 1957; D. Carter to S.G. Kolmakova, 10 September 1957.

179 Boyd interview; John Boyd, comments on manuscript by Jennifer Anderson, April 2008.

180 Hunt explained that his English name and mannerisms helped him to book speakers and make other arrangements for the association. Hunt, interview.

181 Although it is difficult to be certain of the statistics, letters to the editor in the Dyson Carter fonds at LAC seem to suggest that many of his readers had immigrated to Canada from Eastern and Central Europe. As previously mentioned, an AUUC survey in 1965 found that many young AUUC members enjoyed *Northern Neighbors*. LAC, MG 28-V-154, vol. 27, file 14-18, "Poll of Participants of the AUUC National Youth Conference, July 9–11, 1965, Ukrainian Camp Palermo," Toronto.

Chapter 6: The "Pink Tea Circuit" or "Dreams of Equality"? Women and the CSFS

1 Ronald Williams, "The Reds' Pink Tea Circuit: The Communist Front Fools a Lot of Women," *Financial Post*, 9 June 1951, transcribed in an RCMP report, LAC, RG146, ATIP request A-2006-00105, 12 June 1951, 109–10; also in photostat original, LAC, RG146, ATIP request A-2006-00098, 32.

2 Ibid.

3 Sangster, *Dreams of Equality*, 124.

4 Ibid., 124–64.

5 Ibid., 55, 124.

6 Ibid., 146–53.

7 The CPC-LPP defined women's oppression in society as a by-product of capitalism, linked to the system's class-based inequalities. Therefore, nothing short of a revolution could alter women's position, and postwar campaigns led by women on the left for price controls, peace, and women's rights received only "lukewarm support" from their male counterparts. This type of feminism at times paralleled the women's suffrage movement and at other times criticized women's movements for being too "bourgeois." On how women on the Ukrainian Canadian left articulated a particular feminism, see Rhonda L. Hinther, "'Sincerest Revolutionary Greetings': Progressive Ukrainians in Canada, 1918–1991" (PhD diss., McMaster University, 2005). On the issue of ethnic unity and liberation of the ancestral homeland, as well as class interests, taking precedence over issues of women's equality among male leftist leaders, see Swyripa, *Wedded to the Cause*; Linda Kealey, *Enlisting Women for the Cause: Women, Labour, and the Left in Canada, 1890–1920* (Toronto: University of Toronto Press, 1998); and Sangster, *Dreams of Equality*, 88 and *passim*.

8 Hinther, "'Sincerest Revolutionary Greetings.'"

9 The CPSU resolution "On Party Unity" passed in 1921 at the Tenth Party Congress made factions illegal and was one of the most lasting CPSU decisions. On this, see Alexandra Kollontai, *Selected Writings*, with an introduction and commentaries by Alix Holt (New York: W.W. Norton and Company, 1977); and Adam B. Ulam, *The Bolsheviks: The Intellectual and Political Triumph of Communism in Russia* (New York: Macmillan Publishing Company, 1965). For another example of a revolutionary woman challenging this situation in the early years of the USSR, see R.C. Elwood, *Inessa Armand: Revolutionary and Feminist* (Cambridge, UK: Cambridge University Press, 1992).

10 Holt, "Introduction," in Kollontai, *Selected Writings*, 17.

11 VOKS 6:1:36:23, list of "National Council of the C.-S.F.S.," 1951. The women listed here were Dorise Nielsen, Executive Secretary, Mrs. Eleanor Ashworth, Mrs. Wilma Williams, Mrs. W. Savenoff, Mrs. Mary Kardash, Fagel Gartner, Mrs. W. Kugler, Mrs. C. Roberts, Mrs. M. Popoff, C. [Charlotte] Carter, and Mrs. R. McCutcheon.

12 Johnston, *A Great Restlessness*, 228–29, 231.

13 Ibid., 228.

14 Ibid., 228, 231.

15 In the spring of 1957, Charlotte took over the editorship of *Northern Neighbors* while Dyson was in the hospital. VOKS 6:1:55:150–51, A. Tovstogan to G. Ioanisyan, 31 May 1957.

16 VOKS 6:1:36:42, receipts and disbursements, CSFS, November 1950–November 1951, audit report signed by Helen Burpee; 6:1:50:115–18, audit report, 23 November 1954, signed by Helen Burpee.

17 Guard, "Canadian Citizens or Dangerous Foreign Women?"; Julie Guard, "Women Worth Watching: Radical Housewives in Cold War Canada," in *Whose National Security? Canadian State Surveillance and the Creation of Enemies*, ed. Gary Kinsman, Dieter K. Buse, and Mercedes Steedman (Toronto: Between the Lines, 2000), 72–88; Sangster, *Dreams of Equality*, 148.

18 Guard, "Canadian Citizens or Dangerous Foreign Women," 168.

19 Ibid., 178.

20 This could be compared with Guard's discussion of the "overlapping membership" among the Housewives' Consumers' Association, the LPP, and progressive ethnic groups. Guard, "Canadian Citizens or Dangerous Foreign Women?," 179.

21 Kealey and Whitaker, *The R.C.M.P. Security Bulletins: The Depression Years, pt. II, 1935*, 435. In an earlier report, the RCMP identified Dorise's husband Pete as one of the BC relief camp strikers marching to Ottawa. Ibid., 366.

22 Kealey and Whitaker *The R.C.M.P. Security Bulletins: The Depression Years, pt. I, 1933–1934*, 146–47.

23 Peter Krawchuk, ed., *Reminiscences of Courage and Hope (Stories of Ukrainian Canadian Women Pioneers)* (Toronto: Kobzar Publishing Company, 1991), 294.

24 VOKS 6:55:150–51, A. Tovstogan to G. Ioanisyan, 31 May 1957.

25 The best example of this in relation to the CSFS is Nielsen's experience, but other women involved in the CPC-LPP have commented on this. See Johnston, *A Great Restlessness*; Sangster, *Dreams of Equality*, 224–38; Lévesque, *Red Travellers*; Watson, *She Never Was Afraid*, 79–86; and Vance, *Not by Gods but by People*, 61.

26 *Canadian Tribune*, 4 February 1952, 14.

27 Ibid.

28 LAC, RG146, ATIP request A-2006-00124, RCMP report from Toronto CIB Detachment, 26 February 1945, detailing the National Council for the CSFS meeting at Royal York Hotel on 22 February 1945, 175. Besides Margaret Gould, Margaret Spaulding, an active participant in the postwar CSFS, was on the platform at this event.

29 Ibid.

30 Ibid., 174.

31 "Canadian-Soviet Friendship Honors 27th Red Army Date," *Toronto Daily Star*, 23 February 1945, 8.

32 "Urge Canadian Gov't Trade with USSR Now," *Canadian Tribune*, 20 November 1950, in LAC, RG146, ATIP request A-2006-00114, 207.

33 "Nielsen Reports on Soviet Life," *Drumheller Mail*, 13 December 1950, n. pag., clipping in LAC, RG146, ATIP request A-2006-00097, 29.

34 LAC, RG146, ATIP request A-2006-00097, RCMP report, Lethbridge Special Branch, 7 December 1950, 31.

35 LAC, RG146, ATIP request A-2006-00097, RCMP report, Drumheller Special Branch, 14 December 1950, 27.

36 LAC, RG146, ATIP request A-2006-00114, RCMP report, Manitoba Special Section on the CSFS meeting held in Hebrew Sick Benefit Hall, Winnipeg, 4 December 1950, report dated 8 December 1950, 198.

37 Ibid.

38 Ibid., 199.

39 Johnston, *A Great Restlessness*, 229.

40 LAC, RG146, ATIP request A-2006-00101, Dorise Nielsen to Mrs. Carole Laurie, Vancouver, 15 September 1952, 129.

41 "Soviet Friendship Tour: Keen Interest Shown about Life in USSR," *Canadian Tribune*, n.d., in LAC, RG146, vol. 3349, supplement 1, part 2, 128.

42 "'Lasting Peace' Soviet Goal Say Canadian Goodwill Envoys," *Canadian Tribune*, 11 June 1951, in LAC, RG146, ATIP request A-2006-00105, 111.

43 From "The Canadian Delegation in the Ukraine," *Soviet Monitor*, 18 May 1951, transcribed in an RCMP report, LAC, RG146, ATIP request A-2006-00098, 30.

44 Much has now been written on the reality gap between the USSR's promises to women and their experiences with the double burden, stress, access to birth control, daycare, high infant mortality, and divorce. See, for example, Chris Corrin, ed., *Superwomen and the Double Burden: Women's Experiences of Change in Central and Eastern Europe and the Former Soviet Union* (Toronto: Second Story Press, 1998); Paula A. Michaels, "Motherhood, Patriotism, and Ethnicity: Soviet Kazakhstan and the 1936 Abortion Ban," *Feminist Studies* 27, 2 (2001): 307–33; Laurie Occhipinti, "Two Steps Back? Anti-Feminism in Eastern Europe," *Anthropology Today* 12, 6 (1996): 13–18; Barbara Alpern Engel, "Engendering Russia's History: Women in Post-Emancipation Russia and the Soviet Union," *Slavic Review* 51, 2 (1992): 309–21; and Ellen Carnaghan, "Political Attitudes and the Gender Gap in the USSR," *Comparative Politics* 22, 4 (1990): 293–304.

45 Quoted in the Soviet newspaper *Trud* (Labour), 10 September 1952, from the *Current Digest of the Soviet Press*, 25 October 1952, in an RCMP memorandum dated 30 October 1952, LAC, RG146, ATIP request A-2006-00107, 46.

46 Radio Moscow English broadcast, 26 and 27 August 1952, reported in the Monitoring Service for the British Broadcasting Corporation, "Summary of World Broadcasts," no. 343, 1 September 1952, in RCMP report, 4 October 1952, LAC, RG146, ATIP request A-2006-00107, 127.

47 LAC, RG146, ATIP request A-2006-00114, RCMP report, Manitoba Special Section, on the CSFS event held at the Hebrew Sick Benefit Hall, Winnipeg, 21 October 1951, report dated 26 October 1951, 168.

48 Ibid.

49 This information comes from the Monitoring Service of the British Broadcasting Corporation, "Summary of World Broadcasts," no. 456, part 1, 5 October 1953, 41, as quoted in an RCMP memorandum entitled "Canadian Soviet Friendship Society—Visit to Soviet Russia," 23 November 1953, LAC, RG146, ATIP request A-2006-00103, 89.

50 This account appeared as "Sojourn in Uzbekistan of Delegation of Canadian-Soviet Friendship Society," in *Pravda Vostoka* (Truth of the East), 26 September 1953, found in translation in LAC, RG146, ATIP request A-2006-00103, 102.

51 This information comes from the Monitoring Service of the British Broadcasting Corporation, "Summary of World Broadcasts," no. 456, part 1, 5 October 1953, 41, as quoted in an RCMP memorandum entitled "Canadian Soviet Friendship Society—Visit to Soviet Russia," 23 November 1953, LAC, RG146, ATIP request A-2006-00103, 89.

52 This press conference was given on 3 October 1953. This information comes from the Monitoring Service of the British Broadcasting Corporation, "Summary of World Broadcasts," no. 457, 9 October 1953, 40–41, as cited in an RCMP memorandum entitled "Canadian Soviet Friendship Society— Visit to Soviet Russia," 23 November 1953, LAC, RG146, ATIP request A-2006-00103, 89–90.

53 Margaret Spaulding's interview was broadcast by Radio Moscow to North America on 10 October 1953. This information comes from the Monitoring Service of the British Broadcasting Corporation, "Summary of World Broadcasts," no. 459, part 1, 16 October 1953, 36, as cited in an RCMP memorandum entitled "Canadian Soviet Friendship Society—Visit to Soviet Russia," 23 November 1953, LAC, RG146, ATIP request A-2006-00103, 90.

54 LAC, RG146, ATIP request A-2006-00097, RCMP report, CIS Manitoba Special Section, 6 December 1950, 40.

55 "USSR Builds in the Name of Peace," press conference in the editorial offices of *Trud* (Labour), 19 September 1952, LAC, RG146, ATIP request A-2006-00107, 132–34.

56 CSFS, *Canadians Visit Their Northern Neighbours: Picture-Report of a Trip to the Soviet Union* (Toronto: News-Facts, 1953), 4. Thanks to J.E. Baxter for providing me with a copy of this publication.

57 Ibid., 4–8.

58 Ibid., 13–14.

59 Ibid., 15.

60 Ibid., 32.

61 *Vestnik*, 1 December 1954, 6; *Ukrainske slovo*, 17 November 1954, 4.

62 LAC, RG146, ATIP request A-2006-00114, RCMP report, Special Branch, Winnipeg, 15 November 1954, 6.

63 LAC, RG146, ATIP request A-2006-00092, RCMP report, Special Branch, Nelson, 4 April 1955, 11.

64 LAC, RG146, ATIP request A-2006-00121, RCMP "E" Division, Special Branch, Vancouver, Inspector H.J. Spanton to RCMP Officers Commanding in Victoria, Chilliwack, Nelson, Kamloops, and Prince Rupert Subdivisions, 16 April 1956, 179.

65 LAC, RG146, ATIP request A-2006-00121, Inspector C.F. Harvey, RCMP Victoria Subdivision, to RCMP Vancouver Subdivision, 8 May 1956, 171.

66 Kealey and Whitaker, *The R.C.M.P. Security Bulletins: The Depression Years, pt. 2, 1935*, 193, 500, 584.

67 This meeting took place in the Point Douglas Labor Temple, 7 December 1953. Circular letter, LAC, RG146, ATIP request A-2006-00114, 19.

68 Ibid.

69 LAC, RG146, ATIP request A-2006-00107, RCMP report, 9 December 1952, 197. The same report is in LAC, RG146, ATIP request A-2006-00114, 23.

70 Slavenka Drakulic, *How We Survived Communism and Even Laughed* (New York: HarperCollins, 1993).

71 Ibid., 124–25.

72 LAC, RG146, ATIP request A-2006-00107, RCMP report, Manitoba Special Branch, 14 October 1952, 116. A copy of this report is also in LAC, RG146, ATIP request A-2006-00114, 28.

73 *Ukrainske zhyttia*, 12 January 1956, summarized by the RCMP in LAC, RG146, ATIP request A-2006-00104, 17.

74 CSFS announcement of the trade delegation, *News-Facts about the USSR* 26 (1952): 00–00. In most of the publicity, the women were referred to by the prefix *Mrs.* A common practice in those days, the prefix was a sign of a married woman's traditional respectability.

75 LAC, RG146, ATIP request A-2006-00103, letter from Dorise Nielsen and Pearl Wedro (signed as chair of the Toronto CSFS branch) to members and *News-Facts about the USSR* readers, 25 March 1953, 132.

76 VOKS 6:1:36:43–52, Dorise Nielsen, "Report on Organization" to the CSFS convention, 26 January 1952; VOKS 6:1:36:25, circular letter on *News-Facts about the USSR* letterhead, addressed to "Dear Reader," signed by Nielsen, 12 December 1951.

77 LAC, RG146, ATIP request A-2006-00103, "Dear Friend," invitation from Margaret Russell, 31 March 1953, 126.

78 LAC, RG146, ATIP request A-2006-00101, 106, RCMP report, Special Branch, Drumheller, on the meeting of 13 March 1952, report dated 20 March 1952.

79 LAC, RG146, ATIP request A-2006-00114, 32.

80 This meeting took place at the Hall of the Federation of Russian Canadians in Winnipeg on 12 November 1950. LAC, RG146, ATIP request A-2006-00114, RCMP report dated 20 November 1950, 203.

81 LAC, RG146, ATIP request A-2006-00114, RCMP report, Special Branch, Winnipeg, dated 22 January 1952, 37.

82 A *Vestnik* reporter claimed that there were more than 500 people in attendance, but an RCMP report put the number at approximately 350. N. Kuchinksy, "Meeting of the Society of Canadian Soviet Friendship in Winnipeg," *Vestnik*, 6 February 1952, 4, translated and summarized by the Winnipeg RCMP in LAC, RG146, ATIP request

A-2006-00114, 35; LAC, RG146, ATIP request A-2006-00114, RCMP report, Special Branch, Winnipeg, 22 January 1952, 37.

83 This meeting was held on 20 January 1952 in the Hebrew Sick Benefit Hall in Winnipeg. N. Kuchinksy, "Meeting of the Society of Canadian Soviet Friendship in Winnipeg," *Vestnik*, 6 February 1952, 4, translated and summarized by the Winnipeg RCMP in LAC, RG146, ATIP request A-2006-00114, 35.

84 LAC, RG146, ATIP request A-2006-00114, RCMP report, Special Branch, Winnipeg, on the meeting held at the Winnipeg Ukrainian Labor Temple, 14 March 1952, report dated 22 March 1952, 34.

85 LAC, RG146, ATIP request A-2006-00098, RCMP report, 17 April 1951, 88. Referred to as "Mrs. Dewar Ferguson."

86 He was also an LPP member and a leader in the LPP-backed Canadian Seamen's Union.

87 LAC, RG146, ATIP request A-2006-00106, letter signed by Hazel Currie on CSFS letterhead, dated 17 June 1952, as part of the Fort William RCMP detachment report, 21 June 1952, 67–68.

88 Sally Nielsen said that the money in this fund was eventually donated to a local Gravenhurst charity for children. Nielsen, interview.

89 Irja Paul grew up in the Finnish community in Timmins. Her first husband, Bob Paul, had been the campaign manager and common-law partner of Dorise Nielsen for some time in the 1940s. He had known Dyson Carter at that time, and later he and Irja occasionally visited the Carters in Gravenhurst. Johnston, *A Great Restlessness*, 47, 123, 203; Irja Paul (and Irene Kuusela and Marie Rempel), interview with the author, 27 November 2006.

90 Paul (and Kuusela and Rempel) interview.

91 Ibid.

92 Nielsen interview.

93 Ibid.

94 Ibid.

95 Natalia Roudakova and Deborah S. Ballard-Reisch, "Femininity and the Double Burden: Dialogues on the Socialization of Russian Daughters into Womanhood," www.auburn.edu/~mitrege/FLRU2520/Roudakova.pdf.

96 "Soviet Children at Study and Play . . . ," *News-Facts about the USSR* 40 (1953): 8.

97 Dyson Carter, "'A Warless Human Race': That Is What Soviet Peace Policy May Bring for Today's Children," *Canadian Tribune*, n.d., in LAC, RG146, ATIP request A-2006-00103, 113–14.

98 The first issue of *Northern Neighbours*, in December 1956, had the title spelled in the Canadian style, but from then on the title was *Northern Neighbors*.

99 "Women Review Their Rights," *Northern Neighbours*, December 1956, 5.

100 "Where Else?," *Northern Neighbors*, July–August 1968, 6.

101 "Dreaded Smallpox Will Soon Be Exterminated," *Northern Neighbors*, May 1973, 13.

102 Cover and "Soviet Women Are Overtaking Their Men," *Northern Neighbors*, June 1973, 7.

103 "Women's Lib in Ukraine," *Northern Neighbors*, June 1973, 6.

104 On how the Soviet censorship office disguised these figures, see Barbara A. Anderson, Kalev Katus, and Brian D. Silver, "Developments and Prospects for

Population Statistics in Countries of the Former Soviet Union," *Population Index* 60, 1 (1994): 4–20; and Celestine Bohlen, "Russian Women Turning to Abortion Less Often," *New York Times*, 29 March 1999.

105 Anderson, Katus, and Silver, "Developments and Prospects for Population Statistics in Countries of the Former Soviet Union," *Population Index*, 6.

106 "Why They Want NO UNISEX in Socialism," *Northern Neighbors*, December 1974, 3.

107 "There Are No Homely Women," *Northern Neighbors*, January 1978, 3. This article was apparently based upon an interview conducted by Yuri Ivanin with a Moscow hairstylist.

108 Ibid.

Chapter 7: Culture as Political Persuasion: Performing Soviet Friendship

1 Headline of an article from *Ukrainske zhittia* about Carter's recent speech, 14 June 1951, 5, translated by the RCMP in a report dated 16 June 1951, LAC, RG146, ATIP request A-2006-00098, 20.

2 See, for instance, Frances Stonor Saunders, *The Cultural Cold War: The CIA and the World of Arts and Letters* (New York: New Press, 1999); and Hugh Wilford, *The Mighty Wurlitzer: How the CIA Played America* (Cambridge, MA: Harvard University Press, 2008).

3 Here I am influenced by Reiter's contention in "Secular *Yiddishkait*," paragraph 19, that left-wing Jews in Toronto "formed a subculture that unified their ethnic and class identities, and was marked by values and cultural patterns in opposition to the dominant society." This was true in a different sense for most of the progressive groups in Canada, as well as for the CSFS, which tried to work as a liaison among other groups.

4 McKay, *Rebels, Reds, Radicals*, 35, 130. Unfortunately, McKay makes no specific reference to the CSFS.

5 One of the best examples of a Soviet artist with a political role thrust on him, trapped by the vicissitudes of Soviet artistic policy, and consistently promoted as a human propaganda tool, is the composer Dmitri Shostakovich. This quotation comes from Solomon Volkov, "Introduction," in *Testimony: The Memoirs of Dmitri Shostakovich*, trans. Antonina W. Bouis (New York: Harper and Row Publishers, 1979), xxxiii.

6 "Avenues of Friendship," *Canadian Tribune*, January 1952, clipping in LAC, RG146, ATIP request A-2006-00099, 113.

7 "Boost Friendship of Canada, USSR," *Ukrainian Canadian*, 1 January 1952, clipping in LAC, RG146, ATIP request A-2006-00099, 120.

8 Caute, *The Dancer Defects*, 1.

9 Ibid., 3–4.

10 On the publication of Canadian writers in the Soviet Union, and the criteria used to select them, see Joseph Black and J.L. Black, "Canada in the Soviet Mirror: English-Language Canadian Literature in Soviet Translation," *Journal of Canadian Studies* 30, 2 (1995): 5–18.

11 Emil Gartner's participation in Soviet friendship activities predated Carter's presidency. Gartner had been active on the Canadian left as choir director for the Jewish Folk Choir, which often performed at NCCSF events during the Second

World War. LAC, RG146, ATIP request A-2006-00124, RCMP report, Toronto Intelligence Branch, regarding an NCCSF event on 4 May 1944, 230.

12 The outspoken pro-Soviet social activism of Robeson, as a darling of elite educational and sports institutions of the United States, earned him the accolades of Soviet authorities and the criticisms of American state and security officials. There is a photograph of Robeson voting in the USSR in the SovFoto Press Agency Collection at the MacLaren Art Centre, Barrie, Ontario, and his popularity among Canadian union members, UJPO members, and others has been noted elsewhere. See Laurel Sefton MacDowell, "Paul Robeson in Canada: A Border Story," *Labour/Le travail* 51 (2003): 31 paragraphs, www.historycooperative.org/journals/11t/51/macdowell.html; and Reiter, "Secular *Yiddishkait*," paragraph 18.

13 On this, see LAC, RG25, vol. 7117, file 9055-40, and vol. 6829, file 2727-V-40, for analyses originating in the Department of External Affairs as well as the Canadian Embassy in Moscow.

14 VOKS6:1:53:111, I. Kulakovskaya to D. Carter, 17 November 1956; VOKS 6:1:55:55–59, A. Tovstogan to V. Yakovlev, 11 December 1956, with "List of Organizations and Private Persons to Receive Journal *Culture and Life*."

15 The RCMP said that there were 700 people in attendance, and *Ukrainske slovo* reported approximately 900 people there. RCMP report, Special Branch, Winnipeg, 15 November 1954, LAC, RG146, ATIP request A-2006-00114, 7; summary of "Mark the Month of Canadian-Soviet Friendship with a Fine Concert Meeting," *Ukrainske slovo*, 17 November 1954, 4.

16 RCMP report, Special Branch, Winnipeg, 15 November 1954, LAC, RG146, ATIP request A-2006-00114, 6.

17 Summary of "Mark the Month of Canadian-Soviet Friendship with a Fine Concert Meeting," *Ukrainske slovo*, 17 November 1954, 4.

18 Excerpt from *Vochenblatt* (Canadian Jewish Weekly), 28 October 1954, 3; and 4 November 1954, in LAC, RG146, ATIP request A-2006-00114, 9, 10.

19 RCMP report, Security and Intelligence Section, Winnipeg, 19 November 1958, LAC, RG146, ATIP request A-2006-00114, 289–90.

20 "Science and Education in the USSR," *Ukrainske slovo*, 19 November 1958, 4, in LAC, RG146, ATIP request A-2006-00114, 288.

21 "Mark the 41st Anniversary of the USSR," *Ukrainske slovo*, 19 November 1958, 3, in LAC, RG146, ATIP request A-2006-00114, 287.

22 Molly Myers and Pearl Blazer, as quoted by Reiter in "Secular *Yiddishkait*," paragraphs 27 and 24.

23 Ronald Williams, "Reds at Work on 'Friendship': Now Start Photo Propaganda Deluge," *Financial Post*, 5 January 1952, in LAC, RG146, ATIP request A-2006-00099, 114. Buhay's comments were made in the party's journal, *National Affairs Monthly*.

24 Ibid.

25 "President's Speech, January 25, 1952," VOKS 6:1:36:43–52; also in LAC, RG146, ATIP request A-2006-00100, 67–76.

26 VOKS 5:3:32:137–39, F. Taylor to VOKS, May 1951.

27 Three of his paintings completed during the Second World War now hang in the gallery at the Canadian War Museum in Ottawa. For more on Taylor, see John Virtue, *Fred Taylor: Brother in the Shadows* (Montreal: McGill-Queen's University Press, 2008).

28 VOKS 5:3:32:15–18, A. Yanovsky to A. Gerasimov, President, Fine Art Section, VOKS, Moscow, 3 June 1951.

29 "Canadian-Soviet Friendship," *Pacific Tribune*, January 1952 (exact date indecipherable), LAC, RG146, ATIP request A-2006-00099, 65.

30 John Stewart, "'Can't Keep Pace' with Demand for Truth about USSR—Carters," *Canadian Tribune*, 5 November 1951, LAC, RG146, ATIP request A-2006-00099, 141.

31 Ibid.

32 "Eminent Britons Send Greetings to Canadian-Soviet Friendship Parley," *Pacific Tribune*, January 1952 (exact date indecipherable), LAC, RG146, ATIP request A-2006-00099, 64.

33 RCMP, "Memorandum for File" and "Correlated Files (Incomplete List)," dated 17 October 1955, reporting on the Fourth National Cultural Conference of the Labor-Progressive Party, 8–10 April 1955, LAC, RG146, ATIP request A-2006-00104, 37–39.

34 Ibid.

35 Ibid.

36 Ibid.

37 "Radio Moscow Beams Series on USSR-Canada Friendship," *Canadian Tribune*, January 1952 (exact date not noted), LAC, RG146, ATIP request A-2006-00099, 112.

38 The CSFS publications reviewed were Park and Park, *Moscow as Two Canadians Saw It*, and Carter and Carter, *We Saw Socialism*.

39 Editorial, *Vestnik*, 5 January 1952, in RCMP report, LAC, RG146, vol. 3348, part 12, 115.

40 "Show Famous Film Childhood of Gorki," *Canadian Tribune*, 14 January 1952, LAC, RG146, ATIP request A-2006-00099, 82.

41 The Russian spelling of the city Kanev was used in the original source, though today it is referred to by its Ukrainian name, Kaniv. "Canadian Delegation in the Ukraine," *Soviet Monitor*, datelined "Kiev (Tass)," 18 May 1951, in an RCMP report, LAC, RG146, ATIP request A-2006-00098, 29–30.

42 Ibid.

43 Ibid.

44 From the *Soviet Monitor*, 19 May 1951, from a press conference given by the delegation at Friendship House, Moscow, in an RCMP report, LAC, RG146, ATIP request A-2006-00098, 30.

45 Ibid.

46 Ibid., 29.

47 Ibid., 31.

48 LAC, Frederick B. Taylor fonds, MG30-D360, vol. 3, Taylor's reminiscences of his 1951 visit to the USSR. Also see Virtue, *Fred Taylor*, 150.

49 LAC, Frederick B. Taylor fonds, MG30-D360, vol. 3.

50 Virtue, *Fred Taylor*, 150.

51 *Financial Post*, 9 June 1951, quoted in ibid., 151–54. Taylor's brother was the well-known Canadian industrialist E.P. Taylor.

52 See *Ukrainske slovo*, 6 June 1951, 1, translated in an RCMP report, LAC, RG146, ATIP request A-2006-00098, 35.

53 This ad appeared in the *Canadian Jewish Weekly*, 26 April 1951, LAC, RG146, ATIP request A-2006-00098, 82.

54 "What's Doing," *Canadian Tribune*, 21 May 1951, LAC, RG146, ATIP request A-2006-00098, 57, 59.

55 Ibid.

56 RCMP report, dated 2 June 1951, LAC, RG146, ATIP request A-2006-00098, 37.

57 Ibid., 38. Interestingly, the RCMP commented throughout on how closely the Gartners and Penner stuck to the party line.

58 Ibid., 40.

59 The phenomenon of *pokazukha*, which comes from the Russian verb *pokazat'* meaning literally "to show, to display," is sometimes referred to as a "Potemkin village" (idealized false image). For more on the use of *pokazukha* in Russian slang, see Irina H. Corten, *Vocabulary of Soviet Society and Culture: A Selected Guide to Russian Words, Idioms, and Expressions of the Post-Stalin Era, 1953–1991* (Durham, NC: Duke University Press, 1992), 107.

60 "China Blockade Means War, Says Ald. Penner," *Winnipeg Free Press*, 1 June 1951, LAC, RG146, ATIP request A-2006-00114, 192.

61 Summary of report in the Winnipeg newspaper *Dos Yiddishe Vort* (the Israelite Press), 8 June 1951, 1, in an RCMP report, 22 June 1951, LAC, RG146, ATIP request A-2006-00098, 18.

62 "City Rejects Penner Move to 'Screen' Audiences," *Winnipeg Free Press*, 26 June 1951; RCMP letter to the Ottawa Commissioner, 27 June 1951, LAC, RG146, ATIP request A-2006-00098, 16.

63 Summary of report in the Winnipeg newspaper *Dos Yiddishe Vort* (the Israelite Press), 15 June 1951, 2, in an RCMP report, 22 June 1951, LAC, RG146, ATIP request A-2006-00098, 18.

64 *Ukrainske slovo*, 13 June 1951, 3; *Canadian Tribune*, 18 June 1951, 2; RCMP report, LAC, RG146, ATIP request A-2006-00098, 21.

65 Frederick B. Taylor, letter to the editor, "Alleged Anti-Semitism in the USSR," *Montreal Gazette*, 6 November 1951, LAC, RG146, ATIP request A-2006-00099, 136.

66 LAC, RG146, ATIP request A-2006-00099, RCMP report, Vancouver Special Branch, 14 January 1952, 88.

67 Ibid.

68 Interestingly, since the end of the Cold War, Soviet propaganda photos and art have made for provocative exhibitions. Consider the September 2007 exhibition of SovFoto Press Agency photos at the MacLaren Art Centre, Barrie, Ontario, entitled "Broken Promises: Soviet Photography in the Age of Stalin," and "1930: The Making of 'the New Man'" at the National Gallery of Canada, 6 June–7 September 2008.

69 "Captivated by the Oratorio 'The Song of the Forests,'" *Ukrainske slovo*, 18 April 1951, summarized in an RCMP report, LAC, RG146, ATIP request A-2006-00098, 87.

70 LAC, RG146, ATIP request A-2006-00098, from the program for the performance of "Song of the Forests" by the Jewish Folk Choir at Massey Hall, 7 April 1951, 97.

71 LAC, RG146, ATIP request A-2006-00098, RCMP report, 17 April 1951, 88.

72 Ibid.

73 Ibid.

74 Volkov, "Introduction," xxxvi.

75 Ibid., xxxviii.

76 Ibid., xxxvii. Shostakovich was able to speak out more openly against Soviet anti-Semitism after Khrushchev's 1956 speech launched a mild cultural "thaw" in the USSR. In 1962, he composed his Thirteenth Symphony, reworking parts of Yevgeny Yevtushenko's "Babi Yar," a poem describing the Nazi slaughter of Jews outside Kyiv. Ibid., xxxvii; Shostakovich, *Testimony*, 185.

77 The more attention paid to his music in the West, the more fearful Shostakovich became of repressions at home. Shostakovich, *Testimony*, 137. On how well-known but banned poets were made to "dance" for foreign delegations to the USSR, see ibid., 202.

78 I. Nestyev, "On His Fiftieth Birthday: Dmitry Shostakovich," *VOKS Bulletin* 9, 104 (1956): 17–21.

79 For a discussion of why he appreciated Jewish folk music, see Shostakovich, *Testimony*, 156–57; on being "humiliated" by Stalin's order that he attend the Cultural and Scientific Congress for World Peace in New York in 1949, even though his work was banned in the USSR, see ibid., 147.

80 LAC, RG146, ATIP request A-2006-00098, from the program for the performance of "Song of the Forests" by the Jewish Folk Choir at Massey Hall, 7 April 1951, 94.

81 VOKS 5:3:32:153, D. Carter cable to D. Shostakovich, 8 April 1951; VOKS 5:3:32:153, D. Carter cable to K. Perevoschikov and A. Denisov, 8 April 1951.

82 "Elect Delegates to Jan. 25 Parley: Canadian-Soviet Friendship Celebrations across Canada," *Canadian Tribune*, January 1952 (exact date indecipherable), clipping in LAC, RG146, ATIP request A-2006-00099, 80; "Film Masterpiece of Maxim Gorki's Childhood Features at Convention's Opening," *Canadian Jewish Weekly*, 10 January 1952, clipping in LAC, RG146, ATIP request A-2006-00099, 95.

83 "On Soviet Radio 'This Is Canada,'" *Chempion*, 17 January 1952, LAC, RG146, vol. 3348, part 12, 67.

84 "Nationwide 'Friendship Month' Climaxed by Jan. 26 Convention," *Canadian Tribune*, January 1952, LAC, RG146, ATIP request A-2006-00099, 121; *Canadian Jewish Weekly*, 3 January 1952, LAC, RG146, ATIP request A-2006-00099, 119.

85 "Says Democracies Foil Russian Peace Efforts," *Globe and Mail*, 28 January 1952, LAC, RG146, ATIP request A-2006-00100, 36.

86 "Top Soviet Diplomat to Canada Charges 'Big 3' Preparing War," *Ottawa Journal*, 28 January 1952, LAC, RG146, ATIP request A-2006-00100, 83.

87 James McCook, "Russian Embassy Door Creaks Open a Crack," *Ottawa Journal*, 31 January 1952, LAC, RG146, ATIP request A-2006-00100, 3.

88 "Russ Visit Stirs Storm Ban Receptions—Balfour," *Toronto Telegram*, 29 January 1952, LAC, RG146, ATIP request A-2006-00100, 32.

89 LAC, RG146, ATIP request A-2006-00100, 37.

90 "Text of L.F. Teplov Address," *Canadian Tribune*, 4 February 1952, 8.

91 An RCMP transit slip for headquarters use, dated 4 February 1952, signed by Superintendent McClellan, reads "I want two [corrected from "a"] copies of Teplov's address to go to George Glazebrook at External Affairs." LAC, RG146, ATIP request A-2006-00100, 205. It was forwarded with a memo the next day.

92 "Says Democracies Foil Russian Peace Efforts," *Globe and Mail*, 28 January 1952, LAC, RG146, ATIP request A-2006-00100, 36. The *Canadian Tribune* claimed that 6,000 invitations were mailed out to subscribers to *News-Facts about the USSR*, *Photo-Facts*, CSFS members, and associated groups. "6,000 Invites out for Friendship Meet," *Canadian Tribune*, 28 January 1952.

93 "Convention Highlights," *Canadian Tribune*, 4 February 1952, 9.

94 V. Nekrasov, "Around the World: Soviet Artists in Canada," *News* (possibly a version of Novosti for English speakers), 10 May 1954, LAC, RG146, ATIP request A-2006-00095, 18–19.

95 "All Canada Acclaims Triumphant Soviet Artists," *Canadian Tribune*, 10 May 1954, LAC, RG146, ATIP request A-2006-00095, 28.

96 LAC, RG146, ATIP request A-2006-00095, RCMP report, Special Branch, Toronto, 10 May 1954, 2.

97 John Boyd, "A Dual Heritage: How My Ethnic and Left-Wing Background Affected My Life," unpublished manuscript, June 2010.

98 *Ukrainske slovo*, 21 April 1954, 1, 3, in LAC, RG146, ATIP request A-2006-00114, 12.

99 Rose Mickoluk, "Canada Tour Triumph for Artists from USSR," *Ukrainian Canadian*, 1 June 1954, LAC, RG146, ATIP request A-2006-00095, 45.

100 Ibid.

101 "They Fell in Love with Canada," *Canadian Tribune*, LAC, RG146, ATIP request A-2006-00095, 48–49.

102 Ibid.

103 VOKS 6:1:58:35, D. Carter to K. Perevoschikov, 28 May 1954.

104 Richard Kasischke, "Soviet Artists Comment on Canada," *Montreal Gazette*, 9 July 1954, LAC, RG146, ATIP request A-2006-00095, 37–38.

105 Ibid.

106 S. Roy Maley, "Russian Violinist Superb Virtuoso: Audience at Soviet Concert Most Ill-Mannered in Years," *Winnipeg Tribune*, 27 April 1954, LAC, RG146, ATIP request A-2006-00095, 37.

107 Harvey Hickey, "Special Invitation: Soviet Would Welcome Musicians from Canada," *Globe and Mail*, 11 April 1955, LAC, RG146, ATIP request A-2006-00104, 52; Frank Swanson, "Canadian Musicians Get Invitation," *Vancouver Daily Province*, LAC, RG146, vol. 3349, part 20, 54.

108 "On and Off the Record," *Montreal Gazette*, 29 April 1954, LAC, RG146, ATIP request A-2006-00095, 87.

109 VOKS6:1:43:26, CSFS press release, April 1954. Lemoyne was said to work for the Montreal paper *L'autorite*. Later that year Margaret Fairley, editor of *New Frontiers*, the LPP's literary magazine, as well as contributors and CSFS members Avrom Yanovsky and J.S. Wallace, visited Romania. *Canadian Tribune*, 30 August 1954, LAC, RG146, ATIP request A-2006-00093, 88.

110 VOKS 6:1:43:26, CSFS press release, April 1954.

111 *Montreal Gazette*, 10 April 1954, LAC, RG146, ATIP request A-2006-00093, 18, 20, 23, 33. The departure of the Toronto artists was reported in Lotta Dempsey's article "Leave Next Week: Three Toronto Artists Plan Tour of Russia," *Globe and Mail*, 1 April 1954, LAC, RG146, ATIP request A-2006-00093, 50.

112 "What's Going on in Red Culture Takes Six Canadians to Moscow," *Montreal Gazette*, 10 April 1954, LAC, RG146, ATIP request A-2006-00093, 22.

113 Ibid.

114 Ibid.

115 Unfortunately, the RCMP's reasoning is unknown; despite the release of the related documents under Access to Information and Privacy, these particular reports are almost entirely blacked out.

116 "Canadian Artists Going," *Canadian Tribune*, April 1954, LAC, RG146, ATIP request A-2006-00093, 34. MacDonald's decision not to go was also reported in "Composer Unable to Tour Russia," *Globe and Mail*, 6 April 1954, LAC, RG146, ATIP request A-2006-00093, 46.

117 "Le lieutenant Boyczum leur a souhaité 'bon voyage': Quatre pelerins de 'l'amitié canado-russe' sont parties hier de Dorval pour la lointaine Russie," *Montréal matin*, 9 April 1954, LAC, RG146, ATIP request A-2006-00093, 37–38.

118 Ibid.

119 VOKS 6:1:51:113, L. Kon to L. Kislova, 18 January 1955.

120 VOKS 6:1:51:113. Duranty was a pro-Soviet journalist for the *New York Times* who refused to acknowledge that a famine had taken place in the USSR in 1932–33.

121 VOKS 6:1:51:113. The word *drink* and the date that Varley visited the USSR (1954) appear to have been underlined by the letter reader. The letter was forwarded to Perevoschikov (the deputy director of the British Countries division of VOKS) and Chesnokov (the head of the VOKS Medical Section).

122 There was an exchange of correspondence among Taylor, Carter, and VOKS in the summer of 1951. VOKS 6:1:32:76, 77–79, 84, 85.

123 VOKS 6:1:33:46, 55; 36:133; 38:83; 40:63. In January 1952, Dorise Nielsen reported that Taylor's seminars on Soviet art had proven popular. VOKS 6:1:36:54, Dorise Nielsen, "Report on Organization," CSFS convention, 26 January 1952.

124 VOKS 6:1:47:70–71, 3 January 1954. Actually, Grove was born in Prussia in 1879 and died in Canada in 1948. His real name was Felix Paul Greve. Recent research has suggested that Grove lied about many of his experiences, including those described in his autobiography. Klaus Martens, *F.P. Grove in Europe and Canada: Translated Lives* (Edmonton: University of Alberta Press, 2001).

125 VOKS6:1:47:70.

126 Carter might have modelled his writing on Grove's. Like Grove, he used a pedantic style with stereotypically oppressive male characters controlling female characters who sought personal liberty.

127 VOKS 47:12, V. Burdin to V. Bogatyrev, 10 February 1954; VOKS 47:69, K. Perevoschikov to B. Polevoi, Head, Foreign Commission, Union of Soviet Writers, 29 April 1954. In 1947, Grove won the Governor General's Literary Award for *In Search of Myself*.

128 VOKS 47:160, D. Carter to K. Perevoschikov, 5 March 1954.

129 VOKS 47:160.

130 Barker Fairley, *Goethe's Faust: Six Essays* (Oxford: Clarendon Press, 1953).

131 VOKS 47:7–9, V. Burdin to V. Bogatyrev, 29 March 1954; VOKS 47:159, K. Perevoschikov to B. Polevoi, 22 April 1954.

132 VOKS 58:68–71, D. Carter to A. Denisov, March 1954.

133 VOKS 58:68–71; 58:51a.

134 VOKS 47:37, D. Carter to K. Perevoschikov, 1 November 1954. The reference to the clergyman father is especially interesting because Carter's own father was a minister

in the Salvation Army church, and so was James Endicott, spokesperson for the Canadian Peace Congress, linked to the LPP.

135 VOKS 58:68–71.

136 VOKS 47:140; 48:2; 51:28–29; 58:53, 55.

137 VOKS 58:67.

138 Arthur Lower, "So This Is a Free Country, Is It?," *New Liberty* 3, 3 (1953): 15, 92–95.

139 VOKS 48:204–05, A. Lower to A. Denisov, 14 October 1954.

140 VOKS 48:204–05.

141 VOKS 48:203, K. Perevoschikov to V. Burdin, 4 February 1955.

142 VOKS 47:7, 178; 45:21, on Wallace materials sent to VOKS; VOKS 51:75, J.S. Wallace to VOKS, 14 April 1955.

143 VOKS 51:75.

144 VOKS 34:35.

145 Ibid.

146 VOKS 39:91. It is not known whether this review appeared.

147 VOKS 47:10–11, V. Burdin to V. Bogatyrev, 10 February 1954.

148 VOKS 55:11, 39–40, 52–53, 53a.

149 VOKS 55:12.

150 VOKS 31:206–11, Biography of the president of the Canadian-Soviet Friendship Society, Dyson Carter, 1950.

151 VOKS 31:206–11.

152 VOKS 41:5–8, Perevoschikov, 13 April 1953.

153 The description of this first trip appeared as Carter and Carter, *We Saw Socialism*, originally published in two volumes. On the publication of this book, see VOKS 44:51–54, 65–66.

154 A complete list of Carter's publications in the USSR is provided in Black and Black, "Canada in the Soviet Mirror." Black, *Soviet Perception of Canada*, 231, shows that Carter was published in the USSR almost yearly between 1956 and 1983.

155 VOKS 39:105, I.V. Alekseev, 18 April 1953, on the Soviet publication of Carter's *The Future Is with Us* and the Soviet adaptation for theatre; VOKS 48:93, T. Moiseyenko-Velikaya to D. Carter, 19 September 1955, on a review of Carter's *Fatherless Sons* to be published in *Sovetskaya literatura*; VOKS 49:162, A. Tovstogan to V. Vertogradov, 29 May 1956, on the publication of the Carters' *The Science of Health and Long Life in the USSR*; VOKS 55:122, A. Tovstogan to G. Ioanisyan, 20 June 1957, on the release of the Carters' *Cancer, Smoking, Heart Disease, and Alcohol in Two World Systems*. Two copies of this last book, which argued that the Soviet system was handling these ailments better than was the capitalist system, were forwarded by VOKS to the Soviet Ministry of Foreign Affairs. VOKS 55:122.

156 In Soviet literature, Mikhail Bulgakov's novel *The Master and Margarita* (New York: Grove Press, 1967), written "for the drawer" (i.e., not in the hope of publication), was one of the few novels that dealt directly with the tragic situation of artists in the USSR. On Soviet policy on artists, see, for instance, Matthew Cullerne Brown, *Art under Stalin* (Oxford: Phaidon, 1991); Brandon Taylor, *Art and Literature under the Bolsheviks* (Concord, MA: Pluto Press, 1991); Regine Robin, *Socialist Realism: An Impossible Aesthetic*, trans. Catherine Porter (Stanford: Stanford University Press, 1992); Boris Grois, *The Total Art of Stalinism: Avant-Garde, Aesthetic Dictatorship, and*

Beyond, trans. Charles Rougle (Princeton, NJ: Princeton University Press, 1992); and Priscilla Johnson, *Khrushchev and the Arts: The Politics of Soviet Culture, 1962–1964* (Cambridge, MA: MIT Press, 1965).

Conclusion

1 See, especially, Black, "Soviet Tactics and Targets in Canada before and after the Gouzenko Defection," and Black, *Canada in the Soviet Mirror*.

2 Caute, *The Dancer Defects*, 1. Caute argues persuasively for an understanding of culture as political and ideological expressions during the Cold War and identifies VOKS as the organization coordinating many of these encounters. He also mentions that VOKS was known to be "supporting and subsidizing pro-Soviet foreign friendship societies . . . involving a degree of 'interference' in the domestic affairs of Western countries which the Russians themselves would not have accepted" (29).

3 Gaddis, *We Now Know*.

4 Leffler, "The Cold War," 523. This is a review of Gaddis, *We Now Know*.

5 Nancy F. Partner, "Making Up Lost Time: Writing on the Writing of History," *Speculum* 61, 1 (1986): 111.

6 In Russian, Soyuz sovetskyi obshchestva druzhbi i kul'turnoi sviazi s zagranitsei, renamed from VOKS in February 1958.

7 VOKS 6:1:36:43–52, president's speech to the CSFS convention, 25 January 1952.

8 Ibid. Carter was citing Wellington Jeffers, "Finance at Large," *Globe and Mail*, 4 January 1952, 16. According to Carter, Jeffers "tries hard to distort Soviet achievements. But he is forced to say: '. . . I am quite sure that if competent observers could go into Russia, travel in every part of it, and see all as easily as they can on this continent, there would be much more willingness here to pay attention to Soviet bids for peace.'"

9 VOKS 6:1:36:59, president's speech, 27 January 1952.

10 Ibid.

11 Ibid.

12 LAC, RG3120-0-6-E, Association of United Ukrainian Canadians (AUUC) fonds, vol. 27, file 14, 15.

13 LAC, RG146, ATIP request A-2006-00091, RCMP report "The Canadian Soviet Friendship Society, February 1951 to March 1953. Addendum to Brief Ending February 1951," dated 15 April 1953, 116.

14 Ibid.

15 LAC, RG25, ATIP request A-2007-00336, RCMP Research Section report "The Canada-USSR Association," 27 March 1963, 834–45.

16 The RCMP reported that Tim Buck had discussed these changes with authorities in Moscow as early as spring 1959, though the new association was not officially launched until December 1960. Ibid.

17 VOKS 6:2:62:3, M. Lucas to I. Zabrodin, Chief, USSR-Canada Association, Moscow, 10 January 1973. Lucas re-established the association at 55 Bloor Street, opening the doors on 28 June 1972.

18 VOKS 6:2:64:18–19, "Spravka o Kanadskykh obshesvakh druzhbi s SSSR," n.d., but with other documents from 1974, no author listed, probably written by the SSOD representative in the Soviet Embassy in Ottawa.

19 LAC, RG25, ATIP request A-2007-00336, RCMP Research Section report "The Canada-USSR Association," 27 March 1963, 834–45.

20 Ibid.

21 VOKS 6:2:65:26.

22 LAC, RG25, ATIP request A-2007-00336, RCMP Research Section report "The Canada-USSR Association," 27 March 1963, 834–45.

23 Ibid.

24 Lucas, interview.

25 VOKS 6:2:64:18–19, "Spravka o Kanadskykh obshesvakh druzhbi s SSSR," n.d., but with other documents from 1974, no author listed, probably written by the SSOD representative in the Soviet Embassy in Ottawa.

26 Koozma J. Tarasoff, interview with the author, 27 September 2006.

27 VOKS 6:2:64:18–19, "Spravka o Kanadskykh obshesvakh druzhbi s SSSR," n.d., but with other documents from 1974, no author listed, probably written by the SSOD representative in the Soviet Embassy in Ottawa.

28 VOKS 6:2:60:51–52, Mayorov report, 27 May 1973.

29 Canadian Museum of History, Gatineau, QC, Laurence Nowry fonds, 2005-F0016, vols. 977–78.

30 VOKS 6:2:61:40–42, V. Mayorov to A. Masko, 30 April 1973.

31 VOKS 6:2:65:25, List, "Branches of the Canada-USSR Association across Canada."

32 VOKS 6:2:61:40–42, V. Mayorov to A. Masko, 30 April 1973.

33 Tarasoff interview.

34 Adelard Paquin, "Truth Is the Way to Confidence," *Culture and Life* 4 (1988): 29; Michael Lucas, "Facing the Truth," *Culture and Life* 12 (1988): 32. Today Lucas blames Gorbachev for the Soviet Union's demise. Lucas interview.

35 VOKS 6:2:64:18–19, "Spravka o Kanadskykh obshesvakh druzhbi s SSSR," n.d., but with other documents from 1974, no author listed, probably written by the SSOD representative in the Soviet Embassy in Ottawa.

36 VOKS 6:2:62:102–03, I. Zabrodin to H. Dean, 28 June 1973. The band made the trip to Moscow in 1974, but asked about their Soviet tour, members who made the trip preferred not to comment on it for this project. See http://www.kitsband.com/kitshist.htm.

37 VOKS 6:2:64:6–15, "Account of Work of Society USSR-Canada in 1974." This appears to be the text of a speech, perhaps made by Igor Zabrodin.

38 VOKS 6:2:64:16–17, Zabrodin report.

39 VOKS 6:2:61:34, V. Mayorov to A. Masko, 21 April 1973. The festival took place on 20 April.

40 VOKS 6:2:61:63–65, V. Mayorov to A. Masko, 20 July 1973. The Ukrainian delegation was in Canada from 7 to 21 June 1973.

41 VOKS 6:2:65:53–54, V. Mayorov's interview notes with M. Lucas, 9 May 1974, notes dated 21 May 1974.

42 LAC, RG25, ATIP request A-2007-00336, RCMP Research Section report "The Canada-USSR Association," 27 March 1963, 834–845.

43 Boyd, interview.

44 VOKS 6:2:61:31, G. Isachenko, APN, to I. Zabrodin, 30 March 1973.

45 VOKS 6:2:66:252, I. Zabrodin to D. Carter, 20 December 1974; VOKS 6:2:66:246, D. Carter to A. Ledovski, Vice-Chairman, SSOD, 26 November 1974.

46 VOKS 6:2:63:16, D. Carter to I. Zabrodin, 25 May 1975; VOKS 6:2:63:15, I. Zabrodin to D. Carter, 18 June 1973.

47 Black, *Canada in the Soviet Mirror*, 336.

48 On this, see Black, "Soviet Tactics and Targets in Canada before and after the Gouzenko Defection"; also see VOKS 1:6:55:128–29.

49 Edward R. Murrow, "A Report on Senator Joseph R. McCarthy," *See It Now*, CBS-TV, 9 March 1954, transcript available at http://www.honors.umd.edu/HONR269J/archive/Murrow540309.html.

50 Andrew and Mitrokhin, *The Mitrokhin Archive*, 181, 220, 227–28, 532.

51 Ibid., 532.

52 See Black, "Soviet Tactics and Targets in Canada before and after the Gouzenko Defection," and Black, *Canada in the Soviet Mirror*.

53 See Weisbord, *The Strangest Dream*; Callwood, *Emma*; and Scher, *The Un-Canadians*.

54 Palmer, *A Communist Life*, 77.

55 Marcel Fournier, "Fred Rose: Notes pour une biographie," in *Le droit de se taire: Histoire des communistes au Québec, de la Premiere Guerre Mondiale a la Revolution Tranquille*, ed. Robert Comeau et Bernard Dionne (Outremont, QC:VLB, 1989), 296; Callwood, *Emma*; Scher, *The Un-Canadians*; Mark Kristmanson, *Plateaus of Freedom: Nationality, Culture, and State Security in Canada, 1940–1960* (Don Mills: Oxford University Press, 2003); Joyce Nelson, *The Colonized Eye: Rethinking the Grierson Legend* (Toronto: Between the Lines, 1988). The quotation in this sentence is from McDowall, "The Trial and Tribulations of Miss Agatha Chapman," 373.

56 Granatstein and Stafford, *Spy Wars*, 63.

57 There is no Canadian study comparable to Caute's work on fellow travellers in the United States, Britain, and Western Europe; see Caute, *The Fellow-Travellers* Also see Mickenberg, *Learning from the Left*.

58 See VOKS 1:6:49:264–67; 55:150–51.

59 Ibid.

60 VOKS 6:1:55:118–19, A. Tovstogan to G. Ioanisyan, 14 May 1957, detailing the loss of a photo album belonging to Romeo Lafond, who visited the USSR with the CSFS delegation in September 1953. Lafond was described as a "CSFS member and Labor-Progressive Party of Quebec provincial Committee member." He suggested that the album was stolen from his car by a police agent, but it is not clear whether he meant the RCMP or the provincial police.

61 The character and activities of these societies in their respective countries, the VOKS support that they received, and the links among them deserve further study. Important here is Fayet, *VOKS*.

Selected Bibliography

Primary Sources

Oral Interviews

Baxter, J.E., interviewed 8 December 2006

Boyd, John, interviewed 2 August 2006

Hunt, Les, interviewed 2 January 2007

Lucas, Michael, interviewed 27 July 2006

Nielsen, Sally (Thelma), interviewed 28 November 2006

Paul, Irja (with Irene Kuusela and Marie Rempel), interviewed 27 November 2006

Tarasoff, Koozma J., interviewed 27 September 2006

Archival Collections

Library and Archives Canada

Association of United Ukrainian Canadians fonds (MG28-V-154)

CSIS fonds (RG146)

Department of External Affairs fonds (RG25)

Dyson Carter fonds (MG31-D182)

June Callwood fonds (MG31-K24)

Frank and Libbie Park fonds (MG31-K9)

Frederick B. Taylor fonds (MG30-D360)

Cameron Library, University of Alberta

GARF (Gosudarstvennyi arkhiv Rossiiskoi Federatsii/State Archives of the Russian Federation) fonds, 5283

RGASPI (Rossiiskii gosudarstvennyi arkhiv sotsial'no-politicheskoi istorii/Russian State Archive of Social-Political History, Moscow) Collection

VOKS Collection

Canadian Museum of History, Gatineau

Laurence Nowry fonds, 2005-F0016

Research fonds, Jennifer Anderson, 2016-H0036

Global Affairs Canada

External Affairs and International Trade Canada / Department of Foreign Affairs and International Trade, *Documents on Canadian External Relations (DCER)*, vol. 19, *1953*, ed. Donald Barry (Ottawa: 1991); vol. 23, *1956–1957*, part 2, ed. Greg Donaghy (Ottawa: 2002); vol. 25, *1957–1958*, ed. Michael D. Stevenson (Ottawa: 2004); vol. 27, *1960*, ed. Janice Cavell (Ottawa: 2007).

McGill University, Montreal

Louis and Irene Kon Collection, P162

Thomas Fisher Rare Book Library, University of Toronto

Robert S. Kenny Collection

Private Collections

J.E. Baxter

John Boyd

Larissa Stavroff

Memoirs and Other Primary Sources

Andrew, Christopher, and Vasili Mitrokhin. *The Mitrokhin Archive: The KGB in Europe and the West*. New York: Penguin Press, 1999.

Biderman, Morris. *A Life on the Jewish Left: An Immigrant's Experience*. Toronto: Onward Publishing, 2000.

Black, J.L., ed. *Soviet Perception of Canada: An Annotated Bibliographic Guide*. Ottawa: Carleton University Press, 1989.

Boyd, John. "A Noble Cause Betrayed . . . but Hope Lives On: Pages from a Political Life." Originally published as Canadian Institute of Ukrainian Studies Report 64, 1999. Socialist History Project, http://www.socialisthistory.ca/Remember/Reminiscences/Boyd/B1.htm.

British Broadcasting Corporation. *Mindbenders: Propaganda with Facts: Our Soviet Friends*. Director unknown. 1980.

Chernin, Kim. *In My Mother's House: A Daughter's Story*. 1983. Reprint, New York: HarperCollins, 1994.

Documents on Canadian External Affairs, vols. 23 (1956-57) and 27 (1960), ed. Greg Donaghy, Janice Cavell. Ottawa: Foreign Affairs and International Trade Canada, 2002, 2007.

Gouzenko, Igor. *This Was My Choice: Gouzenko's Story*. Toronto: J.M. Dent and Sons, 1948.

Irvine, William. *Live or Die with Russia*. Edmonton: self-published, 1958. Published in Russian as *Zhit' vmeste s Rossiyei* [Live with Russia]. Translated by V.V. Isakovich. Moscow: Inostrannoi izdatel'stvo literature, 1958.

Krawchuk, Peter, ed. *Reminiscences of Courage and Hope (Stories of Ukrainian Canadian Women Pioneers)*. Toronto: Kobzar Publishing Company, 1991.

Laxer, James. *Red Diaper Baby: A Boyhood in the Age of McCarthyism*. Vancouver: Douglas and McIntyre, 2004.

The R.C.M.P. Security Bulletins: The Depression Years, pt. I, 1933–1934, pt. II, 1935. Edited by Gregory S. Kealey and Reginald Whitaker. St. John's: Committee on Canadian Labour History, 1993–1997.

The R.C.M.P. Security Bulletins: The War Series. Edited by Gregory S. Kealey and Reginald Whitaker. St. John's: Committee on Canadian Labour History, 1989–93.

The Report of the Royal Commission to Investigate Disclosures of Secret and Confidential Information to Unauthorized Persons. Ottawa: Edmond Cloutier, 1946.

Shostakovich, Dmitri. *Testimony: The Memoirs of Dmitri Shostakovich*. Translated by Antonina W. Bouis. Edited by Solomon Volkov. New York: Harper and Row Publishers, 1979.

Publications Written or Edited by Dyson Carter (and Charlotte Carter)

Sea of Destiny: The Story of Hudson Bay, Our Undefended Back Door. New York: Greenberg, 1940.

Men, Machines, and Microbes. Winnipeg: Contemporary Publishers, 1942.

Russia's Secret Weapon. New York: Contemporary Publishers, 1942.

Stalin's Life: At Last the True Story. Winnipeg: Contemporary Publishers, 1943.

Booze: The Saboteur. Winnipeg: Contemporary Publishers, 1943.

Atomic Dollars. Winnipeg: Frontier Books, 1946.

Atomic Future. Regina: King's Printer for Saskatchewan, 1946.

Sin and Science. New York: Heck-Cattell, 1946.

Tomorrow Is with Us. Toronto: Progress Books, 1950.

We Saw Socialism. Toronto: CSFS, 1951.

"How *Not* to Be Afraid of Your Heart," *New Liberty*, August 1952, 22–23, 62–63.

Fatherless Sons. Toronto: Progress Books, 1955.

Science of Health and Long Life in the U.S.S.R. Sydney, Australia: Current Book Distributors, 1956.

Cancer, Smoking, Heart-Disease, Drinking in Our Two World Systems Today. Toronto: Northern Book House, 1957.

The Big Brainwash. Toronto: Northern Book House, 1958.

Rising World. Toronto: Northern Book House, 1959.

Future of Freedom. Gravenhurst, ON: Northern Book House, 1961.

Worker Power: Dare We Win? Gravenhurst, ON: Northern Book House, 1970.

This Story Fierce and Tender. Gravenhurst, ON: Northern Book House, 1986.

Secondary Sources

Abel, Kerry, and Ken S. Coates, eds. *Northern Visions: New Perspectives on the North in Canadian History*. Peterborough, ON: Broadview Press, 2001.

Adams, Mary Louise. *The Trouble with Normal: Postwar Youth and the Making of Heterosexuality*. Toronto: University of Toronto Press, 1997.

Ageeva, I.A. "Kanada i nachalo Kholodnoi Voinyi: Delo Gouzenko v sovetsko-kanadskikh otnosheniyakh" (Canada and the Start of the Cold War: The Gouzenko Affair in Soviet-Canadian Relations), in *Kholodnaya Voina 1945–1963* (Cold War, 1945–1963), 369–405. Moscow: Olma-Press, 2003.

Aleksandrov, G.F. "The Pattern of Soviet Democracy" (originally "O sovetskoy demokratii"). Speech delivered in 1946. Translated by Leo Gruliow. Washington, DC: Public Affairs Press, 1948.

Angus, Ian. *Canadian Bolsheviks: The Early Years of the Communist Party of Canada*. Montreal: Vanguard Publications, 1981.

Ankersmit, F.R. "The Dilemma of Contemporary Anglo-Saxon Philosophy of History." *History and Theory* 25, 4 (1986): 1–27.

———. *Narrative Logic: A Semantic Analysis of the Historian's Language*. The Hague: Martinus Nijhoff Publishers, 1983.

Avakumovic, Ivan. *The Communist Party in Canada: A History*. Toronto: McClelland and Stewart, 1975.

Avery, Donald. *Reluctant Host: Canada's Response to Immigrant Workers, 1896–1994*. Toronto: McClelland and Stewart, 1995.

Balawyder, A. "Canada and the Famine in Soviet Russia and the Ukraine (1921–23)." *New Review*, December 1964, 1–10.

Beaumont, Joan. *Comrades in Arms: British Aid to Russia, 1941–1945*. London: Davis-Poynter, 1980.

Black, J.L. "Canada and the Soviet Union in 1945: The View from Moscow." In *Uncertain Horizons: Canadians and Their World in 1945*, edited by Greg Donaghy, 285–302. Ottawa: Canadian Committee for the History of the Second World War, 1996.

———. *Canada in the Soviet Mirror: Ideology and Perception in Soviet Foreign Affairs, 1997–1991*. Ottawa: Carleton University Press, 1998.

Black, Joseph, and J.L. Black. "Canada in the Soviet Mirror: English-Language Canadian Literature in Soviet Translation." *Journal of Canadian Studies* 30, 2 (1995): 5–18.

Black, J.L., and Norman Hillmer, eds. *Nearly Neighbours: Canada and the Soviet Union from Cold War to Détente and Beyond*. Kingston: Ronald P. Frye and Company, 1989.

Black, J.L., and Martin Rudner, eds. *The Gouzenko Affair: Canada and the Beginnings of Cold War Counter-Espionage*. Manotick, ON: Penumbra Press, 2006.

Bothwell, Robert. *The Big Chill: Canada and the Cold War*. Toronto: Canadian Institute of International Affairs, 1998.

Bothwell, Robert, and J.L. Granatstein, eds. *The Gouzenko Transcripts: the evidence presented to the Kellock-Taschereau Royal Commission of 1946*. Ottawa: Deneau Publishers, 1982.

Breines, Wini. *Young, White, and Miserable: Growing Up Female in the Fifties*. Chicago: University of Chicago Press, 1992.

Brookfield, Tarah. *Cold War Comforts: Canadian Women, Child Safety, and Global Insecurity, 1945–1975.* Waterloo: Wilfrid Laurier University Press, 2012.

Burton, Antoinette, ed. *Archive Stories: Facts, Fictions, and the Writing of History.* Durham, NC: Duke University Press, 2005.

Callwood, June. *Emma.* Toronto: Stoddart, 1984.

Caute, David. *The Dancer Defects: The Struggle for Cultural Supremacy during the Cold War.* Oxford: Oxford University Press, 2003.

———. *The Fellow Travellers: Intellectual Friends of Communism.* Rev. ed. New Haven, CT: Yale University Press, 1988.

Cavell, Janice. "The Second Frontier: The North in English-Canadian Historical Writing." *Canadian Historical Review* 83, 3 (2002): 364–89.

Cavell, Richard, ed. *Love, Hate, and Fear in Canada's Cold War.* Toronto: University of Toronto Press, 2004.

Coates, Ken S., and William R. Morrison, "Winter and the Shaping of Northern History: Reflections from the Canadian North," in *Northern Visions: New Perspectives on the North in Canadian History*, ed. Kerry Abel and Ken S. Coates, 23–35. Peterborough: Broadview Press, 2001.

Cohen, Lizabeth. *A Consumer's Republic: The Politics of Mass Consumption in Postwar America.* New York: Knopf, 2003.

Corten, Irina H. *Vocabulary of Soviet Society and Culture: A Selected Guide to Russian Words, Idioms, and Expressions of the Post-Stalin Era, 1953–1991.* Durham, NC: Duke University Press, 1992.

Cruikshank, Julie. *Life Lived like a Story: Life Stories of Three Yukon Native Elders.* Lincoln: University of Nebraska Press, 1990.

———. *The Social Life of Stories: Narrative and Knowledge in the Yukon Territory.* Vancouver: UBC Press, 1998.

Doyle, James. *Progressive Heritage: The Evolution of a Politically Radical Literary Tradition in Canada.* Waterloo: Wilfrid Laurier University Press, 2002.

Drakulic, Slavenka. *How We Survived Communism and Even Laughed.* New York: HarperCollins, 1993.

Endicott, Stephen. *James G. Endicott: Rebel out of China.* Toronto: University of Toronto Press, 1980.

Espiritu, Aileen. "Whither the Northern Natives in Russian History?," in *Northern Visions: New Perspectives on the North in Canadian History*, ed. Kerry Abel and Ken S. Coates. Peterborough: Broadview Press, 2001, 170–71.

Fairley, Margaret. "Our Cultural Heritage." *New Frontiers* 1 (1952): 1–7.

Falsifiers of History (pamphlet). Moscow: Foreign Languages Publishing House, 1948.

Fayet, Jean-François. *VOKS : Le laboratoire helvétique. Histoire de la diplomatie culturelle soviétique durant l'entre-deux-guerres.* Chêne-Bourg: Georg Éditeur, 2014.

Fitzpatrick, Sheila. *Everyday Stalinism: Ordinary Life in Extraordinary Times: Soviet Russia in the 1930s.* New York: Oxford University Press, 1999.

Foreman, Joel, ed. *The Other Fifties: Interrogating Midcentury American Icons.* Urbana: University of Illinois Press, 1997.

Fortin, Gérard, and Boyce Richardson. *Life of the Party.* Montreal: Véhicule Press, 1984.

Gaddis, John Lewis. *We Now Know: Rethinking Cold War History*. New York: Oxford University Press, 1997.

Golitsyn, Anatoliy. *New Lies for Old: The Communist Strategy of Deception and Disinformation*. New York: Dodd, Mead, 1984.

Gonick, Cy. *A Very Red Life: The Story of Bill Walsh*. St. John's: Committee on Canadian Labour History, 2001.

Granatstein, J.L., and David Stafford. *Spy Wars: Espionage and Canada from Gouzenko to Glasnost*. Toronto: Key Porter Books, 1990.

Greig, Ian. *The Assault on the West*. Surrey, UK: Foreign Affairs Publishing, 1968.

Guard, Julie. "Canadian Citizens or Dangerous Foreign Women? Canada's Radical Consumer Movement, 1947–1950." In *Sisters or Strangers? Immigrant, Ethnic, and Racialized Women in Canadian History*, edited by Marlene Epp, Franca Iacovetta, and Frances Swyripa, 161–89. Toronto: University of Toronto Press, 2004.

———. "Women Worth Watching: Radical Housewives in Cold War Canada." In *Whose National Security? Canadian State Surveillance and the Creation of Enemies*, edited by Gary Kinsman, Dieter K. Buse, and Mercedes Steedman. Toronto: Between the Lines, 2000.

Hardt, Hanno. *In the Company of Media: Cultural Constructions of Communication, 1920s–1930s*. Boulder, CO: Westview Press, 2000.

Hewitt, Steve. *Spying 101: The RCMP's Secret Activities at Canadian Universities*. Toronto: University of Toronto Press, 2002.

Hinther, Rhonda L. "'Sincerest Revolutionary Greetings': Progressive Ukrainians in Canada, 1918–1991." PhD diss., McMaster University, 2005.

Hunter, Peter. *Which Side Are You on Boys . . . Canadian Life on the Left*. Toronto: Lugus Productions, 1988.

Iacovetta, Franca. *Gatekeepers: Reshaping Immigrant Lives in Cold War Canada*. Toronto: Between the Lines, 2006.

Irr, Caren. *The Suburb of Dissent: Cultural Politics in the United States and Canada during the 1930s*. Durham, NC: Duke University Press, 1998.

Johnson, Gregory A. Review of *Cold War Canada: The Making of a National Insecurity State, 1945-1957* by Reg Whitaker, Gary Marcuse. *Canadian Historical Review* 78, 1 (1997): 139–141.

Johnston, Faith. "Dorise Nielsen: The Life and Ideas of a Canadian Woman in Politics." MA thesis, Carleton University, 1989.

———. *A Great Restlessness: The Life and Politics of Dorise Nielsen*. Winnipeg: University of Manitoba Press, 2006.

Kameneva, Olga Davidova. "Cultural Rapprochement: The U.S.S.R. Society for Cultural Relations with Foreign Countries." *Pacific Affairs* 1, 5 (1928): 6–8.

Kealey, Linda. *Enlisting Women for the Cause: Women, Labour, and the Left in Canada*. Toronto: University of Toronto Press, 1998.

Kealey, Gregory S. "Presidential Address: The Empire Strikes Back: The Nineteenth-Century Origins of the Canadian Secret Service." *Journal of the Canadian Historical Association* 10 (1999): 3–18.

Kellner, Hans. *Language and Historical Representation: Getting the Story Crooked*. Madison: University of Wisconsin Press, 1989.

Kinsman, Gary, K. Buse, and Mercedes Steedman, eds. *Whose National Security? Canadian State Surveillance and the Creation of Enemies.* Toronto: Between the Lines, 2003.

Knight, Amy. *How the Cold War Began: The Gouzenko Affair and the Hunt for Soviet Spies.* Toronto: McClelland and Stewart, 2005.

Kolasky, John. *The Shattered Illusion: The History of the Ukrainian Pro-Communist Organizations in Canada.* Toronto: Peter Martin Associates, 1979.

———, ed. *Prophets and Proletarians: Documents on the History of the Rise and Decline of Ukrainian Communism in Canada.* Edmonton: Canadian Institute of Ukrainian Studies Press, 1990.

Korinek, Valerie Joyce. *Roughing It in the Suburbs: Reading* Chatelaine *Magazine in the Fifties and Sixties.* Toronto: University of Toronto Press, 2000.

Kramer, Mark. "The Role of the CPSU International Department in Soviet Foreign Relations and National Security Policy." *Soviet Studies* 42, 3 (1990): 429–46.

Krawchuk, Peter. *Our History: The Ukrainian Labour-Farmer Temple Movement in Canada, 1907–1991.* Toronto: Lugus Publications, 1996.

Kukushkin, Vadim. "Back in the USSR." *Beaver* 86, 4 (2006): 33–36.

Leffler, Melvyn P. "The Cold War: What Do 'We Now Know'?" *American Historical Review* 104, 2 (1999): 523.

Lévesque, Andrée. *Red Travellers: Jeanne Corbin and Her Comrades.* Originally published as *Scénes de la vie en rouge: L'époque de Jeanne Corbin, 1906–1944.* Translated by Yvonne M. Klein. Montreal: McGill-Queen's University Press, 2006.

Lindstrom, Varpu. *Defiant Sisters: A Social History of Finnish Immigrant Women in Canada.* Toronto: Multicultural History Society of Ontario, 1992.

Lindstrom-Best, Varpu. *The Finns in Canada.* Ottawa: Canadian Historical Association, 1985.

Lucas, Michael. *Journey for Friendship between Northern Neighbours.* Toronto: North Star Compass, 2010.

MacDowell, Laurel Sefton. "Paul Robeson in Canada: A Border Story." *Labour/Le travail* 51 (2003): 31 paragraphs. www.historycooperative.org/journals/11t/51/macdowell.html.

———. *Renegade Lawyer: The Life of J.L. Cohen.* Toronto: University of Toronto Press, 2001.

MacLeod, Wendell, Libbie Park, and Stanley Ryerson, eds. *Bethune: The Montreal Years: An Informal Portrait.* Toronto: James Lorimer and Company, 1978.

Mann, Robert. *The Petrov Affair: Politics and Espionage.* Sydney, Australia: Pergamon, 1987.

Mastny, Vojtech. *The Cold War and Soviet Insecurity: The Stalin Years.* New York: Oxford University Press, 1996.

May, Elaine Tyler. *Homeward Bound: American Families in the Cold War Era.* New York: Basic Books, 1988.

McDowall, Duncan. "The Trials and Tribulations of Miss Agatha Chapman: Statistics in a Cold War Climate." *Queen's Quarterly* 114, 3 (2007): 357–69.

McKay, Ian. *Rebels, Reds, Radicals: Rethinking Canada's Left History.* Toronto: Between the Lines, 2005.

Meyerowitz, Joanne, ed. *Not June Cleaver: Women and Gender in Postwar America*. Philadelphia: Temple University Press, 1994.

Mickenberg, Julia L. *Learning from the Left: Children's Literature, the Cold War, and Radical Politics in the United States*. Oxford: Oxford University Press, 2006.

Mishler, Paul C. *Raising Reds: The Young Pioneers, Radical Summer Camps, and Communist Political Culture in the United States*. New York: Columbia University Press, 1999.

Nadel, Alan. *Containment Culture: American Narratives, Postmodernism, and the Atomic Age*. Durham, NC: Duke University Press, 1995.

Northern Perspectives 16, 4 (1988). Published by the Canadian Arctic Resources Committee, http://www.carc.org/pubs/v16no4/index.html.

Okulevich, G. *Russkie v Kanade: Istoriya Russkikh Raboche-Fermerskikh Klubov imeni M. Gorkovo (1930–1940) I Federatsii Russkikh Kanadtsev (1941–1952)*. Toronto: publisher unknown, 1952.

Palmer, Bryan D., ed. *A Communist Life: Jack Scott and the Canadian Workers Movement, 1927–1985*. St. John's: Committee on Canadian Labour History, 1988.

Park, Libbie and Frank. *Moscow: As Two Canadians Saw It*. Toronto: Canadian Soviet Friendship Society, 1951.

Parr, Joy, ed. *A Diversity of Women: Ontario, 1945–1980*. Toronto: University of Toronto Press, 1995.

Partner, Nancy F. "Making Up Lost Time: Writing on the Writing of History." *Speculum* 61, 1 (1986): 90–117.

Pashuto, V.T., et al. *Protiv fal'sifikatsii istorii nashei rodiny*. Moscow: Znanie, 1961.

Pechatnov, Vladimir O. "The Big Three after World War II: New Documents on Soviet Thinking about Post War Relations with the United States and Great Britain." Working Paper 13, 1995, Cold War International History Project, Woodrow Wilson Centre.

Penner, Norman. *Canadian Communism: The Stalin Years and Beyond*. Toronto: Methuen, 1988.

Ra'anan, Gavriel D. *International Policy Formation in the USSR: Factional "Debates" during the Zhdanovschina*. Hamden, CT: Archon Books, 1983.

Reiter, Ester. "Secular *Yiddishkait*: Left Politics, Culture, and Community." *Labour/Le travail* (spring 2002): n. pag. http://www.historycooperative.org/journals/llt/49/05reiter.html.

Roberts, Geoffrey. "Stalin, the Pact with Nazi Germany, and the Origins of Postwar Soviet Diplomatic Historiography." *Journal of Cold War History* 4, 4 (2002): 93–103.

Roberts, Glenna, and Serge Cipko. *One-Way Ticket: The Soviet Return-to-the-Homeland Campaign, 1955–1960*. Manotick, ON: Penumbra Press, 2008.

Roberts, Leslie. *Home from the Cold Wars*. Toronto: S.J. Reginald Saunders & Co., Ltd, 1948.

———. "McCarthyism—It's Spreading in Canada—Now." *New Liberty* 31 (1954): 15–17, 78–83.

Roberts, Peter, and Serge Cipko. "Canada and the Khrushchev Government's 'Return to the Homeland' Campaign." Occasional Paper 8, Centre for Research on Canadian-Russian Relations, Carleton University, 2000.

Romerstein, Herbert. "History of the ID." In *The International Department of the CC CPSU under Dobrynin*, edited by Foreign Service Institute, US Department of State, 111–38. Washington, DC: Center for the Study of Foreign Affairs, 1999.

Rouillard, Jacques. *Le syndicalisme québécois: Deux siècles d'histoire*. Montréal: Éditions Boréal, 2004.

Rush, Maurice. *We Have a Glowing Dream: Recollections of Working-Class and People's Struggles in B.C., 1935–1995*. Vancouver: Centre for Socialist Education, 1996.

Sangster, Joan. *Dreams of Equality: Women on the Canadian Left, 1920–1950*. Toronto: McClelland and Stewart, 1989.

———. "Telling Our Stories: Feminist Debates and the Use of Oral History." *Women's History Review* 3, 1 (1994): 5–28.

Saunders, Frances Stonor. *The Cultural Cold War: The CIA and the World of Arts and Letters*. New York: New Press, 1999.

Sawatsky, John. *Gouzenko: The Untold Story*. Toronto: Macmillan of Canada, 1984.

———. *Men in the Shadows: The RCMP Security Service*. Toronto: Doubleday Canada, 1980.

Saxberg, Kelly, dir. *Letters from Karelia*. National Film Board of Canada, 2005.

Scher, Len, dir. *The Un-Canadians*. National Film Board of Canada, 1996.

———. *The Un-Canadians: True Stories from the Blacklist Era*. Toronto: Lester Publishing, 1992.

Schrecker, Ellen, ed. *Cold War Triumphalism: The Misuse of History after the Fall of Communism*. New York: New Press, 2004.

Scott, James C. *Seeing Like a State: How Certain Schemes to Improve the Human Condition Have Failed*. New Haven: Yale University Press, 1998.

Smith, Denis. *Diplomacy of Fear: Canada and the Cold War, 1941–1948*. Toronto: University of Toronto Press, 1988.

Swyripa, Frances. *Wedded to the Cause: Ukrainian-Canadian Women and Ethnic Identity, 1891–1991*. Toronto: University of Toronto Press, 1993.

Tulchinsky, Gerald. *Joe Salsberg: A Life of Commitment*. Toronto: University of Toronto Press, 2013.

Vance, Catherine. *Not by Gods but by People: The Story of Bella Hall Gauld*. Toronto: Progress Books, 1968.

Virtue, John. *Fred Taylor: Brother in the Shadows*. Montreal: McGill-Queen's University Press, 2008.

Watson, Louise. *She Never Was Afraid: The Biography of Annie Buller*. Toronto: Progress Books, 1976.

Watson, Mary Eleanor Barber. "Study of Dyson Carter's Life and Works." Undergraduate paper, Carleton University, 1974.

Weisbord, Merrily. *The Strangest Dream: Canada's Communists, the Spy Trials, and the Cold War*. Montreal: Véhicule Press, 1994.

Whitaker, Reg. *Double Standard: The Secret History of Canadian Immigration*. Toronto: Lester and Orpen Dennys, 1987.

Whitaker, Reg, and Steve Hewitt. *Canada and the Cold War*. Toronto: James Lorimer and Company, 2003.

Whitaker, Reg, and Gary Marcuse. *Cold War Canada: The Making of a National Insecurity State, 1945–1957*. Toronto: University of Toronto Press, 1994.

Whitfield, Stephen J. *The Culture of the Cold War*. Baltimore: Johns Hopkins University Press, 1991.

Wilford, Hugh. *The Mighty Wurlitzer: How the CIA Played America*. Cambridge, MA: Harvard University Press, 2008.

Wolters-Fredlund, Benita. "'We Shall Go Forward with Our Songs into the Fight for Better Life': Identity and Musical Meaning in the History of the Toronto Jewish Folk Choir, 1925–1959." PhD diss., University of Toronto, 2005.

Zembrzycki, Stacey. *According to Baba: A Collaborative Oral History of Sudbury's Ukrainian Community*. Vancouver: UBC Press, 2014.

———. "Memory, Identity, and the Challenge of Community among Ukrainians in the Sudbury Region, 1901–1939." PhD diss., Carleton University, 2007.

Zubok, Vladislav, and Constantine Pleshakov. *Inside the Kremlin's Cold War: From Stalin to Khrushchev*. Cambridge, MA: Harvard University Press, 1996.

Index